Bought at the
Ocean Bookshop

QUEEN ELIZABETH 2

CUNARD

Pride

of the

North Atlantic

A Maritime Trilogy by

David F. Hutchings

" THREE CUNARD LIONS " — THE PRIDE OF THE ATLANTIC!

Subscribers Who Have Put Their Name To This Book

Adams, Brian	Cunard Publicity 1955-1966
Adamson John	Director, Special Events, *Queen Mary*
Baker, John	
Banks, Eric Sinclair	Buckie, Scotland
Baxter, Colin M	Marine Artist, Lee-on-The Solent
Beirne, Jerry	Weymouth, UK
Berry, May	*QE* Crew - December 1946-May 1948
Berry, May	*Queen Mary* Crew - Jan-May 1946
Betts, Eddy	Cardiff, South Wales
Black, Mr Dean A	Southampton, Hampshire
Britton, Andrew	*QM & QE* Devotee
Brocklesby, P	Halesowen
Brown, the late Sir John	Naval Architect on *Queen Mary*
Bruce Grice, R	Redlynch, Salisbury
Cairns, Mr J L	Kirn, Argyll
Cani, Rodney de	Tarvin, Cheshire
Carew, Gregory R	
Catlin, Tony	First Class Waiter
Chandler, Captain P Adrian	Liverpool
Chojnowska (nee Ashton) Hilda	Stewardess *QE*, 1951-1955
Clarke, Adrian	*Pendennis Castle* 71-72
Clarke, Dr Joan	Highcliffe, Dorset
Coulter, John W.B	Engineering Officer, *QE*
Cross, Barrie	Thornton, Lancs.
Curl, Andrew R	Standford, Hampshire
Dalley, Clive	'Masseur' Southampton
Davies, Robin	
Daw, Stuart	Coxswain *QE2* 1985-92, Cardiff
Dickinson, David Rees	Chief Cook
Dryden, Denis G	Southend, Mull of Kintyre
Eagles, Barry J	Chandler's Ford, Hampshire
Evans, Sandy	Passenger, with Daughter Heather *QM*
Fewings, Mr Robert J	Havant, Hampshire
Fielder, Jack	Sanderstead, Surrey
Fisher, Maxi	Liverpool/Southampton, UK
Flint, Paul M	Peterborough
Foster, Nigel	Sheffield
Fricker, Maurice & David	Fond memories of RMS *Queen Mary*
Gilligan, Don	Southampton
Gobell, John	Canberra, Australia
Goddard, David A	Southampton
Goldfinch, Mrs Susan Elizabeth	Downton, Wiltshire
Goold, Mr Reginald W H	Late of Escarie Art Metal London
Grant, Martin	London, SW1
Griffin, John H	Chief Elect Engineer, *QE2* 1987/95
Griffiths, Martin	*QE2* Transatlantic Sept/October 2003
Harding, Ronnie	Weymouth, UK
Hardingham, Roger	Life- long interest in the *Queen Mary*
Hammond, Stewart J	Warsash, Hampshire
Hearn, Terry	BRS
Hicks, David	
Hicks, Remembering William Henry	Served on *QM* and *QE*
Hill, John D	Winchester, Hampshire.
Hollins, Michael	Canberra, Australia, October 2003
Hollowday, Derek	
Holmes, Allan	Chief Radio Officer. *QE2* 1968-1992
Hull, Norman G	Northampton
Huntingford, L	Chief Steward M.N. Retired, Lincs
Jameson, Walter	Gillingham, Kent
Jean, Mr Philippe,	Cherbourg, France
Jones, Geraldine C	Vancouver, British Columbia.
Jory, William and Carolyn	Michelmersh, Hampshire
Kandlbinder, G	Brugge, Belgium
Kegos, Miss Veronica	Ashford, Kent
Kellett, Michael.	Southampton.
Kent, P J	Mansfield, Nottingham
Kibblewhite, Douglas	Colchester, Essex
Kramer, Lovetta	Vice President & Executive Director RMS Queen Mary Foundation
Lackner, Helmuth	Marine Artist, Lee-on-The Solent
Lancaster, J B	Kenilworth, Warwickshire
Lancaster, R J	Warwickgates, Warwick
Langstaff, Mr Alan	Baddesley Clinton, Warwickshire
Lewis, Mike	St Louis, USA
Lilley, Trevor, FCIPD	Warrington, passenger on *QE*
Lotriet, Sandy	Southampton, UK
Mainds, Mr Alexander	Cabinet Maker, Paisley
Mair, Alexander MacKay	Buckie, Scotland
Martin, Isis Mary	Seal Beach, California
Martin, Vera M	Seal Beach, California
Manwaring, Jeffery	*QE2* Engineer
Matusiewicz, Len A	Chief Engineer
Maxtone-Graham, John	
Milburn, Captain D	Tynemouth, Tyne & Wear -*QM* August 1955, *QE* - November 1956
Montgomery Travis	Vice President, RMS Queen Mary Foundation
Moore, Edward	
Murdoch, Robert and Mary	Auchterderran, Fife
Newman, Christopher A	Sendmarsh, Surrey
Ockendon, Mr N D	Ryde, Isle of Wight
Parker, John	*QE* Cabin Class Passenger 1954
Payne, Joe	Senior Masseur, *QE*, *QM* and *QE2*
Poole, J A	Chief Engineer, Thornton-Cleveleys
Poulter, P	Bradley, North Yorkshire
Prevratil, Joseph F	President & CEO RMS Queen Mary Foundation
Prevratil, Robert	Vice President & General Manager of Operations The *Queen Mary*
Richardson, Dr R	Woodfield, Worcester
Riley, Wilf	Weymouth, UK
Robertson, Michael F	
Ruane, John	Lanark, Scotland
Rush, Diane	Former President, *QM* Foundation
Rushton Peter	Uckfield, Sussex
Ryland, David Morrison	Galmpton Ward, Devon Assistant Purser 1963 on *Queen Elizabeth*,
Saunders, Ken	Derby
Scott, Clive B	Falkirk, Scotland
Shotton, Donald W	Newport, Mon.
Sidney, Kevin G	Nottingham
Singleton, Brian	Freckleton, Lancs Radio Officer, *QM*
Smith, J G	Arthurs Hill, Newcastle
Smith, Michael	Hitchin, England
Southern, Mr J B	E.O., *QM* and *QE*
Steamship Historical Society of America	
Stratford, Mr Adam	Eltham, London
Suzuki, Goro	
Sylvestre, Lawrence	Ocean Liner Cruising Con, Truro
Thomas, Dave	Southampton, UK
Vallens, Anne & Mervyn	Ashford, Kent, October 2003
Van der Kemp, Dr J C	Rhoon, Holland
Vard, Ken	Hove, UK
Wallis, Mr Mike	Catering Officer *QE* and *QM*
Wallsgrove, Christine and Colin	Maidstone, Kent
Walmsley, Jim	Ormskirk, Lancashire
Warren, M J	Havant, Hampshire
Webb, Bernard	Crew, *QE* and *QM*, Southampton
Webb, Joe	Crew, *QE*, Southampton
Woodall, Captain R.A	Hoylake, Wirrall, who served on all three *Queen*'s, captaining *QE2*.
Whiteley, D A	Yorkshire
Whitworth, F J, OBE	Cunard Line 1950-1971 Managing Director 1968-1969
Wilkie, M	Sister born on day of *QM* Launch.
Wilkinson, Eddie	Southampton, UK
Williams, Mr Jos	Old Colwyn, North Wales
Wilson, Cynthia Irean	
Wilson, Captain Jim	
Wilson, Stewart W	Banchory, Scotland
Wolseley, George	Finmere, Oxfordshire
Wright, Mark	Winchester, Hampshire

A stunning bow view of *Queen Mary 2* as she undergoes her sea trials.
All photographs of Queen Mary 2 are courtesy of Chantiers de l'Atlantique, St. Nazaire, and John Michael Drake

Introduction

It was in February 1986 that I was delighted to have been invited to write the book that forms the first section of this current volume. Then called RMS Queen Mary 50 Years of Splendour that book set out to celebrate in some small way the Golden Anniversary of what was arguably the worlds most famous liner.

Since then two other volumes followed in celebration of Cunard's other great ships the *Queen Elizabeth* and *Queen Elizabeth 2* the *QE2* and it is with great pleasure that all three books are now presented, with additional photographs and material, as one volume. My thanks for this go especially to both talented marine artist Colin M. Baxter for the loan of recently discovered, glass-plate negatives of the *Queen Mary* leaving the Clyde and arriving in Southampton and to my publisher, Roger Hardingham, for his faith in this combined work.

Indices and acknowledgements are, generally, as they appeared when first published so it is to be regretted that many of those mentioned with such heartfelt gratitude in the original editions have since Crossed the Bar to Fiddlers Green.

A fourth great Cunarder is about to join the élite group of Cunard ships that have borne the names of consorts of British kings the *Queen Mary 2*. It is incredibly breathtaking to realise that the old *Queen Mary*, complete with funnels, could completely fit inside her huge new namesake! It is to welcome her that this book is produced.

Each of the great liners chronicled within these pages have had careers that have been packed with adventure, excitement and tragedy. Let us hope that when her story is finally written that the career of the new Queen of the Oceans, the *Queen Mary 2*, will be as full, at least of interest and excitement, as her predecessors.

David F. Hutchings,
Lee-on-The Solent , November, 2003

Queen Mary is escorted by tugs at Southampton.

W. J. Windebank, courtesy of Barry J. Eagles

Dedication

With love to Cis and Bill; Doris and Frank; Edna and Edgar. To Emma and Alex,
and to my lifelong friend Dick de Kerbrech and to David L. Williams
And to all those who died in the shipyard tragedy at St. Nazaire on 15th November 2003

Main Index

Queen Mary.... 9   Queen Elizabeth....81   QE2....193

Published by

Waterfront

A Division of Kingfisher Productions
**The Dalesmade Centre, Watershed Mill, Settle, North Yorkshire
BD24 9LR England Tel & Fax 0870 747 2983
ISBN 0 946184 67 4**
Copyright David F. Hutchings and Kingfisher Productions 2003
Publisher Roger Hardingham

A Queen In Waiting

Above: The *Queen Mary 2* is almost structurally complete and has just had her funnel lowered into place.
Below: Sitting in the huge dry-dock at St. Nazaire the new Cunarder dwarfs vehicles and men on the dock bottom.

Above: With her name and her proud port of registry emblazoned on her stern, the *Queen Mary 2* is put through her bollard trials.
Below: One of the azipods has arrived from Britain. At first, these pods had to be returned for modification.

Above: A fine aerial view of the new liner, almost complete, sitting alongside the fitting-out jetty at St. Nazaire.
Below: *Queen Mary 2* on one of her sea trials. The liner would return to dry-dock for final painting and fitting out prior to her maiden voyage.

RMS Queen Mary
The Stateliest Ship

Introduction

Queen Mary was more than one of the greatest ships ever built, carrying the rich and the famous between Southampton and New York at great speed. She was more than a prestigious mail-carrying symbol of the country and of the Company that brought her into being.

She represented a nationís hope when she was first designed and laid down; she represented a nationís disappointment when work on her ceased because of the depression; she represented a new hope when she was finally completed and launched, the ultimate achievement of the technology of the age. She represented the embodiment of many dreams.

Ever since her conception she has captured the imagination; ever since her disappearance from the waters of the North Atlantic she has continued to represent in her latter role at Long Beach; the popular ideal of an ocean liner.

In the year that marks the 50th anniversary of her maiden voyage this publication can only hope to celebrate, in some small way, the legend of the *Queen Mary*.

Commodore Geoffrey Marr summed up the impact that not only the *Queen Mary* but also her sister the *Queen Elizabeth* made when he quoted: 'The two *Queens* undoubtedly will always remain the finest ships ever built. They're talking about tankers of 500,000 tons but no tanker, no matter what its size, could ever convey the visual impact of these two magnificent ships, especially when seen at speed, flinging aside the North Atlantic in huge combers, the whole line one of power and splendour: oceanic palaces of magnificent proportions.'

Who could follow that?

David F. Hutchings, Fareham, Hampshire 1986

Dedication
To my late uncle William Way of Cowes, surveyor of lifeboats for the RNLI and an early influence on my love of ships and shipbuilding.

Opposite page: 'To Smooth Your Way Across The Atlantic' - The *Queen Mary* at sea to test her new stabilizers. She couldn'tr find any suitably rough ocean so, by operating the stabilizers, an atificial roll was induced. This roll was then soon subdued by the stabilizers. *The late Captain John Treasure Jones collection*

This page: The *Queen Mary*'s impressive length is illustrated here by this view of the Boat Deck. Cunard's long association with Liverpool is recognised on the side of the lifeboats. *Courtesy, University of Liverpool Cunard archives*

Contents

Chapter One
Lifting The Cloud 10
Chapter Two
A Dream Takes Form 15
Chapter Three
The Wonder Ship 19
Chapter Four
'...behold a city on th' inconstant billows...'..........................31
Chapter Five
You'll Never Get A Better Picture! 45
Chapter Six
Perils and People 55
Chapter Seven
Mary and the Movies..67
Chapter Eight
The Queen Dowager..70
Chapter Nine
A Wonderful, Beautiful Toy 73

Chapter One

Lifting the Cloud

Clydebank on Wednesday September 26th 1934 was grey, cold and very wet. In spite of that is was a special day, not only for the Clydesiders who were taking a specially declared public holiday, but also for the whole of Britain.

After three years of the worst economic depression in world history the country was launching its biggest ship from the Clydeside shipyard of John Brown in the presence of their Majesties King George V, Queen Mary and HRH The Prince of Wales, the latter being there in his guise as Master of the Merchant Navy and Fishing Fleets.

Number 534, the shipyard number by which the new Cunard-White Star liner had been known for so long, was symbolical of the rebirth of a nation. Work on her had stopped a year after it had started and No. 534 had lain uncompleted and rusting on the stocks whilst Britain languished in the years of the Depression and the resulting mass unemployment.

When is was decided to recommence the building of No. 534 it seemed to represent the turning point in Britainís fortunes and her progress was followed with keen interest.

Umbrellas are lowered as the King an Queen aknowledge the cheering crowd prior to proceeding to the launching platform. No. 534 dominates the background 'lofty as a tower'.

Topical Press

To mark this start of a return to normality the Queen had graciously consented to launch the giant liner and in doing so became the first reigning British monarch to perform such a ceremony. John Masefield, the Poet Laureate, had composed a special poem, entitled 'Number 534', to mark the occasion of the launch. It is here reproduced in full:

For ages you were rock, far below the light,
Crushed, without shape, earthís unregarded bone.
Then Man in all the marvel of his might,
Quarried you out and burned you from the stone.

Then, being pured to essence, you were nought
But weight and hardness, body without nerve;
Then Man in all the marvel of his thought,
Smithied you into form of leap and curve;

And took you, so, and bent you to his vast,
Intense great world of passionate design,
Curve after changing curve, braced and masst
To stand all tumult that can tumble brine,

And left you, this, a rampart of a ship,
Long as a street and lofty as a tower,
Ready to glide in thunder from the slip
And shear the sea with majesty of power.

I long to see you leaping to the urge
Of the great engines, rolling as you go,
Parting the seas sunder in a surge,
Shredding a trackway like a mile of snow

With all the wester streaming from your hull
And all gear twanging shrilly as you race,
And effortless above your stern a gull
Leaning upon the blast and keeping place.

May shipwreck and collision, fog and fire,
Rock, shoal and other evils of the sea,
Be kept from you; and may the heartís desire
Of those who speed your launching come to be.

'rolling as you go' and ...all gear twanging shrilly' foresaw with clarity two of the new liner's less amiable propensities.

By the afternoon of the launch day itself an estimated two hundred thousand people, at least, many paying fifteen shillings for a seat in specially constructed stands, converged onto the shipyard and into the fields on the banks of the Clyde, opposite to the shipyard. The river had been newly dredged over a length of 1800 ft from the slipway and had been widened to take the length of the ship.

Continuing rain had deadened the preceding and worrying wind but the mass of black umbrellas was lowered as the royal party, passing 'yards of ermine and gold braid' as one observer put it, ascended to the glass enclosed launching platform.

For the first time, too, the launching ceremony was being broadcast to an eager nation and after Sir Percy Bates, the Chairman of Cunard-White Star, had welcomed the royal guests the King made his speech:

'The sea with all her tempests, will not be readily bridled, and she is stronger than man; yet in recent times man has done much to make the struggle with her more equal.

Above: With propeller edges protected with old rubber tyres the *Queen Mary* is inspected before launching day. The supporting shores are still in place and the slipway has been cleared of all obstructions.

Below: The mass of timber that formed the fore poppet was needed to support the liner's forward end during the crucial seconds of launching.

'Today we come to the happy task of sending on her way the stateliest ship now in being. I thank all those here and elsewhere whose efforts, however conspicuous or humble, have helped to build her. For three years her unaccomplished hull has lain in silence on the stocks. We know full well what a misery a silent dockyard may spread among a seaport and with what courage that misery is endured. During those years when work upon her was suspended we grieved for what that suspension meant to thousands of our people.

'We rejoice that, with the help of my Government, it has been possible to lift that cloud and to complete this ship. Now, with the hope of better trade on both sides of the Atlantic, let us look forward to her playing a great part in the revival of international commerce.

'It has been the nation's will that she should be completed, and today we can send forth, no longer a number on the books, but a ship with a name, into the world, alive with beauty, energy and strength.

'Samuel Cunard built his ships to carry the mails between the two English-speaking countries. This one is built to carry the people of the two lands in great number to and fro so that they may learn to understand each other. Both are faced with similar problems and prosper and suffer together.

'We send her to her elements for the good will of all the nations as a mark of our hope in the future. She has been built in fellowship among ourselves. May her life among great waters spread friend-ship among the nations.'

The King's fine epithet 'the stateliest ship', was to remain with the liner during the ensuing years.

The Queen then stepped forward and, possibly forgetting that the launching was being broadcast, whispered 'Which buttons do I press?' She then made her eagerly awaited speech and, in naming the ship ended years of popular speculation. Because of the well-kept secret the letters of the liner's name had not yet been riveted to the hull. Many suggestions had been put forward as possible contenders for the No. 534's name - *Victoria*, *Britannia* and many others, usually with the 'ia' suffix that had been given to the majority of Cunard ships in the past. However,

because of the recent amalgamation between the Cunard and White Star Lines it was felt politic not to offend the White Star interests whose ships had traditionally used the suffix 'ic' (*Britannic*, *Olympic*, *Majestic* etc) and the final choice pleased both shipping lines and the country as a whole.

'I am happy', the Queen spoke clearly making, this, her first public speech, 'to name this ship *Queen Mary*. I wish success to her and to all who sail in her.' Then, with a pair of golden scissors, the Queen cut a pink ribbon which sent a bottle of Australian wine arcing across the void between platform and ship to shatter its contents against the towering knife edge of the *Queen Mary*'s bow. Her Majesty then turned to the King and asked, 'Was that right?'

The Queen then pressed the first of two electric buttons, which set in motion the results of four years of complicated calculations and model experiments. Six triggers, that had been holding back the *Mary*'s 35,500 ton launch weight on the inclined slipway, were released. The second button, when pressed, started six hydraulic rams that began to push the grey-painted ship backwards on her sliding cradle with an ever-increasing motion towards the Clyde.

As the liner's bow, still encased in its wooden and steel cradle (the 'fore-poppet'), dipped from the edge of the slipway into the river, 2,350 tons of drag chains, connected in bundles to various points along the giant hull, crashed and slid in clouds of rust after the liner, their great bulk and resistance gently bringing the *Queen Mary* to a halt. It had been calculated that the liner would, on this first and

Top: Bundles of dray chain and carefully laid out cable are prepared in readiness to halt the liner once launched into the Clyde.

Left: With her bow snugly held in the fore poppets and her hull still supported by shores, 534 is almost ready for launching. The launch platform appears ready to receive the royal guests.
Courtesy, University of Liverpool Cunard Archives

perhaps most critical journey of her career, travel 1,194 feet before being brought to a halt. In fact, she travelled just two feet more than calculated, a marvellous verification of the naval architectís art.

The ship had also needed a considerable amount of internal shoring to give her additional stiffness during the launch and hundreds of tons of steel girders and wooden shores had been erected inside her. To maintain strength in her superstructure the windows had not yet been cut along her Promenade Deck.

Between the 100 seconds of her first faltering movement to the time that she was brought to a halt the spectators had given her a tumultuous reception, even those who had tried to keep clear of the resulting flood-wave that hit the opposite shore. The ceremony and launch had lasted a mere fifteen minutes and, on its completion, the King and Queen descended the platform steps to meet the men who had built the *Queen* and then to attend a reception in the shipyard's mould loft.

The *Mary*, herself, was gently towed to her fitting out berth in a strengthening wind that made the job increasingly more difficult. This berth would be her home for the next eighteen months whilst engines, boilers and many thousands of items that go to make an ocean liner were installed.

Right: The newly named *Queen Mary* picks up speed as she moves along the most dangerous few hundred yards of her life.

Below: Safely afloat the liner is brought to a halt by bundles of drag chains. Their restraining cables attached to the ship pulled taut by the applied forces of launching.
Courtesy, University of Liverpool Cunard Archives

Above: Immediately after the launch the *Queen Mary* was carefully edged alongside the fitting-out berth. The wetness of the day can be judged from the jetty planking. The tug *Paladin* is to the right.   *Courtesy, University of Liverpool Cunard Archives*

Below: A bevy of tugs busily take charge of the giant hull in order to edge her to her fitting-out berth.   *John and Marion Clarkson collection*

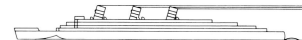

Chapter Two

A Dream Takes Form

The seeds of the idea that germinated into the *Queen Mary* had been sown in 1926 when a preliminary design for a long sought after thousand foot liner was sketched out in Cunard's design office.

Taking into account modern shipbuilding methods and materials, marine engines, types of fuel available (oil, coal or pulverised coal), numbers of passengers and classes to be carried, availability of building slips, dry-and wet-docking facilities etc, the designers had evolved a three-funnelled ship of fairly conventional appearance but with one advantage over all other existing ships - speed.

Later, in 1929, a Cunard committee began to seriously investigate a replacement (or replacements) for the ageing *Mauretania* of 1907, *Aquitania* of 1914 and the *Berengaria*, the latter having been the German liner *Imperator* of 1912 and taken over by Britain as part of the reparations after World War 1.

Until this time, three liners had been needed to maintain a weekly sailing between Britain and the United States but now two large, fast ships were being contemplated to provide the same regularity of sailings. 27½ knots was the minimum speed required to maintain this service, but a greater speed would be required to make up time lost through adverse weather conditions. An added factor would be one of prestige as such a pair of ships would be faster than the express ships of other nations and would attract the cream of the travelling public. Sir Percy Bates discounted any idea that the ships would be built to gain the coveted Blue Ribband, saying that the ships being proposed would be the smallest and slowest ships that could provide the envisaged service.

After the initial idea had gone through several changes of design it was decided that a ship of nearly 1,020 feet in length and with a beam of 118 feet would best be suited to the companyís requirements. The choice of boilers had posed one particular problem but, eventually, water tube boilers gained preference over the originally proposed 'Scotch' boilers. This had upset the calculations of the ship designers, as a lot of weight would be taken from low down in the hull where it was most needed to provide sufficient stability. A complete redesign was avoided, however, when a new system of piping, using lighter pipe materials, was adopted in the higher realms of the ship, thus compensating for any weight lost below the waterline.

The contract for the first of the two new liners was awarded to the renowned John Brown Shipyard on Clydeside and was executed on 1st December 1930. The ship was given a building number in the builders' books and became popularly known to the world by that number, 'No. 534', until the very day of her launch.

The keel of No. 534 was laid on 27th December and the first rivet was driven home by an ex-apprentice who had become the Shipyard Manager, Mr (later Sir) Donald Skifflington.

For the following twelve months the ship grew in stature as frames were erected and plated and beams and decks were laid. Progress on the building proceeded well, so well, in fact, that Sir Percy Bates thought that the ship would be ready for launching in February 1932, four months ahead of schedule and thus be ready for sea by mid-1933. So, according to this estimation, the giant liner (at 73,000 tons - later revised to 83,000 tons - she was half as big again as the previous largest liner, the *Majestic*) was within five months of being ready for launching when a devastating blow fell 'like a bolt from the blue'.

The world had slid into a general economic recession

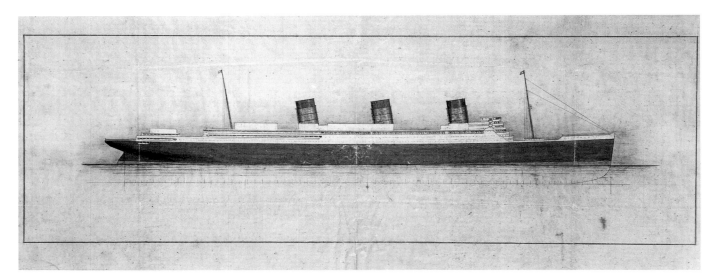

One of the early proposals for the *Queen Mary*'s design, was based on the design of the *Berengaria* (ex-*Imperator*) and the *Aquitania*.

National Maritime Museum

that became known as 'The Depression' but Cunard had been able to soldier on bravely through its early months, even managing to show a profit. It was then found that the available money was needed for insurances, depreciation of the existing fleet, maintaining services and that little or no money was available to compete No. 534 and to finish the ship would prove to be an unbearable burden on the company's resources. The liner had not been subsidised by the British government as it was not anticipated that she would be used in time of war as had, for example, the *Lusitania* and *Mauretania* which had been built to Admiralty specifications.

The Cunard Company therefore had no other choice than to suspend any further work on 534 and this suspension, coming into effect on Friday 11th December 1931, meant dismissal for 3,000 men who worked directly on the ship and a further 6 to 7,000 more who were employed in various sub-contracting industries ranging from steel forgings to cutlery producers and from carpet weavers to potters. The cessation of work also symbolised the

onslaught of the worst of the Depression to the people of a maritime nation who had followed the ships' construction with avid interest, feeding on all the superlatives that the contemporary press could offer.

Whilst the ship languished so did Britain and it was popularly believed, like the search for some holy grail, that as soon as the work restarted on 534 so would Britain find its way back to full employment and prosperity.

For 27 long, hard months the liner lay rusting on the stocks accumulating 130 tons of rust along with innumerable nests of birds that found the man-made cliffs of steel an ideal breeding place.

Smoke and mist hung in a pallid veil over the quiet, hungry town, the usual staccato rhythms of riveting silenced, a silence that spread its meaning of unemployment to all corners of the country.

But in one corner, in the chamber of the House of Commons, this silence was challenged. David Kirkwood, Labour Member of Parliament for Dumbarton Burghs, demanded the resumption of work on 534 to alleviate the

Top: For 27 months No. 534 remained silently on the building slip collecting 130 tons of rust.

Above: Sir Percy Bates, Chairman of the Cunard Line.

Left: Almost complete, the stern (overhanging the Clyde at high tide) awaits the fitting of the rudder and propellers.
Courtesy, University of Liverpool Cunard Archives

unemployment in his constituency. He said, 'I believe that as long as No. 534 lies like a skeleton in my constituency so long will the depression last in this country. To me it seems to shout Failure! Failure! to the whole of Britain....' At first, his cries went unheeded but gradually sympathetic ears listened to his pleas and took up his cause.

The problem was, how to finance the idea. The government refused to subsidise Cunard and Cunard could not afford to restart work from its own finances. After lengthy and complex discussions a solution was found and the government agreed to make Cunard a repayable loan under certain conditions.

The making of a loan to build an express ship was in itself most unusual in that all foreign competition to 534 had been built with state aid and had been, or would be, run with state subsidies, the ships themselves being loss-makers for the sake of being prestigious national symbols. Not only would 534 be paid for from private capital (albeit via a loan) but would be run on a profit-making basis, making her unique amongst her contemporaries.

To add to the financial complexities of the government loan to Cunard it was stipulated, as part of the agreement, that the company should take over the ailing White Star Line as a running mate.

This steamship line had been founded in 1867 and had run many fast and famous ships in the late 19th century but had latterly built for size and comfort. In 1902 the Line had been purchased by the American owned International Mercantile Marine Company although the ships of the line remained under the British flag manned with British crews, (in case of requisition in time of war). However, from 1927, the White Star Line once again became purely British when it was purchased by the Royal Mail Steam Packet Company, adding it to its vast empire of financially interwoven shipping companies under the chairmanship of Owen Phillips, Lord Kylsant.

Above: The enormity of the construction can be seen as Deck beams and the shadow of frames make a gigantic lattice work.
Courtesy, University of Liverpool Cunard Archives

Because of the complexity of its financial arrangements RMSP found itself in difficulties (Lord Kylsant himself was imprisoned as a result) and White Star was once again offered for sale. Cunard was interested but was dubious about the financial pitfalls that would accompany the purchase and the company 'backed-off'. The British government stepped in to champion White Star and made it a condition of the financial loan to Cunard that the two companies should merge. Thus came into being Cunard White Star Ltd., but Cunard consoled itself by the fact that they now had £9.5 million, - £3 million to complete 534, £1.5 million to provide working capital for the new company and a further £5 million for the construction of a long awaited sistership to the liner already under construction.

So, on Tuesday 3rd April 1934, four hundred men, led by a band of kilted pipers, marched through the jubilant streets of Clydeside and back to the open gates of John Brown's Shipyard to start clearing the rust from the hull of No. 534. Formal notice to restart construction was received by the yard on 26th May and thus the campaigning of David Kirkwood MP, along with the shrewd business acumen of Sir Percy Bates, had brought about the impossible dream - the mammoth liner was to be completed. Clydeside was back at work and, taking heart from the renewed vigour in that one shipyard, Britain herself became revitalised.

Left: Advertisement in 'Shipbuilder and Shipping Record' of the Clydebank Works.

Men disembark in their hundreds at the end of a day's work.

Courtesy, University of Liverpool Cunard Archives

Chapter Three

The Wonder Ship

From the time of her conception the *Queen Mary* was planned to be the ship of the age - 'The Wonder Ship'. Everything about her was to be big both in quantity and quality and, without apology, this chapter sets out to list a few of the statistics and superlatives that made her 'The Big Ship'.

From the turn of the century the public, always thirsty for details of the glamorous big liners that plied their trade back and forth across the Atlantic, were supplied with comparisons as each new ship entered the lists.

Photographs, or artist's impressions made when a photograph was not possible, abounded depicting the current liner that was having its virtues extolled shown in most unlikely poses in order to give an idea of its size in comparison with famous buildings or landmarks. Upended against the Eiffel Tower or the Empire State Building, having locomotives driven through a cavernous funnel or seemingly to have run aground along one side of the Great Pyramid of Cheops, all served to astound the hopefully potential traveller who would be attracted to the biggest or the fastest ship of the day.

In this, the *Queen Mary* was no exception. One famous illustration showed the ship with her bows in Whitehall, her starboard bridge wing almost dislodging Nelson from his column in Trafalgar Square and her stern creating mayhem at the Coliseum Theatre in St. Martin's Lane. Londoners, seeing his huge vessel blocking their streets, do not seem to be over-perturbed. Another sketch illustrated the ship with the top of her forward funnel as being four feet above the centre of the clock face at Westminster.

Although such visual cliches were commonplace to preceding generations that grew up when the liner was the only way to cross the oceans and carried the interesting, the rich, the famous, the notorious as well as the ordinary work-a-day folk, it is worth repeating some of the superlatives that caught the public's imagination when No. 534 was being built and came into service.

The first big item was her cost - £5 million. She was to be the first liner to be over 1,000 feet long, (the White Star had a thousand-footer on the stocks but this was cancelled and the French pipped the British at the post when their Normandie was finished before the *Mary* - she had been subsidised by the French government throughout the years

Rivetters fix boundary plates that will take the ship's superstructure bulkheads. The shape of the Bridge can be seen as a backdrop.
Courtesy, University of Liverpool Cunard Archives

of depression) she would be 1,019½ feet in overall length and her beam 118 feet. Her original gross tonnage was to have been 73,000 but this was later increased to 81,000 following a competition in increased tonnages between her and the French liner(each company seemed to find extra tonnage as that of the competition was periodically revised and announced). In the evolution of her hull design twenty two models, each almost 17 feet long, were made and with these eight thousand experiments were run in testing tanks, a total of one thousand miles being travelled.

The hull during construction on the stocks embodied 35,500 tons of steel by the time of launching, the stern frame alone weighing 190 tons and the rudder 180. Ten million rivets (4,000 tons) held the vessel together; the plates forming the hull and decks measured form 8 to 30 feet in length and weighed in from 3 cwt to 3 tons each. Painting the outer hull consumed 70,000 gallons of paint, before which four coats of anti-corrosion paint was applied, that was hoped would last for forty years. Two thousand portholes and windows were cut into her sides and these used two and a half thousand square feet of thick, strengthened glass.

The liner had twelve decks and was divided into 160 watertight compartments.

The main features of the liner, her funnels, came under particular scrutiny. The distance from keel to the top of the forward funnel was 184 feet, (the funnel heights diminished aft to give a 'racy' look) was 30 feet in diameter and the distance between each funnel was 138 feet. The whistles, two on the fore and one on the middle funnel, were 6 feet 7 inches long and weighed one ton each. The beautiful, deep-throated note (more like a roar!) that exuded from these whistles was said to be 'A', two octaves below the middle 'A' on the piano'. However, even to the unmusical ear the sound produced never failed to thrill and could be heard at least ten miles away with the reverberations felt many times that distance away.

To propel the ship four 20 feet diameter, four bladed propellers, each costing £7,000, were fitted. These were made from 50-ton 'Tubiston' castings which took fourteen days to cool. The final propellers each tipped the scales at 35 tons which exceeded the largest propellers previously made by 10 tons.

The propellers were driven by four sets of quadruple

Above: One of the enormous castings that had to be moved from Darlington to Middlesbrough before being shipped to the Clyde. The casting took the width of three railway tracks and the railway had to be closed for the weekend. It seemed as if all of Darlington turned out for the event.

Courtesy, University of Liverpool Cunard Archives

Below: One of four 20-foot diameter proplellers that would be fitted to the liner.

Left: An avenue of frames with attached brackets stand erect in readiness to receive beams that will support each deck.

expansion, reduced-geared turbines having in total 257,000 blades - all hand set. Developing 50,000 horsepower they turned at 3,000 rpm, this speed being reduced to 200 rpm at the propellers by a reduction gear that was itself 14 feet in diameter. The steam for the engines was provided by twenty-four Yarrow-type water tube boilers, fuelled by oil from tanks holding 75,000 gallons, giving a working pressure of 400 pounds per square inch. Low-pressure steam for heating and cooking was provided by three double-ended 'Scotch' boilers. Power to light the thirty thousand electric light bulbs, operate the twenty-two lifts, five hundred and ninety six clocks, etc, was supplied by seven turbo-generator sets that developed 10,000 kilowatts (enough to power a town of 150,000 people) and was distributed through the ship by four thousand miles of electric wiring!

The ship could be secured by the then largest anchors at 16 tons a piece; their cables (chains) of 165 fathoms (990 feet) a further 145 tons. The anchor cables, along with other cables and wire hawsers, would have measured four miles if laid end to end!

For the safety of passengers and crew twenty four lifeboats would be carried, twenty of which were 36 feet long, 12 feet wide and each with a capacity for 145 people. These were built by Hugh McLean and Sons Ltd. of Glasgow.

Passengers carried were up to 776 cabin (first) class, 784 tourist (second) and 579 third. 1,101 officers and crew looked after the safety and welfare of the ship and passengers.

After the heady statistics of the *Queen Mary*'s construction, the shopping list for this incredible ship would make any land-based housewife quake:

Ten thousand meals a day for four days had to be prepared but the catering staff could chose their menus from stores that included: 20 tons of fish, 20,000 lbs of poultry (chicken, duck etc.), 70,000 eggs, 3 tons of butter, 4,000 lbs of tea and coffee, 4,000 gallons of milk, 70 tons of meat (various!), 50,000 lbs of vegetables, not including 50,000 lbs of potatoes - 115,000 various bottles (including 20,000 of beer, 14,500 of wine and 5,000 of spirits), 2,000 lbs of cheese and 6,000 gallons of draught beer.

Although her vital statistics attracted some to travel in the *Mary* the details of her construction meant little to many of her passengers. It was too 'chic' to travel in the biggest and fastest of ships to worry about such detail but the interior decor of the liner also proved to be a great pull.

Again more statistics, but some which had more immediate appeal to the travelling public because these items affected the passengers for the four days of their voyage.

The length of No. 534 necessitated an extention to be built to the slipway. The additional structure extended over a railway creating a tunnel for the shipyard's locomotives to pass underneath.
Courtesy, University of Liverpool Cunard Archives

In the restaurants 16,000 items of silver plate were provided, including many pieces transferred from the old *Mauretania* when the latter was sold for scrap. To keep the passengers comfortable at night 30,000 sheets and 31,000 pillow cases had to be produced; altogether there was a half million items of linen. 200,000 pieces of earthenware, glass and china were on board, again much from the older ships, and underfoot there was six miles of carpeting. For deck and cabin use ten miles of blankets were made, for which 6,000 marino sheep unselfishly gave 16 tons of wool.

Since the advent of the French Line's *Ile de France* the decor of ocean liners had tended less to be copies of palaces or famous country mansions than to reflect, or even inspire, the tastes of the age into which they were launched. 534 was to be no exception. In fact, to some commentators, she may have gone too far and her 'modernity' of the mid-30s had started to jade by the late 40s. But in her day she did set trends, starting a vogue of 'Ocean Liner' decor that could be seen in the Odeon cinemas with their curvilinear art-deco architecture, 'porthole' windows, ship-rail style banisters set on sweeping stairways and so on.

To panel the bulkheads and pillars over fifty types of wood were used for the veneering, some never having been used before and some since declared extinct. Woods were imported from all over the Empire, from Africa, from Asia and America. Their very names conjured up exotic places, seemingly yet to be discovered. There were four types of ash, six of mahogany, four of oak. There was zebrano, rosewood, myrtle and satinwood, thuya, makore, cedar and cherry and many, many more, all finished with a high degree of polish.

It is possible, within this short book, to describe only a few of the public rooms on board the *Mary* but the rooms that the veneers, mentioned above, adorned included one of the - if not *the* - largest room afloat. This was the Cabin Class Restaurant on 'C' Deck, 143 feet long, extending the full width of the ship (118) feet and 27 feet, maximum, in height. Other rooms included childrens playrooms, a library, galleries, smoking rooms, drawing rooms, lounges, shops (W.H. Smith, Austin Reed and a souvenir shop), ballroom, the first synagogue afloat, an observation lounge and a gymnasium, squash court, swimming pool, turkish bath and 'frigidarium' amongst the facilities catering for the health conscious or those just wishing to work off those extra pounds gained in the restaurants!

The Cabin Class Lounge, 96 feet by 70 feet, with is 'autumnal gold' decor could be converted from the main

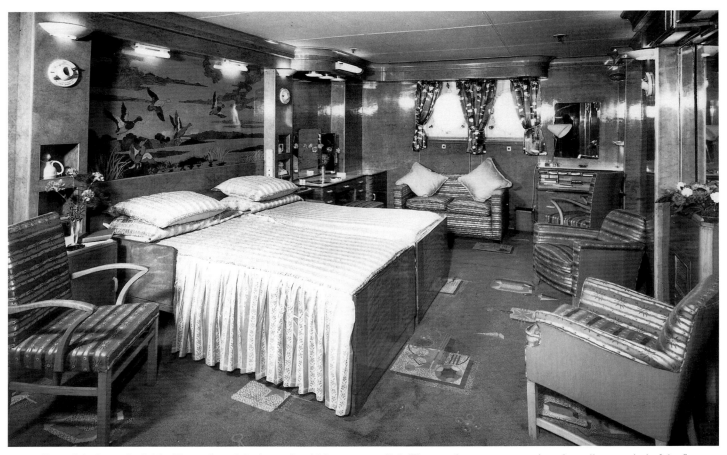

Above: A bedroom in Cabin Class reflected the luxury in which many travelled. The superb marquetry panel on the wall was typical of the fine workmanship employed throughout the liner.

Below: The Entrance Hall on the Promenade Deck which clearly shows Queen Mary's personal standard and the large medallion depicting the royal personage.

Courtesy, University of Liverpool Cunard Archives

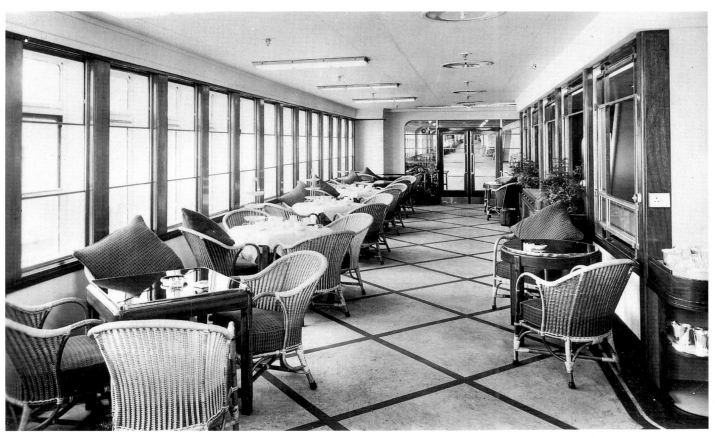

Above: The Garden Lounge, one of two - port and starboard. These would be converted for other uses after the war.
Below: The Verandah Grill at the aft end of the superstructure was an exclusive haunt for exclusive patrons.

Above: The Main Lounge that extended up through three decks with a sparkling cavern of glass and polished veneer.

Below: One of dozens of commissions that adorned the liner's public rooms with stylised Art Deco motifs.

W. J. Windebank, *courtesy of Barry J. Eagles*

Above: A decorative map of the North Atlantic was designed by MacDonald Gill, FRIBA. A silver clock with crystal numerals is placed high in the centre and a lit, crystal model of the *Queen Mary* followed the ship's track along the map to correspond with the ship's position on the ocean.
Below: The forward looking Observation Lounge, resplendent in silver and red lacquer.   *Both, W. J. Windebank, courtesy of Barry J. Eagles*

Above: First Class Main Lounge - note circular windows high up as a reference point.

Below: The exclusive Grill Room with its black carpet and red curtains spangled with gold stars was the glittering gathering place of the rich and famous where dining (at an additional cost) and dancing carried on until the small hours. Note the after mast as it passes through the room!

Both, W. J. Windebank, courtesy of Barry J. Eagles

Above: Fitting-out of the *Queen Mary* is well underway. Windows have been cut into the superstructure along the Promenade Deck. Painting of the hull has started as can be seen around the ship's name at the stern. *Courtesy, University of Liverpool Cunard Archives*
Below: Three funnels fitted and painted in Cunard-White Star colours show that the liner is nearing completion. *Courtesy, University of Liverpool Cunard Archives*

Many of these rooms were adorned with original works of art especially commissioned by Cunard. Thirty-six of the best contemporary British artists were invited to submit works, the *Mary* was not to be a museum ship! Sir Stanley Spencer declined to prepare anything ('I only want to paint what I like and not what people want me to paint') and Duncan Grant's quasi-erotic works were rejected by Cunard's chairman with a suggestion as to what the directors could do with them..... 'Give them to the blind school' was the retort!

Magnificent marquetry, designed by C. Cameron Baillie, adorned walls from third to first class; styled paintings by Kenneth Shoesmith graced the Roman Catholic altars in Cabin and Tourist Classes ('Madonna of the Atlantic' and 'Madonna of the Tall Ships') as well as a beautiful group scene in the Cabin Class Drawing Room; various murals in metals by four sculptors - Messrs. Stanton, Lambert and the Gilbert brothers; Doris Zinkeisen's mural in the Verandah Grill; and Edward Wadsworth whose painting 'The Sea' contained symbolical allusions to that element complete with the *Queen Mary* appearing on the horizon and a pink ribbon draped

first-class social gathering spot during the day to a ballroom at night simply by rolling back the huge Wilton carpet.

The aftermost deckhouse on the Sun Deck housed the elegant Verandah Grill with its stunning black carpets, stylish murals and exotic deep red, gold-star-spangled curtains. This room was 'the place' to be seen on the ship and to dine and dance here would carry an additional charge.

The *Queen Mary* is brought to a halt in the King George V Graving Dock in Southampton. Remains of launch gear can be seen low on the bow and this would soon be removed.
Colin Baxter collection

around a central pillar: this ribbon should have been blue to represent the Blue Riband but the artist decided that there was too much blue on the ship and painted it pink! Much of the outfitting was photographed in colour by Mdm Yvonde, her four-colour camera once apparently fused the entire ship!

For the forward bulkhead of the Cabin Class Restaurant MacDonald Gill designed a decorative and stylised (24 x 15 feet) map of the North Atlantic complete with a crystal model of the ship that moved to show the current position of the liner. At the opposite end of this room was a tapestry-style painting by Philip Conrad depicting English life and at the base of this hung a magnificent pair of finely worked bronze doors.

A marble plaque, designed by Lady Hilton Young,

showing HM The Queen, was hung in a panel of walnut burr and placed at the head of the main staircase facing the Main Hall and shops. Queen Mary's framed personal standard would also be added in this vicinity.

In the tourist Class Smoking Room there hung a magnificent painting by marine artist Charles Pears. This depicted the old *Mauretania*, smoke belching from her funnels and still painted in rust-streaked cruising white, masts cut down to pass under the Forth Bridge, en-route to the shipbreakers at Rosyth.

Thus an old Cunard favourite was shown sailing to her fate whilst the hull that carried her picture like a miniature of a departed loved-one was ready to sail at the beginning of her own reign of the Atlantic.

Above: The *Queen Mary's* First Class Swimming Pool as photographed in June 1964.
Below: In another area deep inside the ship's hull is the Engine Room. Here is the control platform.

Both, W. J. Windebank, courtesy of Barry J. Eagles

The Spirit of the Age

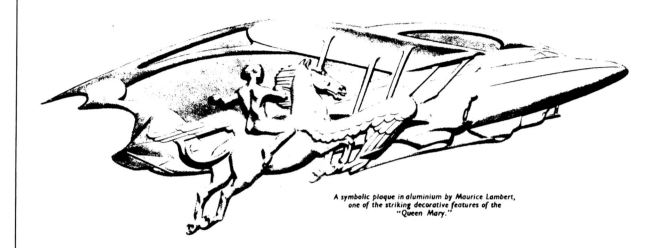

A symbolic plaque in aluminium by Maurice Lambert,
one of the striking decorative features of the
"Queen Mary."

Wonders of the "Queen Mary"

The massive form of Britain's finest shipping
achievement is in itself a symbol of the age
. . the result of all the marvels of modern
scientific research, industry and art. The
immensity and dignity . . . steadiness and stability
. . . beauty in design . . . the wonderful artistic
conception of decoration . . . unprecedented
luxury and comfort . . . qualities which do not
aim at mere effect but which combine to fulfil the
purpose and service of the world's greatest liner.

For further details apply to any Cunard White Star office or agency.

Cunard White Star

'...behold a city on th' inconstant billows...' Henry V Act 3

The *Mary* continued her fitting-out alongside the jetty at John Browns' Shipyard and, because her stern extended some 100 feet beyond the end of the fitting-out berth and into the river, protective piles were driven into the bed of the Clyde to protect her from any possible collision damage. These piles had previously been some of the internal stiffening beams used during her launch.

Other ships were still being built, of course, at the yard and launched whilst the *Queen* was fitted in her finery. One vessel, the Anglo-American Oil Company's tanker *Comanche*, had an additional 480 tons of drag chains attached along her port side. Consequently, when she was launched the extra weight caused her to swing away from the *Mary* prior to dropping her anchors to prevent drift.

Other than attending the launching Edward, Prince of Wales, visited the ship twice whilst she was on the Clyde. Once at the instigation of David Kirkwood MP, who urged him, whilst having a lengthy interview with the King, to visit the ship and town during the depression to see for himself the hardships being caused by the suspension of construction and a second visit was paid during Edward's brief reign as King. To the grief of the nation, King George V, the 'Sailor King', had died on 21st January 1936, the Prince succeeding him as King Edward VIII and as such visited the ship for a

Top: Some of the many men involved in building the *Queen Mary* watch with pride - and perhaps a little sorrow - as she leaves the place of her creation.

Above: With scaffolding still in place, the liner's name is now clear for all to see.   Both, *Courtesy, University of Liverpool Cunard Archives*

lengthy tour of inspection on 5th March. The King upset the official tour that was planned by insisting on seeing, not only the first class areas that he was usually shown, but the crewsí quarters and where they ate.

As the royal visitor and his entourage left the shipyard the siren of Britain's greatest liner sounded for the first time in salute to the King Emperor of the World's greatest Empire.

During the period of fitting-out thousands of sightseers flocked to the Clyde's opposite banks along the shores of the confluence of the Clyde and Cart rivers to inspect recent progress. They saw the letters, two and a half feet high, of the lineris name being fixed to either side of the bow and to the stern; they saw the funnels being fitted one by one and they saw the hull being painted; superstructure in white, the hull a gleaming black and the funnels in Cunard's orange-red with black tops and bands. The painting signalled another important step in the *Mary*'s career - her imminent departure from the care of those who had skilfully and unsparingly built her with an affection that had been interrupted by so much suffering.

As the day gradually approached on which the *Queen Mary* would leave her birthplace an excitement gripped the country.

The French Line had finished their own mammoth liner, the *Normandie*, well before Cunard White Star had completed 534. Although the keel of the French ship had been laid down a month after that of the *Mary*, she had been finished earlier (due to the more far-sighted financial policy of the French government) and had made her record-

Above: A dramatic view of a worker suspended half way down one of the funnels as he applies a coat of Cunard red.
Below: One of a series of dramatic aerial photographs showing the Queen slewed across the Clyde during her brush with near disaster.
C. M. Baxter Collection

breaking maiden voyage a year ahead of her British rival - and rivals they were. To start with, the *Normandie* was given an overall length (tip of bow to stern) of 1,030 feet as opposed to the 1,019.5 feet of the *Queen Mary*, but length overall was purely 'cosmetic' as such extra length could be built into almost any ship via a finely raked bow or style of stern but was useful for publicity propaganda. The length that mattered, at least to designers, was waterline length or even length between perpendiculars. For the *Mary* this was 1,004 feet (making her the first true thousand-footer), for the *Normandie*, 962 feet. On her maiden crossing to New York, the *Normandie* had achieved the Blue Ribband, that allegorical symbol of speed. But what the British public wanted to know was: would the *Queen Mary* wrest the honour form her archrival on her own maiden voyage? Cunard would not purposely attempt to do so, Sir Percy Bates insisted, as the *Queen* would only use sufficient speed to maintain her tight schedule and, besides, Cunard was not interested either in speed records or in racing as the company had always put safety first.

Six weeks after King Edward's visit to the ship the *Queen Mary* was ready to sail. At 9.45am, Tuesday 24 March 1936, four blasts from her mighty sirens boomed out across Clydebank to announce to one and all that she was ready to go. This was one hour earlier than expected due to a freshening wind which might cause problems as the liner attempted to navigate the bends in the river.

Over the previous weeks many thousands had travelled far just to see the liner fitting-out but for her departure schools had closed and a Clydebank holiday had been declared. So, on this special day an estimated one million people had travelled by rail, motorbus, car, bicycle, foot, or by any other means, to line the banks of the Clyde to watch the sailing of that river's greatest creation - 'Britain's Masterpiece' as Cunard so aptly called her, the phoenix of Britain's ordeal by Depression.

Five tugs of the Clyde Shipping Board, the *Flying Falcon*, *Flying Kite*, *Flying Eagle*, *Flying Spray* and *Flying Foam*, were accompanied by the *Romsey*, that had come up from Southampton, and the locally based *Paladin*, a tug-tender belonging to the Anchor Line. *The Paladin* had been chosen to lead the *Mary* during her journey down the Clyde and would later be purchased by Red Funnel Steamers of Southampton, coming south ten years later in 1946 to join her massive charge.

Slowly, the great ship was lead astern into the Clyde and partly into the deepened River Cart before her head was turned downstream and seawards at around 7 knots.

The liner was under the joint command of Captains Duncan Cameron and John Murchie, two of the best-known men in Clyde pilotage. The journey was fraught with tension and this reached a climax as the *Mary* approached a bend in the river near Dalmuir. A gust of wind caught the ship and swung her stern across the river so that her enormous length almost blocked the stream ('We skidded', said an unflurried Captain Cameron). Her stern was aground for several seconds until the tugs had her off but, during that brief period, people on shore had chatted to those on board. The incident got her an entry into the daily casualties list at Lloyds!

The crowds cheered her for the fifteen miles of her river passage until, at last, the Clyde widened and the *Mary*, with her gaggle of tugs, arrived off Gourock where she let go her anchors. This was to be one of many trials of her equipment that she was to carry out here including adjustments to her compass. She also took onboard her

Tugs struggle to stop the great ship from grounding across the width of the Clyde in a very anxious moment.　　*C. M. Baxter Collection*

lifeboats. Only two had been carried as emergency boats during her journey from the shipyard as (neither had her furniture been loaded nor had much fuel been taken on) this was to reduce her draught as much as possible.

The *Queen* stayed for two nights off Gourock.Each evening she was brilliantly lit along her entire length through myriads of gleaming portholes and windows and, with her huge deep orange funnels floodlit, she provided an unforgettable spectacle to the thousands who viewed her from the shores or from pleasure craft splashing around her sparkling bulk.

By the early hours of the morning of the 26th the various trials had been completed so, at 2.30am, she weighed anchor and set course for Southampton.

In Southampton preparations had been going on for years to receive the *Queen*. At first it seemed as if the town would not become the choice British port for the liner as the Southern Railway Company, under the chairmanship of Sir Herbert Walker, was reluctant to build a £1.85 million dry dock that would be big enough to accommodate a ship that would only use it, perhaps, twice a year, bringing in, at the most, £10,000 in dues. In the end, Sir Percy Bates, told the railway company 'No dock, no ship!' and intimated that either Liverpool would become the home port or else Cunard would build its own port on the South Coast in rivalry to Southampton.

His subtle blackmail worked, Southern Railway relented and the 1,200 foot long King George V dry dock was built. The dock, at the northern end of a vast new dock area built entirely on reclaimed land, was officially opened on 26th July 1933 by the King (after whom it was named) and Queen, sailing into the huge new basin on board the Royal Yacht *Victoria and Albert*.

Anchored off Gourock with the Highlands behind her, the *Mary* prepares to take on her lifeboats which had been left off the ship to decrease weight and draught.
Courtesy, University of Liverpool Cunard Archives

The populace around the southern shore were as excited at the prospect of receiving the 'Stateliest Ship Now In Being' as the Clydesiders had been in building her. Local newspapers had been publishing features about the vessel for weeks ahead and, by Friday 27th March, thousands from all over Hampshire, the Isle of Wight and beyond, prepared to make the day a holiday, flocking to line the shores of Spithead, The Solent and Southampton Water.

The liner, it was reported, had touched 29.3 knots on a short spurt, without being pressed, during her trip from the Clyde - this with some launch gear still attached and a marine-growth foulded bottom!

Hundreds of items had been produced to foster the public's interest in the liner. *Queen Mary* berets featured a profile of the liner on the top of the hat; chocolate *Queen Mary*s; *Queen Mary* jig-saws; magazines, booklets and pamphlets; a *Queen Mary* board game where small models of the ship were raced around Britain at the shake of a dice; models and give-away photographs of the liner were amongst the souvenirs to whet, but seemingly never to satiate, the appetite of the public.

The *Queen Mary* arrived in majesty to anchor off Cowes at 7am on Friday 27th (many of the important dates in her career seemed to feature the 27th!) and she was to remain there until midday. Private vessels and paddle steamers sloshed around her during her stay there, with aeroplanes circling her Gulliver-like form in the sky overhead as sheawaited the next high tide.

By noon an estimated three-quarters of a million people had amassed on the surrounding shorelines to witness her regal procession from The Solent up Southampton Water to Southampton Docks. Pilots Captain Wallace Caws

and then Captain George Bowyer had taken charge of the *Mary* during, this, her first arrival in the South.

She sailed past the outward-bound German liner *Bremen* (an ex-Blue Ribband holder), dressed overall with code flags but also flying the Swastika. (Many passengers would eventually take their patronage from the German liners with their Nazi over tones to join the sparkling new *Queen*). The captain of the *Bremen* signalled: 'Our heartiest congratulations for the completion of our youngest and biggest companion at sea. May our first meeting be the beginning of a long, good co-operation. Commodore Ziegebein, Officers and Crew'.

The brotherhood of the sea was a work and any idea of what was to happen to that 'long good co-operation' was still a distant dot on the horizon of world history. Captain Sir Edgar Britten made reply:

'Please accept from myself, officers and crew our warmest appreciation of your kind message. The *Queen Mary* will, we all feel sure, be a worthy successor of those fine ships which have preceded her in the waters of the North Atlantic and of which your noble vessel is one of the brightest examples. Kindest greetings.'

Hundreds of craft surrounded the *Mary* as she approached Southampton Docks with ferries and pleasure craft carrying thousands to view the liner close to. Twelve thousand people were in the Southern Railway's docks as well as thousands more who saw her from the shore.

Greetings were sounded from the liners berthed in the Eastern Docks, and in the Western Docks (the new 7,000 feet of docks completed on the reclaimed Millbrook Bay) she passed by the four-funnelled *Windsor Castle* and the *Majestic* (once a White Star liner and now awaiting sale and possible

Above: The liner has now its compliment of lifeboats on board.   *C. M. Baxter Collection*
Below: Arriving in the South for the first time, the *Queen Mary* passes the German liners *Bremen* and *Hamburg*.   *Frank O. Braynard*

Above: The *Mary* approaches her berth as she has just passed Hythe Pier in Southampton Water on her first arrival in the 'Gateway to the World'.

Below: Then came the entrance into the brand new King George V dry-dock in the Western Dock area. The liners *Majestic* and *Windsor Castle* are dressed overall to greet the new Cunarder. *Both, C. M. Baxter Collection*

scrapping. She did, in fact, become a boys' training ship, HMS *Caledonia*, only to burn three years later) on the bridge of which was a future captain of the Queen and Commodore of the Cunard, Donald MacLean. Then there was the *Shepperton Ferry*, a new train ferry, still laid-up waiting for cracks in the new Dover terminal to be repaired. Many hundreds were on board her for the day.

Finally came the entrance to the enormous King George V dry-dock, flooded and with gate opened. The *Mary* arrived here at 2.20pm, expertly eased into the dock and in place by 2.45. The dock gate (caisson) was closed and pumping commenced with millions of gallons of water being emptied from the man-made gorge into the confluence of the river Test.

By 7pm the *Queen* was high and dry on the dock blocks. She was to stay in the dock for two days longer than originally anticipated, until Wednesday April 8th, but during that time her bottom was cleaned and painted, any remaining launch fittings removed and new propellers fitted in readiness for her speed trials, thousands coming to view her as she towered above the surrounding terrain.

On Sunday 29th alone, it was said that twenty five thousand people paying one shilling (5p) a head came to view the ship and for ten hours, braving the cloudy, chilly weather, an endless stream of spectators walked the three-quarters of a mile around the dock. Cars had arrived to wait outside the dock gates in the small hours of the morning and eighteen special trains brought eight thousand people from all over the country. By the end of the *Mary*'s sojourn in dry dock hundreds of signatures covered her new propellers.

On April 8th the *Queen Mary* was floated out of the dock and carefully assisted to the Ocean Dock (ex-White Star dock and later to be known as the Ocean Terminal) where she moored opposite to the venerable, twenty-two year old *Aquitania*, again with thousands watching her progress.

She remained here until the 15th April when, on completion of fuelling, she was ready to return to the Firth of Clyde for her speed trials off the island of Arran.

For this, the liner carried some special guests including Lord Aberconway, chairman of John Brown and Co. Ltd., Clydebank.

After a 48 hours steaming test in the Irish Sea the *Queen Mary* anchored off Gourock and some of the guests were landed by tender to return to London by special train. The ship was generally described as 'perfect' and Sir James Lithgow commented on her 'vibrationless qualities'. Lord Burghley, the athlete, had tried to set up his own record by running around the Promenade Deck in 58 seconds; a brass plaque was set up to mark the event but this was to disappear during the forthcoming war.

At 4.30 on Saturday morning the ship left her Gourock anchorage and from 6.10 in the morning until 3

The newly opened KGV dry-dock awaits the *Queen*. the dock itself was built in recently reclaimed land as can be seen from water which still has to be pumped away.
C. M. Baxter Collection

in the afternoon the *Mary* made fourteen runs over the measured mile off Arran. Each run took around 4 minutes to complete with 10 minutes at either end to lose momentum or build up speed with half an hour between each run. Speeds from 20 knots earlier in the day to the last of 32.84 knots were recorded by those on shore. What the land-based observers did not know was that the *Mary* traversed the course diagonally, thus in reality, achieving a greater speed.

During the day, Lord Aberconway sent a telegram from the liner, its recipient being David Kirkwood MP whose efforts had done so much in enabling the *Queen Mary* to become a reality:

'We are travelling at full speed off Arran. The directors and staff of John Brown's desire me to inform their workers at Clydebank and Sheffield, also their neighbours on Clydeside and their friends elsewhere who have shown such a deep interest, sympathy and support during the building of the vessel, that the speed and other trials of the *Queen Mary* concluding today have been in every way successful and that the performance of the vessel had amply fulfilled our expectations.'

The liner returned to Gourock at 6pm after other steaming tests and sailed southwards once more at 9.40, giving three blasts on her siren in farewell to her native river. It was thought that she would never return, but events three years later would change that opinion.

The *Queen* returned to Southampton and continued to take on the furniture and carpets that still remained to be fitted.

On May 12th the flag of John Brown was lowered in a brief ceremony and the Cunard White Star flags raised as the *Queen Mary* was officially handed over to her owners.

Thursday May 14th saw the *Queen* once again sailing from Southampton for what was called an 'Inaugural Cruise'. This was to be a 24-hour 'thank you' cruise to the Lizard with Cunard White Star acting as hosts to representatives of the liner's builders, outfitters and various other contractors who had helped to create the greatest of all British liners. The ship returned to Southampton at seven in the evening on Friday.

Above: A wonderful view as the liner is now almost two thirds into the dock. The Eastern Docks and the distant Southampton Water are clearly visible in the background.

Below: The area of Southampton named Millbrook is in the distance and the ship immediately to the right of the *Mary*'s stern is the new train ferry the *Shepperton Ferry*.

Both, C. M. Baxter Collection

Above: With workmen and others around the dockside being completely dwarfed by the ship, lines are attached to warp the liner the last few yards. Paddle steamers still list under the weight of hundreds of sightseers.

Below: No time was wasted in getting the liner ready for its Sea Trials and eventually her maiden voyage. Using the water receding levels to their advantage, workmen scrub the hull clean.

Both, C. M. Baxter Collection

On the 21st, 22nd and 23rd the finished liner was opened to the public and there was a great demand for the tickets. Fifteen thousand people paid five shillings a head (25 pence) to be shown over the *Mary* and the proceeds were donated to seamen's' charities.

Perhaps to see what the opposition to their *Normandie* was up to, the French Line's *Colombie* brought a party of 300 visitors from France to tour the British contender for the honours of the Atlantic.

For a final visit to the *Queen Mary* as King, Edward flew down to Southampton on Monday 25th May where he met his mother, Queen Mary, his brother the Duke of York and the Duchess of York with their two delightful children the Princesses Elizabeth and Margaret Rose, the Duke and Duchess of Kent and the Duchess of Gloucester. The King, wearing a flannel suite and a jaunty straw hat, was severely reprimanded, King or no King, by his mother: 'You would not have dressed like this if your father had been here, David.'

The ship had been cleared of all people not concerned with the royal visit so that the distinguished party could roam where they pleased. It was Queen Mary's first visit to the liner since she had launched the vessel and the Queen was impressed with what she saw. She visited the kitchens whilst the young princesses watched Mickey Mouse cartoons and played on the slide with their Imperial uncle. The King later ventured to the Verandah Grill to see the mural there. On his first sighting of the mural during a visit on the Clyde he had noticed an elderly lady painted as if watching the viewer. 'Oh dear! How like Mama!' he remarked. He noticed now that the figure had been changed.

On leaving the ship the King and his mother presented signed portraits of themselves and the Queen presented her standard, measuring 3 feet by 1½ feet, in pure silk. It was mounted and fixed to the bulkhead beneath the relief medallion of herself on the cabin main staircase.

At teatime, 4.30pm, on 27th May the *Queen* left the Ocean Dock at the outset of her maiden voyage. Again, thousands blackened the local shoreline or else followed the liner in an excited white flurry of accompanying pleasure craft of all kinds; yachts, motor boats and paddlesteamers all jockeying for position in an attempt to keep up with the liner as she headed down Southampton Water, past the Isle of Wight towards Cherbourg (where she was delayed for two hours) and then New York.

David Kirkwood was again remembered when Sir Percy Bates wrote:

'On the *Queen Mary*'s sailing day it seems appropriate that I should write a line to you to express my appreciation of your faith and help in this great work. This is only your due.

'I sail in her today a thankful and a hopeful man.'

On board were Henry Hall and the *Queen Mary* Orchestra (he had to play for fourteen live broadcasts, no matter what the hour at sea, to an eagerly listening, tea-time public somewhere-or-another in the world), the mouth-organ virtuoso, Larry Adler, and Miss Frances Day, the singer, who had brought her own chickens on board (they were cooped near the dog-kennels) along with a Rolls Royce in which to process down Broadway.

The entire maiden voyage was 'A long festival, a joyful cruise experience', as young commis-waiter Edwin Praine remembers, (he had celebrated his 18th birthday on board two weeks earlier) and there was champagne for everyone - including the crew! The liner was considered to be a happy ship from the outset.

Above: The mighty stern of the *Queen Mary* towers above the dock. The missing paint was eroded by the speed of the ship through the water.
Below: The *Queen Mary* on full power whilst on speed trials on the measured mile off the Isle of Arran.

RMS Foundation, Queen Mary Archive

The prevading atmosphere of great excitment is very evident in this view from the ship towards the shore-based Berths. This was the maiden voyage of the liner so keenly awaited since the early 1930s. 27th May 1936.   *C. M. Baxter Collection*

Amongst souvenirs of the voyage, passengers were given a commemorative medallion and the lady passengers were presented with a silver plate powder compact bearing an enamelled portrait of the ship.

As with many new ships on their maiden voyages, the *Mary* had her teething troubles. The minor ones were to do with the service (she was so big) and the smuts from her funnels; the major ones dealt with her design. Firstly, she vibrated badly at the stern, secondly she rolled - according to the experiments on the models she should not do that - and later had additional stiffening fitted into her which was a major alteration and involved some of her main public lounges being stripped, stiffened and rebuilt, much to Cunard White Stars' embarrassment. Propellers were also changed and monitored. The cure was slow and expensive.

The *Queen* did well on her first crossing and all bode well for her to beat the *Normandie* but on the Saturday afternoon she ran into fog (in which a wreath was quietly dropped in the vicinity where the White Star liner *Titanic* had foundered on her maiden voyage in 1912 after striking an iceberg at night), and speed was reduced. She passed the Ambrose Lightship at 9.03am on Monday, June 1st, having steamed from Cherbourg breakwater at an average of 29.13 knots but not enough to break the *Normandie*'s record of 29.68 knots of June 3rd the previous year. The *Mary* had been beaten by just two hours and thirty-three minutes but, as Cunard White Star had insisted she had not been built for records!

A photo opportunity on the maiden voyage as proud passengers parade along the Boat Deck wearing their lifejackets. *C. M. Baxter Collection*

The *Mary* pulls away from the quayside to commence her maiden voyage. This occasion is easily identifiable due to the padded area on her bow which was to prevent any damage from the tugs' cables chaffing her pristine white paintwork on this auspicious departure.

Courtesy, University of Liverpool Cunard Archives

The incredible view from the stern of the *Queen Mary* as she plies in state down Southampton Water on her maiden voyage still followed by well-wishers. The paddle steamer looks well loaded as she heels over from the weight of her sightseeing passengers. A troopship lays at anchor in the distance off Netley.   Three officers take time to watch the spectacle.   *C. M. Baxter Collection*

The *Mary* did beat the *Normandie* that August but, again expressing their (tongue-in-cheek) disinterest in breaking records, the company stated that they were undertaking speed experiments with the *Mary* to obtain engine data for a sister ship, approval for which had been given by the British Government. The sister, No. 552, would become the *Queen Elizabeth*.

The *Mary*'s arrival in New York proved to be one of the most spectacular in that port's history with a flotilla of craft and airships following the arriving liner. A DC-3 aircraft flew over the ship and cascaded her with flowers, a romantic motion that was to be repeated many years later on another gala occasion. Cheering crowds and bands waited on the quayside and for days afterwards the crew was fêted by New Yorkers, either in their homes or in public.

A new £2 million pier had been build (earlier exorbitant rates had been reduced in the port by kind permission of the late Depression) and an estimated 30,000 visitors came aboard the liner and, in return, an unlimited number of moveable and unscrewable souvenirs went ashore!

On a sad note, Sir Edgar Britten, who took the *Mary* on her maiden voyage, collapsed on board a few months later and died in Southampton General Hospital.

One of the failings of the *Mary* as mentioned earlier was her ability to roll. This had not been accounted for and handrails had

Perhaps not the maiden voyage, but a pervading gala-like atomsphere usually existed in the holiday season when the *Mary* sailed through the Solent off Cowes.
Courtesy, University of Liverpool Cunard Archives

not been fitted in main passageways and neither had bulky furniture been bolted to the deck. After a few voyages workmen travelled on the ship fitting handrails and bolting heavy furniture down to prevent it from moving. Potteries made a small fortune after each crossing. The *Mary*'s rolling had an unsettling feel about it, in more ways than one! She would roll, hold for a moment or so and then continue the roll as if she wouldnít stop. After an anxious moment she would steady herself and repeat the movement to the other side. An officer in the early '50s said that when she rolled the horizon on the opposite to the side of the bridge wing on which he was on duty would appear above the Bridge roof! This was a problem that would remain with the ship for twenty years.

Becoming a more comfortable ship after her major rebuild, the *Mary* became popular with one character of traveller whilst the *Normandie* was the darling of another. The two ships vied with each other until the *Mary* finally took the record in August 1938 with a westbound crossing of 30.99 knots and eastbound 31.69, almost half a knot better than the French liner.

The *Queen* reigned supreme.

The triumphant arrival in New York on 1st June 1936. Fog had delayed her but her welcome was magnificent.

Courtesy, University of Liverpool Cunard Archives

Chapter Five

You'll Never Get a Better Picture!

The *Queen Mary* finally wrested the Blue Riband from the *Normandie* in August 1938, defeating the French ship by half-a-knot with a speed of 31.69 knots. The *Normandie* conceded defeat, but only in speed. Due to structural alterations to alleviate the vibration from which she, too, had suffered the French liner still came out the larger of the two ships both in tonnage and overall length. She was also the more sophisticated of the two, epitomising French chic with grandiose yet comfortable luxury. Her hull design was outstanding and nothing short of revolutionary, nothing had been seen like it before, whereas the *Mary* was evolutionary in design although she was more 'jazzy' with her art-deco interiors and that appealed to the Americans. But this modernity was soon to date her. Still, the rivals were a fairly matched pair and the two shipping lines sensibly agreed to sailings of their superliners on alternate weeks. The luxury of speed was also expensive, as the *Mary* would burn 1,300 to 1,400 tons of oil per day at speed instead of 1,000 tons per day for normal steaming. Cunard had also said sometime before that the *Mary* would be eventually run at high speed on the odd occasion in order to glean valuable information for use in the construction of the sistership No. 552 that would be built on the Clyde.

By 1939 the sinister spectre of Nazism had spread its insidious cloak from Germany to cover other states in Europe. Although Nevil Chamberlain had victoriously waved his piece of paper promising 'Peace in our time', in front of the newsreel cameras, realists knew that a war with Germany was imminent if the Third Reich was to be stopped.

By August, Americans were leaving Europe in droves, returning to the United States in fully booked ships. The *Mary* would sail packed to capacity on the westward run but returned almost empty.

Far away, whilst the *Queen* was heading towards Southampton after leaving New York on 23rd August, Hitler signed his non-aggression pact with Stalin and passengers on board the liner expected at any moment to hear that war had been declared. This generated an air of uncertainty and this was intensified when the ship was blacked-out at night and egress to the outer decks was prohibited from late each afternoon.

The *Queen* leaves New York for the first time en-route to Sydney. The degaussing strip has not yet been fitted. A vessel of the Holland America Line is in the distance painted with neutrality markings. *Imperial War Museum*

The usual BBC news broadcasts were stopped, announcements being made instead on the ship's broadcasting system. It was felt by many that war must have had already broken out whilst the ship was still at sea.

Elsie Greenman, a teacher who had been on holiday in Canada, was returning to England on the *Mary*. Sometime later she found out during a chance meeting (at her school near Newchapel) with an ex-pupil and currently serving petty-officer from HMS *Hood* that the battlecruiser had shadowed the Cunarder across the Atlantic, keeping her distance during the day and closing-in at night which made her presence unknown to the liner. The sailor, Frank Wheeler, was later lost with his ship.

The *Queen* arrived back in Southampton on Monday 28th August to find that war had not yet actually been declared. She sailed again on the 30th with 2,332 passengers. This was to be her last departure from the port for six years.

As the liner approached New York news arrived that war had been officially declared on Sunday 3rd September 1939. She had sailed with extra life rafts on board and with sealed Admiralty orders.

Captain Irving had heard that at least two German pocket battleships were on the prowl and now two warships could be seen on the horizon as the *Queen* approached the American port.

These, to the great relief of all on board, turned out to be HMSs *Exeter* and *York*. The men-of-war were waiting for the *Bremen*, with whom the *Mary* had exchanged cordial signals when she sailed on her maiden voyage, to break out of New York where she had been deliberately delayed by the authorities until war had been declared. The *Bremen* did sail shortly after the *Aquitania* and, avoiding the British blockade, eventually managed to get back to Germany only to burn in harbour and eventually to be broken up.

On arriving at Pier 90 on Monday 4th September the *Mary* berthed and was immediately laid-up. Many of her crew returned home on other Cunard ships as the *Queen* was too valuable, too big a target for the Luftwaffe for her to return to Southampton and basically, no one knew what to do with her.

Partially obscured by smoke (Captain Bisset threatened to do something down the tugs' funnels when they made too much smoke!) the *Mary* arrives in Sydney Harbour.

Courtesy, University of Liverpool Cunard Archives

A working party remained on board preparing the ship for any long journey that might be required of her. Junior Third Officer Geoffrey Marr (later to become a Captain and then Commodore of Cunard) stayed on her for six months of this enforced inactivity, but the crew were well entertained by the hospitable New Yorkers. Orders were received, eventually, to paint the exterior of the ship in a drab grey, her ports and windows having been so covered on her last trip over.

Voices in the House of Parliament were critical of the *Mary* and her consort then still completing on the Clyde. 'Too big and too costly to be risked', was typical of the tirades raised against the ships but the critics would soon be proved to be so very wrong.

Berthed next to the *Queen Mary* was her peacetime rival, the *Normandie*, also laid-up but still in French Line livery. She and the *Mary* had canvas caps fitted atop their funnels to keep the worst of the weather out of their boilers.

Meantime, back in Britain, Cunard White Star had received a surprise telephone call at 8pm on the evening of 1st March, from the Ministry of Shipping. This was to advise Cunard that the Ministry wanted their ship! She had been called-up.

Six days later the citizens of New York also had a surprise for there, sailing up the Hudson, for the first time, was the newest, biggest liner in the world, the *Queen Elizabeth*.

She had left the Clyde estuary on 2nd March ostensibly destined for Southampton. Word had got back to

Germany that packing cases had arrived at Southampton containing items for the new Cunarder and the Luftwaffe subsequently paid a visit to the town on the day that the ship was due to arrive, hoping to score a blow for the prestige of their regime. But the *Elizabeth* had sailed in utmost secrecy for the States. The crew were told at the very last moment, to avoid idle dangerous talk, and any crewmember who declined to go was 'detained' until the *Queen Elizabeth* was safe. Even her pilot was unprepared for more than a short sea journey.

So the three largest liners in the world, the 'monsters', were there side by side in New York. For two weeks they remained there until, on 21st March, the *Mary* (having had the silt that had accumulated under her keel blown away) broke up the slumbering trio and in doing so unknowingly bade a final farewell to the *Normandie*.

Laid-up in New York at the outset of war the *Normandie* was seized by the US on 15th May 1941. During her conversion into a troopship after America's entry into the war bought about by the bombing of Pearl Harbour, she caught on fire on 9th February 1942 and capsized at her berth due to the weight of water that had been pumped into her upper decks. She was eventually to be raised, towed away and scrapped. A tragic waste and an ignominious end for what was, perhaps, the most beautifully proportioned and decorated liner that ever plied the oceans.

On leaving New York the *Mary* headed south, crossed the South Atlantic, surprised the citizens of Cape Town and then sailed for Sydney.

Captain 'Bill' Bisset who took over command of the liner in February 1942.   *Imperial War Museum*

Her surprise arrival there, like all her sailings and arrivals during the war, was secret - a point not missed, according to Staff Captain, later Captain, Harry Grattidge who tells of a local guide finishing his patter about local landmarks in Sydney Harbour with '.... and on my starboard side, ladies and gents, the greatest phantom you have ever seen. For why? Because you may THINK it is the *Queen Mary,* but officially it aint!'

She stayed there for two weeks, being partially converted to a troopship, having extra kitchen, stores and sanitary arrangements fitted and putting much of her furniture ashore for safe storage.

From Sydney she took 5,000 Anzac troops to Gourock, an anchorage, it was thought, she would never see again after completing her trials back in 1936. The *Mary* could now carry up to 5,500, an increase on her peacetime capacity of an additional 3,361 passengers. Because she had been built purely as a North Atlantic liner

As the *Queen* approached waters that were haunted by U-boats, an anti-aircraft cruiser and anti-submarine destoyers would meet and escort her to safety - if they could keep up! This photograph was taken from HMS *Figi. Imperial War Museum*

and not for hot weather cruising she was not consequently fitted with air-conditioning and there were several riots on board and deaths through heat exhaustion as the heat became unbearable during her voyages in the Indian Ocean. On her first trip from Sydney hundreds of troops went absent without leave in Simonstown and their sentences imposed at the court martials that followed were sensibly later rescinded.

She sailed with troops for Singapore to help bolster that garrisonís defences and whilst there the *Queen* dry-docked for machinery overhauls and was given additional armament and other protection. She was dry-docked in Singapore twice, running a shuttle service in between from Sydney to Bombay or Trincomalee where her troops were transhipped to the threatened deserts of Egypt.

On one occasion, whilst in Singapore, a rowdy section from a temporary element of her crew, wrecked the dormitories that they had been given ashore, broke into a canteen and wrecked the bar. The worthy inhabitants of the city were more than glad to see the *Mary* leave! The *Queen Elizabeth* subsequently had a very cool reception when she, in turn, arrived there for her conversion.

The *Mary* carried on with her journeys to and from Sydney and when it was deemed safe in the Red Sea area she took her troops direct to Suez. These voyages continued until November.

After the Japanese attack on Pearl Harbour on 7th December 1941 Australia was in danger of invasion and because most of the Australian troops were in England or Africa, American soldiers were needed - and quickly - to defend Australia. Leaving the Indian Ocean the *Queen Mary* went to New York, arriving there on 12th January 1942. Twenty-five days were spent upgrading the troopship's capacity to 8,500, standee bunks, some five deep, being fitted wherever there was space, with more armament, stores and even more showers being fitted.

Loading 8,398 troops at night she sailed on the 18th February for Sydney.

Her first port of call was to have been Trinidad where stores and her new captain, 'Bill' Bisset, awaited her. But U-boats had managed to make their way to the area and the

Reinforcements were urgently needed in Europe and the *Mary* sailed after taking on 9,880 troops, (with 875 crew this made it the first time ever a ship had sailed with more than 10,000 people on board) who embarked on the night of 10th May, and steamed at 25.5 knots to Gourock in Scotland.

Another change of orders. Suez via the Cape to reinforce the Allied defence against Rommel's attack on Egypt, 9,357 troops, stores and payroll cash - 1 /2 tons of it! The run from the Cape to Suez - 6,200 miles - was the longest haul ever done by the ship and there were yet more deaths through heat exhaustion in the Red Sea.

She returned to New York on 23rd June with passengers including German prisoners of war and sailed on 2nd August with the incredible total of 15,125 troops (and 863 crew) almost 16,000 people on one ship - an entire army division. By now the liner's berthing capacity had reached 12,500 standee bunks so 'hot bunking' was brought into operation; when one man left his bunk another climbed into it! This high number of troops could only

Above : The giant Cunarder dwarfed the various vessels that came alongside to load fuel and stores   *Imperial War Museum*
Below: British and US gunners 'close-up' at the double during and exercise on the Clyde.
                                                                 Imperial War Museum

Mary was diverted to Key West, Florida, where she anchored well out to sea. Captain Bisset joined her there. His first voyage in the *Queen* turned out to be one of the eventful voyages of her wartime career. On one occasion a ship ten miles astern was torpedoed in an area through which the liner had just passed, perhaps leaving one very annoyed U-boat captain when he realised what he had missed. A story said that Herr Hitler had promised a large financial reward and the Iron Cross (with oak leaves) to the person who could sink either of the *Queens*. There was also a fire that lasted for two hours in mid-South Atlantic and a Japanese radio report stated that the *Mary* had been sunk. Captain Bisset, always ready with a glib comment, said to his Senior Wireless Officer who had reported the Japanese claim: 'Keep it under your hat. Don't let the troops know that we've been sunk. It might worry them'.

The Queen Mary arrived in Sydney on 28th March and disembarked the troops in seven hours. She stayed in the harbour for nine days before she left for New York with just fifty-eight passengers. In the convoy that she joined she met her sistership for the second time at Sydney Heads.

She arrived in New York, the only port where she could berth alongside instead of anchoring, on 7th May and received order to divert to her natural environment - the North Atlantic - to begin the famous 'GI Shuttle'.

be carried in the summer months and needed a great deal of discipline.

Reaching Gourock on 7th August 1942 the liner reported a narrowly missed explosion explained by the probability of an acoustic mine being detonated just as the *Mary* zigzagged, a procedure that she used throughout the war to confuse submarines.

On these high speed GI shuttle dashes across the Atlantic a cruiser would, as usual, meet the *Queen* off the

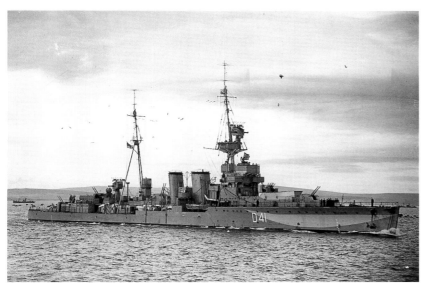

northern coast of Ireland to escort her through the potentially dangerous waters to Scotland. The escorting cruiser would act as an anti-aircraft defence ship and six destroyers would provide anti-submarine cover.

On 2nd October HMS *Curacoa*, the 4,200 ton cruiser that had been sent as escort vessel, saw the smoke of the *Mary* appear above the horizon so she turned about and started at full speed towards the British coast, knowing that even at full speed the *Mary* would soon catch her up and overhaul her. The two ships met off the part of the northern Irish coast known, appropriately, as Bloody Foreland.

The *Queen Mary* maintained her zigzag; 'Number 8' zigzag was being used which involved four minutes steaming on a mean (straight) course, then a 25° turn to starboard for eight minutes, 50° port for eight and then a 25° turn brought her back to her mean course. The *Curacoa* got in rather close. Later, witnesses said an officer on the bridge was taking photographs of the *Queen* and was told 'You'll never get a better picture!'

What happened next has long been a matter of debate. The *Curacoa* should have been watching the *Mary* carefully but somehow she had manoeuvred in too closely alongside the *Mary*'s starboard side and either a wrong helm order or else, as was suggested later by tank model experiments, the interaction between the two vessels pulled the cruiser in front of the rushing, knife edge of the *Queen Mary*'s bow.

People on the *Mary* either felt nothing, a slight jolt or else they believed that they were being bombed as the liner's bow knifed through the cruiser at 28 ½ knots. The time was 2.10pm.

During the awful moments that followed the cruiser's stern section sank quickly, followed a few minutes by the bow. Those brief moments of the disaster claimed the lives of 331 officers and men, only 101 surviving the calamity. The cruiser's commanding officer, Captain John Boutwood was amongst the latter.

In spite of the anguish of those witnessing the event from on board the *Queen Mary*, the liner could not stop. She could not risk the lives of 15,000 people by attempting a rescue in waters known to be frequented by U-boats. To stop could easily court a greater catastrophe.

Horrified troops on the *Queen*'s decks threw lifejackets overboard as her mighty bulk steamed through the wreckage of ship and men. She notified the escort destroyers which then sped to rescue those thrashing about in the oily water.

The troopship's speed was reduced by half - to 14 knots. Her bow had been split to the height of the cruiser's weather deck and had also, fortuitously, been forced back and to one side as she cut through the warship, thus practically sealing the huge wound in the damaged stem. Water entered the ship but its force of ingress was reduced as the ship slowed. The forward collision bulkhead held and was stiffened by the hurriedly applied wooden shores on the after side. The liner made Gourock

Above: The cruiser, HMS *Curacoa*, photographed in better times - later to be sent to the bottom of the sea after a tragic collision with the *Queen*. *Imperial War Museum*
Below: The *Queen Mary* dry-docked in Boston, Mass., for emergency repairs to the damage caused by her collision with HMS *Curacoa*.

safely, leaving many observers on shore wondering what had happened. They would be left wondering for a long time as the incident was hushed-up until the War's end when, after a series of inquiries, appeals, claims and count-claims blame for the accident was apportioned ⅓ to the *Mary* and ⅔ to the *Curacoa*, mainly for negligent watch keeping. The *Queen*'s captain, Gordon Illingworth, normally a popular and unassuming man, was to be frequently haunted by the incident in the years to come.

The crumpled bow of the superliner was temporarily patched up with cement and she returned to the States at around 24 knots, her speed still her best defence against submarines and (other than well-aimed) torpedoes. She dry-docked in Boston where a new stem section had been constructed from templates rushed over from Britain and carried on the liner's foredeck.

So the *Queen Mary* continued to shuttle American soldiers to Britain for training in preparation for D-Day, and its aftermath. Her longest trip of the war was designated ''The Long Voyage'' and had lasted between her departure from New York on 8th December 1942 and 16th June 1943 when she finally berthed once again alongside Pier 90. From New York she had travelled to Gourock, Freetown, Cape Town, Aden, Suez and onto Australia, back again to Gourock and then to New York. In all she had steamed 46,865 miles, carried 45,614 passengers and consumed several million pounds of stores.

From June of 1943 to August 1944 the *Mary* did a complete series of trooping voyages from New York (except for one from Halifax, Nova Scotia) to Britain.

Each loading of troops took place at night and had been practised earlier on full-size mock-ups of the ship at Fort Kilmer so each man know where to go and what to do when he arrived on board. The ship was also divided into 'Red', 'White' and 'Blue' sections and a soldier would be punished with extra duties if he trespassed into the wrong section. On leaving New York (she never sailed when there was a full moon) with thousands of men on board the *Mary* was in special peril. With the additional weight of human cargo she drew an extra 2 feet of water and the men were ordered to stand still in their quarters whilst the ship left harbour. If they had been tempted to rush to wave farewell to the Statue of Liberty then the ship would have listed at least 10° and would have increased her draught on the 'deep' side by 4 feet. This would have been enough to rupture the sub-river tunnels beneath the Hudson.

As the troops travelled they indulged themselves in several activities which were not to Cunard's or the authorities' liking - amongst these were playing dice ('craps' was a great favourite) and as far as the ship's company was concerned the chewing of gum was unpopular - it was difficult to clean off bulkheads and decks - as was the carving on initials in the teak-wood handrails. The latter was eventually tolerated and as Captain Bisset later wrote '.....I decided not to make a fuss about this. These men might soon be going into battle, and some of them would never return to their homes and loved ones. Let them amuse themselves!' These carvings would later become treasured relics.

To the American soldiers, the *Queens* were so huge that they believed that only the United States could have built them!

The Main Restaurant became the Main Mess Hall and, in place of 800 peacetime diners, 2,000 troops could be fed at one sitting.

Imperial War Museum

Amongst the celebrities who travelled on board the liner during the war one in particular should be mentioned. This was a gentleman who travelled under the pseudonym of 'Colonel Warden'. He travelled three times on the *Mary*, partly because of being affected by tuberculosis at one time which prevented him from using aircraft. He always travelled with a large retinue and used the chance of sailing in the Cunarder to make several important decisions. The *Mary* would wait for him (at one time for eighteen days) to rejoin her and he was always appreciative of her crew and qualities and even cabins were especially refurbished for his use. The man in question was Winston Churchill.

During the war HRH Queen Mary did not forget the ship that bore her name and messages were exchanged between the two. One in particular was sent by Her Majesty from her shelter in the country just before D-Day:

'Since I launched the *Queen Mary* nearly ten years ago, almost half of her life has been spent on active war service. Now, as the war enters upon this decisive phase, I send my warm greetings to the Captain, Officers and the Ship's Company, and to all those who sail in the ship that bears my name.

'It is always a source of pride and of pleasure to me to receive news of the magnificent work the *Queen Mary* is doing in the transport of troops from every quarter of the Empire and Commonwealth, and from the United States of America, to the theatres of war. I pray that before very long it may be her joyful duty to carry the victorious soldiers of the United Nations back to their homes and families in many parts of the world.

'My earnest hope is that the many friendships born on board the *Queen Mary* during the years of war will continue into the happier years of peace to come, and that she will always prove herself a strong link, and a messenger of goodwill between the great English-speaking Nations.'

The Queen's speech reflected and qualified some of the statements made in her husband's, the late King George V's, speech at the launching ceremony of No. 534 ten years previously and her sentiment '..... may be her joyful duty to carry the victorious soldier..... back to their homes....' would soon be realised. When the *Mary* arrived in New York on 4th April 1945 she was laid-up for several weeks and dry-docked until it was decided that she would no longer be needed to transport American soldiers to Europe.

VE (Victory in Europe) Day was celebrated in the States, as elsewhere, after the German collapse on 7th May and by this time both the *Mary* and *Elizabeth* were in New York and they joined in the port's armistice celebrations by adding to the crescendo of sound with their beautiful sirens.

The *Mary* did several more trips to Gourock but this time the numbers of eastbound passengers were low but westbound the numbers reflected the huge numbers of troops previously carried, but this time they were going home. With 14,777 GI's on board the liner had a tremendous reception in New York with aircraft, boats, bands and crowds cheering her in. It was, at the time, the largest contingent of soldiers to enter the port on one ship and to the *Mary* fell the honour of taking the first US units home.

During the war years the *Mary* had carried 810,730 passengers and steamed 661,771 miles. Winston Churchill felt that the *Queens* contribution to the war effort had shortened the conflict by a year and in his tribute to both of the *Queens* he said: 'Built for the arts of peace and to link the Old World with the New, the *Queens* have challenged the fury of Hitlerism in the Battle of the Atlantic. At a speed

An impressive view of the *Queen Mary* at anchor in the Clyde, off Gourock. Her troops were disembarked into what had been peacetime pleasure steamers for tranference to shore bases.   *Imperial War Museum*

Looking a little worse for wear, it seems incredible that the liner was just 6 years into her lifetime on the oceans when this photograph was taken.   *Imperial War Museum*

never before realised in war they carried over a million men to defend the liberties of civilisation. Often, whole divisions at a time were moved by each ship.... To the men who contributed to the success of our operations in the years of peril..... the world owes a debt that it will not be easy to measure.'

Zigzagging and blackouts ceased and on Saturday 11th August 1945 the *Queen Mary* made her first post-war return to Southampton, again watched by thousands, berthing at 2pm accompanied by aeroplanes and boats, with the Southampton Police Band and civic dignitaries welcoming her back.

The *Queen Elizabeth* had been the first Cunarder to be released from war work on (6th March 1946) whilst the *Mary* continued to repatriate American troops and the 'GI Brides', British girls who had married American servicemen and also girls who had married Canadians (the latters' wives were taken to Halifax, Nova Scotia). In all the *Queen* carried 30% of all the service wives, numbering 9,118 women and 3,768 children. Special facilities had been installed on onboard and an attempt, during a dry-docking, had been made to try and return the *Mary* to some sort of pre-war standard. Standee bunks, armour etc. were removed and by now the funnels had been painted in the cheery Cunard White Star colours.

The *Mary* was finally 'demobilised' on her return to Southampton on 29th September 1946 to begin a ten-month refit. Ten thousand items of furniture had to be

The two *Queen*'s were not supposed to be in the same place at the same time, but here they are in Port Tenerife. The *Queen Elizabeth* photographed from the *Queen Mary*. *Courtesy of Cheif Engineer Willie and Mrs Denny Farmer*

An impressive view showing the splendour of a liner at speed. The *Mary* has just had her funnels repainted in Cunard colours but still retains her degaussing belt.
Courtesy, University of Liverpool Cunard archives

brought from storage from the New Forest, Australia and New York where they had been sent ashore in the early part of the war for safe keeping. These had to be renovated and collated and this was done at automobile manufacturers Ford's which had huge sheds at Eastleigh near Southampton. A new stem was fitted, degaussing strips and their protective steel shielding removed from around the sheer line, murals renovated and ten thousand other tasks had to be completed to get the ship ready for sea. Men came from the Clyde to work on the liner and 120 lady french polishers were employed.

During the refurbishment the *Mary* benefited from experience gained from the *Elizabeth*. She had two Garden Lounges built on either side of the First Class smoke room, a permanent Cinema converted from the starboard Gallery on the Promenade Deck, a Cocktail Bar now greeted passengers in the entrance to the Main Restaurant and the Gymnasium was moved to amidships on the Sun Deck. Tourist Class now had their own self-contained section of the Sports Deck between the first and second funnels and the crew had new accommodation. To aid in the navigation of the ship 'Seascan' radar was also fitted.

The *Queen Mary* was reconditioned by John Brown, her builders, as the main contractor and John I. Thornycroft of Southampton was the main sub-contractor. Fifteen hundred men from Clydeside camped at Chandler's Ford and were taken each day to the liner. When the *Mary* was dry-docked her propellers were removed, her shafts drawn

out for inspection and her underwater hull was scaled and coated with 3,000 gallons of anti-fouling paint.

When the *Queen Mary* had returned to Southampton at the commencement of her refurbishing she had passed the *Queen Elizabeth*, newly refitted, pristinely painted and ready for her own, long delayed commercial maiden voyage.

Sir Percy Bates had sadly died on the very eve of the *Queen Elizabeth*'s maiden voyage which took place on 16th October and was thus denied the chance of seeing the realisation of the concept which he had supported and fought for so long ago - the two ship, weekly express service across the Atlantic.

By mid-July the *Mary* was ready to re-establish herself on her intended route and she was well booked for her post-war debut.

The week before she sailed for New York she combined a trials trip to test her services with a short cruise, so on Thursday 25th July she left Southampton with 500 guests on board.

She returned the next day but anchored in Cowes Roads whilst the *Queen Elizabeth* sailed by, the two mammoth liners exchanging greetings in a spectacular meeting. The *Mary* then entered Southampton Docks, occupying the berth recently vacated by her newer sister.

She sailed for New York on the following Thursday with 2,000 passengers. The *Queens* had at last laid claim to their rightful domain and together they would rule it in splendour for the next eleven years.

On 29th September 1946 the *Queen* arrived in war-torn Southampton prior to being renovated for peacetime work. The *Queen Elizabeth* has already been refurbished and is ready to sail for New York.

Courtesy, University of Liverpool Cunard archives

Chapter Six

Perils and People

In spite of numerous model experiments that had shown the *Mary* would be steady in almost any sea-state, she proved her confident forecaster, like the lady she was, to be presumptively wrong. She rolled badly. The crew would even come to say that she could roll the milk out of a cup of tea!

When she had appeared fresh and untried from her builders she had not even been fitted with safety storm rails along her corridors, such was Cunard's errant confidence in her. After a few voyages that had involved rough weather - and not a few injuries that brought ambulances to the quayside to meet her - workmen travelled on the ship to discreetly fit the missing safety rails.

One particular traveller during the war was obviously greatly influenced by the rolling liner. The traveller was Paul Gallico and it was he who was to later write a novel, 'The Poseidon Adventure', about a badly rolling liner that capsizes after being hit by a tidal wave. The book was later made into a film with a model of the *Queen Mary* starring as the SS *Poseidon*.

One famous statesman arriving in New York after a particularly rough crossing on the *Mary* was met by a bevy of news cameramen who had congregated at the Pier to meet him. But when they saw the storm damage to the *Queen*, - bent stanchions, crushed ventilators, ladders carried away, broken windows etc - their cameras were directed towards the ship.

The crew did not complain that their quarters had also been flooded. They just got on with the job and repaired the damage as best as they could until more permanent repairs could be made at a later date.

The insurance companies complained about the *Mary*, especially in the winter months. Broken crockery, furniture and people's legs caused the insurers to double their premiums and if this wasn't enough for Cunard, female passengers increasingly declined to travel on the liner in winter, especially as aircraft could provide an equally uncomfortable but quicker passage. Women were terrified of the ship in rough weather so, as a trial, the shipping company had stabilisers fitted to their new *Media* in February 1952. To everyone's consternation the *Media* started to roll quite happily during the experimental voyage and obviously the stabilisers were not working as they should. When the liner arrived in New York a diver was sent down to inspect them and the reason why the ship had rolled so badly soon became apparent - the stabilisers had simply disappeared!

However, undaunted, Cunard had stabilisers fitted to the *Queen Elizabeth* but the officers of the *Mary* thought that their ship would never allow herself to succumb to such trickery.

Sir William Denny, the inventor of the stabiliser, travelled on the ship to observe her motion and he talked to the officers in the Engineers' Ward Room. He even demonstrated his ideas, with the aid of scale models, showing where he would fit two pairs of stabilisers to the ship to reduce its rolling.

Work was started in the King George V dry-dock on fitting the Denny-Brown stabilisers in 1957 and a few months and half-a-million pounds later the task was completed in 1958 by John I. Thornycroft. The modification was a success and a roll of 10 degrees could be dampened to a fraction within seconds. The ladies, reassured by leaflets promising 'To Smooth Your Way Across the Atlantic', soon returned to the *Mary* whose roll was now almost a thing of the past except at high speed when the effect of the stabilisers was lessened.

Almost a thing of the past but not quite: In the autumn of 1964 the *Queen Mary* sailed from New York. The American meteorological office had forecast a typhoon and the liner's course supposedly took her well clear of it. Unfortunately, the typhoon had inconsiderately veered off its predicted course and, about two in the morning, struck without warning.

The Bridge had no time, or failed, to notify the Engine Room that trouble was imminent when the ship was suddenly caught in the vicious onslaught of a strong and continuous wind. As the liner was on her second day out from port she had settled down to her normal, fair-weather, engine room routine. Amongst the calm-weather procedures one of the two turbo-feed pumps in each engine room had been switched off. These pumps maintained a pressure of feed water that kept the boilers 'topped-up' from either side and during moderate weather only two pumps were

Leaflets enclosed with brochures extolled the virtues of the Denny-Brown stabilisers fitted to the *Queens*. The operating machinery on the *Mary* was fitted vertically due to space limitations.

Above: Operators are busy in the *Queen Mary*'s Radio Receiving Room.   RMS Foundation, Queen Mary Archive
Below: Shipyard workers look on as the port side forward stabilizer fin is lowered into position.   RMS Foundation, Queen Mary Archive

Above: The extensive Promenade Deck is buzzing with activity as passengers enjoy the sporting facilities.
Below: Another hive of actrivity - this time in one of the kitchens as chefs prepare some of the tens of thousands of meals required every day the liner was at sea.

Both, RMS Foundation, Queen Mary Archive

The 'eyes and feet' of the liner were the Bridge (left) and Engine Room (right), linked by the telegraph signals with with their distinctive clanging.

Courtesy, University of Liverpool Cunard archives

necessary to maintain feed to the boilers.

But when the typhoon struck the *Mary* listed 20° to starboard and was held there by the force of the wind. As a result, the boilers tilted with the ship and water went to one side of the boiler top drums whilst leaving the port side low. The automatic, or 'robot', valves controlling the feed-water levels detected this happening on each of the 24 boiler top drums (12 each port and starboard) and the starboard valves stopped feeding water which was perfectly acceptable. But the port side level was still low due to the continuing list and demanded more water (despite unrequired water on the starboard side still being available) which put an additional strain on the two operating feed pumps. In their efforts to supply water the pumps came close to overspeeding and tripping the turbo governors. The feed water pressure fell to just above the boiler steaming pressure: if the two needles indicating both pressures met and then suddenly passed each other it would be only a matter of seconds before the boilers melted down and blew.

The Boiler Room engineers watched the convergence of the needles and could only stand by, terrified. For some, prayer seemed to be the only solution.

By then the Bridge had got control of the situation and had turned the *Mary*'s head into the wind and as the list decreased the water pressures normalised just as the Engine Room engineers had got the other two turbo-feed pumps into operation.

In the wake of the night's events the morning brought its own aftermath. A bright but turbulent dawn broke as a few passengers and crew ventured out onto the still heaving deck. An elderly lady passenger fell and injured herself as the *Mary* continued to roll. Looking over the ship's side the stabilisers could be seen as they were rolled out of the water by the ship's motion, indicating the severity of the swell.

A dismal sight greeted an engineer when he returned to his cabin in the Engineer's quarters that had been built above the Verandah Grill shortly after the maiden voyage. The force of the gale had completely torn a steel-window cover away from its housing and another hung precariously from one hinge. To another engineer, 'Jack' Horner, an even more serious disaster had only just been averted:

He had left a bottle of whisky on the shelf above his wash basin and this, due to the rolling of the ship, had jumped over the fiddley surrounding the shelf, fallen through the sink (leaving a neat round hole in its wake) and ended up - unbroken - on the cabin floor, there to be rescued with the aid of glasses from any other provocation of fate by the engineer and his friends.

Fog, too, presented a great danger to the ship even after she had been fitted with radar. Bad seamanship on the part of other vessels was always something to contend with so during fog extra lookouts were posted on the bridge wings, watertight doors closed and the Engine Room put on 'Stand By'.

The *Queen Mary* would especially reduce speed to around 20 knots when, on her westward crossing, she crossed the 100 fathom line which indicated the edge of the Newfoundland Banks and an increased possibility of meeting fishing vessels. In years gone by many fishing vessels had gone missing, unreported by the fast ships that had possibly - perhaps unknowingly in light of the *Curacoa* incident - run them down. If another vessel's siren could be heard in the fog then the *Queen* would veer away at 45° from the siren's direction for ten minutes before resuming course. But one particular problem had been foreseen in John Masefield's poem 'No. 534'

Above: The mighty *Queen Mary* passes Hythe as she steams down Southampton Water at the start of another voyage to New York.
Right: A close-up of the ship's sirens, the deep and beautiful sound of which could be heard many miles away. A set of these sirens were shipped over from the liner at Long Beach on board *QE2* and will be fitted to the new *Queen Mary 2*.
Lower: Queen Mary sits proudly in the King George V dry-dock in Southampton during a maintenance period.

All, W. J. Windebank, courtesy of Barry J. Eagles

Above: Polished binnacles, telegraphs, ship's wheels, voice pipes and shimmering wood made the liner's Bridge a picture of nautical perfection.
Below: Looking aft from the starboard Bridge Wing. The large ventilation cowls were constructed with only the centre stiffener. When the liner was converted to a troopship during the War the additional outer stiffeners were fitted to support gun tubs that would be mounted atop the cowls.
Both, W. J. Windebank, courtesy of Barry J. Eagles

The 29th March 1958 and *Queen Mary* steams back into Southampton following stabiliser trials. *I. Bovey*

'.... and all gear twanging shrilly as you race....'

for when the captain and senior officer on watch listened out for other ship's sirens from their posts on the *Mary*'s bridge wings during fog they fought a losing battle. A ship's siren should be able to be heard from many miles away but this distance was reduced to a mile (thus decreasing the *Queen*'s ability to manoeuvre in time) due to the interference of the whistling created by the *Mary*'s own rigging.

As in any township the *Queen Mary* contained within her walls the extremes of human emotions - birth and death.

For the latter, allied soldiers and prisoners-of-war suffered the ultimate pain when they succumbed to heat exhaustion when the *Mary*, during her trooping days, voyaged in the Indian Ocean and especially into the Red Sea.

And in the normal sailing days of peacetime her company was not immune from accidental death. One crewmember fell down a funnel, whilst a young Third Officer, Marshall, was found dead with a fractured neck at the bottom of the officers' stairway in 1948. It was supposed that he had turned to look at the clock at the top of the stairs whilst he was rushing to get ashore in New York, missed his footing and fell.

Burials at sea also took place with the ashes of former crewmembers being committed to the deep.

On one such occasion, a greaser, having been told to empty a gash-can over the side noticed an officer gloomily and reproachfully looking at him. Later, the officer telephoned the engineer who had given the instruction to empty the can: 'Did he realise', the officer asked 'that ashes of a deceased crew member had been committed to the deep just before the gash from the engine-room had been sent to join him?'

To redress the balance of death on board, the *Mary* also acted as s maternity ward to babes who became known as '*Queen Mary* citizens'. As is sometimes the case, a child born on a ship will take the vessel's name as his (or her) own, but when twin daughters were born on the *Mary* (one name solved) the dilemma of the other child's name was resolved by christening her Elizabeth.

The *Mary* also saved life and on more than one occasion, sailors had the giant liner, her crew and medical staff to thank for their salvation. Even her presence gave ships in danger a feeling of security when they saw the *Mary* steaming towards them.

Unfortunately the *Queen Mary* was also once 'duped'. A radio call informed the Captain, Commodore George Morris, that the skipper of a Greek ship was ill and that his symptoms were bad. The ship turned around and found the vessel with the 'injured' skipper at around two in the morning. There was blood all around the Greek skipper's cabin and he was taken on board the Cunarder. Once the liner was underway, the skipper made a remarkable recovery, probably aided by suitcase full of money that he had brought with him. This episode had cost Cunard £5,000 and the *Queen Mary* twelve hours extra steaming.

The 'Big Ship' herself was endangered more than once. The first major occasion was when the liner had unhappily cut down and sank HMS *Curacoa* in the Second World War and depth charges on the stricken cruiser could well have exploded as the naval ship sank around the *Queen*.

The second such occasion occurred on New Year's Day in 1949, although only briefly reported, or not mentioned at all, in the press and in subsequent biographies of the ship, it greatly affected the captain and officers of the liner who were the main participants in the drama. This has been borne out in subsequently published autobiographies and later reminiscences recalled in personal conversation.

The *Queen* was due to sail from Southampton on New Year's Day 1949 and blustery squalls were blowing in from the direction of the New Forest to the west. The *Mary*'s Captain, Harry Grattidge, had only taken over the command of the liner three days before and to him fell the awesome responsibility to decide whether to sail in such weather. Around one in the afternoon there was a lull in the gales and, as tugs were available, the captain decided to leave with Jack Holt, the pilot, taking over the ship as far as the Nab Tower.

Picking up the French pilot, off the Brittany coast, the ship's company was reassured that the coast would provide some shelter. In order to pick up passengers arriving from Paris, there being no suitable overnight accommodation for them in Cherbourg, the Captain decided to enter Cherbourg Harbour, always difficult and still wrecked after the war, and anchor at 6.30 on that dark evening. Both anchors were dropped in the outer harbour.

The westerly wind had now changed to west-south-westerly, gale force 6 to 7 and by 8pm the passengers were on board. The captain ordered 'All hands to stations' and for the ship to get underway. The anchors, held taut by the force of the wind, were taken in and as the port anchor was housed safely the pilot, Guy Frielaut, ordered the engines slow ahead. Then the starboard anchor came into sight clutching a long black, shiny object in it flukes. 'Oh, look! There's a sea serpent on it!' a crewmember was heard to call.

Pull as the captain might, the anchor could not get free of this obstacle and the pilot ordered full astern on both engines to ease the strain on the cable but still the anchor held fast. The wind increased in intensity and squalls blotted out the working party on the bow under the direction of Chief Officer Marr, who found it increasingly difficult to communicate with the Bridge over the noise of the wind.

The recalcitrant anchor was once again let go, engine manoeuvres executed and again an attempt was made to weigh the starboard anchor.

This time the anchor had two or three of the black lines on it and these, it was realised, were the remains of 'Pluto', the Pipe Line Under The Ocean, that had been laid to deliver petrol to the Allied invasion forces in France. Unsuccessfully, Geoffrey Marr tried to report to the Bridge but heard the captain say 'Tell the Chief Officer there is nothing we can do for him now!' The port anchor was dropped as the *Mary*, continuing her astern drift, just missed rocks near the breakwater.

By now the captain had said, 'All right, Pilot, I'll take over', as tugs that had been signalled for had not appeared and the ship was still held by the tentacles of the pipeline on her dragging anchors.

At 9pm there was a gentle bump and the liner stopped. A manoeuvre with the engines did not move her and a signal was at once sent for tugs which, again, did not appear. The liner was obviously aground.

Above: The buckled keel plates of the *Mary* after grounding on the table-sized Seleine Bank in Cherbourg Harbour.

Below: The damaged plates cut out and dumped on the side of the King Geroge V Graving Dock, Southampton. November 1949.   *Both, National Maritime Museum*

Low water was due in half an hour and plans were made to transfer oil to barges and to get the passengers ashore to reduce draught as Geoffery Marr had his men got busy with flame torches to cut the ship free of the pipelines grip. Ultimately the passengers remained on board and much of the oil was transferred to other tanks.

The ship had grounded at the western side of Cherbourg Harbour on a pinnacle of hard sand. only a few feet wide. called the Seleine Bank. By now the pilot, chain smoking and frantic, told the captain that at low tide the *Mary* would break her back. But, perhaps luckily, the liner had grounded on one of the few strong parts of her keel - between the two forward propellers.

By seven the next morning, after a night of hacking and burning, the pipeline was finally cut away. By now the four propellers could be seen as the tide had supposedly dropped by seventeen feet. Staff Officer (later Commodore) MacLean was to say years later that he had been told that the drop in tide was more like 21 feet!

The next high tide was due at 9.30am but by 8 the liner was thankfully afloat. She went astern out of the harbour, returned to The Solent where she anchored before returning to Southampton for dry-docking and inspection. A few rivets were found to be leaking and the keel was slightly concaved in the area of grounding. With difficulty, sixty tons of cement was poured around the dent inside the ship and three days later the *Mary* continued her broken voyage to New York. Of the 1,700 passengers on board only three had decided to continue their journey by air. Dame Myra Hess and Benno Moiseiwitsch, the internationally acclaimed pianists who were on board, entertained the passengers and many took the chance to explore the ship more fully in what turned out to be ten-day journey.

Perhaps, fortunately, the hours of darkness and the appallingly bad weather that had covered the period of grounding and refloating, had deterred any curious news photographers.

Other perils threatening the well being to the *Mary* were man-made, especially those times when she had to be docked in New York without the aid of tugs due to local strikes. This happened, firstly, before the War in 1938 when Commodore Sir Robert Irving, the Laird of Bonshawe, took her in and again in 1953 when the diminutive, but highly respected, Captain Donald Sorrell (he was 5' 3" but wished he was 6' 3") took her in using a home-made sighting device 'my piece of wood' (made of wood and nails) previously constructed for use should such an event occur. At such times the *Queen* would wait for slack water, use the knuckle of Pier 90 as a pivot and pull herself in on her hawsers, previously landed by ship's boats. A very difficult and precise operation that brought telegrams of congratulations and herds of press-photographers hoping for a major crash that would interest their readers. Captain Irving's action actually broke the tugmens' strike.

Over the years of the *Queen Mary*'s seagoing career many hundreds of people worked in her. Many famous passengers asked for their favourite steward, etc, to look after them during a voyage and this loyalty was repaid in many ways with holidays or medical bills for the crewmember being paid for by the well-attended passenger. From commis-waiter to officer, all of these people have often fascinating stores to tell and a picture gradually grows of what life was like on board an ocean liner.

Due to space limitations only two stories can be told of the many varied duties performed by the crew.

The day of a young commis-waiter such as Edwin Praine (who had joined the Empress of Britain as a bellboy at the age of 14 in 1932, then joined the *Queen Mary* on her maiden voyage in 1936), began when he woke at 5am ready for a 5.30 start. His first duty was to collect a bucket of water and a pair of 'kneelers' and scrub the linoleum in the companionways. At 7.30 there was muster for a clean hands inspection prior to laying tables and then serving breakfast in the Main Restaurant, when long, white, starched continental aprons were worn. Breakfast finished at 10am so a change of clothes was necessary either to serve lunch or to clean silver cutlery or brass portholes. Lunch continued until 2.30pm

Above: Tinkerbell proudly on display on the Promenade Deck in August 1965.
Below: On the Bridge of *Queen Mary*, Capt. Divers no doubt discusses maritime affairs with Bob Manry, who crossed the Atlantic from the USA to England in *Tinkerbell*.   *Author's collection*

and afternoon teas were served every other afternoon in the lounge. Alternate afternoons Edwin Praine had free unless, as a punishment for being late, more portholes had to be cleaned. Dinner was served until 10pm and the young waiter came off duty at 11pm, tired out but ready to start all over next morning at 5am!

Peter Jackson (later to captain the *Queen Elizabeth 2* on her journey to South Georgia during the Falklands war of 1982) joined the *Queen Mary* in November 1948 as Junior Third Officer having just obtained his Master's Certificate. Everything on board the liner was still spanking new after her post-war refit and her 100th voyage had passed un-remarked.

To explain his routine to him Staff Captain Donald MacLean took Peter Jackson to one side and said, 'You've just got your Certificate and we don't want you getting lost if there is an emergency; so, to help you find your way around the ship, you will be my representative on the midnight, 2-4

Above: The liner in dock, framed by a dockside crane and gangway, rises above the quayside.

Left: The Engine Room blackboard with chalked notes for the information of those on watch or their successors.

Below: Another Engine Room scene photographed by Colin Walker on his accompanied visit before the liner was withdrawn.

Colin Walker courtesy of Southampton Museums

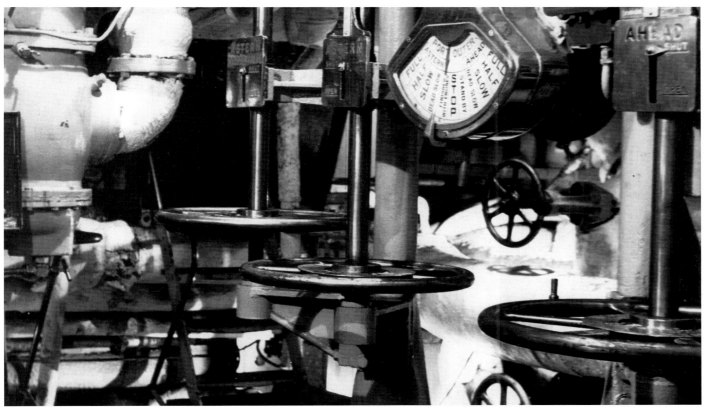

Above: Well-polished gauges and steam control hand wheels in the Engine Room.
Below: A quiet night time dockside scene with little activity going on. *Both, Colin Walker courtesy of Southampton Museums*

and 6am rounds and report back to the Bridge 'Rounds Correct' at the end of each round. Don't call me at, say, 3.30am unless there is a real emergency!' Each night, walking these rounds, meant that seventeen miles were covered and the ship's layout soon became familiar. Things such as burst pipes had to be sorted out with the source of the flood stopped and the water baled out. Occasionally, bad weather would smash a porthole and the deadlight (the steel version of the glass port) would have to be secured over the aperture. One's way was soon found around the ship and problems were dealt with sensibly as they arose.

Whilst on night watch during the few spare moments that presented themselves Peter Jackson would practice on the magnificent Steinway piano in the early hours of the morning. He was given a spare key for this instrument on which he played his favourite Chopin and Beethoven. Unbeknown to him, Wally Adams, a fruit-storeman, would quietly enter the lounge and sit listening, discreetly, from behind a pillar.

Another officer who enjoyed playing was First Officer Noel Jones. Because of the many Joneses at sea he was known as 'Mendelsohn' Jones. Another Jones was known as 'Corpus' as his family had an undertaking business back in Wales!

Association with passengers was forbidden and although navigating officers had their own table in the Main Restaurant they were not allowed then to dine with passengers. Officers were also not allowed in the lounges unless on security patrol but they could invite passengers to their Wardroom for afternoon tea.

So the *Queen Mary* carried on with her work, giving practical experience to those who wanted it, work to many who valued it (some jobs were often handed from father to son), and the ship in return receiving love and loyalty - crew members from the *Queens* were proud of their ships, had their own tie, formed their own clubs and were jealous of their own *Queen*'s reputation. They even had their own car club badges for the various organisations that had branches or chapters on board.

With such loyalty and devotion the *Queens* would surely prosper.

Top: A group photograph of staff in the hospital on board, Jean Edwards is in the front on the left.
Centre: On the occasion of his retirement Captain Donald Sorrell is flanked on his left and right by Arthur Bebe and Dr Mackay.
Below: To say farewell to Captain Sorrell, some crew members line up for a scrapbook photograph. In the centre is Captain Sorrell shaking hands with Jean Edwards. On her left is 'Jonny' Johnson, Jean Woods, John Baines, Dr Mackay and an unidentified member of the crew. On the left of the picture is nurse Mairi Allen. *Jean Edwards collection*

Chapter Seven

Mary and the Movies

Born into an age when the ocean liner was the only way to travel great distances in both relative safety and great comfort the 'Big Ship', the *Queen Mary*, attracted the big names.

Over the years the *Queen* carried hundreds of thousands of passengers and numbered amongst these were the rich and the famous, helping to give the ship an aura of glamour. The curious public were fed with news of important arrivals of people of note by reporters who themselves were 'characters' and sometimes somewhat flamboyant: Jack Frost (who co-authored excellent biographies on the *Mary*, *Elizabeth* and *QE2*) with his straw boater and bow tie (he became a personal friend of passengers and crew alike) and Hannen Swaffer, were both commentators on the coming and goings of the famous and rich in pre-'jet set' days. Their reports in the national newspapers were widely read with avid interest.

Politicians, sportsmen, ministers of governments and churches, musicians, royalty (including the Duke and Duchess of Windsor until they transferred their loyalty to the *United States*) and titled worthies, movie stars as well as the infamous and unfamous, all travelled on the *Mary*. Household names of the day such as Montgomery of Alamein, Lord and Lady Louis Mountbatten, Sir Winston Churchill, Sir Thomas Beecham, Lord Beaverbrook, General and Mrs Eisenhower, voyaged along with perhaps not-so-well known bankers, millionaires and industrialists.

But it was the movie stars who created the greatest stir when they disembarked at, or sailed from, Southampton in the 1930s, 40s and 50s, those times when the cinema provided a major source of entertainment with its performers often idolised.

Some of the crew became compulsive autograph hunters and many a menu, photograph or album was dedicated and signed by the famous passengers.

Sir Cedric Hardwick, sailing on the *Queen*'s maiden voyage with his family, was one of the first film stars to travel on the ship. He would be followed in later years by Henry Fonda, Charlton Heston, John Mills, Victor Mature, Elizabeth Taylor, Rex Harrison and Kay Kendall, Michael Wilding, Katherine Hepburn, Richard Burton, Deborah Kerr, Robert Ryan, Johnnie Ray, Bette Davis, Robert Mitchum, Karl Malden, Claude Rains, Anna Neagle, Margaret Rutherford, Charles Boyer and many more - all of whom sailed on the *Mary* at one time or another, some of them returning time and time again to the ship they loved.

Stories abound about the stars, some humorous, some sad, some scandalous so, to accompany the reproduced photographs of a few of the film-stars who favoured the *Mary*, a tale or two would not be amiss.

After dining well in the Main Restaurant, Spencer Tracey was asked by one of the chefs if the actor would sign his autograph book. Feeling more mischievous than truthful Spencer Tracey wrote 'Thank goodness for Alka Seltzer!' before adding his signature.

The world-renowned pianist Liberace, voyaging on the *Mary*, would often play for the passengers and on one crossing one his many sequinned coats shed its shimmering embellishments. Stewardesses volunteered to sew them back on, all three thousand of them! Whilst Liberace was waiting for his jacket, two other members took the opportunity to obtain his autograph and presented him with sugar models of his piano and candelabrum.

Phil Silvers travelled on both *Queens* when he was at the height of his popularity as the scheming television Sergeant Bilko. One of the engineers was due to be introduced to Mr and Mrs Silvers and was quite nervous at the prospect. He kept on telling himself that he must say 'Mr Silvers' and not 'Mr Bilko'. When the introduction was effected he managed 'Good morning, Mr Silvers' quite well, but let himself down with 'Good morning, Mrs Bilko'!

Some of the travelling celebrities would go down aft to the crew's own pub, by tradition called 'The Pig and Whistle', and join in the crew's weekly show. Ted Heath and His Band played for them and Nancy Sinatra sang for them.

Photographed on board R.M.S. QUEEN MARY.

Bob Hope, June 1951 apparently ready to tee-off from the ship!   *Author's collection*

Gracie Fields was a great favourite and she loved to sing for the crew and Dorothy Lamour followed in the steps of royalty by sitting amongst the crew to watch the performance.

Alec Guinness, that most talented of English actors, wrote on a photograph, taken on board, that had caught him blinking '...... not really as drunk as I look!'

Joan Crawford journeyed with her two daughters and seemed to be the perfect mother ñ the girls even wrote 'Thank you' notes to the captain at the end of the trip. The revelations made years later by one of her daughters would shock the world.

These are stories, too, about the other passengers and these are just as interesting, just as humorous as the yarns about the people in the limelight.

One such story is told by Mike Smith, who became the captain's 'Tiger' or personal steward, whilst waiting on the prestigious Captain's Table.

One of the guests at the Captain's Table was a millionairess who had risen from humble beginnings but never forgot her Cockney background - or accent.

Quickly perusing the menu with its enormous selection of dishes the lady in question spotted the addendum at the bottom of the page informing the passengers that if they could not see what they required on the menu all they had to do was to inform their waiter and arrangements would be made to obtain what was wanted. So the wealthy woman said:' 'ere, Mike! I'd like fish 'n' chips wrapped up in 'The News of the Worldi!'

A not unreasonable request but as the ship was only a day out from New York the English Sunday newspaper posed a bit of a problem.

Undeterred, Mike Smith scoured the crews' quarters until an old, crumpled edition of the newspaper was found, which with the application of an iron, was made presentable. With great aplomb the fish and chips, wrapped in newspaper and accompanied by a huge bottle of vinegar, was presented to the delighted gourmet who proceeded to consume it with great relish.

Good service was always appreciated and as the lady left the table she tipped the resourceful waiter - with a $100 dollar bill!

One of the most popular passengers ever to sail with the *Queen Mary* was Her Majesty Queen Elizabeth the Queen Mother. She had sailed to the United States, for a tour after her husband's death, on the *Queen Elizabeth* three weeks earlier and for the return trip Cunard arranged for Commodore Ivan Thompson, captain of the *Elizabeth*, to transfer his flag to the *Mary*. This was an unpopular decision with the *Mary*'s crew as they felt it was a slight on their own beloved captain, Donald Sorrell.

Geoffery Marr was at this time Staff Captain of the *Mary* but he was asked to act as liaison officer between the royal party and ship and to arrange an on-board itinerary for the Queen Mother. After her energetic American tour it was thought that Her Majesty would like a restful trip. Not a bit of it! The Queen Mother wanted to see everything and meet as many as possible.

On the first night out the Queen Mother chose to dine in the Main Restaurant and the room was full to capacity for the occasion. As she entered, dressed in a gown of blue and gold, the entire assemblage rose to its feet.

The Queen loved films, and each evening Geoffery Marr would call for her as soon as the cartoons were over.

On the last night out Her Majesty held a small, sparkling dinner party in the Verandah Grill and afterwards invited her guests back to her suite. The Staff Captain thought it was merely to bid her guests 'Goodnight' but coffee and liqueurs awaited them. Geoffery Marr recited John Masefield's poem about lighthouses for Her Majesty as the *Queen Mary* was due to pass Bishop Rock that very night.

On arriving at Southampton on Tuesday evening, 23rd November, at 8.30 the Queen Mother asked to see the liner docking so Geoffery Marr escorted her to the port Bridge wing where he could describe what was happening.

The Royal traveller left behind her a ship full of happy people. She had presented gifts to several of the crew - a silver crested comb for Senior Sister Moy in the surgery, a portrait in a leather frame and a silver cigarette case for Mrs Geoffery Marr; she had been, as Geoffery Marr recalls '..... so very charming and gracious and made you feel so much at home.'

Stories about the celebrities who travelled on the *Queen Mary* could fill books - and have. The *Queen* also seemed to change peoples' attitudes to one another once they were on board. Hard-line politicians softened to those of dis-similar leanings and businessmen relaxed and clinched many an important deal whilst on board.

The *Queen Mary* carried stars and made stars. She, herself, became a star of films and television shows proving that once 'on stage' she could not be 'up-staged'.

Frank Sinatra co-starred with the liner in 'Assault on a Queen', made in 1965, when she played herself. Luckily, it was the only time in her career when a U-boat got the better of her! She took on a character part in 'The Poseidon Adventure', the first and best of a spate of pseudo-disaster movies, that was based on Paul Gallico's book. In this she played the fatally unstable SS *Poseidon*, although mainly in model form. Parts in various 'soap' television detective series followed but she has taken to her recent screen roles with the ease of a gentle lady in distress.

To be associated with the *Queen* in those days meant a measure, however small, of success.

The Duke and Duchess of Windsor in February 1952 at an on-board press conference.

Celebrity actress, Margaret Lockwood, poses in the First Class Main Lounge.

British Prime Minister, Winston Churchill used the two *Queen* liners to ply between Britain and the United States for talks with his American counterparts.

All photographs courtesy of
RMS Foundation, Queen Mary Archive

Gracie Fields was another of the celebrities to sail regularly on the *Queen Mary*. She dines with a friend in the First Class Restaurant.

David Niven was a very familiar face on board over many years.

Chapter Eight

The Queen Dowager

In the eleven years following their post-war refits the two *Queens* were an enormous success. Cunard, its emblem a lion holding the world in its paws, also carried the 'lion's share' of the North Atlantic passenger trade. Of this share the giant sisters laid claim to a sizeable proportion. A one million peak was reached in 1957. The two Cunard lionesses were the pride of the Atlantic.

The *Mary* had lost the Blue Ribband to the *United States* in July 1952. This liner beat the *Queen* by a comfortable margin with 35.59 knots but her maximum speed was kept a secret. She had been built on warship lines and it has since been revealed that she could achieve 40 knots! In that same year members of the *Mary*'s crew were plagued by the anti-Communist witch-hunt that was sweeping the States. Questions and questionnaires assailed the crew each time that the liner docked in New York and many a witty answer was provided. 'What are you? - 'I'm a commis!' - commis, pronounced 'commy', was an assistant

to a waiter but sent the questioning officer into paroxysms of rage!

With the ships making money 'hand over fist' the Cunard management of the day became complacent in many ways. They ill advisedly refused to recognise the aeroplane as a serious threat to sea-travel and also a large shore staff was built up, administrating from several offices in each country of operation. Money was being made but it was also being spent almost recklessly.

However, in 1958, the ascending problem at last stared Cunard in the face, for this was the year in which the number of passengers flying the Atlantic by the fast, ever-increasing jet aircraft equalled the number travelling by sea, one million to one million. By 1964 the figures showed that four million had travelled by air but in the same period Cunard's carrying capacity had fallen to 650,000. A particular voyage, November 1961, became typical of winter travel with the *Mary* carrying just over 470 passengers out of

The *Mary* is docked at Berth 46 whilst the Ocean Terminal is under construction.   *Southern Newspapers*

her capacity of over 2,000! Crew numbers still remained at the same level at over 1,000.

To help reduce costs, the summer dry-docking was omitted from 1963 onwards. These had always occurred during the *Queens'* peak season but, by cutting the two annual overhauls to just one in the winter, Cunard gained the revenue from an additional summer voyage and saved the cost of the peak-season lay-up.

Realising that fewer passengers were travelling during the winter months Cunard decided to put the *Queens* to cruising. For the *Mary* this meant making the first cruise, in February 1963, that a Cunarder had made from Britain since 1939. During the ensuing years she cruised from Southampton to Las Palmas and from New York to Nassau and the Mediterranean. Because of her draught and breadth she could not moor in many ports and she could not traverse the Suez or Panama Canals to further lucrative markets (this was eventually and spectacularly remedied by the *QE2)*. Her lack of air-conditioning was also a great drawback.

One cruise was charted by the British Sunday newspaper 'News of the World' was offered as a prize to those of its readers who could correctly place various features of cruising in the correct order. The ship sailed on 23rd December 1965 in a gale of Force 5 to 6. By the time the *Mary* had reached the notorious Bay of Biscay this had increased to Force 9. A heavy sea crashed over her and a one ton ventilating cowl was torn off its seating, crashing into a ¾ inch thick glass plate window on the Promenade Deck, shattering it and badly cutting a passenger who had fortunately just had time to shield his young son. After Finisterre the gale subsided and the Christmas cruise was enjoyed from then on, the preceeding bad weather becoming only a half-remembered incident.

By 1966 the *Queen Mary* was still fast, still showing her fighting spirit, when she crossed the Atlantic at 29.68 knots. That same year saw the disastrous seamen's strike that lasted for six weeks and cost Cunard nearly £4 million.

Calls at Cobh were instigated in 1967 but in spite of new ports of call, new itineraries for cruising, the *Queen Mary* was by now losing up to £8,000 a day.

A new chairman had been appointed by Cunard in 1965 and his new philosophy was intended to make the line pay, no matter how drastic or unpopular his proposals would be.

As a consequence, Captain William Laws opened a sealed envelope on board the *Queen Mary* on 8th May 1967. Contrary to what previous Cunard chairmen had said about the long-term viability of the *Queens*, Sir Basil Smallpiece announced:

'It is a matter of great regret to the Company and to me personally, as it will be to friends throughout the world, that these two fine ships, the *Queen Mary* and the *Queen Elizabeth*, must shortly come to the end of their working lives. They hold a unique position in the history of the sea, and in the affections of seafaring people everywhere. But we cannot allow our affections or our sense of history to divert us from our aim of making Cunard a thriving company and no other decision will make commercial sense.' These great liners were, after all, just tools to forge prosperity!

It was therefore decided to put the *Queen Mary* up for

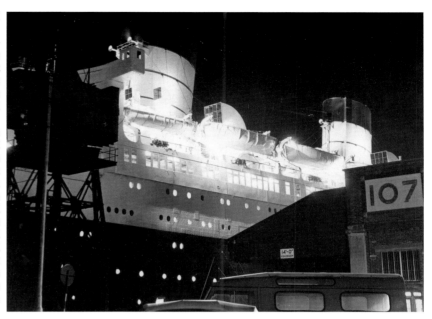

In readinss for her final sailing, the *Queen* docked alongside Berth 107 in the Western (or 'New') Docks.   *Colin Walker, courtesy of Southampton Museums*

sale. Cunard did not particularly want her to go for scrap but neither did they want her to be operated in competition with them.

After many bids, with many a strange suggestion as to the ultimate usage of the *Queen*, Cunard accepted a $3,450,000 offer from the City of Long Beach in California, the deal being signed on 18th August by representatives of Cunard and the Corporation of Long Beach. The ship would be used as a maritime museum, conference centre and hotel.

So, after years of faithful service, the *Queen Mary* was to be pensioned off. Her initial building cost of £5 million had, over the years, earned Cunard £132 million. She had sailed just over 3,790,000 miles, had carried 2,114,000 passengers and had won herself an immortal place in the affections of a nation - ask any schoolboy, even now, to name an ocean liner; his answer'?

The *Queen Mary* left New York on 22nd September 1967, at noon, amidst momentous and tearful farewells. Despite a two-day storm she arrived at Southampton on 27th September, having achieved 27.86 knots on this, her 1001st crossing, amidst a welcoming reception of fireboats, small craft and a mostly silent crowd on shore. The mood was subdued.

The *Mary*'s master for her last Atlantic voyage was Captain John Treasure Jones, one of the most natural public-relations orientated captains that Cunard had ever had. He had had a varied and interesting career starting with White Star - he had been made redundant from this company as he had less than fifteen years experience with the line which would have guaranteed him continuing employment after the amalgamation with Cunard; he had stevedored in Liverpool; had joined Cunard White Star; became a naval commander during the War after being torpedoed and commanding anti-submarine patrols; and, as a commander, became Divisional Sea Transport Officer in the Dutch East Indies; re-joined Cunard after the war and joined the *Queen Mary* for the first time as Chief Officer in 1953.

His favourite ship was '..... the one that I was currently Captain of,' - and it fell to him to be captain of the *Mary* during her last days at sea.

When he was asked by Cunard if he was surprised at the *Queen Mary*'s forthcoming disposal, John Treasure Jones replied, 'No, I'm not surprised. I'm just surprised that you've kept her going for so long and losing so much money!'

During her ultimate crossing the *Mary* met her younger sister the *Queen Elizabeth* command by Captain Bill Laws, the ships 'closing in' to within one mile of each other. At ten minutes past midnight on 25th September the two largest liners passed each other on the dark Atlantic, brilliantly lit and with funnels floodlit, providing an unforgettable experience to the few who braved the lateness of the hour and the wind. This last poignant meeting was over in just a few minutes as the liners sped by each other at a combined speed of 60 knots.

Never again would they meet.

The *Mary* in all her glory at speed in the North Atlantic.   *Author's collection*

Captain Law on the *Queen Elizabeth* raises his cap in farewell to the *Queen Mary* on her final voyage to New York. This close encounter was pre-arranged to ensure both liners passed each other in close quarters.

Chapter Nine

A Wonderful, Beautiful Toy

Ten thousand people watched the *Queen* sail from Southampton on Tuesday 31st October 1967.

The day before, the Port's floating crane had lifted two red London buses onto the liner where they were secured aft on the Main Deck. These were going to be used to transport visitors from the centre of Long Beach to the ship once she was operational in her new home town.

The City of Long Beach in Orange County, California, had bought the *Queen Mary* and her value quoted on her export licence (other information: *Queen Mary*; Numbers 'One'; Description of package 'One ship'; etc) was $3,450,000.

Cunard had agreed to deliver the ship and to supply the minimal crew to do so and the fuel to get there on a slow speed voyage. But the new owners did not want that alone, they wanted the delivery trip to become a high profile publicity cruise, in spite of the ship not having facilities for hot weather voyaging. She would also have to go via Cape Horn with its inherent dangers. So Long Beach arranged for Furgazy Travel to sell the trip as 'The Last Great Cruise' in order to recoup some of the $650,000 delivery costs. In the event 1,093 passengers paid up to $9,000 each and a profit of $125,000 was realised. 806 crew were taken on (119 deck, 98 engine and 589 catering staff) but they would be overworked and only after strong representations would overtime be paid.

4,700 tons of fuel and 8,560 tons of fresh water for various purposes would be loaded but this would have to be replenished *en-route* as the *Mary* had been designed for the Atlantic route and not for the 14,559-mile journey she was about to undertake. Seven stopovers had been arranged for the ship at ports that were capable of handling her.

HRH Queen Mary's personal standard had been taken off the ship and stored safely until it could be installed on the new *QE2*.

So, at 9.30am on 31st October with pilot Jack Holt on the Bridge for the final time, the Band of the Royal Marines playing 'Auld Lang Syne' on the quayside, with fourteen naval helicopters flying in anchor formation overhead and a 310 foot long pennant flying from her main mast the *Queen Mary* left Berth 107 in a tearful farewell. Shop staff in the city climbed to the roofs of their stores to witness her passing and, as the *Mary* passed by, the *Oriana* signalled, 'Adieu, great Queen'. The liner replied, 'Thank you, thank you, thank you very much and good luck to you all.'

Tears ran down the face of the *Queen*'s Master At Arms, 'Oh! That was a grand, grand goodbye', as crowds waved and vessels blew their sirens as the *Mary* sailed by.

Passing by Cowes for the last time the *Mary* read a signal from the exclusive Royal Yacht Squadron, 'I am sorry to say goodbye. Very best wishes.'

The passage to Lisbon, her first port of call, was rough and took about two days. In the English Channel *en-route* she passed HMS *Hermes*, the British aircraft carrier whose company line the flight deck to cheer the *Queen* rousingly.

At Lisbon a stowaway, Stacy Miller, secretly joined the ship and the next stop was Las Palmas where nearly 6,000 tons of oil fuel was taken on.

The *Queen* had to make a slow passage (which chagrined many a misunderstanding passenger) of around 20 knots. This was done to conserve fuel; she would use 1,100

The *Mary* approaches the famous Manhattan skyline of New York at the end of one of her 1001 crossings of the Atlantic.

Courtesy, University of Liverpool Cunard Archives

The *Queen Mary* at her berth in Southampton in June 1960.

W. J. Windebank, courtesy of Barry J. Eagles

tons on the North Atlantic to maintain her high speed, but this would consume the fuel up too quickly so two engines and half the boilers only were operational. As a result, only 550 tons of fuel were burnt daily.

The journey to Rio de Janeiro from Las Palmas would cover 3,540 miles and once there the *Queen* was again refuelled with 2,460 tons of oil.

Early on the morning of her arrival at Rio, on Monday 13th November, the death occurred, through cerebral haemorrhage caused by heat stroke, of fish cook Leonard Horsburgh, aged 56, who had been known as 'Lobster' to his friends because of his ruddy complexion.

By the time of the arrival at Rio the 'Mermaid Bar' had been reduced to using paper cups, through pilferage of

glasses, and had become known as the 'Lily-cup Bar'. At the port, funds had been raised amongst the crew for a representative to go ashore to buy drinks for use on board. When the time came for the *Mary* to sail the assignment had not arrived and the purchaser was beginning to feel that he might become none too popular.

As the ship sailed a tug raced out of Rio and the *Mary* slowed as a cargo port was opened and various boxes were taken on board. These were detailed as 'Ship's stores' but were, in fact, the belated packages of 'crew's booze'!

At 11.15am the burial at sea took place of Len Horsburgh and his body was committed to the deep. The captain had in all good faith chosen this relatively late hour for the commitment to show the passengers what a burial at sea was like. Unhappily, the crew did not see it this way and were offended when cameras clicked as the burial progressed, the passengers treating the event as an additional spectacle not included on the published itinerary.

As the ship headed south the captain found it increasingly difficult to communicate with Cunard in England, long delays frequently occurring. Eventually Cunard told Captain Treasure Jones, 'Get her there by yourself and don't try to contact us' and he was thus left to his own devices. Far from being daunted, he welcomed the enhanced responsibilities thrust upon him and said later that being in sole charge of the *Mary* was like having '.....wonderful and beautiful toy that you had to be very careful with!'

One Sunday 19th November the *Queen* passed Cape Horn in mid-afternoon. No one knew what the weather was going to be like but it turned out to be cloudy, clear, with a moderate northeast wind creating a slight swell. For four hours people queued and paid $1 to ride on a London bus around the infamous Horn! The proceeds went to an orphanage in Valparaiso and certificates were given out to mark the 'Rounding'. One man dived into the swimming pool to say that he had swum around the Horn whilst another pedalled away on a bicycle in the gym!

That night, the weather blew up just to show what the Horn could really offer.

The rest of the journey up the West Coast of South America towards Valparaiso continued to be rough and she arrived at the port on 23rd November having completed the longest part of her journey, 3,895 miles.

The *Queen Mary* glides down Southampton Water in the company of mainly Red Funnel vessels packed with onlookers. Both liner and tugs are dressed overall for the occasion.
Keith McLean

The next stopover was at the old sailing ship port of Callao on the 28th and then Balbao where 3,500 tons of bunkers were taken on.

Acapulco came next on 5th December and she anchored off the fashionable resort overnight. All the crew had shore leave (save for safety parties) and, for a change, the *Queen* was fêted.

Champagne cocktail parties had been held since Valparaiso with caviar and Havana cigars being freely distributed. This was due not so much as to the party spirit prevailing on board but to various US import restrictions of foodstuffs and to a ban on Cuban imports.

500 miles form Long Beach a DC-9 jet met the *Queen* and, in imitation of an incident on her maiden arrival in New York, bombarded the liner with flowers, most of which missed. However, the airliner's captain, A. Heimerdinger, later sent Captain Treasure Jones a framed and signed photograph of the event.

The arrival at Long Beach was nothing short of spectacular as 'Eight thousand if there was one!' boats came to meet the ship fifteen miles out in order to escort her in to her berth. The craft kept well clear of the liner as her course had been well publicised by the authorities and her sea-lane was made into a Federal waterway with a year's imprisonment or a $2,000 fine for those who infringed it.

By 11.30am, Saturday 9th December 1967, amidst the noise and cheering of an estimated million people, the ship came alongside her berth. At 2.50pm the passengers began to disembark and at 4pm two stowaways were landed into the care of the FBI. (The second stowaway had boarded at Acapulco.) At a brief dockside ceremony the captain was presented with a flowered key to the city and he handed over the Cunard houseflag.

The crew were flown home almost immediately as their 72-hour visas would not allow them much time for sight seeing.

A sombre crowd in Southampton, many afloat, gathered to bid 'farewell' to a great ship. *Colin Walker, courtesy of Southampton Museums*

On the following Monday a slightly delayed ceremony took place on board, aft of the Verandah Grill. A telephone linked the ship with Cunard in London and Lord Mancroft informed Captain Treasure Jones that the '....Long Beach cheque was a good one and had not bounced!' As the American flag was raised to take the place of the British ensign the Captain felt a lump in his throat, realising that "it was all over".

So ended the long, eventful and honourable career of the Royal Mail Ship *Queen Mary*. She was to become, after a planned $8 million (later to be slightly increased to $100 million plus!) conversion, a 'building' - reliant on lines from the land to supply power and water - and is now known as The Hotel Queen Mary. She was later joined by Howard Hughes' giant wooden flying boat, the *Spruce Goose*, enclosed in a huge dome just along from the ship. The

'*Goose* would later be moved with changing plans for the area.

A local politician expressed his hope that the *Queen Mary* would be safe for at least three hundred years - but in the first 30 of these years the ship has experienced changing fortunes. She has changed hands several times with her management passing from the Wrather Corporation, to Disney (complete with dancers dressed in huge menu cards cavorting around the deck - after all, Disney's business is to entertain rather than extol historic attributes!); then back to the City of Long Beach. Tideland oil revenue was supposed to keep the ship going but she still had to make a viable profit.

Often embroiled in local politics and preservation battles from both city and on board - the old ship has survived batterings that could equal the storms that tried to claim her at sea!

In 1992 it was proposed to dispose of the ship in one way or another whether by scrapping, selling or mothballing etc. A firm of naval architects produced a thick report and one proposal set the alarm bells ringing around the world. This gave the very feasible option of towing the vessel out to sea, sink her, sell the filming rights to Hollywood and then use the wreck as both a submarine tourist attraction and artificial reef!

A group comprised of horrified businessmen, politicians, ex-seafarers, authors and publishers formed 'Project Queen Mary' in Southampton (other similar groups were also formed in other countries) and started a campaign to bring the ship back to the port.

The Southampton group finally petitioned Sir James Sherwood (he had just pulled out of a deal with Portsmouth Historic Dockyard) and, after a long interview during which he was presented with a copy of the original edition of this book, 'Queen Mary - 50 Years of Splendour', he agreed to offer £1 for the ship but backed it up with £15 million!

Each bid had to be accompanied by proposals as to the future use of the ship and Southampton proposed to dock her near to the Town Quay and one of the uses for her would be as an hotel for passengers boarding the *QE2* after bringing them to Southampton on the Orient Express.

When approached for permission to berth the ship in Southampton the Port's owners, Associated British Ports, said an emphatic 'No!', they didnít have room, but added '......but if she is halfway up Southampton Water then there would be nothing we could do about it!'

Long Beach decided after all to keep the ship where she was but did not act on any of the ideas for her use. That is until now, as she will become a staging post for passengers sailing on the *Queen Mary 2*.

The *Queen Mary* is now suffering from the fatigues of

Above: Boats and planes great the *Queen* at Long Beach after the mammoth voyage.

RMS Foundation, Queen Mary Archives

Below: The *Queen* pictured just a few days after arrival in the sunny climes of California. Her berth was at Pier E in Long Beach harbour - and so began another eventful career.

Roger Hardingham

old age. Her boilers were scrapped when she arrived at Long Beach and the removal of this enormous weight from where it was very carefully calculated to contribute to the strength of the ship has resulted in the ship hogging (bending). As a result her expansion joints have opened and other technical problems are becoming apparent. A decayed lifeboat also fell in the water and the London buses that went out with the ship ended up in a local scrapyard.

There is in existence a $6 million plan put forward by a Californian engineer (he even built a working scale model of one of the ship's boilers that actually runs on the correct Bunker 'C' grade of fuel!) an ambitious and laudable plan to build a replica boiler room in the present empty cavern, complete with associated sounds and smells.

The docking machinery on her aft deck has also been cut away to make more 'sunning room'. Fortunately, an admirer of the ship bought it before this important machinery could be scrapped

In an attempt to remedy leakage from the upper decks the teak planking was lifted, carefully cut to reduce its thickness and re-laid onto a plywood base. It seemed to work but an occasional leak still occurs but now its source cannot be traced because of the ply. A later plan would have had the liner sent to Japan for refurbishment with the possibility of her remaining in the China Seas as a gambling den! Preservationist opinion was appalled!

But she still remains a monument to the ingenuity and craft of British shipbuilding; a memorial to the thousands of soldiers who travelled in her during desperate times of war, many of whom did not return; and she became a symbol of peace between two great nations who have so much in common.

Those who sailed on her, saw her or just even only heard of her still lovingly remember the *Queen*. Special Anniversaries of launch and maiden voyage are commemorated by themed sailings of the *QE2* and excursions from the UK to visit her at her berth are regularly organised. The 50th anniversary of the maiden voyage saw HM the Queen Mother on board *QE2* for a luncheon and

Above: A Yellow cab indicates the importance to Long Beach of the *Queen Mary*.

Below: Exterior with propeller 'box' showing. This allows visitors to view the propeller from inside the vessel.

Right top: The *Mary* in her location at Pier J Long Beach. All the services are attached from ship to shore to sustain the liner's new tourist business.

Right bottom: Taken from the rock barrier around the ship, this early morning photo shows her current state externally.

All, Roger Hardingham

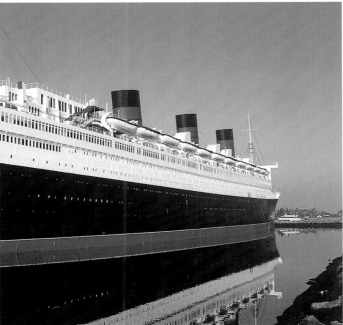

Left: A 1990s shot showing the then sad state of the decking.

Above: A start being made to renew - by recycling old teak decking. A layer of plywood was put down first before the renovated, original teak was re-laid. Any leakage that occurs now is difficult to locate as the plywood dissipates the water making its source difficult to locate.

Below: A large section of the Boat Deck after the new deck had been fitted.

All, Roger Hardingham

Acknowledgements

In the researching of this brief history of the *Queen Mary* many people were either interviewed for first-hand information or else offered assistance by the loan of cherished photographs or mementoes of the ship.

I would especially like to thank Commodores Donald MacLean and Geoffrey Marr and Captain John Treasure Jones for their invaluable assistance, the former two amplifying many instances contained within their most readable autobiographies. Thanks also to Captain Peter Jackson for relating his experiences as a Junior Third Officer on the *Mary*, Edwin Praine (a young commis-waiter at the time of the maiden voyage), Wally Adams for the use of his photographs of the stars who travelled on the ship and Harley Crossley, the excellent marine artist from Sherborne in Dorset, for permission to use his work.

Amongst others to whom I am indebted are: Rod Baker, Len Betts, Norman Blundell, Frank O. Braynard, Bob Bruce Grice, Jean Edwards, David Easton, Mr C. English, Miss Freda Ferguson, Miss Elsie Greenman, Keith Gould, John Havers, Jack Horner, Judith Jacobs, Susan Leatherbarrow, Bill Mitchell, Sylvia Mitchem, Bert Moody, Mike Smith, Sandy Vinter, Peter Walters and Jean Woods - and also the wives of the interviewees who kindly gave me tea!

Amongst the organisations I would single out Nigel Overton of the Southampton Maritime Museums, Peter Ashton of the Southern Evening Echo and representatives of the National Maritime Museum, Imperial War Museum, The University of Liverpool (for the Cunard Archives), The Illustrated London News and the Cunard Line (Public Relations).

My sincere thanks also go to Roger Hardingham of Kingfisher Productions for his enthusiasm and assistance and for the honour he did me in inviting me to write this Golden Anniversary tribute (now revised for this 2003 edition) to the greatest of all ocean liners.

A driving force behind the design of the *Queen*, John Brown, meets Joseph Prevratil in 1994 on occasion of the 60th anniversary of the launch visit to the ship in Long Beach. John Brown would receive recognition of his work through a knighthood shortly before he died weeks before his 100th birthday.

Roger Hardingham

Bibliography

Benstead, C R 'Atlantic Ferry'   Methuen & Co. Ltd.   1936

Bisset, Comm Sir James 'Commodore' Angus & Robertson   1961

Bonsor, Noel 'North Atlantic Seaway Vol.1' David & Charles 1975

Braynard, Frank O 'Lives of the Liners' Cornell Maritime Press 1947

Coleman, Terry 'The Liners'   Penguin Books Ltd   1976

Cunard Line booklets 'Art on RMS Queen Mary' - 'The Stateliest Ship Now In Being' 'Launch of the Queen Mary' 'The Cunarders'

Grattidge, Capt Henry 'Captain of the Queens' Olbourne Press 1956

Harding, Steve 'Grey Ghost - the RMS Queen Mary at War' Pictorial Histories Publishing Company Ltd. Montana   1982

Hughes, Tom 'The Blue Riband of the Atlantic' PSL   1973

Hyde, Francis E 'Cunard and the North Atlantic 1840-1973' The Macmillan Press Ltd.   1975

Kludas, Arnold 'Great Passenger Ships of the World, Vol.3 1924-1935' Patrick Stephens Ltd.   1976

Lacey, Robert 'The Queens' Sedgwick & Jackson   1973

MacGuire, Joseph B 'The Sea My Surgery' Wm Heineman Ltd. 1975

MacLean, Commodore Donald 'Queens Company' Hutchinson 1965

Marr, Commodore Geoffrey 'The Queens and I' Adlard Coles   1973

Miller, William & Hutchings, David 'Transatlantic Liners at War - the Story of the Queens' David & Charles   1985

Ocean Liners of the Past 'The Cunard White Star Quadruple Screw Liner Queen Mary' Bonanza Books, New York

Potter, Neil and Frost, Jack 'The Queen Mary' Harrap   1961

Various contributors 'Railways, Ships and Aeroplanes' Odhams Press

'Shipbuilding and Shipping Record'

Southampton Corporation   'The Queens'

'RMS Queen Mary - the Log of Voyage No. 516'

Harvey Barton - St Stephens Publications

Steamship Historical Society of America 'The Stateliest Ship'

Time Life Books 'The Great Liners' Time Life Books   1978

Tute, Warren, 'Atlantic Conquest' Cassell   1962

Wheeler, Harold (editor) 'The Wonderful Story of the Sea' Odhams Press

Winchester, Clarence 'Shipping Wonders of the World' Fleetway House Ltd.   1957

RMS Queen Elizabeth
- From Victory To Valhalla

Foreword

About twenty years ago, when it was announced that the *Queen Elizabeth* was to follow her older sister into retirement, Noel Mostert wrote an article for the "US Travel News" called "Farewell to the Great Ships" in which he said, "The two older *Queens* undoubtedly will *always remain* the finest ships ever built," and these words have reverberated through my mind over the years whenever I have thought about my last command. After mentioning the 500,000 ton tankers being built at that time he concluded: "No tanker, no matter its size, could ever carry the visual impact of these two magnificent ships, especially when seen at speed, flinging the North Atlantic aside in huge combers. Their whole line, one of power and splendour, oceanic palaces of staggering dimensions."

Many people tend to compare the *Queen Elizabeth* unfavourable with the *Queen Mary* when it comes to the internal decoration of her public rooms but it must be remembered that whilst her decorations were designed in the late 1930s they had to be completed in that period of austerity and material shortages that followed World War Two.

But to me, the *Queen Elizabeth* was always a ship of great dignity, and the beauty and symmetry of her lines when viewed from the beam have never been surpassed.

Her destruction by fire in Hong Kong harbour on 9th January 1972 was a great tragedy but as I said at the time, at least she had a Viking's funeral, and if there is a Valhalla for ships she will occupy a place of honour, as we who knew her, in fair weather and foul, salute her.

So it is with great pleasure that I introduce David Hutchings' book, which I hope will revive many memories of the ship which played such an important part in my life.

The late Geoffrey T. Marr. DSC, RD, CDR, RNR (retired) Commodore (retired) of the Cunard Line and the last captain of RMS *Queen Elizabeth*.

Introduction

I started work on the rough draught of this book shortly after finishing 'QE2 - A Ship for all Seasons' thinking that I had, by then, simultaneously researched most of the information that I needed for the new volume.

But the more I wrote the more I discovered until this volume grew to become the largest (and a year late in publication because of it) of the ship biographies that I have produced for Kingfisher Publications.

Perhaps this is appropriate. Not only was the *Queen Elizabeth* the largest passenger liner ever built but she also held, for many years, the distinction of being the largest ship in the world. She was also the flagship of 'The Cunard', flying the flag of the Commodore of the world's premier passenger fleet,. Surely such an eminent vessel deserves the largest tribute!

The delay in publications has also fortunately meant that the book will, also appear in time for Cunard's 150th anniversary, although missing a few months the 21st anniversary of the ship's final voyage in Cunard service.

And to those readers who have awaited publication (and my wife who suffered the extended authorship!) with patience - thank you.

David F. Hutchings Lee-on-The Solent, Hampshire , June 1990

Dedication

To Dorothie (the Late Mrs. Geoffrey Marr) and all other wives of the sea who have patiently waited.

Left: The last refuelling at night in Southampton of the *Queen Elizabeth*, 7th November 1968. *R. Bruce-Grice*

Contents

Chapter One
The Noble Mission 82
Chapter Two
Sisters, Not Twins 87
Chapter Three
The Making Of A Queen..90
Chapter Four
Flight Of An Empress..99
Chapter Five
"The Furye Of Her Enemies"......................................107
Chapter Six
"The Years Of Peril" 113
Chapter Seven
"The World's Fresh Ornament"....................................124
Chapter Eight
"Thank You To This Englishman"................................135
Chapter Nine
A Large Withdrawal From The Bank 139
Chapter Ten
Jobs, Yarns And Cabin 52 143
Chapter Eleven
In Luck's Way 154
Chapter Twelve
Lovely To The Last 164
Chapter Thirteen
The Most Mighty of Pyres ... the Roaring Flames Mingled with Weeping 180

Chapter One
The Noble Mission

er Majesty, Queen Elizabeth, stood on the launch platform that had been decorated in blue and gold. With the Royal Coat of Arms placed centrally its canopy and glass front protected her from the dull September day, the earlier drizzle having fortunately stopped.

Standing discreetly behind the Queen were various dignitaries and officials including Lord Aberconway, chairman of the shipyard which had built the ship that stood before them and Sir Percy Bates, chairman of the shipping company for whom it was being launched. To her right stood two little princesses – her daughters Elizabeth and Margaret Rose, both dressed in rose pink – excitedly looking up at the pencil-slim bow of the huge ship that their mother had come to launch towering 80 feet above them.

Four years and a day had passed since the Queen's predecessor, Queen Mary, had similarly come to Clyde-

bank to launch her own very successful namesake that was even now ploughing its way across the North Atlantic at record-breaking speeds.

Now, on Tuesday 27th September 1938, it was the turn of her daughter-in-law, consort of her son King George VI, to stand at the head of the same slipway on which the *Queen Mary* had been built and sent into the Clyde with such genuine national rejoicing. The completion of the *Queen Mary* had symbolised, by the resumption of her interrupted building, the end of the Great Depression in Britain during which millions of people had been forced out of work.

Earlier, thousands of cheering, flag waving children had greeted the Royal party shortly after its arrival and reception at the south end of the jetty a few minutes before 3 pm.

Almost ready for launching, the *Queen Elizabeth*'s raked bow looms above the platform from which Her Majesty Queen Elizabeth will perform the launching ceremony.
Stewart Bale Ltd/Queen Elizabeth Historical Society

As yet without the letters of her name attached 'No. 552' awaits her launch, looming above an as yet quiet shipyard.

Stewart Bale Ltd/Queen Elizabeth Historical Society

However, the excitement that hung over Clydebank that day as the Queen – herself a daughter of Scotland which doubly endeared her to the waiting crowds – approached the launch platform contrasted sharply with the tension that hung over the rest of Europe. It was this tension that had kept the King at home in London at the request of the Prime Minister.

The mood of grim expectancy that gripped Great Britain and its continental neighbours had found its roots a few months earlier when the dictatorial German Chancellor, Adolf Hitler, had ordered his troops to march into Austria as part of his politically coerced annexation of that country, thus making it a satellite of his expanding Nazi empire.

Now, in September of 1938, in a crescendo of fear, tyranny and propaganda he had cast his hungry eyes eastwards towards the young state of Czechoslovakia claiming its western province of Sudetanland as Germany's, using as his pretext the falsely laid charge that the German minority living there were being persecuted by the Czech government.

Hitler's secret aim, however, was the eventual destruction and take-over of Czechoslovakia as an independent state, and the political crisis that was developing – even as the Queen stepped forward to launch the largest liner in the world – would lead Western Europe to turn its back on Czechoslovakia in a futile attempt to appease Hitler in the hope of avoiding a European war. (This would be all neatly expressed a few days later in the Munich Agreement which assured 'peace in our time'.)

Even so, war seemed to be very much a likelihood. A mobilisation that had been ordered had even gone so far as the secret withdrawal from service of many liners in readiness for a possible outbreak of hostilities. The Cunard's *Aquitania* was so affected, eventually arriving in Port Said laden with troops after a mysterious and sudden disappearance from her North Atlantic duties.

The King had, however, sent a message which the Queen, after the playing of the National Anthem and being presented with a bouquet, incorporated into her speech that she delivered after hearing a speech of welcome:

Queen Elizabeth, Princess Elizabeth and the then Mr Stephen Pigott, watch the launch of the *Queen Elizabeth* at the Clydebank on 27th September 1938.

Shipbuilding and Shipping Record

'I thank you for the kind words of your address,' she said, and continued: 'the King has asked me to assure you of the deep regret he feels at finding himself compelled, at the last moment, to cancel his journey to Clydebank for the launching of the new liner. This ceremony, to which many thousands have looked forward so eagerly, must now take place under circumstances far different from those for which they had hoped.

'I have, however, a message for you from the King. He bids the people of this country to be of good cheer in spite of the dark clouds hanging over them and indeed over the whole world. He knows, too, that they will place entire confidence in their leaders, who, under God's providence, are striving their utmost to find a just and peaceful solution of the grave problems which confront them.' The rest of the speech was the words that the King would have spoken had he been present.

'The very sight of this great ship brings home to us how necessary it is for the welfare of man that the arts of peaceful industry should continue – arts in the promotion of which Scotland has long held a leading place. The city of Glasgow has been for Scotland the principal doorway opening upon the world. The narrow waters of the Clyde have been the cradle of a large part of Britain's mercantile marine, so it is right that from here should go our foremost achievement in that she is the greatest ship that plies to and fro across the Atlantic, like a shuttle in a mighty loom weaving a fabric of friendship and understanding between the people of Britain and the peoples of the United States.

It is fitting that the noblest vessel ever built in Britain, and built with the help of her Government and people, should be dedicated to this service. I am happy to think that our two nations are today more closely linked than ever before by a common tradition of freedom and a common faith.

'While thoughts like these are passing through our minds we do not forget the men who brought this great ship into being. For them she must ever be a source of pride and, I am sure, of affection. I congratulate them warmly on the fruits of their labour. The launch of a ship is like the inception of all great human enterprises – an act of faith. We cannot foretell the future, but in preparing for it we must show our trust in a divine providence and in ourselves. We proclaim our belief that by the grace of God and by man's patience and goodwill order may yet be brought out of confusion, and peace out of turmoil. With that hope and prayer in our hearts, we send forth upon her mission this noble ship.'

But the launching ceremony that was being broadcast to the nation by radio did not go without incident.

The timber shoring, that had supported the liner's 40,000 ton launching weight during building, had been removed the day before the launch, lowering the liner onto the greased sliding ways. Only a few timbers remained in place and these would be knocked away shortly before the launch.

The hull of the ship that had been also specially stiffened internally by temporary wooden shores to strengthen her for what would possibly be the most critical journey of her career, was held in place by triggers. Her weight was now mainly supported by the heavily greased ways (the grease comprised ten tons of tallow and soft soap) with her bows cradled in a strong wood and steel support known as the fore-poppet.

Rams would be used to give the ship an initial push should she not gather sufficient momentum once the triggers had been remotely released from the launching platform. Conversely, to prevent the liner from gathering too much speed – and also to prevent her from ramming the opposite bank (should she veer from her astern course towards the specially dredged River Cart that joined the Clyde opposite to the yard) – eighteen bundles of chains would slow her progress. These bundles, of between 55 and 70 tons each, and totalling 2,350 tons, were secured to the ship's side by steel cables attached to eye bolts, and would be pulled into action to maintain the launch speed at a safe and manageable rate: the liner would reach a speed of 15 miles an hour during launch. Even these bundles of chains had historic maritime antecedents as some of them came from that daring (but at 16,000 tons far too big and advanced for her time) creation of Isambard Brunel – the *Great Eastern*.

As the moment arrived for the launch the *Queen Elizabeth* was delicately balanced on the ways and for many hours previously, because of the removal of most of the supporting timbers, an almost imperceptible movement had already taken place which would be magnified into magnificent action once the restraining triggers were released.

As Scotland's poet Robert Burns once wrote 'The best laid schemes o' mice an' men gang aft a-gley' so events in the shipyard almost took a different course to those planned.

After the formal speeches had been completed there was a pause as high tide was awaited. During the pause the Queen was presented with a sixteenth century inlaid casket from Saxony containing an album of photographs of the ship's building and the princesses played with a small model of the ship on her ways that had been used to explain the launching. Suddenly a crash of breaking timbers was heard and No. 552, on her own volition, started on her un-named journey towards the Clyde.

'She's away!'

At around the same time the Queen's microphone failed but, with great presence of mind, Her Majesty quietly and almost unheard by those around her said 'I name this ship *Queen Elizabeth* and wish success to her and all who sail in her.' Then, with the pair of gold scissors that Queen Mary had used to perform the launching ceremony of her namesake, she cut the red, white and blue ribbon which sent the bottle of Empire wine to break, just in time, against the liner's accelerating bow.

After the ceremony the Royal party departed but the other guests adjourned to the shipyard's Mould Loft (where more usually the lines of ships' frames were converted from scale drawings to faired, full size shapes on to a large floor. Wooden templates were then formed around these lines from which the steel frames etc were shaped) which had been specially laid out for the post-launch tea.

After almost launching herself the liner is sent down the ways to join her natural element for the first time.

Winchester Publications

During his speech Sir Percy Bates, chairman of the Cunard – White Star Line, recalled the circumstances in which the *Queen Elizabeth* – which was even now being towed and gently nudged into her fitting-out berth – and her elder sister, the superb *Queen Mary*, had come into being.

The liners were a result of Sir Percy's own initiative which was itself a fulfilment of a long cherished dream held by many ship owners: that a weekly transatlantic ferry service should be maintained by two ships rather than by the three, or even four, (sometimes mismatched) vessels that had previously – and expensively – maintained the same timetable.

As Sir Percy said in his speech,

'The ship you have just seen launched is no slavish copy of her sister. I described the sister, the *Queen Mary*, as the smallest and slowest ship that would do the job.' Sir Percy then briefly described the changes that made the *Elizabeth* an improvement on the *Queen Mary*: 'Naval architecture and marine engineering have not stood still since we contracted for 'No. 534' (the shipyard contract number of the *Queen Mary* by which she popularly known until the very moment of her launch) 'and we tried hard to make use of their progress to get the functional requirements for the sister ship expressed in a smaller hull. We found it impossible. For our schedule we need no more speed than the *Queen Mary* has got.' (The twenty-seven boilers in the *Queen Mary* had been reduced to twelve in the *Elizabeth* as one result of technological changes.)

Sir Percy elaborated: 'There is no sense in having one-half of a weekly service faster than the other. Yet technical advances made it absurd for us to repeat what we had done. There had to be changes. These changes have cost us little or no money. They can hardly be needed in speed, though I think 'No. 552' – the *Elizabeth* – 'might travel a little faster than 'No. 534', but they can be expressed in economy in the weekly job of crossing the Atlantic.'

The two *Queens* would also differ uniquely from their superliner contemporaries. 'Ships of State' of other lines,

especially foreign, had been built with state aid and run with state subsidies. The *Queens* were different. They had been built with repayable loans and would run with great profit.

Meanwhile, as the tea progressed, the sparkling new *Queen Elizabeth* rested on the waters of the River Clyde, resplendent in her livery of white, black and red (strangely the same colours adopted by Hitler and his nefarious gang for the Nazi party which would soon so dramatically influence the Queen's career). But unbeknown to those present (or if they did foresee the future they did not voice their fears) it would be a long time before the *Queen Elizabeth* would become the ambassadress of the 'Noble Mission' of which the Queen had spoken.

Immediately after her launch the newly named *Queen Elizabeth* is taken to her fitting-out berth.

UCS Records/Glasgow University archives

Chapter 2
Sisters, Not Twins

The idea that was to evolve into the *Queen Elizabeth* had been sketched out just over ten years previously, in 1926.

It was then that the original plans for her elder sister that was to become the *Queen Mary* were first quantified: the first vessel of the hitherto elusive two-ship North Atlantic express service.

Planning, preparation and building of the *Queen Mary*, the first of the giant thousand-foot liners (then popularly known solely by her shipyard number of '534') went bravely ahead. During the course of her construction the world was beset by the economic plague of the Great Depression. As a consequence of this, Cunard was forced to suspend work on the liner just before Christmas 1931.

The enormous, almost completed, hull of No. 534 had lain rusting on the stocks for over two years until the spring of 1934. By then the Labour Member of Parliament for Dumbarton Burghs, the Hon. David Kirkwood, aggrieved by the unemployment in his shipyard constituency, had petitioned the Government for assistance to enable the Cunarder to be completed, thus providing work for his constituents. This in turn would rekindle employment in the multitude of sub-contracting industries and spearhead Britain's recovery from years of financial limbo.

Kirkwood's appeal was heeded and the liner became a majestic and popular symbol of the British revival from the Depression as 'Bankies' (Clyde-bankers) marched triumphantly back to work on 3rd April 1934.

Work on the ship began with clearing tons of rust and thousands of birds' nests that had accumulated over the months of idleness in readiness for the construction to restart.

For its part in this daring rescue package the Government had agreed to advance Cunard a total of £9.5 million (1938 value) on condition that the Cunard merge with the famous, but ailing, White Star Line.

The advance was broken down into three parts, the first of which was a payment of £3 million to complete '534'. Secondly, £1.5 million was to be provided as working capital for the newly formed company of Cunard – White

Star Limited which would manage the new ship and the combined fleets and, thirdly, a loan of £5 million would be made available, when requested, for a sister to 'No 534'.

Surrounded by a eulogizing publicity campaign that satiated the public's appetite for superlatives, details and the promise of the grandeur to come (everything, it seemed, except for the actual name of the liner) No. 534 blossomed into completion, towering above the smokey, revitalized town that was giving her life.

Finally, on a rainy 26th September 1936, their Majesties King George V and his consort, Queen Mary, came to Scotland to launch the 1019 foot liner.

An impressive view of the *Queen Elizabeth*'s elder sister, the *Queen Mary*, on speed trials off Arran.
'Wonderful Story of the Sea'

After the King's speech, during which he magnificently described the liner being launched as 'the stateliest ship now in being', the Queen cut a ribbon (using a pair of gold scissors which would be used in two later launches of regal Cunard liners) that sent a bottle of wine crashing against the ship's bow, naming the liner after herself – *Queen Mary*.

A few months previously, in February 1936, a preliminary announcement was made of Cunard's intention to build a sister to the ship then currently building on Clydeside. But not until the promised money had been obtained from the Government would a builder be selected and the *Queen Mary*'s performance – and that of her competition – studied in detail.

The *Mary* sailed on her glittering maiden voyage on 27th May 1936, surrounded by a blaze of well-earned publicity. This had been preceded by a triumphant cruise off the southern coast of Britain, providing the population with a splendid view of the new ship whilst giving members of the various sub-contractors a memorable cruise by way of thanking them for their hard work.

Shortly after the *Mary*'s entrance into service she soon disproved some of the optimistic theories that had accompanied her building.

Being over a thousand feet long it was anticipated that she would be steady on even the longest Atlantic swell – but she still rolled miserably in rough weather.

Fleets of ambulances would sometimes meet the berthing liner at Southampton or in New York to take off

The magnificent but revolutionary French liner *Normandie* seen here tendering at Spithead. It was the clean upperdecks of this liner that influenced the design of the *Queen Elizabeth*.   *Red Funnel Group, Southampton*

people injured during rough crossings. Handrails were hurriedly installed (these had been omitted due to the faith put in her stability) and during her first winter refit she underwent an enormous internal rebuild with additional stiffening added in critical areas.

She emerged a steadier ship but she would still continue to roll, particularly with a following sea even after leaving rough weather well astern. Her crew said that 'she could roll the milk out of a cup of tea!'

She was, nevertheless, a supremely popular ship right from the outset, continuing to command the interest that had been afforded her during her construction. Royal visits undertaken by the Prince of Wales at Clydebank and by Queen Mary and members of the Royal Family shortly after the liner's arrival at Southampton, all helped to build up the fervour of excitement prior to the *Queen Mary*'s introduction into service.

The maiden voyage was broadcast to eager radio listeners all over the British Empire with, amongst other attractions, Henry Hall and his Orchestra playing the specially composed 'Somewhere at Sea' at all hours of the day to suit tea-times all over the world.

Cunard approached the Government, then represented by the Chancellor of the Exchequer Neville Chamberlain, and asked for the release of the third part of the promised loan for its intended purpose: the financing of the second of the two intended thousand foot liners, anticipated since the keel laying of the *Queen Mary*.

In the second half of June 1936 in reply to a question in the House of Commons, the Chancellor said 'I have received a reply from the Cunard–White Star Company for authority to use the sum available under the North Atlantic Shipping Act for the construction of a sister ship .... I have agreed in principle.' The Chancellor added that Cunard had received preliminary tenders from various yards and were negotiating in the first instance with John Brown and Company as they had a slip that was almost ready for the work, other than adding or replacing piling to the existing No. 4 slip, and their experience in building giant liners was second to none.

The Financial Secretary to the treasury, Herbert Morrison, made an announcement in the House on Tuesday 28th July to the effect that the Chancellor had given his final assent to the money being released after receiving ample evidence from Cunard that their choice of yard had been the correct one.

A little while previously and perhaps as an inducement to Cunard, Lord Aberconway, chairman of John Brown's

Clydebank shipyard, said that if his yard were entrusted with the work they would hope to build an even better ship than the *Queen Mary*, of which they were all proud.

The Scottish yard had apparently been Cunard's choice from the start as Sir Percy Bates had privately intimated as much to Lord Aberconway at the launch of the *Queen Mary*.

The contract was signed on October 6th 1936.

Cunard was determined that their new ship would not be an evolutionary development of previous ships – as the *Mary* had been – but would be based on the latest revolutionary developments that had taken place in naval architecture and marine engineering.

To this end Sir Percy Bates would not be rushed. As he had said in his post launch speech, after the *Elizabeth* had been offered to the elements, that she would be '..... no slavish copy of her sister.' And to achieve this Cunard had looked elsewhere for inspiration other than relying wholly on their own experience, invaluable, though, that this had been.

And what better ship to study than the *Queen Mary*'s arch-rival in the North Atlantic stakes – the French Line's superb *Normandie*? After all, the two ships had been carrying on a contest as to which was the larger and the faster. To obtain first-hand observations of the French ship, Cunard booked passage for one of their designers who travelled as a grocer! Taking care not to ask too many technical questions that would expose his assumed identity, the information that he obtained proved to be of great use in the design of the new ship. Various structural changes had been effected on both the *Normandie* and the *Queen Mary* since their introduction into service and a rivalry existed to prove each ship the faster. Cunard, of course, denied that there was any rivalry on their part to gain the speed record, saying that any attempt to do so was merely to gather information needed for the design of the *Mary*'s forthcoming partner.

However, the two companies did have a sensible working arrangement whereby it was ensured that their sailings were alternated. The *Queen Mary* was also running a weekly service with her elder cousin, the four funnelled *Aquitania*. As a result, the latter ship was hard pressed, her turn-round times in the terminal ports being reduced to a minimum in order to maintain her half of the service.

The *Normandie* had one edge on the *Queen Mary* in being aesthetically more pleasing to the eye through her revolutionary streamlining and lack of visible deck 'clutter'. Costing almost twice as much as the *Mary*, the French liner was perhaps also that more lavish in her first class appointments.

But the *Mary* had a slightly better hull and the two ships vied with each other to achieve the cream-of-the-trade appeal of being the fastest afloat.

For two years the competition raged, with the honours passing to and fro. Structural changes helped to reduce the effects of vibration in both ships as did improvements to propulsion systems which honed up speeds by valuable fractions of a knot.

As a triumphant fanfare to the launch of the *Queen Elizabeth* the *Mary* captured the Blue Ribband – although Cunard refused to acknowledge the recently introduced Hale's Trophy as a tangible symbol of their achievement – in August 1938 with a speed of 31.69 knots, a record that would stand for 14 years.

Sir Percy Bates was determined that the *Elizabeth* would be able to exceed her sister's performance but sensibly refuted the suggestion that the two ships would compete with each other. This would be expensive as well as nonsensical.

For many years warships of His Majesty's Royal Navy had used watertube boilers of the Yarrow design to give them short bursts of high speed. This design had been bravely adopted for the *Mary* where sustained, all-year-round high speed was required to maintain her timetable and to ensure that a reserve of power would be available to make up time lost during adverse weather conditions.

Sir Percy had also wisely waited for other anticipated improvements in boiler design to occur. As a result only twelve boilers would be placed in the *Queen Elizabeth* rather than the twenty four that the *Mary* needed to raise the same amount of steam in order to produce the same amount of power.

The reduction in boiler room space had several follow-on effects. A smaller boiler room resulted in more space being made for additional passengers (crew numbers were also increased to cater for these); two funnels were erected instead of the three as on the older ship and were self-supporting, having their stays on the inside of the stack, thus taking up less passenger deck space; fans of a newer design were also mounted inside the ship giving the new liner a cleaner, uncluttered upper deck. The prominent square ventilation cowls on the *Mary* were also dispensed with on the new ship.

Another obvious difference between the two ships was the lack of a forward well deck on the younger liner. This had been included on the *Mary* to spend the force of any heavy sea that might break over her bow before the water could damage the superstructure front. This anticipated event had never occurred and was considered very unlikely to occur, so the well-space area was plated in and used for additional revenue.

The bow, unlike that of the *Mary*, was heavily raked. This enabled a third anchor, the bower, to be carried allowing the anchor to fall well clear of the stem; it also made it possible for the ship to ride at anchor without the problem of the anchor cable chaffing the stem plates when the ship swung due to changes in wind and tide.

The rake also gave the *Elizabeth* a longer overall length: 1,031 feet as against the 1,019.5 feet of the *Mary*.

So gradually designs were completed and approved, orders for steel plate, machinery and a host of items for kitchens, restaurants, cabins, lounges, etc., were placed and on Friday 4th December 1936, without ceremony, the keel of No. 552 was laid.

Sir Percy would later describe the giant liner as '.... human audacity in steel.' But on the European continent the evil power of Adolf Hitler grew concurrently with the new liner. This human audacity in terror would eventually rob the new *Queen* of her youth.

Chapter Three

The Making Of A Queen

It was almost a foregone conclusion that the two Cunard liners would be the queens of the Atlantic. With the *Queen Mary* already in service it was popularly assumed, even before Her Majesty the Queen gave her royal assent to do so in February 1938, that Shipyard Number 552 would become the *Queen Elizabeth*. The liner thus, if unofficially, had a name by which she could be known during the course of her building. In contrast Number 534 had not become the *Queen Mary* until the very moment of her launch.

With the keel of No. 552 laid on slip No. 4 and construction proceeding beyond the laying of the keel plates and the erection of vertical keel, floors, tank tops and frame legs etc. (all carried out by shipwrights – '*The* Ship-builders'), other trades moved in to make a start on the outfit of the gradually rising shell. Pipework for steam, oil and water; electric cable runs; ventilation and air-conditioning trunking runs were 'lined-off', their locations being marked in thin, white paint lines.

Employment once again rose in the shipyard as materials arrived for forming.

Drawings for the ship had been transferred from their scaled paper conceptions to full sized curves on the mould-loft (or scrieve board) floor, their graceful shapes being etched (scrieved) into the giant black board-like floor. From these curves, 'faired' to perfection, the steelworkers would make templates which would then be used as a guide when hot steel sections were hammered into shape to become the frames of the ship.

As these frames were erected, reaching upwards like out-stretched giant fingers cupped to catch the sky, so transverse beams joined opposite frames to provide the supports for deck plates, pillars connected beams of one deck to those of the deck above to provide support and strength.

A week before keel laying the last few timbers are laid on slip No. 4. The wooden building blocks would eventually have to support 40,000 tons of steel.

UCS Records/ Glasgow University Archives

Other templates of wooden battens were taken from the erected frames and, using these, huge steel plates were cut, shaped and drilled with rows of holes corresponding with lines of rivet holes drilled into the frames.

The plates were then offered into position and bolted through an occasional hole to hold the plates temporarily in place whilst riveters fastened the plate permanently into place. The noise of their rivet guns sent their familiar staccato rhythms, typical of pre-war shipyards everywhere, over the yard's walls into the town and surrounding countryside. By their noise the rivet guns told all and sundry that employment was once again in the proud Scottish town which was now building the largest liner that the world had ever seen.

The lesser sound of caulking guns would also be heard as the edges of adjoining plates were caulked to ensure watertightness.

But it was not only in Clydebank that No. 552 brought employment and prosperity. Many of the products that would be built into or used on the new Cunard liner would either be of United Kingdom manufacture or come from one of the various globe-scattered countries that constituted the British Empire.

From Glasgow and all over the British Isles came huge castings for propeller brackets along with stern, bow and hawse-pipe castings, four 32-ton manganese bronze propellers, steel plates and sections of various shapes, machinery, electrical generators and switchboards, four anchors at 16½ tons apiece, a 140 ton rudder with its own inspection door, ten million rivets, twenty-six lifeboats and their motors, two thousand portholes, twelve water tube

Above: Watched by two bowler-hatted managers, the first keel plates of 'No. 552' are laid on Friday 4th December 1936.   *UCS Records/Glasgow University Archives*

Right: Supported by timber shoring the framework of the after double bottom tanks begin to show the fine lines of the liner's hull.
UCS Records/ Glasgow University Archives

Above: Almost nine months after the laying of the keel plates the side frames of No. 552 veer up from the slip. The bridge in the foreground was originally constructed over the shipyard railway to support the bow of the *Queen Mary* during her construction.

UCS Records/Glasgow University Archives

Left: As the erection of frames is completed shipwrights and rivetters fit the shell plates to the skeleton of the ship. This midship section shows the plating method adopted.

Stewart Bale Ltd/Queen Elizabeth Historical Society

The strengthened brackets for the inner propeller make an impressive sight.
Stewart Bale Ltd/Queen Elizabeth Historical Society

An hydraulic riveting machine makes life a little easier for the contemporary workmen. March 1938.
UCS Records/Glasgow University Archives

boilers, fans, navigational aids, glass, silver-ware, carpets, curtains, chairs, tables – the list was almost endless. The weight of steel in the hull and machinery alone would be in the region of 50,000 tons.

Items, such as much of the machinery, would come from John Brown's own works and from the area around

This photograph clearly shows the bridge built over the ship-yard railway. A locomotive whistles a warning as it prepares to pass under the liners bow.
Stewart Bale Ltd/Queen Elizabeth Historical Society

Glasgow but many contractors and sub-contractors were huddled around Manchester, Birmingham, Sheffield and London.

From Dundee in the north to Belfast in the west; from Norwich and Ipswich in the east to Cowes and Fowey in the south, the British Isles produced the essential items that eventually found their ways converging through the gates of John Brown and Company, Shipbuilders.

Apart from the leather from a thousand hides of cattle that became furnishings and wall panels, and the use of satins for decorative, quilted wall-padding, the most exotically sounding of the decorative – as well as practical in some cases – materials were, as on the *Mary*, provided by the woods used on board.

Dozens of exotic, rare and unusual timbers were used as either decking, bulkhead linings in public rooms and first-class cabins, in furniture or for the revitalized art of marquetry. Fine examples of the latter art would be found in the more expensive cabins and in the public rooms of all classes.

These woods came from all over the Empire and some would be used solely in a large piece of marquetry that would hang (in pre-war days) in the Main Lounge.

This piece of woodwork combined the skills and art of the designer with those of the woodworker. Entitled 'The Canterbury Tales', it had been designed by George Ramon

Above: By the beginning of April 1938 much of the hull steelwork is complete. The men standing on the after structure are dwarfed by the construction work surrounding them.

UCS Records/Glasgow University Archives

Left: Looking forward, the bare frames and deck beams contrast starkly with the deck plates being fitted in the foreground.

UCS Records/Glasgow University Archives

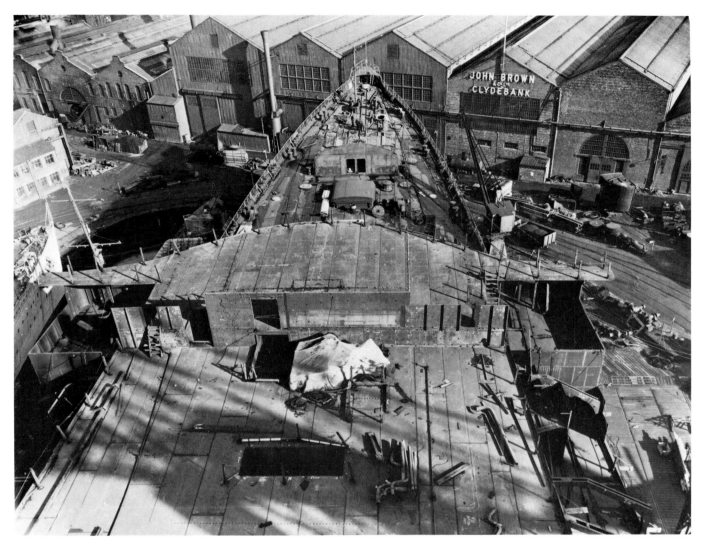

Above: With the construction of the bridge underway the bow of 'No. 552' points proudly towards the workshops that are bringing her into being. The bow of the submarine depot ship, HMS *Maidstone,* can be seen to the left of the photograph.
Stewart Bale Ltd/Queen Elizabeth Historical Society

Right: By the end of August 1938 the propeller cones (or bosses) are ready to be bolted into position onto one of the port propellers. *UCS Records/Glasgow University Archives*

in response to a call for something that typically depicted Britain (he originally thought of 'Fog'!); the work was executed by A.T. Dunn and family.

Woods used on and in the ship included London Plane, Scottish Pine and blackened, centuries-old 'Bog Oak' (retrieved from the peat bogs of Ireland). Also from Britain came Sycamore, Laburnum, Acacia and Wych Elm.

From the forests of the Dominion of Canada came Birch and Blistered – and Bird's Eye Maples. From Australia came Silky Oak and the native Bean Wood. A thousand tons of Burma Teak was used as deck cladding and for other carpentry work. Laurelwood, Coralwood and

Above: As the painting of the hull reaches completion so the scaffolding is taken down. The upper superstructure can be painted later using platforms slung from the upper deck.
Stewart Bale Ltd/Queen Elizabeth Historical Society

Left: A view from amidships looking aft shows the completed hull of 'No. 552' free of scaffolding and with work continuing on the superstructure.
Stewart Bale Ltd/Queen Elizabeth Historical Society

Left: Yet without the letters that will make up the liner's name and part of registry, the stern of the *Queen Elizabeth* looms above the launching ways. Old car tyres protect the sensitive edges of the enormous propellers.
Stewart Bale Ltd/Queen Elizabeth Historical Society

Above: The balanced rudder (with its bolted access hatch) and a tyre-protected propeller flanked the carefully painted draught marks.   *Stewart Bale Ltd/Queen Elizabeth Historical Society*

Prima Vera came to grace the ship. Cherry was used in many fine carvings.

From North and South America, from French Guiana, the Indies and Scandinavia came Satina, Sandalwoods and Coromandel; black and figured Ebonies, Thuya, Mahoganies and Zebrano, Rosewood, Purple Heart, Almond and the curious sounding Colo Bolo. Lignum Vitae (black and yellow and denser than water), Tulipwood, Beefwood, Olivewood and Walnut; scented Camphor, Orange and Palm. The galleys of old never carried a richer cargo.

From the Palace at Hampton Court came a Virginia Creeper that was 120 years old; perhaps, most romantic of all there was the 'Waterloo Elm'. The veneer of this lined the Captain's cabin and was, in fact, Wych Elm that had been used as piling under the Waterloo Bridge of 1811. Bleached grey by water and time it had been removed from its position in 1936 and a small brass plaque was placed in its final resting place to record its pedigree.

Lower class accommodation and crews' quarters were generally lined with enamel-painted plywood, 5/8 inch thick.

As the ship grew upwards in stature from the building blocks so more men were taken on at the shipyard, finding employment in the various outfitting trades.

After the *Queen Mary* had been launched many men had been saved from unemployment by the contract awarded to their yard to build the Royal Naval submarine dept ship HMS *Maidstone*. Not only did the construction of this ship keep many skilled men on the payroll until No. 552 was ready for building, but the launching of the naval ship served as a scaled experiment for the launch of its

larger merchant sister. Amongst other information gleaned the pressures on its hull during launch provided much important data.

The giant liner was constructed on No. 4 slip by using (quite astoundingly, looking back now over half-a-century) 5 ton derrick cranes and a 10 ton tower crane that had been erected at the forward end of the slip for the construction of the *Mary*. Heavy castings were erected by using derrick poles or sheer legs.

Steam locomotives would deliver steel plates loaded on low wagons to the building slip but lighter items such as pipes, ventilation trunking, timber etc. were brought by horse-drawn lorries. The horses belonged to a local haulier who stabled them across the road from the shipyard. Careful, painstaking and satisfyingly creative work was being carried on, it seemed, to the patient beat of horses' hooves.

To ensure that good progress was maintained during construction the General and Shipyard Managers met all the various departmental head foremen at the gangway every Friday.

This 'Glee Party' – as it was known to the men – then toured the vessel deck by deck. Any problems that were encountered were resolved by the foremen concerned by sending in extra men to assist temporarily with the work that had fallen behind and bring the construction plan back to its timetable.

Very little overtime was worked on the ship before launch. Sam Campbell, a joiner who had worked on the outfit of both *Queens*, recalls that a skilled craftsman received £3.2s.0d (£3.10) for a 47 hour week, although

Supported by wooden shores (most of which would be knocked away a day before the launch) and flanked by the 5-ton gantry cranes the hull dwarfs the shipyard around it. *Stewart Bale Ltd/Queen Elizabeth Historical Society*

such apparent occasion occurred in mid-1939 when a two week demarcation strike was held by 350 plumbers who walked out in protest at a claimed encroachment on their field of work by coppersmiths; the plumbers claimed that the copper piping being used by the coppersmiths came under their jurisdiction.

By the time that her launch day arrived the *Queen Elizabeth* had a weight on the slip of 39,400 tons. She measured 1,031 feet in overall length, had a waterline length of 1,004 feet and was 965 feet between perpendiculars. Moulded breadth, measured to the inside of the shell plating (or outside face of frames), was 118 feet. The liner stood 132 feet from her keel to the top of her superstructure and her Promenade Deck was 724 feet in length. Her hull, embracing fourteen decks, would have a draught of 39 feet 6½ inches once finished and stored for sea.

The public had already had a chance to see what the new liner would look like once completed as an eighteen foot model of the ship had been on display at the Empire Exhibition in Glasgow opened a year before the launch.

On the day of the launch the Royal party visited the Exhibition before going on to the shipyard and Princess Elizabeth became the Exhibition's millionth visitor.

After her launch the liner was towed to her fitting-out berth. A barrier was then constructed around the ship to shut her off from the river. This was to prevent Clyde-borne silt building-up around and under the vessel thus making her a grounded prisoner even before her first voyage.

the steelworking trades made this up to £4 per week by piecework.

As an indication of the worsening European situation the keel of the Royal Navy's newest battleship, HMS *Duke of York*, was laid on 5th May 1937, on the adjoining slip to the rapidly growing liner.

The building of the warship would decrease the number of spectators (attending the launching of the Cunarder) who could be accommodated on the starboard side of the slipway. To overcome this, extra stands were built on the west side of the fitting-out basin. An estimated 250,000 would attend the launch with stands, enclosures and special steamers being used as vantage points.

Fortunately very little industrial unrest was encountered during the building and fitting-out. The only

For almost five years the shipyard had carried on a correspondence with the Clyde Navigation Trust, dealing with the safe navigation of the liner on her one and only journey to the open sea.

This would involve a great deal of dredging and the removal of rock outcrops that might hazard the ship's safe progress. The river was also widened in places, especially at Dalmuir. It was here that the *Queen Mary*, caught by a gust of wind on her journey downriver from the shipyard, swivelled about and temporarily ran aground for many anxious seconds that could have proved disastrous for both ship and for future river traffic.

Meanwhile, however, the *Elizabeth* lay alongside her jetty, cosseted with careful attention that would make her the new sovereign of the sea.

Chapter Four

Flight Of An Empress

During the fourteen months that followed her launch the interior and exterior of the *Queen Elizabeth* steadily approached completion.

Large windows that would give panoramic views of the passing ocean were cut into the steel plating along the Promenade Deck and into the gracefully stepped curves of the superstructure front. These areas had been left as uncut steel structures in order to maintain strength and stiffness along the upper part of the ship during the brief, critical moments of the launch.

The *Queen* took on her identity as the letters of her name were fixed on either side of her bow and, also along with 'Liverpool' as her port of registry, on the upper part of her black hull around the stern.

The letters at her bow were each two and a half feet high and the name *Queen Elizabeth* occupied a length of nearly sixty-eight feet.

In overall charge of the vessel's interior decoration was G. Gray Wornum and within his sphere of supervision came the artistic talents of many people whose works would be on display in many of the better cabins as well as in the thirty-seven public rooms of all classes.

In the space of this book it is only possible to describe a few of these rooms with an emphasis on the Cabin Class, renamed First Class in post-war days.

The large and airy Main Lounge, on the Promenade Deck, in which hung George Ramon's 'Canterbury Tales' marquetry, was panelled with a tawny pink Canadian maple burr veneer. The wood was put into relief by other panels covered in leather of light grey, pale blue and buff. Aft (portside) of this room was a writing room, the alcoves of which were also lined with leather.

Two fine paintings ('Elsinore' and 'Dover Harbour') by Norman Wilkinson, the famous marine artist, were displayed in the Main Lounge and these would be hung in place the day before the liner left Clydebank by joiner Sam Campbell.

The carpet in the lounge represented a broad swirl of rope (a theme often repeated in the ship's decor) woven in tan on a darker background.

The restaurants of the three classes were placed on the same deck, interspaced with the appropriate kitchens, and thus named the deck on which they were situated (Restaurant Deck).

Snug alongside her fitting-out berth the *Queen* is kept company by two warships. The launch of the submarine depot ship HMS *Maidstone* (right) provided much valuable data for the launch of the giant Cunarder.　*UCS Records/Glasgow University Archives*

This needlework tapestry designed by Miss E. Esmonde-White, assisted by Mr Leroux S. Leroux, was destined to be hung in the Main Restaurant.   *Southampton City Museums*

The Cabin (First) Class Restaurant was carpeted with a shadowed hexagonal pattern weave and over the room's entrance hung the royal cypher carved in lime by Bainbridge Copnall. The Queen had requested that a portrait of her should not be hung in the ship so, as a compensation, her coat of arms with its three lions and three bows (representing the family arms of Bowes-Lyon) was suggested in lieu.

The main dining room of the Restaurant was one hundred and ten feet long by one hundred and fifteen feet wide and was panelled in myrtle cluster.

Above an alcove was set a clock, the numbers being represented by radial dashes. Next to each of these dashes was a beautifully carved sign of the Zodiac, again carved by Bainbridge Copnall, giving a garland effect.

On another wall hung a tapestry depicting Venus in the waves with four large sea-horses and three 'mer-children' in front of her. The tapestry, although woven in England, was the work of two South African designers – Miss Eleanor Esmonde-White and Mr Leroux Smith-Leroux.

Having its own kitchen and perhaps the most exclusive room on board, the Verandah Grill was decorated in ivory coloured veneers and peach coloured velvet curtains. Confronted by a small dance floor – for those who liked to dance as well as dine – a small stage stood against the forward bulkhead of the room.

The daytime sea views obtained from the grill (other than for when it was foggy!) proved a great attraction to those who were willing to pay an extra charge for the privilege of dining in the grill. Cunard would capitalise on this asset when, almost thirty years later, their second ship to be named after the Queen Mother (as Queen Elizabeth would become) had all her restaurants built into the higher

The First Class Observation Lounge and Cocktail Bar as it would later appear.   *Southampton City Museums*

The centre portion of the First Class Main Restaurant as furnished in post-war years. *Southampton City Museums*

As the ship is gradually fitted out so she assumes the fittings of luxury. The Ballroom here is almost complete.

UCS Records/Glasgow University Archives

Miss Esmonde-White's large tapestry hangs in-situ in the Main Restaurant, as yet not fitted with tables or chairs. This and other interior photographs following were taken on the liner's arrival in New York, March 1940.

UCS Records/Glasgow University Archives

A Third Class cabin with twin bunks as completed.
UCS Records/Glasgow University Archives

Part of the Cabin (First) Class Gymnasium.
UCS Records/Glasgow University Archives

sections of the ship; an advantage also made possible by built-in stabilisers.

The other restaurants on R Deck were sited low in the *Lizzie* as it was expected that any untoward motion would be least felt there, an assumption soon upset by the tables left unoccupied during rough weather.

The Smoke Room was described as '.... magnificent .... with its atmosphere of quiet dignity'. The four distinct

Above: The beautiful wood veneers in the Cabin (First) Class Library can be seen here to full advantage.

The University Archives, the University of Liverpool

Right: Tourist/3rd Class Dining Room (photographed in New York April 1940).

UCS Records/Glasgow University Archives

veneers were all cut from one giant walnut tree that had grown in the Isle of Wight.

Above the triple electric fireplace in this room was a series of bas-reliefs, one placed on each of nine veneered panels. The reliefs were individually carved or cast from the principle materials used in the building of the liner – lead, glass, white metal, steel, wood, rubber, aluminium, bronze and copper – each one cleverly represented the source, production or abstract spirit of the material presented.

Carvings representing Hunting, Shooting and Fishing as well as a clock were displayed in the Smoke Room, all carved by Dennis Dunlop. A map, designed by Macdonald Gill, occupied another bulk-head. Models of the two *Queens* were supposed to move on this map to reflect the relative positions of the two ships at all times of the day. The carpet contained both the colours of the Cunard Line and of the sea, all set against a tawny background. Armchairs were in light cobalt blue and fawn. Outboard on either side of the Smoke Room was a garden lounge both of which had direct sea views.

The Salon, also on the Promenade Deck, with walls of quilted satin and a gilded ceiling was used as a perfect setting for dances. Opposite to the stage a deep recess contained a lively jungle scene of tropical birds, antelope and monkeys. Designed by another South African, Jan Juta, the work had been executed by Fred Barker in painted glass and enamel. Twelve panels of fish carved in wood and covered in silver foil completed the decor.

The cinema/theatre could be used by Tourist as well as by Cabin Class (Third Class had their own). Seating three hundred and thirty eight the room suggested the national colours of those three nations between whose ports of Southampton, Cherbourg and New York the Queen would travel. A blue carpet, furnishings of vermilion and walls of ivory white presented a very comfortable room.

The two higher classes each had its own swimming pool but Cabin Class was the only class to have a dedicated library – Tourist for instance had to make do with a few bookshelves in their lounge – but four thousand volumes in total were carried on board.

Forward of the Main Lounge was the Main Entrance Hall, both rooms extending over the width of the superstructure. In the entrance hall w as a bronze statue of a female figure swimming through the arms of her male companion, both figures surrounded by dolphins: the whole seeming to balance on one leg of the male figure.

Inspired by the music of Sibelius and entitled 'Oceanides' the piece had been sculpted by Maurice Lambert and was not originally intended for the ship – George Ramon had seen it in the artist's studio during a visit and had subsequently asked Sir Percy Bates to come along and view it. Sir Percy was impressed (which was more than he was when he recommended that some paintings intended for the *Queen Mary* should be given to a blind home!) and the work was purchased.

The forward port of the Promenade Deck housed the Observation Lounge and Cocktail Bar. Set in the forward curvature of the superstructure the lounge had forward views over the bow to the seas rushing towards the ship.

Panelled in sycamore that had been dyed lobster red, the lounge contained more George Ramon marquetry, this time of circus scenes. At the after end of the lounge was a cocktail bar panelled in silver Sycamore studded with metal stars.

It should be finally noted that the public rooms of the Tourist and Third Classes, although not so sumptuous as those in Cabin, were light, spacious and well-appointed. The Winter Gardens in Third were particularly delightful. Fresh enamel paint, an occasional hint of highly polished veneer and a variety of plants gave the room an airy appearance. Placed in the lowest superstructure deck forward it had its own promenade on the fore deck of the ship.

When considering the comfort of those on board the Company had decided against the installation of stabilisers. The Times said in their special 'Cunard – White Star Supplement' of Tuesday 27th September 1938, that '... no practicable installation of this type '(ie gyro-stabilizers)' could possibly be of the slightest use in vessels of the size of the *Queen Mary* and *Queen Elizabeth* .... to date the safest and easiest crossings are secured by sheer size and huge transverse inertia, coupled with a good form design, bilge keels of practicable dimensions and careful experienced seamanship. The stability of the *Queen Mary* has proved ample at all times to make the ship as safe and comfortable as it is possible for any vessel to be when passing through an Atlantic storm'.

Cunard and The Times had obviously temporarily forgotten the devastation on board the *Mary* caused by stormy weather when crockery and limbs alike had been broken and fleets of ambulances had met the ship on arrival!

But all this luxury (along with 3,603 people) had to be propelled across the North Atlantic at an average speed of 29.5 knots if the *Queen Elizabeth* were to maintain her half of the express weekly schedule.

To do this twelve Yarrow-type high pressure water tube boilers were built into four boiler rooms. In the *Mary* twenty four boilers had been equally divided in four boiler rooms (two rows of three placed athwartships in each) with three Scotch boilers in their own compartment, providing steam for the ship's hotel services.

However, the oil-burning boilers in the *Elizabeth* were to be sited only two abreast. Four of the boilers (two on No. 1 and two in No. 3 boiler rooms) were fitted with desuperheaters and reducing valves to provide steam for the hotel and in-port services, thus doing away with the need for dedicated boilers as on the *Mary*.

Two boilers were placed in Nos. 1 and 4 boiler rooms with four apiece in Nos. 2 and 3. Two compartments, containing air-conditioning plant, electrical generating plant and water-softening equipment, separated Nos. 2 and 3 boiler rooms.

The boilers, the largest such marine installations ever built, were constructed under licence by John Brown and Co. They each had a combustion chamber volume of 3,220 cubic feet; a steam generating surface of 20,530 square feet; a superstructure surface of 10,120 square feet; air pre-heating surface area of 27,300 square feet and produced a working pressure of 425 pounds per square inch (400 on the *Mary*) at a final steam temperature of 750 degrees

Photographed in July 1938 this picture shows the lower part of the forward funnel in position atop a ventilation intake. The design of these intakes (inspired by the *Normandie*) ridded the liner of the upper deck clutter of the *Queen Mary*'s square cowls.

UCS Records/Glasgow University Archives

Fahrenheit, 50 degrees more than the *Queen Mary*.

Because of the larger boiler units it was felt certain that the *Elizabeth* would prove to be more successful and economical than the *Mary*.

The steam from the boilers fed into four Parsons single reduction geared turbine engines placed two each in the forward and after engine rooms, astern of No. 4 boiler room. The two engines in the forward room drove the two outer propellers whilst the inner propellers were powered by the after engine room.

Each engine consisted of one high-, two intermediate-, and one low-pressure turbine, the steam from which exhausted into a condenser where it was cooled back into re-usable water.

The total output of the engines, each of which could be used independently, was 160,000 s.h.p. (shaft horse power).

Electricity came from four 2,200 kilowatt turbo-generators at 250 volts. These, along with four main and forty-three auxiliary switchboards produced enough power to light 30,000 lamps through 4,000 miles of wiring; operate 700 electric clocks; 800 telephones; drive 21 lifts (11 for passenger use and 10 for stores and services); keep

43,000 cubic feet of cold storage space suitable for meat, fish, fruit, vegetables, dairy produce, wines, beer, etc; and power kitchen machinery such as the potato peelers, meat mincers and choppers, raisin stoners, ice-breakers, fruit juice extractors, silver burnishers, dish washers, etc etc; and operate the 38 watertight doors in an emergency as well as keeping the 26 lifeboat motors ready warmed. Many improvements were made on the *Queen Elizabeth* from lessons learnt on her elder sister. For example, the engineers had originally been quartered near the engine rooms on the *Mary* but soon special quarters were built for them atop the Verandah Grill at the aft end of the superstructure. The *Lizzie* had custom-built accommodation for the engine room department, complete with ward room, forward of the Veranda Grill on the Sun Deck.

Whilst all this grandeur, power and luxury was being created on Clydeside the European situation gradually worsened.

Men and materials were taken away from the liner as Admiralty work took priority and the pace of work on board slowed down.

On 22nd August 1939 it was announced that the maiden voyage of the *Queen Elizabeth* was intended to

At noon on 16th November 1939 (a month after the outbreak of World War II) the first lighting of a boiler is undertaken.

UCS Records/Glasgow University Archives

commence on 24th April 1940. However, after war was declared between Great Britain and Germany on 3rd September 1939 and work slowed on the mighty Cunarder, the date of the anticipated maiden voyage became doubtful.

Questions were asked in Parliament as to what possible use the two vulnerable Cunard leviathans could be in wartime. Suggestions extended from laying-up the *Elizabeth* in a sheltered loch to selling her to the Americans; from converting her to an aircraft carrier-cum-plane transport (for which plans were later drawn up showing a cut-down superstructure and only one funnel forward and placed to starboard) to converting her to a cargo ship. The two ships' real potential had not yet been realised.

Churchill, still First Lord of the Admiralty, expressed his fears on the safety of the *Elizabeth*.

The *Queen Mary* was by now laid-up in New York having reached there on Monday September 4th, the day after war was declared, and Churchill feared that the still completing *Elizabeth* would fall victim to Nazi bombers. On 6th February, he ordered that the *Elizabeth* ' ... should keep away from the British Isles ...'.

Consequently a special licence was granted in early November for the supply of valuable steel and labour to complete the liner. This would allow work to progress sufficiently to enable her to sail to somewhere safe, wherever that was.

Also, the liner's fitting out berth would soon be needed for the battleship *Duke of York*, due to be launched on the 16th September 1939.

On the same day the last section of the liner's 44 x 29 foot elliptical, 80 and 78 foot high funnels was lifted into position. The two funnels (the forward taking the gases from 1 and 2 boiler rooms, the after one taking the rest)

were self-supporting having not the external steel wire rope guys of the *Mary* but internal cross-rod bracing tie bars. Steam pipes were also carried internally to the three whistles (one aft, two forward).

These one-ton whistles were toned 'two octaves below middle A' and the deep, rich, glorious sound that bellowed forth would never cease to thrill – even ten miles away! Pulses from the melodious, vibrating roar could be felt up to twenty miles from the ship.

The ship was practically mechanically complete when ten days later, at noon on the 16th, a light smoke curled upwards from the funnels as the boilers were lit for the first time. In December, two days before the end of the old year, the engines were turned under steam.

Bollard and other tests could now be carried out on the engines of the stationary ship. Three months later the vessel was ready to sail for, it was rumoured, Southampton, the only British port with a dry-dock large enough to take the *Queens*.

The Luftwaffe learnt of these arrangements, which were supported by the arrival of crates of equipment in the Hampshire port marked with the ship's name and the forward booking of local hotel rooms for shipyard personnel, and they planned a warm reception for the liner.

His Majesty the King, accompanied by his wife, finally managed to visit the liner when he visited the shipyard to launch the *Duke of York* (his title before he became King) on 16th September 1939.

Monday 26th February was a dull, misty day and not many people saw the giantess slip from her berth and head down river.

The *Queen* was about to make her debut in history.

Chapter Five
"The Furye Of Her Enemies"

At the time of the *Queen Elizabeth*'s launch a letter to the London Times quoted a passage written four centuries before:

'The ship called the *Elizabeth Jonas* was so named by her Grace in remembrance of her own deliverance from the furye of her enemies, for which she was no lesse myraculously preserved than was the prophet Jonas from the belly of the whale.'

This passage described the first ship to be named after another royal Elizabeth – Queen Elizabeth the First of England (but not of Scotland) – at the time of the Spanish Armada.

And now, four hundred years and many generations of maritime progress later, another similarly named ship was about to face greater perils than ever imagined by the earlier Elizabethan adventurers.

The choice of the Queen's name for No. 552 was challenged however, by the owners of another *Queen Elizabeth* – a 91 gross ton pleasure steamer built in 1924, official number 147670 on the British register, and operated on the Thames by Joseph Mears Launches and Motors of Richmond, Surrey!

In 1940 there would be only two days in the entire year on which a high enough tide would be available giving a sufficient depth of water in the Clyde for the *Queen Elizabeth*'s a safe departure.

The second such occurrence, six months later, could possibly be too late as Glasgow came within the range of enemy bombers. More especially, the *Queen*'s fitting-out berth was required for HMS *Duke of York*. The *Queen* would move out on the first tide of the day and the *Duke* would be moved in on the second.

So shortly after noon on Monday 26th February, after many weeks of correspondence between Cunard and John Brown (much of it secret) – and the subject of much speculation around Clydebank as to the ship's eventual destination – the *Queen Elizabeth* was moved slowly away from her berth, well before the high tide needed to take her downstream.

The order (from the First Lord of the Admiralty, Winston Churchill – concerned at the huge and valuable

liner's vulnerability) directing that the vessel should stay away from British waters '... for as long as this order lasts' was about to become a reality.

It took about an hour for the tugs to manoeuvre the liner's head downstream towards the sea and soon word spread amongst the citizens of the town that their ship was off.

Gradually the crowd increased from a few dozen to several hundred as people rushed to vantage points along the Clyde to watch their pride slip quietly – almost furtively – by.

To many her appearance must have come as a bit of a surprise for no longer was she in her pristine Cunard paintwork of black hull and gleaming white superstructure. The one funnel that had been painted red with black bands and a black top had, along with the rest of the ship and the hitherto unpainted funnel, been repainted with a dull uniform Admiralty grey that would give her an anonymity on the broad expanse of the late-winter North Atlantic.

The *Elizabeth* had also been fitted with four miles of rubber coated copper cable, wound around her enormous girth. This coil, suspended almost untidily alongside her fore deck before rising to run beneath the projection of the Promenade Deck, was known as a 'degaussing' coil (named after Dr. Gauss, a nineteenth century expert on magnetism, whose theories had enabled the Germans to produce their new, lethal magnetic mines). Electrically charged it had the effect of neutralising the magnetic field that had been induced in the ship's hull by the constant hammering incurred by the steel structure whilst she was on the slip being built. The object of fitting the coil (one of the first to be so fitted) was hopefully to render the ship immune from the recently introduced menace of the magnetic mine.

Nearly five hours after leaving Clydebank the liner reached the Tail o' the Bank where she anchored.

During her slow and careful trip downriver she had been caught by the flood of the incoming tide and her accompanying tugs had to fight for nearly an hour before the giant could be persuaded not to bury her head into the

For the very first time smoke curls upwards from the *Lizzie*'s forward funnel.

UCS Records/Glasgow University Archives

Lacking her lifeboats and with a degaussing cable temporarily fixed around her the grey painted mighty *Queen* is eased away from her fitting-out berth.

UCS Records/Glasgow University Archives

bank of the river. Ironically this happened near the spot where the *Queen Mary* had been caught by the wind and, pivoting around, had touched the bank on both sides of the river. She had then earned an entry at Lloyd's as being officially aground, even if for just a few hair-raising minutes.

The next afternoon at a short ceremony held in the Tourist Class Lounge, the *Queen Elizabeth* (official number: 166290) was officially handed over to Cunard – untested and untried. Over the next three and a half days the anchored liner would take on all but eight of her twenty six lifeboats. These had been floated downriver in order to help reduce the liner's weight and thus reduce her draught during that short, critical journey. Even so, the new *Queen* had several thousand tons of weight more than did the *Queen Mary* during that ship's similar journey.

Just over four hundred crew (mostly from the *Aquitania*) joined the *Queen Elizabeth* under the command of Captain Jack Townley, signing articles for a short, coastwise voyage that would ostensibly terminate in Southampton where a hurriedly prepared docking plan – forwarded by the drawing office at John Brown's – had been received by the authorities in the southern port.

Crowds gradually form on the banks of the River Clyde as the *Queen Elizabeth* is carefully escorted from the shipyard to the Tail o' the Bank on Monday 26th February 1940.

Imperial War Museum

A magnificent view of the *Queen Elizabeth* at the start of her flight to safety taken from a British patrol aircraft.

Imperial War Museum

Shipyard workers and officials, using special passes, boarded the ship as she lay at the Tail (if they had not been on board for the short trip) in an attempt to bring some of the hundreds of uncompleted jobs to a satisfactory stage of completion before the ship sailed. The compass was adjusted and many tests were carried out on machinery and other items as the *Queen* waited to sail.

On the 27th, at a boat drill, the assembled crew were told of Churchill's earlier order that the ship was to leave British waters.

This meant that the crew had to sign new foreign articles for an ocean-going voyage. They demanded £50 per man danger money-cum-bonus but were given £30 plus £5 a month extra pay.

Those crew members who, for family or other reasons, declined to sign the new articles were taken off the liner, sworn to secrecy and subsequently spent many hours, practically interned, on board the Southampton tender *Romsey* in a nearby loch.

Not until after the *Elizabeth* had sailed was it considered safe to release them.

The King's Messenger was also constantly awaited as he would bring the order to sail – whether the ship was completed or not. At seven in the morning of Saturday 2nd March the Messenger finally arrived with sealed orders that were only to be opened when the liner was safely out at sea.

The *Queen Elizabeth* weighed her bower anchor half an hour later, at 7.30 am, after putting ashore those remaining shipyard personnel who would not be travelling with the ship.

Joiner Sam Campbell had been put ashore the night before and he recalls that his last sight of the *Lizzie* was from the tug that ferried him to Gourock Pier. As the tug pulled further away the giant liner seemed to disappear into the mist.

Underway at last the *Queen* slipped through the anti-submarine boom that stretched across the Clyde between the Gantocks and the Cloch Lighthouse and headed out to sea. The liner was escorted by aircraft and by four destroyers that would accompany her as far as the Northern Irish coast before she headed into the Atlantic and her

The 'Empress Incognito' arrives in New York on 7th March after her secret Atlantic dash.   *Southampton City Museums*

unknown destination, (as yet only still a speculation but in the minds of a well-informed few there were only a few ports in the world that could take a vessel of such a size).

Still having the remains of her launching gear attached to her hull beneath the waterline (this would be removed during the first available dry-docking) it was considered that the liner would be fast enough, if the situation should arise, to outrun any lurking U-boat and avoid any but the most fortunate of well-aimed torpedoes.

Speed would be her best defence in the trying years to come. She was untested, unarmed and – other than for pill boxes and sand bags on the bridge and stern – unprotected.

At eleven o'clock that evening as the liner approached the position where convoys gathered before heading either west or south, Captain Townley opened the sealed orders which had been delivered to the ship shortly before she sailed. After weeks of speculation her destination was at last known: New York! Three hundred and ninety-eight men were scattered around the immensity of the seemingly empty and ghostlike ship, as they settled down to making life on board as pleasant as possible. There were still many unfinished areas in the crew accommodation, some of the men having to make do with bare steel decks. Many electrical cables were unconnected, light fittings still hung unsecured from the deck heads and the lack of heating was keenly felt by those on board.

Carefully edged into her berth by tugs of the Moran fleet, the *Queen Elizabeth* joins her elder sister for the first time and, alongside her, the *Normandie* – still in civilian colours in readiness to hopefully be the "first off the mark" when hostilities finish. Cunard's *Mauretania* is to the right having vacated her berth for the new arrival.   *Southampton City Museums*

The three largest liners in the world cast their shadows onto a murky River Hudson. *Normandie* and *Queen Mary* sport funnel covers to protect their propulsion machinery from the elements. *Southampton City Museums*

Other parts of the ship, however, were finished and in those areas the passengers and crew luxuriated in beautiful carpets and decor. Much of the furniture was covered in dust sheets, giving the interior a feeling of a giant hotel closed down for the winter.

The *Elizabeth*'s call sign was, appropriately enough, GBSS and radio silence was enforced but the wireless room did receive one call at least. This was a signal to alter course in order to avoid a convoy, a precaution against the discovery of the position and course of a *Queen* fleeing into voluntary exile.

Living up to the image of his profession, the purser organised many of the officers and shipyard officials on board into a club called The Unruffled Elizabethans'. With its own printed constitution and with Captain Townley as president, the spirit of the club would seem to remain with the ship throughout the dark years to come: '.... that true Twentieth-Century Elizabethans are able to remain under all conditions completely unruffled'.

During the Atlantic dash members of the club would entertain one another with stories, musical recitals and so on.

One of the members of the 'The Unruffled Elizabethans' was Captain Duncan Cameron. He was the pilot who had taken the *Mary* down the Clyde and was Cunard's choice to do the same for the *Queen Elizabeth*.

After the short trip down the river he had disembarked at the Tail o' the Bank but Cunard insisted that he rejoin the ship for the start of her coastal journey to Southampton: part of the ruse to throw enemy agents off the scent as to her actual destination. Captain Cameron was well and truly

unprepared for the subsequent Atlantic dash, having as his only luggage '... a pocket handkerchief'! However, others on board donated various items of clothing to make up a small and very mixed wardrobe.

There was still plenty of work for the men to do during the few days of the crossing. Tests, inspections and attempting to alleviate a little of the mass of unfinished work that remained in many areas of the ship helped to pass the otherwise uneventful days that blended one into the next.

Some of the men would help the look-outs, constantly on duty, in scanning the sea, sky and horizon for any suspicious movement as the liner sped along between 25 and 27½ knots on a zig-zag course.

At night a strict black-out was observed and to aid this all the windows and portholes had been painted over in the same monotonous grey in which the ship had been coated.

On 7th March, the first sign of outside human existence was observed when a TransWorld Airliner was spotted flying over the ship. This plane carried several reporters and was piloted on this special occasion by the vice-president of the airline company.

The only signs of life on board the ship that the newsmen could see from their vantage point were the figures of just two men waving up at them from the stern of the ship.

Much to the consternation of the crew, New York already seemed to know that the new queen of the ocean, the 'Empress Incognito' as the New York Post called her, was on her way. Listening to a forbidden radio, a crewman had picked up the BBC broadcast which repeated the telling announcement relayed from New York. Suspicions that the *Queen* was on her way must have been strengthened earlier after Cunard's New York office had received orders to move the *Mauretania* from her position on the north side of Pier 90 to another pier further south.

The south side of Pier 90 was occupied by a grey-painted *Queen Mary* and, in the berth next to her, was the French Line's *Normandie*, still resplendent in her peacetime paintwork.

As the *Queen Elizabeth* approached the United States with the steady certainty of 83,000 tons travelling at 30 miles an hour, she steamed by the first ship that had been seen for five days. The sludge-carrier *Coney Island*, outward bound from New York with her loathsome cargo that she was eager to discharge well out to sea, blew three blasts on her single whistle as a courtesy to the grey *Queen* looming ahead of her. As an acknowledgement, the liner replied with a similar signal that boomed forth from her own three deep, richly vibrating sirens.

Five days, nine hours and 3,127 miles after leaving her anchorage in Scotland, the *Queen* passed the Ambrose Channel Light just before 9.30 am, local time.

During that most unusual of maiden voyages her engines had performed beautifully.

After taking on the Sandy Hook Pilot, Captain Townley anchored his ship at Quarantine at 11 am for four hours to await a suitable slack tide that would allow his ship to be safely docked. The stem anchor once again proved its worth.

By now word had spread around the city that the arrival of Britain's newest and mightiest liner was imminent and thousands of people from New York and New Jersey made their way to the vantage points on either side of the River Hudson to watch her come in as planes circled about her and joyous tugs had their high pitched toots regally acknowledged. She docked smoothly and without incident just before 5 pm.

Her Majesty the Queen was delighted to hear of her name-sake's safe arrival and signalled:

'I send you my heartfelt congratulations on the safe arrival in New York of the *Queen Elizabeth*. Ever since I launched her in the fateful days of 1938, I have watched her progress with interest and admiration. Please convey to Captain Townley my compliments on the safe conclusion of her hazardous maiden voyage.

Elizabeth R.'

Churchill was more brief: 'Splendid! Very good indeed. I never had any doubt about her getting over.'

The New York Times succinctly, but admiringly, summarised many pro-British thoughts:

'The world has come to expect naval feats of the British, but there is a quality of sharp surprise and mischievous daring about the *Queen Elizabeth*'s first voyage that electrifies the pulse. The British can take well-justified satisfaction in an opportunity so courageously seized and so adroitly carried out ...'

The article continued, almost lyrically '....Many sagas have begun and ended in our harbour; but can the old-timers remember anything to compare with the unheralded arrival of the biggest and fastest liner in the world, after the most daring of all maiden crossings? It did not matter that the *Queen Elizabeth* wore a drab coat of grey on her first visit to New York or that no brass bands went down the bay to meet her. The interest of New Yorkers was echoed by the admiration of Americans everywhere for those who built her, sailed her and sent her on her way.

'She was due to be launched on that terrible September day in 1938, when the Munich crisis reached its height. The British fleet was mobilised, and peace hung in the balance, too. But no crisis could keep this sea *Queen* from her schedule. For the past six months British shipyards have been crammed with war orders and workers have been pressed relentlessly into war industries; but war was not enough to prevent her or delay her being made ready to sail.

'Neither could the threat of submarines and mines keep her from her first voyage and now she lies safely in a harbour where German bombers cannot harm her.

'Any landlubber can see that the *Queen Elizabeth* is a fine ship, as sleek and graceful as a yacht; a credit to the British merchant marine. Her distinction is not only in being the largest ship in the world; she is also new in design, as the *Queen Mary* was not. The *Queen Mary* was planned before the crossing of the *Bremen*, the *Rex* and the *Normandie*. The *Queen Elizabeth* is the first super-liner to embody the lessons of these maritime pioneers of our streamlined era. The British were right in not leaving such a ship at the mercy of air attack at home. Their luxury liners will have a job to do when the war is over. The dramatic maiden voyage of the *Queen Elizabeth* proves that the British are looking ahead to the days of peace and to the laurels of peace which must be won.'

It was laudable that the New York Times considered that Great Britain and her Allies might be the eventual victors but it was equally strange that they should almost dismiss the super-liners' role as being effective only at the anticipated end of the war.

The arrival of the *Queen Elizabeth* provided those working in and around the city with a unique sight.

For not only had the *Elizabeth*, the grey-painted 'Empress Incognito', joined her elder sister (also painted in similar sombre, but business-like, grey) but the berth next to her intended running companion contained the French Line's chic *Normandie*, the peace-time beauty of the French liner showing slight signs of neglect. She had been laid-up in New York since 20th August the previous year, the gaiety of her lounges silenced, her carpets covered with moth-repellent powder, her furniture draped in sheets.

The world's three largest liners – plus the *Mauretania* – were now together for the first and, as events proved, the last time. Three giants, totalling a quarter of a million tons, dressed in khaki and chiffon but with 'nowhere to go', awaiting the fate imposed upon them by politicians as far dispersed ideologically as they were geographically. By order of the neutral American government (in accordance with the Geneva Convention) only maintenance or construction work of a non-belligerent nature could be carried out on the liners moored along the New York waterfront. The *Queen Mary* had, however, been 'called-up' on 1st March and in the afternoon of 21st March she quietly left her berth: her military career about to begin.

The two sisters would not meet again for another year.

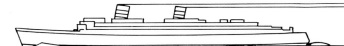

Chapter Six
"The Years of Peril..."
(Churchill)

The *Queen Elizabeth* was now the sole companion of the *Normandie*, a ship to which she owed a debt for her own sleek looks.

The Cunarder was soon transferred to the berth since vacated by the *Queen Mary* and now shared the same rectangle of murky Hudson water as her French counterpart. The latter ship seemed to ignore the young arrival's presence, perhaps secretly resenting the emulation of her own uncluttered upper deck and terraced after decks. She might also have secretly sneered at the *Elizabeth*'s exposed clusters of deck machinery and fittings on the latter's foredeck, a family characteristic that both the *Elizabeth* and her sister shared in common.

The majority of the already reduced crew of the *Queen Elizabeth* left for home on the smaller (20,000 gross tons), twenty year old *Scythia*, also of the Cunard Line. A skeleton crew of just 143 men remained with their charge to maintain her and to oversee the American workmen who now came on board. This labour force came from the nearby Todd Shipyard in Brooklyn and had been contracted to further the completion of the British liner. It was emphasised that no work of a military nature would be undertaken that might affect America's status as a neutral nation.

As a result, the liner found work being carried out on her that would bring her towards completion as the largest merchant ship in the world.

Wooden decks had to be caulked and much of her equipment, which had been brought over as cargo, fitted. Many of the shipboard services such as electric cables still had to be connected, light fittings screwed to deckheads, bare steel castings galvanised, ad infinitum. A lot of her furniture and unnecessary fittings were taken ashore at night to be stored until the day came when they could, hopefully, be reinstated.

The crew, although separated unexpectedly from their families and having had no chance of making their farewells, found – as did their counterparts on the *Mary* – friendship and hospitality from amongst the New Yorkers. However, their shipboard conditions did not compare with those enjoyed by their 'sister-shipmates' who lived on their ship surrounded by her full splendour.

Photographed in New York shortly after her arrival the open upper decks of the liner can be seen to good advantage.
UCS Records/Glasgow University Archives

After leaving her brief lay-up in New York the *Queen Elizabeth* sailed for dry-docking in Singapore. She is seen here at Cape Town *en-route*.

John Eaton and Charles Haas

Free passes to theatres, invitations to private homes, the absence of rationing – all contributed towards compensating for being away from home.

Towards the end of the year additional crewmen arrived in New York, having travelled to the city via the British Dominion of Canada. The ship's complement was brought up to four hundred and sixty-five, just sufficient to operate deck, navigating and engineering departments.

The New York newspapers speculated that something was about to happen and, sure enough, on a wet, grey 13th November, at almost 3.30 pm, the *Queen Elizabeth*, heavily laden with fuel and water, quietly slipped out of New York and headed south.

As a final accolade as she pulled away from her berth, a waterside stevedore shouted, almost affectionately: 'Goodbye and good luck, you great big Limey son-of-a-bitch!' His cheer was heard and remembered by Doctor Joseph Maguire who had just joined the liner and who would remain with her throughout the years of her trials – and longer.

Her departure left the *Normandie* alone once again; languishing and, it seemed, left to fend for herself.

The French liner almost seemed abandoned.

But that was not to be. After the Americans were rudely awakened by the unheralded Japanese attack on Pearl Harbour on 7th December 1941 and their consequent entry into the war, the *Normandie* was seized by the U.S. five days later on 12th December.

Work commenced, under the supervision of the Navy, to convert her to a troopship, renaming her U.S.S. *Lafayette*.

Due to the rush, disorganisation and disregard of French routine on board, she caught fire on 9th February 1942, when conversion work was almost complete, capsizing at her berth, top-heavy due to the prodigious amounts of water that had been pumped into her upperworks by the unco-ordinated fire-fighting tugboats.

After providing training for a new generation of naval salvage divers the *Normandie* was later cut-down at the superstructure, righted, towed away and scrapped. An untimely and sordid end to a fine ship whose contribution to the war effort – had things gone right – would surely have equalled the splendid war records of the British *Queens*.

A little while previously, at a meeting held in New York between Cunard and British government officials, it had been decided that the *Queen Elizabeth* should follow in the wake of the *Queen Mary* and become a troop transport. The *Mary* had made her first trooping voyage from Sydney to Scotland on 5th May and, as the *Elizabeth* sailed, rumours as to her destination varied from 'just moving her berth' to 'sailing to Halifax, Nova Scotia.'

But before the second *Queen* could become one of His Majesty's Troop Ships (HMTS) she had to have the remains of the launch gear removed from her bottom plates which would then have to be cleaned and painted. She had been in the water, continuously, for two years.

The liner needed to go into a dry dock somewhere to have this work done and the nearest such facility was in Singapore, then still colonially British. There were only five dry docks in the world that could take liners of the *Queens'* size. The one in Southampton, especially built for the sisters, was unusable because it was within range of Nazi bombers; the use of the American dock at Bayonne was denied because of U.S neutrality; the Esquimalt dock on the west coast of Canada was too far away and the French dock at St. Nazaire (built for the *Normandie*) was out of the question.

To get to Singapore the *Queen Elizabeth* would have to make two stops to take on fuel and water; she had been designed as a five-day voyager.

The liner's first stop would be at Trinidad where she rendezvoused with an oil replenishment tanker five miles off shore to avoid any unwelcome attention.

Then, after steaming across the South Atlantic with a few John Brown men on board as passengers, she arrived at Cape Town in the British possession of South Africa, anchoring off the naval base at Simonstown.

At first the people of Cape Town thought the two funnelled *Mauretania* had returned to their waters, this liner having been there a few weeks previously. As soon as the true identity of the new ship became known, large crowds gathered to look at her.

Sailing from Cape Town, suitably revictualled, the *Lizzie* arrived in Singapore three weeks after leaving New York, for a seven-week lay-up for conversion into a troopship. The lessons learnt from the conversion of the *Mary* both in Singapore and in Sydney would be incorporated in the *Elizabeth*'s transformation.

The *Queen Elizabeth*'s reception in Singapore was far from cordial. Dr Maguire felt 'sickened by the complacency of the people' there and they in turn regarded the arrival of the liner with suspicion.

The suspicion stemmed from the *Mary*'s term in the dockyard's dry-dock when some undesirables from the crew (not regular Cunard crewmen, it was hastily pointed out, but a contingent 'from the slums of Glasgow' who had been taken on in a hurry because of the war emergency) broke into the NAAFI bar next to their sleeping quarters within the dockyard. After stealing quantities of alcohol and cash these tearaways proceeded to wreck the bar and other buildings.

As soon as she was in dry-dock the *Queen Elizabeth* was fumigated, ridding the liner of the rats which had managed to sneak aboard in New York.

The ship did not have an adequate water supply whilst in dock and under the hot sun began to take on an unpleasant aroma as hundreds of perspiring dockyard workmen and native labourers clambered to convert her into the world's largest trooper.

The ship's passenger capacity was increased to enable five thousand troops to be carried. Amongst other jobs steel covers were welded over the glass-panelled engine room skylights. Although affording the engine rooms some protection from the war, the temperature in these compartments would rise to unbearable levels under the heat of the tropical sun. Guns, too, were fitted along the upper decks.

During the refit a Liverpudlian fireman was fatally injured when, whilst helping to carry a heavy cylinder across a narrow gangway, he lost his footing and fell to the dock floor.

After the man's funeral some of the rough element of the *Elizabeth*'s irregular crew returned to the ship and seriously assaulted a cook because the food he served was not to their liking. A similar element on board the *Mary* had even put a cook into his own oven, the poor man later succumbing to his injuries.

After several more incidents with these men they were taken off the *Queen Elizabeth* and, under armed escort, returned to the UK.

While in Singapore many of the crew frequented a pub called the 'Pig and Whistle'. The name of this establishment so caught their fancy that crew bars on all Cunard ships were subsequently named in its honour.

On arrival in Singapore the great liner is warped into drydock there to prepare her for war. *Imperial War Museum*

Singapore was glad to see the *Lizzie* sail and the ship's men were glad to see the last of Singapore. The inhabitants of that small State might have wished for the ship's presence a few months later as they clamoured to leave their beleaguered city.

The *Queen Elizabeth*, now with black-painted hull and grey superstructure, sailed for Sydney, Australia.

The security and secrecy that usually surrounded the *Queens'* departures and arrivals went completely by the board when the *Elizabeth* arrived in Sydney. Half the city, it seemed, was aware that the ship was on her way, lining the surrounding coastline and crowding the famous bridge to watch her arrival, bringing all traffic to a halt. Cars stopped while their drivers gaped at the sight moving below them.

As the liner anchored in the Bay and listing ferries closed in to give their passengers a better view, one Australian, confused by the appearance of a second giant after the arrival of the *Mary* a while previously, was overheard to exclaim: 'Gawd they're clever these Pommies! What camouflage! They've even taken away a funnel!'

In Australia the *Queen Elizabeth* would undergo further conversion work with workmen from the Cockatoo Docks and Engineering Company also putting to rights what they considered to be sub-standard work that had been carried out in Singapore.

By the end of the refit the *Elizabeth* was ready to join her sister which had already made five trips to the Middle

The *Queen Elizabeth* tendering in the Clyde estuary. Many American G.I.s were surprised at the idyllic surroundings as they disembarked from the liner prior to their training for 'D-day'. *Imperial War Museum*

The speeding liner made a grand sight for those on board the ships send out to escort her homewards. Unfortunately, the cruisers could not always keep up with her! *Imperial War Museum*

East transporting urgently needed Australian troops to bolster the defences of Egypt against the enemy's incursions into North Africa.

More than a year after the two *Queens* had last met in New York they sailed in company for the very first time in April 1941. But, as Sydney Harbour was not big enough to allow both ships to anchor at the same time (ie each anchored vessel required a swinging ground of 1,100 feet in radius), one would load her human cargo via tender, usually at night inside the Harbour, whilst the other would lie off in Largs Bay waiting for her partner.

Carrying 5,600 troops on the *Elizabeth* and 6,000 on the *Mary* for the outward trip, the two ships met with other large, but slower, ocean liners to form a spectacular convoy.

Ile de France of the French Line, making a mockery of the 'no-smoking-on-deck-after-dark' routine with a persistent glow emanating from the top of her funnels, Holland America's *Nieuw Amsterdam*, Cunard's own venerable four funneller *Aquitania* (now experiencing duties in a second war) and *Mauretania* plus other famous ships kept the *Queens* company.

Although the *Queens* could easily manage 27-28 knots by themselves, even more when danger was believed to be in the vicinity, they were reduced to the common speed of the convoy of around 20 knots.

Relying on speed and the presence of fast naval cruisers for their defence, the most luxurious liners of peacetime accompanied each other through the Indian Ocean to the Red Sea carrying thousands of troops to stem the eastward ambitions of Nazism and Fascism.

On the return journey the ships carried allied wounded, internees or enemy prisoners-of-war, stopping off at Trincomalee in Ceylon (now Sri Lanka). The Nazi prisoners proved to be particularly arrogant and often gave their despised salute. One Luftwaffe major, who spoke fluent English, decided to boast of his part in the devastating air-raids on Coventry. A young British lieutenant, who had lost his mother and two sisters in these raids, visited this major and subsequently provided Dr. Maguire and his hospital staff with a sudden case of 'unexplained' injuries sustained by the German.

The *Queen Elizabeth* made one welcomed trip to Hobart in Tasmania where their welcome made the ship's complement feel that they were actually appreciated.

Other casualties were caused by the extremely hot weather in which the ships sailed. As the ships were designed for cooler climes there were many cases of deaths caused by heat stroke or by injury caused by frayed tempers in both crew and passengers. Methods were devised to 'cool' such outbreaks, and it also took the *Queens* two and a half days to cool down themselves after arriving at Suez.

Security at sailing and arrival and the safety found in high speed was always paramount and any breach found its lesson learnt in later ventures.

But one particular breach of security that occurred in the Pacific sent shivers down the spines of many. Dr. Maguire wrote of the incident that occurred a day out of Trincomalee.

'..... I awoke suddenly because the engines were slowing down. I slipped into shorts and shirt and went on deck.

Viewed from an escorting cruiser the largest troop transport in the world speeds towards Scotland. *Imperial War Museum*

'My eyes almost refused to believe what they saw.

'The three great ships – the two *Queens* and the *Ile de France* – were stationary. They were huge sitting targets in a hostile ocean. The cruiser (HMAS) *Canberra* had lowered a pinnace which was cruising calmly around collecting bags of mail from each.

'At that moment I remembered that the cruiser, HM(A)S *Sydney* had been sunk by the *Kormoran* without a single survivor a few days before, not so far from our present position. (Her last shells hit the German raider which was abandoned on fire from stem to stern.)

'Now the *Canberra*'s boat crawled around like a sea slug. Time never passed so slowly. At last the pinnace hooked on and a cheery farewell hoist ran up the cruiser's yardarm as she turned for home. I never did find out who was responsible for that risky mid-ocean mail collecting. I know it was the last time the *Queens* ever stopped at sea in war time.'

Between them, in a year spent shuttling between Sydney and Port Tewfik in the Red Sea, the two *Queens* transported nearly 80,000 troops to the war zone.

The *Elizabeth* had quite a lucky escape in August 1941, when steaming through the Red Sea. Enemy spotter planes often flew over the area during the day to provide information of potential targets for their bomber flights which would then arrive at night. On this occasion the *Queen Elizabeth*, completely blacked-out, was steaming astern of the hospital ship *Atlantis* which was brightly lit to identify her as a ship of mercy.

John Havers, a Supply Officer travelling on the *Atlantis*, heard later that an enemy aircraft had flown in low to inspect the hospital ship and in doing so had actually passed between the *Elizabeth*'s funnels!

With Japan and the United States entering the war after the debacle of Pearl Harbour on 7th December 1941, the *Elizabeth* was laid up in Sydney for seven weeks. The Pacific was too dangerous for her with both German and Japanese submarines on the prowl. The Australians also needed what remained of their depleted army for their country's own defence in case of Japanese invasion.

The *Mary* meanwhile had returned to the Clyde but it was decided to send the *Elizabeth* to Canada for dry-docking (that facility in Singapore now being unavailable) as the large amount of tropical growth that fouled the liner's bottom plates needed to be removed. It was estimated that the growth that had attached itself to the hull reduced the ship's speed by a good 2 knots.

Two stops were required for refuelling and watering en route, the first call being made in New Zealand where even the bath tubs of the cautious were filled with fresh water.

The second stop necessitated a call at one of those tiny specks in the vast Pacific, the Marquesas group of islands. A secret rendezvous had been arranged with an American tanker but as the *Elizabeth* steamed into the narrow fjord-like entrance of one of the islands, Nuku Hiva, and sounded her whistle she received no reply. Some natives appeared and promptly disappeared, and a few anxious officers on the Bridge began to wonder where their supplies were. As far as they knew the U-boats that were active in the Pacific could have denied the m the means to continue on the last leg of their journey to Canada.

Ten anxious minutes later the tanker appeared around the headland of the tiny island.

The tension on the liner's Bridge was relieved when one of the officers shouted 'What the hell kept you?' but the tanker's crew were not amused. They had come a long, difficult way; some of their own supplies had run out en route and their flour had gone sour, but their mood eventually mellowed when the larger ship passed over some welcome liquid stores as, being an American ship, the tanker was 'dry'.

Fuelling took eight hours to complete, – an 'orderly rush' – as a report was received that there was a Japanese raider in the area.

Sailing on to Victoria on Vancouver Island, British Columbia, the *Queen* arrived only to miss the tide due to a miscalculation by the ship's officers and had to steam around off the island awaiting the next. When she again came to enter the dry-dock her paravane chains fouled and knocked over some dock-blocks and once more she had to cruise around for twenty-four hours whilst the dock was pumped dry, the blocks reset and the dock re-flooded.

Whilst in Esquimalt dry-dock the ship's bottom was cleaned, the interiors fumigated, guns fitted and the groundwork for the de-gausing coil that was to be given a permanent, plated-in position (more or less on a level

with 'B' deck) was carried out. The final plating-in of the coil would be completed in Scotland.

After Esquimalt the *Queen Elizabeth* sailed for San Francisco and, on arrival, briefly ran aground near the Golden Gate Bridge.

During a conference on board, the U.S. military was told how many men had been transported on the ship on each Sydney-to-Suez trip.

The Americans were characteristically amazed:

'Are you crazy? Only five thousand in THIS monster? We'll fix to send you eight thousand!'

Within five days carpenters had removed the Australian hammocks and bunks and in their place fitted fold-down 'Standee' beds, (made of tubular steel and easy-to-clean canvas webbing) two, three or five to a tier, into every available space. Two days later the *Elizabeth* left in a small convoy bound for Sydney via, once again, the Marquesas with eight thousand American GI's on board needed to bolster Australia's depleted defences until some of their own troops could be recalled from the Middle East.

After disembarking the troops at Sydney, the *Queen Elizabeth* waited for thirteen days until decisions were made as to her future. With a mutually nostalgic farewell the *Queen* sailed out of Sydney on 19th April, with a group of nurses on board destined for Fremantle where they were disembarked.

This was a strange decision as 180 US servicemen, badly wounded in the fighting in the Philippines, had been embarked at Sydney for New York.

German prisoners of war and their Polish guards came on board at Cape Town heading for internment in the USA.

At Rio the ships' searchlights scoured the water around the liner to prevent any escape attempts by the POW's. Armed guards in two motor launches patrolled around the ship but no one had told them that the hospital on board had been allowed to open its portholes whilst in port for ventilation purposes. Subsequently, when one of the patients put his head through the port to get a breath of fresh air, bullets ricocheted from the hull around him!

At last the *Queen Elizabeth* arrived in New York to begin what became known as the 'GI Shuttle', her first such trip departing 5th June.

But another conference took place on board the liner – 'Only eight thousand in a big ship like this? Next trip you sail with ten thousand.'

And so she did. But after the first round voyage the *Queen* would be fitted with a total of twelve thousand Standee bunks (including some along the Promenade Deck) with a special dispensation granted for the gentler Atlantic summer months when an additional three thousand five hundred men could be carried. Many of these men could sleep on the top deck in the open air or else they could 'hot bunk', that is use the Standee bunks on a rotational basis – one soldier using a bunk once it had been vacated by another.

After the *QE*'s arrival in Gourock with her first load of GI's she was then sent to Suez on 17th June, (via Freetown and Simonstown) with reinforcements for the British Eighth Army to help stem Rommel's advances towards the Canal.

The liner returned to New York on 19th August via Capetown, Simonstown and Rio de Janeiro to begin her regular GI shuttle work in earnest. Sometimes she diverted to Halifax, Nova Scotia, to transport Canadian troops to aid in the defence of the Motherland.

In the US the GI's would be gathered at Camp Kilmer in New Jersey for training and instruction on how to board the liners, how to find their cabins, where to stow their kit bags and so on. Giant mockups of the *Queens'* gangway, entrance halls and cabins were built or lined-out for this purpose.

The troops would board which ever of the two ships was berthed at Pier 90 during the late evening hours under cover of darkness after being transported to the Pier by either ferry or bus. The *Queens'* night-time sailings were planned to avoid full moons.

On boarding the *QE* or *Mary* each GI was given a coloured disc or card (red, white or blue) and this indicated the section of ship in which he must remain during the voyage. If he strayed into another section then he was 'fined' by having to assist the crew with their tasks.

Another essential rule was that each man, regardless of rank, should wear or carry his lifebelt when outside his cabin at all times. A transgressor had to forfeit a shoe when caught, having then to hobble back to his cabin to collect the missing belt before being able to retrieve the confiscated footwear.

On leaving New York every soldier had to stand stock still in his allotted cabin until the ship was out to sea. A rush of men to either side to view the famous skyline or the Statue of Liberty would have caused the ship to list. It was calculated that such a list would increase her draught by between two to four feet (with possible damage to both ship and under-river services) and possibly detrimentally affect the ship's stability.

Feeding 10,000 to 16,000 men (depending on the season) twice a day for five days proved to be a mammoth task. A well-narrated shopping list for one trip comprised:

155,000 lb meat and poultry
124,300 lb potatoes
76,000 lb flour and cereal
53,000 lb butter, eggs and milk powder
31,400 lb tea, coffee and sugar and the same amount of canned fruit
29,000 lb fresh fruit
18,000 lb jams
4,600 lb cheese
(2.2046 lb = 1kg)

31,000 eggs at breakfast were boiled in six clean dustbins into which steam hoses were played for the usual four minutes or so.

US Captain Bill Williams of Kentucky, the messing officer on board *QE* throughout the war, would call the six sittings each of forty-five minutes, 2,000 troops at a time, for the two meals a day (breakfast 6.30 am to 11 am, dinner from 3 pm to 7.30 pm) in his Southern States accent:

'This is the last call for the first sitting in the troops' mess hall. Fahwm yo' lines. This is the last call for chow!' The troops would be then given a pack of sandwiches after breakfast to last them through the day until dinner time.

Although one hundred British and one hundred American full time and voyage-only gunners were carried and regularly exercised, the *Elizabeth* never fired a shot in anger.

Even so, one captain at least would keep the troops below decks during his time in command in 1942 during the voyages from New York to Gourock. Captain Eric Ashton-Irvine (then First Officer) recalled:

'The troops were never permitted on deck during my voyages. Soon after we passed The Narrows in New York harbour, they were sent below and then only to reappear five days later, just after we passed the Clyde lighthouse in Scotland. Only the gunners were permitted on deck. Understandably, should the upper decks be littered with humanity during an attack, the gunners simply could not reach their stations. We would have been lost ...'

During the voyage the troops would keep themselves amused in several ways. The favourites were cards and dice. These games seemed to be never-ending with a man's place in a game quickly being taken should he leave.

On board the *Mary* (and one can assume it was the same on the *QE*) Captain Bisset requested that, as part of keeping the ship clean, the troops should refrain from chewing gum as discarded pieces were difficult to remove from the deck. The practice of carving initials into the ship's teak railings was not discouraged as Captain Bisset resignedly thought: 'Some of them (the troops) would never return, and they knew it. I did not begrudge them the pleasure of carving their initials on the teakwood rails.'

The safety of the troops during these solo, high-speed trooping dashes across the Atlantic was not considered to be paramount in the minds of those at the top. 10,000 men could, perhaps, be carried in safety according to the lifeboat and liferaft capacity of the ship but it was considered that the extra 5,000 men who were carried in summer and not provided for in life saving capabilities was worth the risk, based on the liner's existing records of speed and reliability.

In November 1942, the *QE* was involved in an incident that still remains the subject of much speculation.

The *U-704*, under the command of Kapitan Horst Kessler, was wallowing in a Force 8 gale off the west coast of Ireland heading south returning to base in France.

Early in the afternoon of the 9th a large, two-funnelled steamer was seen through the varying visibility, six to seven miles away.

The submarine dived and the captain identified the ship as the *Queen Elizabeth*. Four torpedoes were fired and the U-boat followed their course. One detonation was heard.

Apparently the torpedo had exploded well away from the ship. The *Queen Mary's* captain, Bill Bisset, was travelling on the *QE* at the time as a passenger; he said after the war 'There was an explosion near us .... we got up to 31 knots without any trouble!'

Apparently the steamer, observed by Kessler, had been travelling at speed, stopped and, a few minutes afterwards, proceeded on her way.

Kessler has always maintained that the ship was the *Elizabeth* and later, after the war, a Cunard officer told of a detonation near the ship on that same day (all Cunard records from that period have apparently been lost) and

At the end of the war American G.I.s board HMT *Queen Elizabeth* via tender at the Tail o' the Bank for their triumphant return home.

Imperial War Museum

the liner was stopped for fifteen minutes – a forbidden action but obviously considered necessary.

However, to stop the ship would take a considerable time as the superheated steam would need to be cooled to normal working temperatures before slowing the ship could even be considered. This would take an hour at least plus many miles that would not have allowed her to stop within Kessler's observation.

However, rumours had reached New York that the *Queen Elizabeth* had been sunk with the likelihood that she had taken many men down with her.

Staff Captain Harry Grattidge of the *Queen Mary* had heard the unconfirmed reports whilst presiding over lunch-time drinks in his cabin as the liner lay alongside her berth in New York.

The resulting gloomy lunch-hour was just coming to an end when the telephone rang. It was the girl at the Cunard Exchange on the Pier Head.

Harry Grattidge wrote of the conversation in his auto-biography, 'Captain of the *Queens*':

' "Captain," she gulped, "Oh, Captain – the *Queen Elizabeth..*"

' "I know," I said patiently. "It's terrible news."

'She almost squawked in her excitement. "No, no, you don't understand. Oh Captain, it was all a rumour ... She's here. She's just anchored at Quarantine ...."

' "Gentlemen," I said, replacing the receiver, "will anyone refuse a glass of wine when I tell then that the *Queen Elizabeth* is with us now, safe and sound?"

'There was not a dissenting voice. We charged our glasses. It was Henry Morganthau who raised his first: "To the two great ladies of the Atlantic – the *Queens*' "

Five weeks before this incident the *Queen Mary* had been involved in a more tangible, more substantial accident. On 2nd October, the three-funnelled liner was approaching the north coast of Ireland en route to Gourock from New York with thousands of GI's on board.

The Royal Naval cruiser HMS *Curacoa* had come out to meet and escort the liner into home waters and, as usual, set off in the direction of England at high speed as soon as the smoke from the *Mary*'s funnels was sighted over the horizon.

The Cunarder soon caught up, both ships maintaining their synchronised zig-zag.

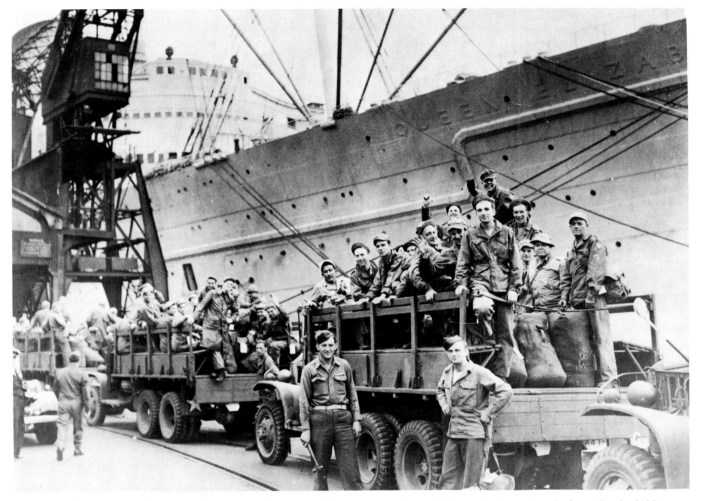

After the *Queen*'s first visit to Southampton in August 1945, the repatriation of G.I.s took place directly from the dockside.

Imperial War Museum

The cruiser's zig-zag gradually went out of phase with that of the liner and soon the upset pattern decreed that the naval ship should cross the path of the oncoming troopship.

Unhappily, fortune took a sad turn and the *Queen Mary*'s bow sliced through the cruiser's hull like a knife through butter.

The liner, with buckled stem and flooded fore-peak, had to carry on at reduced speed whilst four other destroyer escorts remained behind to pick up survivors from the two quickly-sunk sections of the cruiser. Out of four hundred and ten sailors on board HMS *Curacoa* only seventy-two survived.

The comfort and well-being of the men on the *Queens* was considered as far as it was possible to do so – but the North Atlantic itself was still a force to be reckoned with.

On one particular crossing from Gourock to New York the *Lizzie* ran into a very heavy storm when two days out into the Atlantic.

Fortunately, being on a westbound trip, the liner was not full carrying, amongst others, British service personnel to various postings in the United States. Some passengers helped to pass their days by helping the crew with anti-submarine lookout duties.

Charles Harrison, on his way to a naval posting, remembered that amongst the civilian passengers on board was Irving Berlin who played the piano and sang some of his own songs.

The storm was particularly violent and the *Queen* hove-to for about two days, making under 10 knots. Doctor Maguire recounted what happened in his autobiography 'The Sea my Surgery':

'We were driving far to the north, risking heavy weather we would normally have dodged on a peace-time run. Head-seas smashed heavily against our 83,000 tons of ship.

'My wrist-watch showed eight o'clock in the morning and I was thinking of getting up. My mind was suddenly made up for me.

'We suddenly hit a freak sea, a great mountainous mass of green water. The *Queen Elizabeth*'s bows rose skyward and then disappeared down into a vast trough. As she did so another enormous roller came from nowhere and punched her bows even further downwards. We just continued to go down. I was thrown clean out of bed and could not stand upright.

'This is it', I thought, even though I couldn't believe it. There was a deafening roar like nothing I have ever heard before. Every plate vibrated as our propellers rose up out of the sea and raced in thin air. For a measureless moment the ship seemed to stand up on her nose. Finally, slowly, so very slowly, she dragged her fore-part from the water, and I found I had been holding my breath.

'Then the loud-hailers started booming, calling for carpenters and joiners from the troops we were carrying to New York. Every skilled man was needed – fast.

'That colossal sea had punched the ship's fore-deck down and out of shape by six inches. The fore-peak was flooded. Every forward capstan was out of commission. Both anchors were jammed.'

As will be remembered, the *Queen Mary* had a forward well-deck in which green seas could spend their force before breaking against the bridge. As this eventuality had never arisen the well-deck had been omitted on the *Queen Elizabeth*, an omission that was now to be regretted. Doctor Maguire continued:

Eager to get home, American soldiers clamber on board at Southampton. *Imperial War Museum*

'The second vicious sea had also smashed squarely against the bridge, shattered the thick plate-glass windows, washed the quartermaster from the wheel-house to the wing of the bridge.

'The Staff Captain, whose cabin was immediately under the bridge, had been shaving when it struck. A block of plate glass from his window was stove in, in one piece, ricocheted from a panel, hit him flat, and knocked him down. In two seconds he was sitting, dazed, waist-deep in water.

'When I went up to attend to him I talked to a white-faced officer on the bridge. He was suffering from minor shock. His line of vision, he told me, as the *Elizabeth* went down and down towards the bed of the ocean was from the bridge window, through to the crow's nest on the fore-mast to where the ship's bows should normally have been. The hawse-pipes, like huge frightened eyes, must have been staring straight down towards the bottom of the Atlantic.

'And from that frightening episode, I had two minor casualties!'

From the officer's description of looking through the crow's nest from his position on the bridge, the liner must

have been heading to possible destruction at an angle of around 60°

Some men weren't so lucky on another rough crossing the previous Christmas. Dennis Money had boarded at Gourock and recalled that only five hundred of those passengers on board attended Christmas lunch.

'One of the most bizarre experiences still vivid in my mind was attending the Christmas Eve carol service in what was the first class lounge – lush even in wartime garb. Those attending were seated in wicker armchairs, the splayed feet of which sank into deep-piled carpet. Midway through the service, the ship suddenly heeled over in excess of 30° and like some fantasy, all the passengers slid towards the bulk-head. Needless to say, the programme continued. After-wards, we learnt that the sonar had picked up a submarine sounding and the helm of the *Queen Elizabeth* was flung over – the ship making a 45° change in direction.

'The culmination of events occurred when the *Queen Elizabeth* was caught between the crests of some 40 ft waves during the night and dropped bodily into the trough, resulting in many injuries, including three fatalities, when those manning the guns on the upper decks plunged to their deaths as the ship plummeted down. Among the most seriously injured were those accommodated in the troop quarters aft in five-tiered bunks. When the ship literally dropped, many of those in the upper bunks crashed down on the deck below. Fortunately, I was housed in one of the adapted first-class cabins and landed with a jolt safely on my bunk. The severity of the accident was clearly visible the next morning. The huge steel stanchions to the foremast had been torn away together with all the 'Carley floats' attached to them.'

After this horror it was a special pleasure to arrive safely in port, especially one like New York. Denis Money recalls:

'After the months of black-out experienced in and around the UK it was like a fairyland to sail into the tranquil waters past the Statue of Liberty and to see the twinkling lights of the renowned New York skyline.'

The sheer pleasure of arriving in a lightened, bustling, bomb-free city on board the world's largest ship after a pleasant Spring crossing is also remembered by Denis Morrell of Barking:

'At the age of 67 (in 1987) I can look back with great pleasure and affection at my one and only encounter with *Queen Elizabeth*.

'At the age of 20 I had departed from Nottingham for the Royal Navy, a snotty-nosed kid whose main thrill in life had come from sundry day trips to Skegness.

'I had completed my telegraphist training at HMS *Royal Arthur* (ie Butlins Holiday Camp, Skegness – "Our True Intent Is All For Your Delight"), spent eighteen months on a Submarine Depot Ship, resting on a pile of empty corned beef tins in the Firth of Clyde, and had successfully swapped a draft to HMS *Flamingo* (ie Bombay) for a mysterious assignment called, I think, JX232.

'We left Chatham Barracks in April 1943, on this unknown venture. We found ourselves heading for Glasgow. Before much time had elapsed we were on a small boat heading for a grey hulk in the middle of the Clyde. The small, grey ship soon became enormous.

'It was indeed the *Queen Elizabeth*, newly fitted out and given the job of transporting the Army, Navy and Air Force between the Old and New Worlds. It (the ship) went so fast that there was very little likelihood of a U-boat confrontation.

'What a wonderful ...crossing that was! We were given the job of washing up after hoards of airmen had gorged themselves on the magnificent food which was available. We were quartered down below in the bows where bunks rose and fell six feet as the giant sped along. Although it was April, and the North Atlantic, I do not remember ever feeling cold.

'There was a joyous atmosphere everywhere on board. Could it be that we were all delighted to get away from war-torn Europe, at least for a little while? At night the upper decks were filled with music from guitars or mouth-organs. The snotty-nosed provincial kid was overwhelmed with happiness.

'And then came the early morning sight of New York. As a child I had time after time considered that if ever I got to Heaven it would be going round Woolworth's in New York, and there it was, perhaps the most dramatic vista in all the world's history.

'We cruised up the Hudson River to Pier 90, passing the terrible sight of the *Normandie*, burnt out and on its side near one of the piers. We left the *Queen Elizabeth* and I never saw her again until the newsreel shots of her ... in Hong Kong harbour.

'But it was the *Queen Elizabeth* that took me to a magic world of Frank Sinatra singing "I Couldn't Sleep a Wink Last Night", to Harry James, to Fred Waring and his Pennsylvanians, to Boris Karloff acting in "Arsenic and Old Lace", to the top of the Empire State Building. It was the *Queen Elizabeth* that introduced me to the overwhelming generosity and kindness of the American people.

'Later there was Asbury Park, and meeting two Dorothy's either of whom I could have married; there was Montreal and the River-class frigate *Barle*. There was Jeanette Macdonald in an important operatic debut in Montreal. There was St. John's and Halifax, the return to Europe, Gibraltar, a new ship – the destroyer *Kempenfelt*, and Scapa Flow.

'Later still there was Naples, and the Suez Canal, and Anzio and D-Day. There was demob and marriage and children and the Civil Service and several houses. After *Queen Elizabeth* there were 44 years of the ups and downs of life. But the memory of that Atlantic crossing in that great ship burns brightly always in my memory.'

Other passengers were less enthusiastic at seeing the 'twinkling lights of the New York skyline' for the first time. These were the German POW's travelling, 4,000 at a time on both *Queens*, to internment in the United States. They had been informed, through Nazi propaganda, that a blacked-out New York skyline was in bombed ruins. What a surprise they had!

Altogether the *Queen Elizabeth* made thirty-five crossings of the Atlantic during which time, and for a while after, she was under American control through a lease-lend arrangement. She had, however, remained all the while under Cunard management with British officers and crew.

Throughout the years of the 'GI shuttle' the two *Queens* had never been in the same port at the same time and avoided full-moons whilst at Gourock. They had quietly left New York, steaming by the sad hulk of the *Normandie* gradually decaying through the final act of salvage, impressing many New Yorkers as they efficiently went about their business.

Heading for Gourock and their safe anchorage amongst the magnificent hills of the Scottish countryside they would disgorge their whole battalions of GI's into paddle steamers and other tenders for onward transmission to camps dispersed throughout the British Isles. Here the GI's would wait and train before taking part in the enormous achievement of D-Day – the Invasion of Europe – and the ultimate defeat of Hitler and his insidious reign of terror.

After being cleaned by a small army of cleaning ladies and being replenished with fuel and stores, the *Queens* would then take on a lesser number of returning wounded, POW's and British civil and military passengers heading for the USA, Canada and other destinations.

By the end of May 1945 the *Queens* had carried between them, in both directions, a staggering 1,243,538 passengers. On the North Atlantic alone totals of 869,694 people had been carried eastwards and 213,008 transported between Gourock and New York. The *QE* had, between April 1941 and March 1945 steamed 492,635 miles and carried 811,324 'souls'. The highest number she had carried at any one time was 15,932 passengers and crew but the record for the highest number ever carried in one ship went to the *Mary* with 16,683!

Many famous people travelled to and fro on the *Queens* during the period of the war en route to political or theatrical engagements. Winston Churchill, unable to travel by 'plane due to a tubercular complaint, travelled on the *Mary* to meetings in the US and Canada on three occasions. Perhaps the most famous visitor to the *Elizabeth* was the self-exiled ex-king Edward VIII (Duke of Windsor); he visited the liner in New York between trooping voyages.

The *Queen Elizabeth* happened to be in New York both on VE Day when her whistle joined that of the *Mary* in the noisy celebrations of the joyous occasion. She was also there on VJ Day three months later.

It now fell to the *Queens* to transport back to their homelands many of the hundreds of thousands of GI's they had brought to Europe and, in the *Mary*'s case, transport some 25,000 American servicemen's 'War Brides' and their children to their new home country.

And so, on 24th June 1945, the *QE* left Gourock with her first load of returning GI's. Their welcome in New York was, to say the least, tumultuous with a 'blimp', bands on small ships and a ticker-tape shower cascading from the waterfront buildings welcoming 'the boys' home.

The *Elizabeth* left Gourock for the last time as a troop-ship on 7th August, bringing to an end a long and close association that had been surrounded by maximum security, because of its vital importance. As she left she signalled, simply but sincerely, 'Thank you, Gourock'.

The next time the *Queen Elizabeth* would berth in the United Kingdom it would be in Southampton, the port which should have received her six years previously.

At last, she was coming home.

Chapter Seven
"…. the World's Fresh Ornament"
(Sonnet I)

In a dull, steady drizzle the still grey-painted *Queen Elizabeth* carefully steamed past the Nab light tower into the eastern approaches of Spithead.

Soon the three, dome-like, stone structures of Palmerston's forts – his 'follies' – passed the ship astern off Bembridge. She sailed on into the Solent and towards Cowes where she turned to starboard to glide between the Brambles and Shingles sandbanks that guarded the entrance to Southampton Water.

Another turn, this time to port, brought the ship's bow around Calshot Spit, before she headed up the water towards Southampton Docks.

The Red Funnel tug which had met the huge liner off Ryde remained with her just in case her services were needed.

The day, Monday 20th August 1945, was an auspicious – if underplayed – day. Four and a half years late,

the liner was making her first visit to the port which had been deceived into believing that the *Lizzie* was on her way there back in February 1941. For its enthusiasm the port had, instead, received a visit from an equally deceived Luftwaffe.

Now all was forgiven. 'Southampton's Baby' – as the Cunarder was described later in the day by the city's mayor – was at last coming home.

But the reception that bomb-torn Southampton proffered differed greatly from that given to the ship when she arrived in New York carrying the first batch of fifteen thousand returning heroes.

With other ships in the port sounding the three dots and a dash of the 'Victory-V' morse sign on their sirens the *Queen Elizabeth* slid into her berth on the River Test just before midday.

The *Queen Elizabeth*'s first departure from Southampton in August 1945 was marked by a fly past of eight Meteor jets; almost 16,000 returning G.I.s were on board the liner.
Imperial War Museum

The fourteen-piece Southampton Borough Police Band played on the quayside. Cunard's house flag, flanked on either side by the flags of Great Britain and the United States, hung rain-sodden and limp from the adjacent passenger shed.

The small crowd of spectators fell silent as the tugs gently brought the great, grey, cliff-sided vessel alongside the quay.

As the British and American national anthems came to an end the band packed up and hurried off. And that was that! The Mayor of Southampton and other civic dignitaries boarded the vessel and made speeches of welcome. Captain E.M. Fall, who had succeeded Captain Townley and had commanded the QE throughout much of the war, replied on behalf of the ship.

Three days later the Commodore of the Cunard–White Star Line – and recently ennobled – Sir James Bisset ('Bill' to his friends) took over the command of the Queen Elizabeth on Captain Fall's retirement.

Commodore Bisset had previously been in command of the Queen Mary, joining that ship in 1942 and sailing with her throughout much of the 'GI Shuttle'. During this period he had taken over command of the Elizabeth for two voyages in 1942. It was during his absence that the Mary, under Captain Illingworth, had cut her escorting cruiser – HMS Curacoa – in half. Trained in sail, as most Cunard skippers then were, Bill Bisset had many years earlier been Fourth Officer on the Carpathia, the ship that had responded to a famous distress call in April 1912, subsequently rescuing survivors of the great White Star liner Titanic which had struck an iceberg and foundered on her maiden voyage with great loss of life.

Happily, the Queen's first departure from Southampton was more of a celebration in the grand style. Full of GI's happy to be returning home the liner was given a send-off to match the occasion. Eight 'Meteor' jets provided an exciting military salute, flying in formation over the liner as she pulled away from her berth.

The 14,996 passengers – which included thirty civilians amongst the war's bravest GI's (a bravery that had earned them the right to be the first to be repatriated) – was USAF Colonel James Stewart – famed film star in the days of peace but an 'All American' airforce hero during the war. Amongst the embarked civilian passengers was the Queen Elizabeth's first actual fare-paying passenger, Mr Sam Berlin.

The QE would make three voyages from Southampton repatriating US servicemen until Britain requested her return to British control to repatriate British and Dominion personnel. The Queen Mary would continue under American guidance for a while longer carrying thousands of 'GI Brides' to their new homes in the States.

During the Elizabeth's turn around in New York on her second GI trip from Southampton, Commodore Bisset had the liner's grey funnels repainted in Cunard's red and black on 24th September. The result brightened up the ship considerably '... after the years of drabness' and seemed to reflect the anticipated joys of the peaceful years to come.

On the QE's last such trip she carried what was believed to be her greatest number ever – 15,077 GI's and other passengers and 855 crew – a total of 15,932.

From 22nd October, the Queen's job would be to repatriate thousands of Canadian soldiers home from defending the Motherland.

It was considered appropriate that a British ship should be used for repatriating British citizens, Canadians outwards and British Far East Prisoners of War home eastwards (the latter men travelling across Canada from Vancouver where they had arrived from the Far East). It was, however, also considered unpractical for the Queen to venture further abroad to other ports in other countries which might either not be able to accommodate the liner or the ports themselves might be in states of disrepair or mined. The reduced numbers likely to be carried on longer voyages also tipped the balance in favour of purely North Atlantic voyages.

The Canadian Government had hoped that the Queen Elizabeth would be able to disembark their soldiers at Halifax, Nova Scotia. And so it was to this port, easy of access and on a shorter route than New York, that the Queen triumphantly arrived on 26th October with 12,517 jubilant passengers and 864 crew, four days after leaving Southampton where the soldiers had showered cigarettes and coins on to the crowd of spectators.

However, Commodore Bisset, although delighted with the reception given to his ship, was not happy with the location of the quay alongside which the QE was berthed. He considered the site too exposed should a strong southeasterly wind spring up; this would cause his ship to range back and forth, possibly breaking her moorings, causing damage to both ship and quay.

In spite of understandable Canadian protestations that they wanted their soldiers to step directly onto Canadian soil, Bill Bisset recommended that future repatriations should be either to New York or to Boston from where the Canadian citizens could be transported back to Canada by rail. The Commodore considered the safety of his ship to be paramount and he would not be persuaded otherwise.

On the return from the first trip to Halifax the Queen carried the Canadian Prime Minister, the Honourable Vincent Massey, his wife and state officials. Amongst the other passengers were many British POW's returning from internment in the Far East.

Typical of these was A.C. Humphries of Sholing, Southampton.

He remembered the Lizzie with affection, writing to the Southampton Echo at the end of her career:

'It is October 1946 in Halifax, Nova Scotia. 1200 men are returning home from a living Hell, from 3½ years of captivity under the Japanese. We helped build the 'Railway of Death'; had been shipped to Japan; had smelted zinc; mined coal; laboured on the Docks. Had been beaten, starved and humiliated. Now we were coming home, on the finest ship the World had ever seen, a British ship, and we were proud to be British.

'As this Giant of the Seas eased slowly away from the quayside, we were finally on the last lap of our long journey home.

'We have not been accustomed to such luxury, quite a change from prison camps.

'Commodore Sir James Bisset is in command and the Right Hon. Vincent Massey, Mr Philip Noel Baker,

Flag bedecked, the *Queen Elizabeth* arrives in New York for the first time with thousands of returning G.I.s on board.
Author's collection

In October the *Queen*, with funnels repainted in Cunard colours, delivered a shipload of Canadian soldiers back to their homeland. In spite of the welcome her skipper was not happy with the exposed berth at Halifax, Nova Scotia.
Author's collection

General Sir Hastings Ismay and 'Wee' Georgie Wood are sailing with us.

'English food, English beer, English cigarettes, the first for four years – we were in clover. November in the North Atlantic didn't worry us, we were coming home.

'Four days went by quickly, but not quickly enough. 'Wee' Georgie organised and compered a concert, and the captain and the VIPs addressed the audience with words of welcome and encouragement. Nearly everyone attended a church service, voluntarily, to give thanks for our deliverance.

'Monday November 5th is 'The Day'. Everyone is up on deck bright and early to catch a first glimpse of England, to be met by a thick November fog. As she slowly edged her way up Southampton Water, her deep siren blaring out its warning I was constantly being asked "Where are we now?" or "How much farther?", but I couldn't see through the fog to tell them.

'The Dock Head came into view, then the turn to starboard, tugs manoeuvred her into the berth, a military band played us in. A "Welcome Home" speech by the Mayor of Southampton was followed by one from South-ampton's new M.P. Dr. Horace King.

'Many of the men unashamedly allowed a tear to trickle down their cheeks as the full realisation came that we were really home and remembered those that we had left behind, never to return.

'Of all the hundreds of thousands of miles she sailed in her long career, that was probably classed as just another uneventful trip, but to that small band of men, of whom I was privileged to be one, it was the 'Journey of a Lifetime'. For me the *Queen Elizabeth* will always be "The Ship That Brought Me Home!" '

On arrival in Southampton the *Queen* was dry-docked, using for the very first time the King George V dock which had been specially built for her sister and herself more than ten years previously.

The *QE*'s first Christmas of peacetime was spent at sea, en voyage for New York. The trip was unfortunately rough and not all the 13,272 Christmas dinners that had been prepared were eaten!

Quite often on the return journey from New York the *Elizabeth* would carry fewer than a thousand passengers.

The liner's first departure from Southampton in the New Year of 1946 found a special VIP amongst her 12,314 passengers. After successfully directing Britain's war as Prime Minister against the now crumbled malignant influence of Nazism, Winston Churchill found himself voted out of office and en route for a three month holiday in Florida.

Boarding the ship dressed in his Trinity House uniform of yachting cap and brass-buttoned coat and clutching an inevitable cigar, he and his wife posed for the cameras at the top of the gangway.

It would be Churchill's first voyage in the *Queen Elizabeth*, although he had travelled on the *Mary* on several occasions during the war heading westwards for top-level conferences in Canada and the United States.

Now, on the day before berthing in New York, he broadcast a special, but typical of his style of oration, speech to the troops on board although it went unreported by the press: 'My friends and shipmates in the *Queen Elizabeth*!

'For most of you it is homeward-bound. It has been a good voyage in a great ship, with a fine Captain – or indeed Commodore. We have not got there yet, but I am quite sure he will find the way all right. At any rate, he has been over the track before, and, as I can testify myself, having been several times with him, in those days there used to be U-boats and things like that. They all seem to have dropped off now and we don't have to worry about them at all. Something has happened. The seas are clear, the old flag flies, and those who have done the work, or some of it – because the British did some – turn home again, their task accomplished and their duty done.

'What a strange fearful, yet glittering chapter this war has been! What changes it has brought throughout the world and in the fortunes of so many families! What an interruption in all the plans each of us had made! What a surrender of the liberties we prized! What a casting away of comfort and safety! What a pride in peril! What a glory shines on the brave and true! The good cause has not been overthrown. Tyrants have been hurled from their place of power, and those who sought to enslave the future of man-kind have paid, or will pay, the final penalty.

'You Canadians, many of whom served in the Canadian Fifth Division, no doubt have your minds filled with the victorious war scenes of Italy and the Rhine. But we Englishmen always think of the days of 1940, when the Canadian Army Corps stood almost alone in Kent and Sussex, and the Germans had twenty-five divisions ready to leap across the Channel and wipe Great Britain out of life and history. I think about those days, too, sometimes, and how fine it was to see everyone, at home and throughout the Empire, moved by the same impulse, so simple, so sublime – "Conquer or die!"

'Victory in arms, or in any walk of life, is only the opportunity of doing better on a larger scale and at a higher level. Do not be anxious about the future! Be vigilant, be strong, be clear-sighted, but do not be worried. Our future is in our hands. Our lives are what we choose to make them. The great British Commonwealth and Empire, emerging from the fire once again, glorious and free, will form a structure and an organisation within which there will be room for all, and a fair chance for all.

'Yesterday I was on the bridge, watching the mountainous waves, and this ship – which is no pup – cutting through them and mocking their anger. I asked myself, why is it that the ship beats the waves, when they are so many and the ship is one? The reason is that the ship has a purpose, and the waves have none. They just flop around, innumerable, tireless, but ineffective. The ship with the purpose takes us where we want to go.

'Let us therefore have purpose, both in our National and Imperial policy, and in our own private lives. Thus the future will be fruitful for each and for all, and the reward of the warriors will not be unworthy of the deeds they have done.'

Churchill's words had provided meaningful inspiration and hope during the war years for countless millions. Now, in what was perhaps the last of many such fine orations,

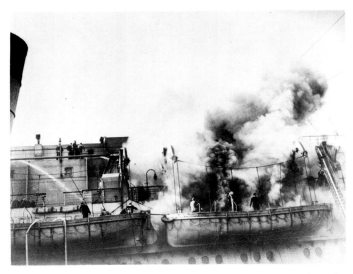

Two days before her demobilisation a fire broke out on board the liner. Firefighters and their equipment were lifted to Boat Deck level using the ship's boats as lifts.

Imperial War Museum

he was quietly exiting the world's stage, leaving behind his final encouraging words of peace.

During the recent conflict the *Queen Elizabeth* had carried much valuable cargo (other than for 750,000 troops, as Commodore Bisset was proud of relating). After safely delivering Winston Churchill to American shores the liner returned to Southampton carrying one of the most priceless pieces of cargo that she had ever carried – the Lincoln Cathedral copy of the Magna Carta.

Stored in a copper lined metal case it was due to be stored in a safety deposit box placed within the liner's strong room. Unfortunately the deposit box was just half-an-inch too large to fit into the assigned strong room safe so Commodore Bisset decided on another place of safe storage-in his own cabin under his bed!

The *Lizzie* made two further trips to New York repatriating Canadian troops.

On 6th March, when the liner arrived back in Southampton, the Ministry of War Transport announced that the *Queen Elizabeth* would be the first ocean going passenger ship to be released from His Majesty's Government service. She was to become to a post-war Britain what the *Mary* had represented to the country after the Great Depression – a national symbol of recovery from adversity.

For the *Lizzie* the war was over. Together, the *Queens'* war records stood second to none. Sir Percy Bates said that he liked to think that the *Queens* had, by their troop carrying capacities, shortened the war by a whole year. Churchill agreed, succinctly summing up the Cunard liners' important contribution:

'Built for the arts of peace and to link the Old World with the New, the *Queens* challenged the fury of Hitlerism in the Battle of the Atlantic. At a speed never before realised in war, they carried over a million men to defend the liberties of civilisation.

'Often whole divisions at a time were moved by each ship. Vital decisions depended upon their ability continuously to elude the enemy, and without their aid the day of final victory must unquestionably have been postponed. To the men who contributed to the success of our operations in the years of peril, and to those who brought these two

The *Queen Elizabeth* was transformed from a drab troopship into the world's most luxurious liner whilst laying at anchor at the Tail o' the Bank. Thousands of men and tons of equipment were ferried out to her. The Royal Navy's newest battleship, HMS *Vanguard*, is seen passing the moored liner *en-route* from completion at John Brown's shipyard to her own trials.

George Outram & Co Ltd, Glasgow

great ships into existence, the world owes a debt that it will not be easy to measure.'

So much for the cynics who, in the early days of the war, prophesied that the *Queens* would lie uselessly alongside their safe pier in New York for the duration of the war!

As a preliminary to the normality of peace that the *Queen Elizabeth* had not yet known, two hundred and fifty tons of fittings – including 10,000 standee bunks and 12,000 lifejackets – had already been taken off the ship in New York. Now, back in Britain, the major job of converting the liner into a passenger ship – including completing work that had been left unfinished by John Brown's in 1941 – was to be undertaken.

During the months preceding the end of the war Cunard and the shipyard had been corresponding, discussing the anticipated conversion. Timetables drawn up by Cunard were considered to be arbitrary by John Brown's as it had been tentatively agreed that the *Queen Elizabeth* should spend twelve weeks on the Clyde (at her old wartime anchorage off Gourock as she could not now reach the ship-yard) plus ten weeks alongside Berth 101 in Southampton's Western or 'New' Docks and in the King George V dry dock.

Half the ship's crew was paid-off and went on leave whilst around four hundred remained with the ship for maintenance, fire watch and to sail the ship on the coastwise journey to the Clyde.

But before any of the complex plans for conversion could be realised the *Queen*'s future was almost denied to her only two days before her release from active service.

The *Queen Elizabeth* had just come through five years of warfare and its aftermath relatively unscathed other than for the wear and tear of the active service on which she had been employed.

True, some minor attempts of sabotage had been made. Bombs had been found on board in New York in the early days of the war (these had been thrown overboard before it could be determined whether they were dummies or 'for real'); bottle caps had reportedly been found blocking hoses and holes had been drilled into some lifeboats. The *Queen*, however, escaped the sad fates of the *Normandie* and *Empress of Britain* and many other fine liners lost either through enemy action or accident.

But at 8.50 on the morning of Friday 8th March 1946, two waiters, Barlow and Cartright, saw smoke pouring from the one-time Isolation Hospital on the Promenade Deck. The hospital had not been used as such for some time and had recently been used as a medical store room containing, amongst other things, bottles of ether, methylated spirit and other inflammable substances. The room was also, apparently, the only room on the ship not to have been fitted with automatic sprinklers!

Fire bells alerted the Commodore and crew and, before fans could be shut off, smoke crept into the ventilation trunking, finding its way into other areas of the ship.

Fire doors were shut and the crew attempted to fight the fire with hoses connected to deck hydrants. But the smoke was too dense to get near the seat of the fire and the firefighters were few – many of the trained men having gone home on leave.

Within minutes, it seemed, fire appliances from Southampton's Fire Brigade arrived on the dockside; other units were called from surrounding towns in Hampshire and Wiltshire. Bournemouth, Salisbury, Winchester, Eastleigh, Totton, Lyndhurst, New Milton and Hythe sent engines to help fight what could easily become a major disaster. Fire floats from Southampton and the Isle of Wight were also alerted.

Other large liners were in the berths adjacent to the *Elizabeth* – the *Mary* and *Aquitania* were due in over the next few days – and, as sabotage was the initial summation, guards were brought into the docks.

As the dense smoke continued to billow into the sky from the threatened liner the shore firemen tried to reach the seat of the fire by using their telescopic ladders. Unfortunately the ladders could not reach high enough for the firemen to direct the water jets efficiently onto the seat of the fire. Luckily Commodore Sir James Bisset was a resourceful man and he ordered that the lifeboats in the vicinity of the fire be lowered; he then had the firemen, with their immediate equipment, clamber into them. The lifeboats were then hoisted to Promenade Deck level from where the firemen could easily tackle the fire from an effective point of attack.

Water was also played into the cabins and public rooms bordering the seat of fire in order to cool them. It took three hours to extinguish the blaze.

Damage sustained by the liner consisted of several heavy steel beams (supporting the Boat Deck) warping and bulging the deck above into a huge blister. Damage to other parts of the liner had been caused by smoke and water and the final cost of damage was £14,000 (in 1946 terms).

'Sabotage' was the favourite word of the day but, after studying photographs of the damage and the available evidence, Dr R. B. Firth (the UK's foremost fire expert who had been called in to investigate the fire) thought otherwise. He concluded that it had 'probably' been caused by a workman who had gone into the Isolation Hospital for a quiet smoke not noticing – or ignoring – the fumes emanating from a broken bottle of medical spirit!

The *Elizabeth* lay at Southampton with her small caretaker crew and three hundred men from John Brown's (there was a drastic shortage of local skilled men) on board taking off as much of the ship's wartime fittings – such as temporary toilets, wash stands, associated piping, etc. – prior to the ship sailing north for her major reconditioning.

On 30th March, she sailed, arriving and anchoring at Gourock the next day.

It was out of the question for the *Queen* to sail up the Clyde to the shipyard so it was planned that men and equipment would be ferried out to the liner as she lay anchored at the Tail.

The shipyard manager, William MacFarlane, would have preferred the *Queen* to have anchored alongside the jetty at Gareloch where direct rail access was available, but Cunard objected to the plan as, like Halifax, it would expose the liner to danger if a strong wind blew from a particular quarter.

Cunard's engineering department was concerned at the length of time that the *QE* would be anchored at the

Tail o' the Bank as the liner would need to have the engines, that were not under survey, running. This would enable the liner to be manoeuvred if necessary but it would also mean continuous operation that might place too great a strain on the machinery.

Cunard had allowed the shipyard just ten weeks to complete the mammoth task of restoring and completing the ship's structure – the largest ever such task to be completed afloat. In spite of the shipyard's protestations and pleas for more time it was done.

According to one estimate the liner had experienced the equivalent of 25 years of normal wear in five years because she had not had the chance of a proper overhaul and refit. The Ministry of War Transport would pay for the repair of the wear and tear of the war years to bring her back to her pre-war condition and John Brown's undertook to finish off those jobs interrupted by the liner's dash to a safe refuge. Cunard would pay for any extra work required to be done in addition to their original specifications.

One of the first jobs to be undertaken was to remove the de- gaussing coil and its protective steel-plate housing, to clear the hull ready for chipping and repainting. Wooden decks were replaced where damaged, panels smoothed down and repolished, kitchens refurbished and public rooms and cabins restored. Most striking of all, as the *QE*'s battledress of grey was chipped away and the hull given a coat of anti-corrosion paint, the liner was gradually painted (in stages from stem to stern) in gleaming Cunard colours: black hull, brilliant white superstructure and that marvellous deep orange funnel colouring surrounded by a broad black top with two thin black bands on the orange/red of the lower funnel. Thirty tons of paint was used in the restoration.

Two thousand portholes were also scraped clean of grey paint; four thousand miles of electrical cabling was checked, tested and renewed where necessary. Deep down in the ship firebricks were replaced in the boilers and thousands of turbine blades were surveyed.

Just abaft the bridge a structure, looking rather like a water-tower, was removed. This, as on the *Mary*, had contained an early type of radar equipment, amongst the first to be fitted to merchant ships.

To achieve all this restoration work two thousand 'Bankies' had to be ferried out to the ship as she lay at the Tail along with all the equipment and materials that they needed.

The refit was not free from labour troubles. As the *Queen Elizabeth* would finally be fitted-out with her furnishings in Southampton the Scottish joiners reckoned that they should be paid at the same rate as their Southern counterparts. Cunard resisted the idea on the supposition that other unions would expect similar treatment. Another result would be detrimental increases in the cost of future new buildings.

The man directly in charge of the massive job of reconditioning the *Queen* was Shipyard Manager William McFarlane. He had been in a similar position during the construction of the *Mary* and would also oversee the post-war reconditioning of the elder ship in Southampton on her release from government service.

To further the completion of the *Elizabeth* he later came south to supervise the final stages of her restoration. The liner arrived back in Southampton on 16th June.

A thousand Clydebankers also came south to alleviate the acute shortage of local skilled labour. Two thousand people, all told, would be involved in the last, essential stages of fitting the *Queen Elizabeth* in her civilian finery.

During their stay in the south (a period which included the *Mary*'s refit between October 1946 and July 1947), the Scots were billeted in the hutments of Velmore Camp at Chandlers Ford. Each day they were bussed to and from the Docks by a fleet of thirty or so double-decker Corporation buses. One hundred female french polishers had also come south but they stayed nearer to the Docks, lodging in Portland Terrace near the city centre with its bombed Civic Centre.

The John Brown men were also entertained. On one occasion Dr. Horace King (the local Member of Parliament) and his concert party did the honours.

A flurry of criticism emanating from uninformed quarters of the country deplored the channelling of precious post-war resources and materials into the purpose of transporting a privileged few in luxury. The Times thundered to the rescue in defence of Cunard by reprinting its pre-war 'special' about the *Queen Elizabeth* which showed that the material being used in the liner had been in existence since before the war and that any new input into the liner using scarce post-war materials would be kept to a minimum.

The revitalizing of the *Queen* became the focal point of Britain's recovery from the human, material and financial ravages of war. She was the first British liner to be restored; she became, in essence, a Ship of State. She became 'The Wonder Ship'.

During her conversion for war the *Elizabeth* had undergone various refits to prepare her for troopship duties and unnecessary items of her peacetime outfit were removed and sent ashore. So it was that furniture and fittings from the liner found refuge in New York, Singapore and Sydney.

All these globally scattered fittings had to be brought to Southampton for refurbishment, assembly, sorting and fitting. The old *Aquitania* brought much of it from storage in New York directly to Southampton and those items stored in Sydney were returned via Liverpool where they were temporarily stored at Pilsworth in Lancashire. Fittings which had been intended for the *Queen* but had had their installation interrupted by the war had been stored at Brockenhurst and Lymington in the New Forest and at Woolston near Southampton for the duration of the war.

All the items were collated, processed and stored in two large aircraft hangars at Eastleigh on the outskirts of Southampton prior to being transported to the *Queen Elizabeth* and installed in their proper places as she lay alongside Berth 101.

Over 21,000 pieces of furniture were fitted into the liner. 4,500 settees, chairs and tables; 4,000 mattresses; 50,000 items of bed and table linen; 6,000 curtains which represented three miles of material; six miles or 2,000 carpets and rugs; and 1,500 wardrobes and dressing tables were included amongst the restored items.

Works of art were also renovated by the original artists and, in some cases, replaced where the original had 'disappeared' during her days as a troopship. The liner was also fitted with three radar sets of varying ranges, supplied by the electrical firm of Cossor.

On 7th August, the *Queen* went into the King George V dry dock, her entry being postponed for twelve hours because of strong winds.

Her 140 ton rudder was inspected (internally, as well as externally, as access doors had been built into the structure); propellers removed and cleaned; the underwater hull cleaned and painted; anchors tested; and each link of the anchor chain that had been spilled on to the dock bottom was tested and painted.

In total the reconversion had cost £1 million.

Sir Percy Bates visited the ship before she sailed from Southampton on 6th October once more for the Clyde for speed trials, adjusting her compass and testing other equipment at the Nab en route. Sir Percy told Commodore Bisset, retained after retirement to take the liner on her maiden voyage, that Her Majesty Queen Elizabeth would visit the liner at the Tail o' the Bank and remain on board for the measured-mile trials in the Firth of Clyde and that the maiden voyage had been arranged for 16th October.

Sir Percy added, 'We do not expect you to attempt to make speed records either on the trials or on the maiden voyage. The *Queen Mary* still holds the Blue Riband with her eastbound crossing in 1938 at 31.69 knots, and that is quite good enough! We shall be satisfied with crossings in four and a half days, more or less, according to the weather, at average speeds of from 27 to 29 knots, without driving the ships at their utmost speeds ....'

For the two *Queens* to race against one another would not only make commercial nonsense but it would also be a waste of fuel.

After the brief adjustments in the Channel the *Queen* headed north for the Firth of Clyde where she arrived three hours late because of fog early in the morning of 7th October. Sir James took his ship over the measured mile and satisfied himself that she could comfortably achieve 'over 30 knots without straining'.

Anchoring off Gourock at 11 am a party of distinguished guests came on board in readiness for the embarkation of the Royal party the next day. The guests included Sir Percy Bates and his wife; various Cunard directors – also accompanied by their wives; the Minister of Transport, the Right Honourable Alfred Barnes, and Mrs Barnes; Lord Aberconway, Chairman of John Brown Limited, and Lady Aberconway; and several senior officers and heads of departments of the Cunard White Star Line. These included G. M. Paterson, Naval Architect; J. Austin, Superintendent Engineer; and the Chief Marine Superintendent, Captain B.H. Davies. These men, amongst others, were on board to receive the thanks of country and company for the enormous amount of work and worry that they and their teams (probably all fuming because they had not been invited!) had put in to make the whole magnificent project possible.

The guests much admired the scale and detail of the finished liner as they toured the public rooms and peeked

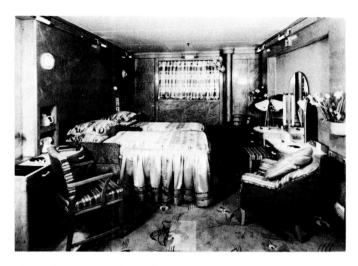

Over the period of refurbishment the liner's appointments were restored to the intended pre-war standards. This First (ex-Cabin) Class stateroom reflects the comfort to be found on board.

After the war rationing still continued in Britain so passengers were delighted to find articles freely available in the ship's shops that were as yet unobtainable or scarce in the mother country.

Both photos The University Archives, the University of Liverpool

into cabins. They admired the marquetry, the polish, the carpets and the feeling of freedom and peace not experienced for many years, all beautifully embodied in this symbol of Britain's determination to win the peace as well as the war.

Sir Percy Bates went ashore the next morning to meet the Royal Party at the start of a carefully timetabled day.

On board, the Commodore, noticing Doctor Maguire's white gloves, realised that he did not possess a pair, so the doctor gave his to Sir James. Lionel Carine, the purser, then gave one of his gloves to the doctor and hoped that nobody would notice that they were holding only one glove each!

The restored First Class Restaurant on 'R' deck.

The University Archives, the University of Liverpool

After disembarking from the Royal train at Greenock Station at 10.30 am, the Queen and her two daughters, Elizabeth and Margaret Rose, were escorted to the gangway of the Clyde steamer *Queen Mary II* laying alongside Prince's Pier. Sir Percy Bates met the Royal party at the foot of the gangway and the ferry's skipper, Captain McGlasham, received the expanded party at the top.

As the ferry pulled away the Queen, responding to the cheers of the crowd of spectators on the pier, asked that the steamer be turned round to make a second pass by the pier to give the loyal Scots a better view of 'their' Queen.

During the short trip out to the liner Sir Percy showed Her Majesty the portrait of H.M. Queen Mary that was hung in the tender's lounge. This portrait had been presented by Cunard–White Star as a token of appreciation for the small ship giving up her name in favour of the mighty *Queen Mary*, then building on the Clyde. The smaller vessel then took on the suffix II.

The *Queen Mary II* arrived at the *Queen Elizabeth*'s anchorage and circumnavigated the huge liner which loomed above the smaller vessel.

The Chairman then led the Royal party on to the larger ship and presented the Commodore to his Royal guests. 'I have been looking forward to this moment so much' the Queen told Sir James. 'I have been watching the ship with great interest throughout the war.' The Commodore then presented his senior officers to the Queen who had a few words with each. The party then proceeded to the Promenade Deck where the Queen and the Princesses showed a great deal of interest in the names and initials that had been carved into the handrails by hundreds of GI's.

Commodore Bisset excused himself and disappeared to the Bridge while the Queen and the two Princesses were introduced to the Cunard Directors and other guests. A tour of the ship's main public rooms was then undertaken.

Meanwhile the liner, dressed overall and with the Royal Standard fluttering at her foremast head, weighed anchor and proceeded out to sea at 11.15.

Three quarters of an hour later Captain Wood, the Staff Captain, introduced H.M. the Queen to a group of the ship's leading ratings: Messrs Frogatt (Bo's'n), Mitchell (Carpenter), Kapper (Engine room Storekeeper), McAteer (Electrical Attendant), Evans (Chief Bedroom Steward) and Mrs Kilburn (Chief Stewardess) were all presented.

Danny McAteer, although described in the day's printed programme as an 'Electrical Attendant' preferred to refer to himself as a greaser, had been 'scrubbed and polished' by his mates with whom he was very popular and then given a tot of rum and a peppermint!

Commodore Sir James Bisset carefully watches a lifeboat drill. This rare photograph, although undated, could have been taken *en-route* between the Clyde and Southampton after the major post-war refurbishment.

Queen Elizabeth Historical Society

On being presented to the Queen he was so overcome that he could only stand there with tears in his eyes, so struck dumb by the occasion that he could not reply to Her Majesty's gentle questions.

The *Elizabeth* passed by the islands of Great and Little Cumbrae at 12.15, by which time her speed had been increased to 20 knots. By now the Queen and her daughters were freshening up in specially prepared suites on the Main Deck before taking cocktails (for the Queen) and lunch.

During luncheon the small island of Pladda at the southern tip of Arran appeared two miles to the north. Ten minutes after lunch, at 2.20 the liner began working up to 30 knots.

Lunch was followed by a short tour of the kitchens. Then, after another brief respite in their suites, the Royal family were escorted to the Bridge at 2.50 pm.

The two Princesses were each given a stop watch to time the liner's speed over the Measured Mile, (the mile was actually a two mile course with each mile marked out). The liner had by now been worked up to the desired speed. The Commodore explained to the party that he was not attempting to ascertain the liner's full speed but wanted to see what she could do with 175,000 h.p.

At 3 pm the *Queen Elizabeth* commenced her northward run in the brilliant sunshine and she covered the first mile in 2 minutes 1.3 seconds which gave a speed of 29,71 knots. The third marker was reached in 2 minutes 1.0 seconds, giving a speed of 29.75 knots.

The ship, completing her first run, turned in a great circle before heading on a southward course over the Measured Mile(s).

During the two minutes exactly that the liner took to cover the first part of the course (the second part of the course could not be accurately timed as the sun was reportedly so bright the mark on the second leg could not be taken), the Queen was invited to take the wheel under the guidance of Commodore Bisset who explained that the 140 ton rudder was controlled so precisely that the slightest movement of the wheel would affect the ship's course. After remarking how easy the wheel was, Her Majesty teased the Commodore 'You know, Commodore, I don't believe this wheel is really steering the ship at all.'

She then handed the wheel back to Quartermaster Campbell: 'I hope I am giving the ship back to you in good condition.'

On completion of the trials the Queen again toured the liner visiting the First Class Library (pre-war Cabin Class had now been renamed First), Observation Lounge, Gymnasium, Squash Racquet Court, First Class Swimming Pool, Turkish Bath and Doctor Maguire's Hospital.

A small crowd of crew members had gathered in the corridor and, as she left the Hospital, the Queen made straight for the group, chatting freely with them.

Meanwhile, after the speed runs, the Princesses had donned blue dust coats and gone down to the Engine Room where they were shown the machines by Chief Engineer John Swanson who had been on the vessel during her secret dash to New York.

Princess Elizabeth showed a special interest in the machinery as she had been a proficient motor mechanic during the war.

The *Queen Elizabeth*'s speed had been reduced to 25 knots after the trials and a course was set to take her back to the Clyde.

At 3.50 pm the huge steamer once again passed the Cumbraes at 20 knots on the inward journey and once again the Royals retired to their various suites until the liner anchored at 5 pm.

By 5.30 pm tenders had come alongside to take off the distinguished visitors and the smiling Queen gave that famous wave of her hand as she and the Princesses left the ship before returning to Balmoral.

Arriving at Southampton from the Clyde prior to her maiden voyage the *Queen Elizabeth* is about to pass the Royal Pier. Shortly afterwards she will pass the *Queen Mary* still in her battledress of grey, seen in the distant Western Docks.

Stewart Bale Ltd/Queen Elizabeth Historical Society

The next day four hundred guests embarked for a festive journey south to Southampton and, after bidding farewell to the Clyde, the *Queen* sailed at 8 pm.

In the Irish Sea a small coastal collier was seen wallowing along at all of 6 knots. The small vessel's skipper hoisted a flag-signal:

'What ship is that?'

As required by law the Commodore obligingly raised the Cunarder's recognition flags 'GBSS'

The floodlit *Queen Elizabeth* docked in Southampton at 11 pm on 10th October. The passengers landed – except for one man apparently ill in his stateroom. Surgeon Maquire was summoned and gave the Commodore his diagnosis: 'He'll be all right tomorrow. He's suffering from blood in his alcohol stream!'

The next day Sir Percy Bates and Sir James Bisset entertained to lunch on board many members of Parliament from both Houses including the Lord Chancellor and the Speaker of the House of Commons. Alan Patrick Herbert, writer and poet, was also invited. Already booked for the maiden voyage he had written a poem in readiness for the occasion: 'Bon Voyage.

'At last young giant, infant of the fleet,

Your medals on, you sail down Civvy Street:
And may you serve the peaceful folk you bring
As well, as nobly, as you served the King!
Here come your passengers; but who will check
The ghosts of soldiers crowding on your deck?'

Another writer summed up the impact that the *Queen* was making on a war-torn Britain (about to face several more years of hardship and rationing) when he wrote of the ship:

'... gleaming like a yacht, vast like a city, towering over the dockside in her enormous grace ... Where once she was grey and secret, now she is carnival with lights. Where once she was stark and stripped, now she is gay and opulent with the warm extravagance of luxury. She is the ultimate in liners, the greatest ship in the world!'

Stocked with food and cigarettes that, being unobtainable in Britain, had been brought over from the States on the ever-faithful *Aquitania*, the *Queen* was ready for her symbolic debut, tangible proof that 'Britain Can Make It' (the name of a manufacturing and trade exhibition that would show the world that the country was now ready to 'win the peace'). But before the liner sailed the Cunard–White Star Line would suffer an unhappy loss.

Chapter Eight

".... Thank You to This Englishman."

The *Queen Elizabeth* was about to depart on her maiden voyage becoming as she did so the first British liner to be both reconverted from war duty and the first to start a regular post-war passenger service.

Among the first to board the liner in readiness for this gala occasion were the well-known British band leaders Bert Ambrose and his wife; Geraldo and his wife; Mr and Mrs Jack Hylton; and the singer Miss Frances Day (she had been on the maiden voyage of the *Queen Mary*).

On Tuesday 15th October 1946, six boat-train specials (drawn by a 'Merchant Navy' – class locomotive) left London's Waterloo Station bringing Tourist Class passengers down to Southampton.

The following day was sailing day and Sir Percy Bates was due to witness the departure from Waterloo of the 10.15 am Pullman Boat Train taking First Class passengers to the ship. Pulled by another locomotive of the 'Merchant Navy' class and appropriately named 'Cunard–White Star', the locomotive was fitted with a special headboard declaring 'RMS *Queen Elizabeth*'.

In all 2,228 passengers had booked for this prestigious premier voyage including some whose original booking for the ill-fated maiden voyage of 1941 had been cancelled.

But the plans of Sir Percy Bates were brought to an unexpectedly tragic end.

Suffering a heart attack, he had collapsed in his office on the day before the eagerly awaited sailing. His passage on the liner was cancelled (as was his wife's) and his luggage was taken ashore.

An announcement later appeared in the The Times (Thursday): 'On 16th October, at Hinderton Hall, Neston, Cheshire, Sir Percy Elly Bates, 4th Baronet, G.B.E. Greatly loved and loving husband of Mary Bates, aged 67 years. Funeral, Chidwall tomorrow (Friday) at 12 noon. No flowers, by request.'

On the very eve of the maiden voyage the cup of success had been dashed from the hands of the man who had made a long-cherished dream become a reality.

News of the chairman's death reached those on board by mid-morning and contrasted sharply with the high feeling of celebration that pervaded the liner, dockside and town.

Sir Percy's successor as chairman, his brother Fred Bates, requested that the company's houseflag flying at the liner's masthead should not be lowered to half-mast as

Sir Percy Elly Bates, chairman of Cunard-White Star and mastermind of the creation of the two *Queens*.

would normally be expected in such circumstances. Commodore Bisset concurred, saying that the late chairman, whom he admired greatly both as a businessman and a gentleman, would not have wished anything should mar the gala occasion.

However, Sir James said that he would hold an onboard service at the same time as Sir Percy's funeral. Southampton Corporation recognised the honour that Sir Percy's vision had bestowed upon their town and the flags at the Civic Centre were flown at half-mast in his memory.

As the sailing of the *Queen Elizabeth* signalled the beginning of a new era of peace, so another occurrence signalled the end of an era of evil that, in a long career of crime, had sought the *Queen*'s destruction. This was the suicide in his Nuremberg cell of Hermann Goering, erstwhile Reichsmarshal and henchman of the megalomaniacal architect of Nazism whose ego had destroyed Germany.

Among the passengers embarked for the maiden voyage (the escape to New York in 1940 was denied by Cunard as being a 'maiden voyage' – the ship was merely moving from one berth to another while still under construction!) were many distinguished people, eminent personages in the worlds of government, diplomacy, the arts and society.

Sir Hartley Shawcross, the British Attorney General and recent Chief Prosecutor at the Nuremberg trials of Nazi war criminals, was sailing with the ship.

Helena Rubinstein, queen of the cosmetics world, was on board and Ludwig Bemelmans, distinguished journalist of The New Yorker and ardent Atlantic traveller also graced the passenger list. Amongst the politicians on board U.S. Senator Conolly was returning from the Paris Peace Conference and the Czech M. Jan Masaryk was travelling in his official capacity to a meeting of Foreign Ministers to be held at the United Nations. The British Secretary of State for Air, Philip Baker, was perhaps interested in comparing sea travel with the still infantile air route across the Atlantic.

Two unpublicised passengers came aboard the ship just before sailing time. Their arrival was surrounded by such a high degree of security that passengers' visitors were not allowed on board for the *de-rigeur* bon-voyage parties.

The first was U.N. bound Soviet Foreign Minister M. Molotov. 'I have great admiration for this great ship,' he

Wrapped against the early autumn chill of the North Atlantic, First Class passengers relish the comfort of deckchairs during the maiden voyage.

Stewart Bale Ltd/Queen Elizabeth Historical Society

told the Commodore. He was accompanied by his comrade colleague Vishinsky.

Promptly at 2 pm under a grey sky but on a calm sea the *Queen Elizabeth* pulled away from the quayside. Lines of flags cascaded downwards at an angle from each masthead as the liner was coaxed into the River Test. In spite of the occasion no band played her away. The Docks and Marine Band had been cancelled because of the passing of Sir Percy Bates.

Seven tugs gently cajoled the *Queen* into the stream to escort her to where the Test blended with the River Itchen to form Southampton Water. The *Clausentum*, *Canute* and *Paladin* of Red Funnel and the *Sloyne*, *Gladstone*, *Wellington* and *Romsey* of the Alexander Towing Company Limited pulled, tugged and fussed about the liner until she was solidly pointing towards Calshot and the Isle of Wight.

Her departure certainly did not go un-noticed. Tens of cheering, waving thousands watched her glide down the Water and into the Solent. Passing the Calshot Spit light-vessel she followed the dredged channel between the Calshot and Brambles sandbanks as she turned first to starboard and then to port as she sailed by Cowes, alive with hundreds of sightseers and where the light caught her so well. Then past the headland of East Cowes with the turrets of Queen Victoria's beloved Osborne House peeping above the woodlands that cascaded down to the water's edge.

Passing through the waters of Spithead between Ryde and Portsmouth she exchanged signals with her Royal Navy namesake, HMS *Queen Elizabeth*, anchored in the resting place of naval ships since ancient days. During the war the two ships had met in the Red Sea and one of the famous

Passengers line the sun deck railings as the liner passes the Battery with the ever-impressive Manhattan skyline looming above it.

The University Archives, the University of Liverpool

136

stories of the sea had the then troopship signalling to the warship 'Snap!'

Escorting paddle steamers and myriads of other pleasure craft escorted her, ploughing the sea into white furrows. Low flying aircraft and a helicopter buzzed the liner as she in turn sounded her magnificent siren, a cloud of steam from the whistles on her forward funnel appearing seconds before that glorious, heart-stopping roar hit those on shore.

Sailing into the English Channel the liner headed straight for New York. This would mean missing a call at Cherbourg, but this was done on two counts: the French port was still in a state of disrepair and the *Elizabeth* was fully booked. Steaming in an arc well off the Isle of Wight she headed into the vast unpredictable expanses of the North Atlantic.

For two days the liner made good progress with a following easterly wind. M. Molotov visited the Commodore in his quarters where he was offered vodka. He gave the reply that would become well-known to the Western world over the next few years: 'No!' But, to another offer, 'Veesky? Yes! Very Good!'

Both men then visited the Bridge where Molotov took the wheel for a few moments.

On Friday the weather changed from the fine conditions experienced previously to a fierce north-westerly gale and a very rough sea and the ship slowed down to ride out the worst of the storm.

Commodore Bisset went ahead with the memorial service to Sir Percy Bates at 11 o'clock with many of the crew present and those passengers who wished to attend. He ordered that the ship's flag be flown at half-mast.

Sir James gave the address: 'Sir Percy Bates was mainly responsible for building two great vessels. He watched them grow from masses of steel plates and girders, children of his brain, lived for them, worked for them and, alas, died for them. He was a man of great integrity, strong purpose and sympathetic understanding. All who worked for him and with him felt that they had lost a firm valuable friend. He loved the sea, loved ships, and loved those who went down to the sea in ships and did business in great waters.'

The Commodore then read Tennyson's poem 'Crossing the Bar', which had moved him so much when it was read at the funeral of another Cunard skipper, Sir James Charles of the *Aquitania*. Sir James had died of a 'broken heart' as he arrived at Southampton before leaving his beloved ship for retirement. Sir Percy's favourite hymn 'Praise, My Soul, the King of Heaven' was also sung, accompanied by the ship's orchestra.

Passenger Sir Warren Fisher summed up the greater influence of Sir Percy's life, beginning with these evocative words: 'Our country may well say thank you to this Englishman...'

Because of a strike by tug-boat men in New York there was a possibility that the *Queen* would be diverted to Halifax. But perhaps because of his experience with Halifax in the past and of the prestigious nature of the maiden arrival of the first passenger liner to enter New York since the war's end, Sir James decided to head for his original destination and dock the *Lizzie* without tugs, if need be, as

the *Queen Mary* had done in pre-war days.

The *QE*'s reserve of power came in useful in making up the time lost by Friday's storm. Ironically, her speed had to be decreased to 10 knots as she approached the New England coast as otherwise she would have arrived too early.

4 days, 16 hours and 18 minutes after passing the Bishop Rock in the English Channel, the *Queen* steamed by the Sandy Hook light just before dawn. She had averaged 27.99 knots and the Commodore later told reporters that the vessel had 'Performed beautifully – just like a sewing machine.'

The day was, appropriately enough, Trafalgar Day – 21st October. The pilot boarded and, once in the Lower Bay, the *Lizzie* anchored off quarantine using her specially installed bower anchor.

She remained anchored for two hours during which time a reception committee came on board headed by New York's 'Official Welcomer'. A hundred and fifty reporters and photographers boarded (80 had travelled westwards with the liner including Jack Frost of the Telegraph) most of whom wanted to interview Molotov. His cabin proved to be too cramped for the press conference so he took his interviewers to the Sun Deck. Perhaps he wanted to see the Manhattan skyline as the ship approached it or perhaps he wanted to show off the ship which had impressed him so much.

Port officials also boarded but many of the immigration formalities had already been settled during the voyage: an officer had travelled with the ship processing around 1,600 documents a day.

The City of New York was delighted to receive the *Queen Elizabeth* on this her commercial debut as she represented, even more so than during the war, employment and profit for hundreds of its citizens, now and for the years to come.

Ships afloat and factories ashore joined in the cacophony of sound that greeted the blimp-escorted, flag-strewn liner as she passed through the confines of the Hudson River on a beautifully sunny morning. 83,000 tons of magnificent proof that the situation in Europe was about to return to normal, progressed regally towards Pier 90 where she docked just before 8 am.

Under heavy guard an unsmiling Molotov was one of the first to leave the ship, being met by an equally unsmiling Andrei Gromyko, then a young Soviet delegate to the UN.

One of the first to board the ship was the mayor of New York, Vincent Impellitteri.

Ten thousand people paid $1 each to tour the liner over the next few days, the monies going to British and American seamen's charities. Amongst the visitors were many ex-GI's who wanted to show their families where they had slept and ate during their transportation to the battle zones. A few even found their carved initials still intact in the teak railings.

The liner stayed in New York, replenishing her stores and entertaining many, for four days until the 5th when, at 6 am, she sailed, bound for England.

On this second leg of her maiden voyage she carried the first two stowaways of her career. The first, ex-GI

With Jersey City in the background the *Queen* is carefully guided into her berth at the end of her maiden voyage.

The University Archives, the University of Liverpool

Kingsley Foster, was eager to join his war-bride and baby in England; the second was a young Canadian, John Dick, who was eager, for some reason, to get a job in Manchester.

The Cunard tried to dissuade the passengers who wanted to contribute towards the two men's fares; they said it would encourage further such attempts in the future. But the passengers had their way although the two men concerned were locked up for a short while as the ship approached English shores.

The *Queen* made the return trip in 5 days 3 hours arriving in her home port at 2 am on the last day of the month.

Ten thousand pieces of luggage were unloaded and Sir James Bisset told a reporter from Southampton's own Evening Echo that the *Queen Elizabeth* could 'not possibly have begun life as a passenger liner under happier auspices'.

The next sailing from Southampton – on 6th November, – set the seal on the liner's reputation as a favourite of the elite when the Duke and Duchess of Windsor sailed with the ship. They had embarked the evening before.

During this particular trip the Commodore conducted Divine Service, as was the usual practice when a Sunday was spent at sea.

The Duke and Duchess were in the congregation and as Sir James began to read Psalm 146 he realised that a particular passage might cause Britain's ex-King, and the woman for whom he had given up his throne, some embarrassment:

'O, put not your trust in princes, nor in any child of man: for there is no help in them!'

Reporters on board cornered Sir James after the service and asked him whether the inclusion of that particular Psalm had been intentional. The Commodore replied in the negative and it took all his powers of persuasion to dissuade the newspapermen from reporting the incident.

As the year grew old, so the liner's honeymoon with the Atlantic came to an end as the winter season brought forth its usual breed of storms.

A particularly stormy encounter with the ocean occurred at the beginning of December 1946. Forty-foot waves left four passengers with broken limbs and twenty-two others with lesser injuries.

But as the liner passed the Bishop Rock on the evening of Tuesday 3rd, a baby daughter was born to Mrs Joan Toley. Commodore Bisset christened the baby a few hours later – Elizabeth Dawn.

The *Queen* would encounter many storms during her voyage – especially during the winter months – and it would not be until the mid-fifties that anything would be done to alleviate the problem.

In the first few months of the *Elizabeth*'s service – up until the end of 1946 – the liner crossed the Atlantic nine times and carried a total of 11,000 passengers westward and 9,000 east to Europe.

Her popularity for the years to come was assured.

Chapter Nine
A Large Withdrawal From The Bank!

Commodore Bisset retired from the Cunard in January 1947, handing over command of the world's largest liner to Captain Charles Ford.

Tall and imposing, Captain Ford had commanded the *Elizabeth* on several occasions during the war, substituting for the Commodore as relief captain whilst the latter went ashore on leave.

Captain Ford would eventually be dubbed 'Foggy Ford' by his crew; ships which he commanded encountered

Staff Captain Thelwell was on the bridge with 'Foggy' Ford and as they approached the shores of the Isle of Wight, Thelwell said: 'I take a bet that none of the appropriate pilots are available'.

On arriving at the Nab the liner was slowed to pick up her pilot and, as the Staff Captain had guessed, it was not her usual pilot, Captain Bowyer, who stepped on board but a substitute, F.G. Dawson.

Although having spent many years with Trinity House

RMS *Queen Elizabeth* outward bound down Southampton Water having just passed the River Hamble and Warsash.

Author's collection

fog in New York on no fewer than thirteen consecutive occasions!

Three months after taking over command of the *Queen Elizabeth* Captain Ford faced an entirely different problem, one that could have finished his career at sea as well as his ship. Leaving the French coast on 14th April 1947, the liner headed towards Southampton – and home – with 2,246 passengers on board.

Unfortunately a thick fog lay on the channel and visibility was down to almost zero.

as a pilot, Dawson had no experience of handling ships as large as the *Queens* which was why Cunard had their chosen pilots to do the work. (Captain Bowyer had previously taken another ship out and had been unable to return to his station because of the weather.)

During the day the troopship *Ranchi* had had to anchor three times in the fog while trying to navigate the Solent and a small Panamanian collier, the *Georgic* of 6,000 tons, had gone aground off St. Catherine's Point at the southern tip of the Isle of Wight.

Above: Watching the attempts to free the grounded *Queen* hundreds of spectators on the surrounding shorelines had their last view of the liner just before a mist obscured the moment of victory. *Frank O. Braynard collection*

Left: Surrounded by tugs and lighters the *Queen Elizabeth*'s bows remained embedded in sand for many hours.
"The Wonderful Story of the Sea"

As the *Queen* progressed through Spithead the fog thinned and a late afternoon sun began to shine through the remaining haze.

Off Cowes the *Elizabeth* turned to starboard to bring her into the Thorn Channel, dredged between the Brambles and Calshot sandbanks.

Senior First Officer Geoffrey Marr – having changed into his shore clothes (other than for his uniform jacket, navy-blue raincoat and cap) – was at his docking post on the after docking bridge.

When the liner was halfway between her first turning point off Cowes and the second at Calshot that would bring her into the entrance of Southampton Water, Staff Captain Thelwell asked the officer of the watch: 'How's it going?' 'About halfway to Calshot lightvessel', came the reply.

From his post aft, Geoffrey Marr saw that the liner was far from safe. Looking forward along the whole length of the ship – which gave him a good idea of how well she was swinging – he could see that the ship, travelling at around 6 to 8 knots, was not keeping to the designated

The operational headquarters of the *Lizzie* – her Bridge. Full of gleaming brass, copper, white enamel paint and varnish this small area experienced many anxious moments. Note the four telegraphs – one for each Engine Room.

Collection of Louis O. Gorman/Queen Elizabeth Historical Society

channel. This fear was confirmed when the liner passed a buoy on the wrong side.

On the bridge the Captain voiced his own fears: 'I don't think we'll make the West approach channel, Pilot. She's turning too slowly.'

The pilot reassured the captain that all was well and continued to navigate the ship.

Suddenly the Captain ordered 'half astern on the starboard engines!' (the liner's port and starboard engines were used to help manoeuvre the ship on difficult bends), but it was too late.

Meanwhile, eighty feet below the bridge, a small motorboat – the *White Lady* out of Cowes – was bobbing around on the Solent.

Archie and Beatrice Turner (of the 'Mayflower' public house in the Island yachting and shipbuilding town) had decided to take their daughter Patricia and some friends out to see the *QE*'s arrival at close quarters instead of from the seafront at Cowes, always a vantage point from which to watch ships passing to and from Southampton.

Whilst waiting at what Archie Turner considered to be a safe point off Calshot, he and his companions were concerned to witness the huge liner practically cut across the bows of their launch.

This experience, frightening in itself, was followed by the *QE* gently coming to a halt. As she did so the occupants

of the motor-boat heard a loud crashing noise as giant propellers thrashed the shallow water into billowing clouds of yellow and black as sand and mud were churned up from the sea bed.

On the Bridge of the liner there was the faint sensation of a slight, lurching jolt which some on board never even felt. The ship shuddered slightly as the forward momentum of the vessel slowed and pushed the bows deeper into the mud.

Somebody said 'We're aground.'

The first indication that many on board had of the grounding was that the shoreline bordering the Solent had stopped 'moving'.

The gentleness of the sensation of grounding also seemed to decrease the further down in the ship that one was sited. On watch in the engine room the Second Engineer remembered a loud scraping noise as the liner dug her nose deeper into the gravel.

The Captain ordered 'Reverse engines' – but to no avail; the liner would not budge. To avoid sucking silt into the underwater inlets the engines were stopped until help became available.

Underwater the *Lizzie* was embedded in mud to a point just below the bridge.

By coincidence she had grounded in almost the same geographical spot that the *Aquitania* had done so, ten years previously almost to the day.

A signal for assistance was sent and – within an hour – company, port and salvage officials were aboard and in conference with the captain.

The tender *Romsey* which had brought the officials out to the stricken ship tried, meanwhile, a solo attempt at pulling the liner off the bank – but the towing line parted under the unequal strain.

By six the next morning, thirteen tugs had arrived from Southampton, Portsmouth Dockyard and Poole and were made fast using the liner's manila ropes. With two tugs in tandem on some of the ropes which were attached to the liner's seven after bollards the first attempt to release the liner from the grip of the mud was made.

Water ballast had been pumped overboard to lighten the ship forward and to lift her bow; little oil remained to be removed after the transatlantic journey, but a barge arrived alongside to take it off if necessary.

The salvage attempt at the first available high tide failed and the *Elizabeth* had to wait until the next day when another suitable tide would occur.

The second attempt at salvage was directed once again by signals given on the liner's whistles with toots of acknowledgement blown in response by the tugs.

With twelve tugs on the ropes and two more tugs on each side of the liner, she was pulled first to port for fifteen minutes, then, on a signal, to starboard for a similar period, thus waggling the ship in slow motion like a giant tooth waiting to be pulled. The treatment worked as a slight movement could be felt as the restraining grip of the mud's suction was broken.

At 8.40 pm on the evening of Tuesday 15th April, with an increasing fog which gradually obscured the lovely evening light that had hitherto illuminated the scene, and on the third 'waggle' the ship's engines joined in the struggle. The ship slid out of her temporary prison, dark smoke streaming from her funnels.

Amidst the cheers from those on board, the liner's freed bows were taken into control by the tugs which had hurriedly scampered forward.

Hearing the whistle booming out from the liberated liner, cheers also went up from the crowds on shore. Thousands of sightseers lined the shore at Calshot, many coming from miles away in coach specials, to see the spectacle; amongst the crowd was retired Chief Engineer John Swanson who thoroughly enjoyed the excitement – and told the Echo's reporter so!

Two more blasts on her whistles indicated that the liner was under her own power but, because of the fog, the spectators on shore could only guess that she was not going to try to reach Southampton that night. They were right; the liner replenished her ballast and retraced her wake of twenty six hours previously, anchoring overnight a few miles away to the south in Cowes Roads.

The next morning she steamed into Southampton – fifty hours late!

A lot of baggage had been sent ashore during the attempt to lighten the ship and her First Class passengers had also been disembarked at 4 pm on the 15th via two local paddle steamers – the *Solent Queen* of Red Funnel and Southern Railway's *Merstone*.

Amongst the First Class travellers were the Duke of Marlborough, Lady Peel (better known as Bea Lillie, the film actress), playwright Terence Rattigan and Randolph Churchill – journalist and son of Britain's victorious wartime leader.

Bea Lillie had been photographed waving obligingly over the ship's side during the period of grounding by an enterprising photographer who had worked his way on to one of the tugs. But Randolph Churchill had no reason to be cheery. He was furious!

As an 'on the spot' journalist his opportunity of a 'scoop' on a story that would make headlines had been thwarted.

After the grounding Churchill found his way to the Bridge – the 'holy of holies' where passengers were definitely not allowed – but Captain Ford refused to give him an interview. Churchill was just 'another passenger' – as far as the captain was concerned – who might just get in the way at that particularly worrying time.

But, in spite of being gently 'warned-off' even by the Staff Captain, the journalist was not to be deterred, He tried once more – and then again as his newspaper clamoured for a story.

Randolph Churchill's frustration was aggravated even further when the radio room was closed down on orders soon after the grounding and his telegram was refused acceptance. This 'unwarranted censorship' that one would have expected only under wartime conditions was later lifted but, even then, only short messages were accepted. Even so, the telegram of one passenger that described the *Elizabeth* as being 'stuck' had the offending word changed to 'delayed'.

The problem of communication was further exacerbated by the ship not having a tannoy system. Passengers were not kept officially informed as to what was happening and many only received information – usually rumour – gleaned from individual crew members.

The day following the *Lizzie*'s delayed but jubilant arrival into Southampton, divers inspected the underwater hull for signs of damage.

Other than for silt found in some inlets there was very little evidence of the grounding. A fifty foot length of one-inch rope was also found to be coiled around a propeller, but otherwise nothing untoward was found in connection with the episode.

Internally the condensers and oil coolant inlets were cleared of shells and gravel but other than having her dignity affronted the *Queen* had come through her ordeal relatively unscathed.

She had however, been entered onto Lloyd's casualty list after refusing to accede to the tugs' first attempts to secure her release. Her hull, machinery and fittings were insured for just under £6 million, with a further value of £255,000 placed on her cargo and the announcement of her grounding was given 'star billing'.

But her reputation was undamaged and ten years of popularity and profit were set to follow.

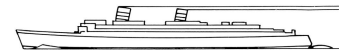

Chapter Ten

Jobs, Yarns And Cabin 52

The *Queen Mary*'s post-war refit in Southampton was completed and, on 1st August 1947, she joined her larger sister to commence the long delayed two-ship Atlantic express ferry service for which they had both been built.

The size, chic and romance of the two beautiful liners (combined with their heroic reputations and Cunard's publicity campaigns) would ensure that the liners would be well patronised, especially during the calmer summer months.

Commodores of the Cunard Line (but other than for Sir James Bisset and Sir Ivan Thompson, none had been bestowed with the knighthood that had been more-or-less customary before the war) – flew their flag on the company's flagship, the largest liner the world had ever seen. A relief captain, the 'bagman', would also act as relief for the captains of the *Queens* and *Mauretania*, the latter ship also acting as a substitute for whichever *Queen* was undergoing refit in dry-dock.

From Townley at the very beginning to Marr at the very end, a succession of skippers had made the 'Waterloo Elm' lined Captain's day-room their home. Caunce, Cove, Divers, Ford, Grattidge, Jones, MacLean, Morris, Snow, Sorrel, Thelwell, Thompson, Watts and Williams were amongst those who had enjoyed sovereignty over a mobile, thriving city of several thousand people. It was a combined hotel, town-hall and factory with the passengers as the guests, the captain and his staff as the management and administrators and the crew seeing to the needs of all those on board.

The 'municipal and industrial' employees under the captain's command changed with the years but a large proportion of the crew had made the sea, the *Queens*, their lives. Indeed, so jealously guarded were the prestigious and respected positions on the *Queens* that sons would find employment on board on the recommendation of their fathers.

During almost two decades following the end of the war, young men in Britain were 'called up' for two years' National Service in the armed forces. An alternative was the option to serve in the Merchant Navy (a vital task during conflict) and the prospect of earning £2 a week in the forces or to be well-paid in the merchant service proved to be a one-sided choice for many youngsters.

Some of the captains of the *Queens* would ultimately write their autobiographies giving accounts of life in perhaps the most famous – certainly the most glamorous – job in the world.

But as not much has been set down about the shipboard lives of other members of the crew, it may be useful to redress the balance – even if briefly.

The hotel staff, as they became known, included bedroom stewards, stewardesses and restaurant stewards – generally known as the waiters. These groups, having direct access to the passengers, were able to make a very lucrative living by supplementing a basic wage with the tips proffered by their well-attended charges, some of whom were generous in their làrgesse – some less so.

For their part the steward was expected, at the end of each voyage, to tip those who in turn supported him in the performance of his duties.

A bedroom steward for example would tip – perhaps £1 each – the linen keeper who provided him with fresh sheets, pillow-cases etc. for his cabins; the larder cook with whom he came to an agreement to feed him during the voyage (meals were taken anywhere convenient and usually eaten standing up as no special messes were available for stewards); he would also tip the 'Glory Hole' steward for waking him each morning and for making his bed (this janitor might serve 4 to 5 dormitories each sleeping 12 to 18 men each of whom would give him a similar tip), and so on.

A restaurant steward would also find tips were expected by the kitchen staff and storemen who provided him with the means for carrying out his duties.

Appointed Staff Chief Engineer of the *Lizzie* in 1964 and Chief Engineer in 1967, Stanley Tattershall had previously served in many of the company's ships. *R. Bruce Grice*

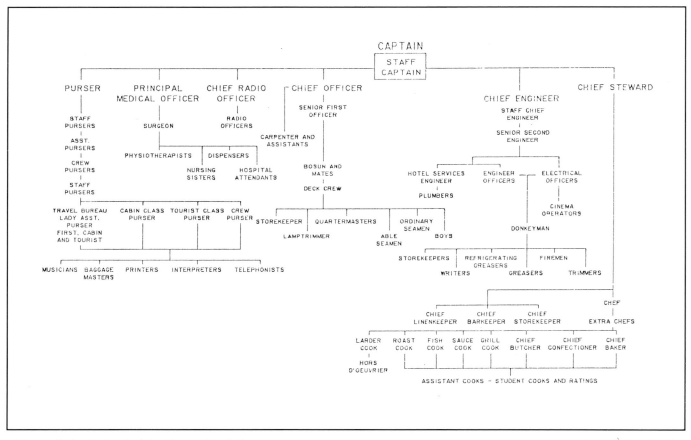

The staff 'family tree' of the *Queen Elizabeth*.   *Cunard/Gary Smith*

If a steward was inclined to be too covetous of his tips then he soon found that the enthusiasm of his back-up team fell away!

Tipping oiled the cogs of a well-run machine; it was the lifeblood of an efficient service. Passengers and crew alike were either 'good bloods' if they tipped well or 'bad bloods' if they did not.

The stewards and other ship's personnel dined on the same fare as the passengers and palates soon become bored with succulent roasts, etc. On making representations to the staff captain a quantity of corned beef was obtained but this somehow found its way to the officers' and pursers' tables. Not until the advent of the *QE2* would proper messes be provided with the 'home cooking' that the crew yearned for.

Through the infra-structure of the *Queens* a man could avail himself of a training that would stand him in good stead should he decide to leave the sea and set up business on shore. To have been a first class Cunard steward was in itself an assurance of excellence, and many such men still thank the Cunard for the experience received.

From bell-boy to Chief Bedroom Steward, there was a steady progression for the right man.

A young boy of fourteen years of age and of less than 5 foot in height (this height requirement was later changed as the school leaving age was increased to 15) could join the company as a bell-boy, undergoing eight weeks' training at the Sea School at Gravesend (usually during the liner's eight week annual winter lay-up and overhaul).

When the *Queen Elizabeth* first sailed after the war the bell-boys had been fitted with tailored uniforms of powder blue with silver piping; the uniform was later changed to maroon. A pill box hat (sometimes useful as an improvised football) was attached to a button on the jacket, and a loop was provided for the stowage of white gloves.

Rising at 5.30 am the boys would be given half- an-hour's PT on the Sun Deck followed by a quick cup of coffee and a change into uniform before breakfast at 7.20. The boys then lined up for inspection on 'R' deck which required personal cleanliness and a smart appearance.

Then it was time to start the day's various duties. A favourite was manning the doors to the First Class Restaurant as tips gleaned per voyage could be in the region of $200 to $300. One of the least popular assignments was duty in the Radio Room awaiting telegrams. Here tips were less frequent but on one west-bound trip a young bell-boy, James Collins (his autograph book always tucked into his tunic), was given a telegram – 'Deliver this to Bing Crosby'.

On its delivery the great singing star took the telegram from the silver tray, signed for it and said: 'Hang on, I've got something for you' and put $100 bill on the salver, the equivalent of several months wages.

A rise from bell-boy to commis waiter (assistant waiter) put a youngster on a course for gradual advancement. Waiters and bedroom stewards progressed upwards through Tourist, Cabin and First Class duties, gradually increasing their skills over the years until a top bedroom steward could be entrusted with his passengers' valuables and be relied on to perform discreetly any task demanded by his 'bloods'

A bedroom steward usually had a block of 44 passengers to look after in 2, 3 or 4 berth cabins.

On sailing days a passenger might hold a party in his or her cabin. Other than for delivering baskets of fruit or flowers (chocolate rabbits and eggs at Easter) to the cabin, the steward (or stewardess) might have to organise trays of canapes for the guests.

For these bon voyage parties Cunard would later find that they had to make a charge for their provisioning. Even so, it was reckoned that the number of parties being held decreased by only 25% from the usual two hundred or so before the charge was made.

It was not unusual for some well-wishers to celebrate a little too well and subsequently miss the last call for going ashore. The reluctant 'stowaway' might then have to be put off on to a tug or even on to the pilot vessel.

On board, some passengers could make difficult demands of their steward. Jim Jone recalls 'one well-heeled but ignorant' First Class passenger, the son of an eminent British jeweller, asking for a smoked salmon sandwich. Particularly difficult to cut in large slices smoked salmon was usually only used on canapes so the Chief Steward (who held the key to the cupboard in which the salmon was kept) asked Jim Jone 'Are you sure?' – 'Yes'. The cold-larder cook whose job it was to prepare the salmon was verbally colourfully less than receptive to the idea of having to slice such large portions.

But nothing was impossible in those days.

At the end of each trip the bedroom stewards would have to vacuum, polish and generally service the cabins in readiness for the next occupants. After each round voyage the portholes would be cleaned with brass rims being wire-wooled and polished to rid them of the effects of salt water. Other crew members who were not busy while in port might lend a hand for a $1 or so.

Accidents occurred at times, but one of the most amusing that happened on the *QE* occurred when a bedroom steward illegally emptied his vacuum bag through an open porthole.

Caught by the wind the contents of the bag were sucked into another open port serving one of the crews' toilets.

This was followed by a dust-covered and very irate chief bedroom steward emerging from the toilet spluttering and threatening vengeance on the perpetrator of the crime!

Part of a bedroom steward's duties was to clean the passageways outside the cabins under his charge. Kneelers and sponges had to be used for this job as the use of mops (sometimes bought ashore with the steward's own money) was considered a breach of discipline. Eventually the company relented and the 'undignified' kneelers were dispensed with.

A bell-boy's life at sea on a great liner could be rewarding in many ways. Here, young 15 year olds Jim Collins (left) and Kenny Ailing man the doors to the first class saloon.
James Collins

A trusted position to achieve was that of a first class bedroom steward. Jim Jone was one of the lucky ones. *Jim Jone*

A waiter, by the time he had progressed to the First Class Restaurant, was a man unequalled in his trade.

An expert at silver service, he could also carve a 40 pound turkey in five minutes, and joint a chicken into five portions in as many seconds! One of the more skilful jobs requiring much practice under expert supervision was to carve meat from the baron of beef contained within the 'Silver Bullet', a dome covered trolley wheeled from table to table in First Class. Cabin and Tourist classes had their meat ready served on a plate.

A waiter would also have other duties. Put in charge of condiments, napkins etc. he would be known as the 'Cruet King', 'Linen King', 'Fruit King' and so on.

Still in uniform, but in a party spirit, engineer Lovell Taylor 'lets rip' at one of the engineers' parties. *Lovell Taylor*

Catering for a small city was a continuous job. Trevor Jones prepares a side of beef for the following day meals.

R. Bruce Grice

It was a good lucrative life for many and one which was jealously guarded.

The crew who did not come into contact with the public were as proud of their jobs as those who did – even if they did grumble on occasion. But it seemed that every few years or so a bad element would manage to find employment on the *Queens* and the presence of such an individual or group of individuals could prove disruptive to the rest of the crew.

However, they were not tolerated and after an incident involving such a group, Commodore Marr refused to sail until the rough element was put ashore, in spite of union protestations.

These groups of men were known colloquially as 'Belfast Men' and once their games of 'Crown and Anchor' or other misdemeanours were discovered they received short shrift from the ship's Master-at-Arms and the company.

Off duty, the crew could fetch beer from the 'Pig and Whistle' and take it back to their 'Glory Hole' as the 'Pig' was not a very comfortable place in which to sit around: it tended to be draughty and the bench seats were hard.

Sometimes a singing star or comedian who was travelling as a passenger would come down to the 'Pig and Whistle' to entertain the crew. It was all summed up by Gracie Fields while travelling on the *Mary*: 'I'll sing f'lads f'nowt, but passengers can pay!'.

Ginger Rogers sang for the 'lads', as did Vera Lynn. Richard Burton and Alan Ladd drank with them. Comedian Frankie Howard gave a well-received performance and afterwards acknowledged the cheers with a deep bow, arm across waist. As he rose his arm waved in a rotating motion, fore and middle fingers extended in appreciation of his applauding audience!

Engineer Lovell Taylor (himself no mean trumpeter who enjoyed many a jazz-session on board) remembers Bob Hope going through his act for which Lovell formed part of the backing band. Lovell recalls:

'After a few bars of his signature tune 'Thanks for the Memory' Bob Hope starts off by saying:

'I've played in a lot of strange places in my time, but I've never played in a sewer before! Good evening rats!', and goes straight into one of his famous comedy routines. The crowds start roaring and stamping their feet, shouting for more'.

Bob Hope's act was followed by 'Jane', a crew member and one of the most famous amateur 'drag' artists afloat.

Of all the jobs on the ship, that of barman was perhaps one of the most lucrative. When on the rare occasion the job changed hands, it was accompanied by a covert payment of quite a large sum of money which, if they had been aware of the practice, those in authority would certainly have discouraged.

The seeking of this sought-after position came to an end when the Cunard complained that their profits from the bars were down. It transpired that the barmen had been buying their own cheaper liquor, keeping it under the bar and selling it in preference to the company's stock!

Even the customers of the 'Pig and Whistle' were not immune from 'private enterprise'. After a severe bout of sickness amongst the crew it transpired that plumbers had somehow managed to get sea water into fresh water pipes during a maintenance job. Unfortunately no one had told the 'Pig's' barman who had hitherto been regularly watering the beer.

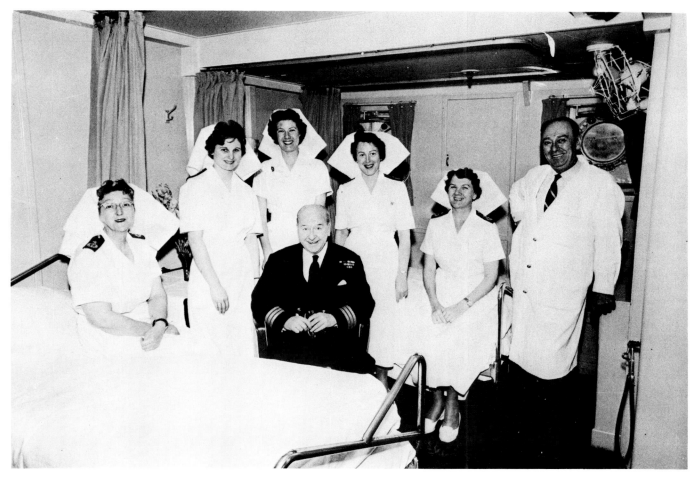

Ready with help and a smile. The *Lizzie*'s hospital staff.

The University Archives, the University of Liverpool

One crew member slightly avenged his mates. He was in the habit of using an innocuous tin mug for his pint of beer which he duly passed over the bar to be filled. One day a pint glass was filled by mistake and, on being transferred to the tin mug, the beer disappeared to well below the rim. His 'pint' mug had held almost 50% more.

Perhaps the most neglected of all the ship's company – the engineers – lived in a world of their own. Completely detached from the cash flow circulating above they had a unique humour and culture, regarding the rest of their 'shipmates' with a 'mutual but friendly contempt'.

The *Lizzie* was generally a popular ship with the crew, being more modern and easier to work than the *Mary*, but she did not fully attain the affection that the latter ship enjoyed.

But, even so, the *QE* was not generally well-liked amongst her engineers.

This was due in the most part to her boiler rooms. Very hot with temperatures sometimes reaching 150°F the huge boilers had to be carefully balanced when in port.

Whereas the *Queen Mary* had three Scotch boilers that had been installed solely to provide power to the ship's hotel services, the *Lizzie* had to use two of her twelve Yarrow type boilers (larger than the 24 similar ones on the

A newspaper was printed and delivered daily. The 'Ocean Times' succeeded the wartime 'The Elizabethan' in bringing the latest news.

The University Archives, the University of Liverpool

Above: World news, private messages, stock market prices, weather and company business were all received and sent from the Radio Room of the *Elizabeth*, call sign GBSS.

R. Bruce Grice

Left: Engineer and electrical officers during an evening in the Ward Room.

Lovell Taylor

A group of children in the play room with Helen Wiltshire.
Collection of Jim Jone

Mary) to perform the same function both at sea and in port.

This meant, in simple terms, that when the *QE* was due to sail or be docked, the other boilers had to be brought into or taken out of line with those already either under steam or 'cold', with a cross connection being made when pressures were equalised in all boilers.

Failure to ensure that the pressures were equal either way would lead either to a loss in pressure or blown safety valves!

Heating or shutting down the boilers was also a lengthy procedure. The *Mary*'s smaller boilers were very controllable and her engineers considered themselves unlucky if shut-down took more than an hour. But with a similar operation on the *Elizabeth* the larger boilers took anything from two and a half to four hours to perform.

Apart from the Staff Chief Engineer's frantic but futile efforts in trying to trace the origins of the aroma of baked potatoes ('Baked Idaho a'la Main Stop') cooking away on a piece of hot machinery in the Boiler Room, there are countless other more often than not humorous stories that tell of life down below.

The *Queen*'s position was often calculated by dead-reckoning and to do this the bridge would want to know the total engine revolutions as indicated by the Chadburn Counters sited on the Engine Room platforms below the board-mounted, brass-contained gauges.

The revolutions indicated by the counters did not always reflect the actual revolutions turned by the propeller shafts so the engineer on watch would sometimes use the palm of his hand to spin the counter round to obtain a more 'reasonable' reading.

On more than one occasion, after the removal of the cover plate and an application of an over-zealous hand, the counter wheels – plus various cogs and springs – scattered over the Engine Room platform floor!

(It was said of the Engine Room floor plates that the only decent de-greaser was locally brewed coffee!)

Six hours before sailing a warming through of engines would take place and, four hours later, the telegraphs and navigational equipment were tested, as were the ship's whistles. The engineers on watch gave a gradual feed of steam to the turbines. This was to prevent localised over-heating on the turbine blades and was usually done by bleeding steam into the ahead and astern inlets of each engine, thus cancelling out any tendency to move.

However, on carrying out the exercise on one particular night, a few hours before sailing the next morning, the 2nd Engineer said to the Junior 5th: 'Do you know what that 'clunk' was?'

The 'clunk' turned out to be the gear-box coupling taking up the load and the accompanying, increasing 'whirring' noise meant that the engines had 'gone live'. The liner was underway whilst still tied-up at the quayside!

Before the engines could be disengaged the *Queen Elizabeth*'s stern had swung away from the quay sufficiently enough to dislodge one of the after storing conveyers that spanned the water between ship and shore leaving it suspended from the open cargo port.

Once the ship was at sea and on course the steering power could be reduced and one or two of the three pumps could be shut down to economise on power.

On one voyage, just after leaving Cherbourg, the duty engineer stopped the electric motor driving one of the steering gear pumps and inadvertently mechanically disconnected the servo control of a 'live' pump.

As soon as this happened the error of his ways was dramatically revealed as the counter-weight of the live – but now uncontrolled – pump took over as a constant hydraulic flow in one direction took place.

This had the effect of pushing the rams, and consequently the rudder pintle, into a maximum position.

The result was a surprise to several hundred unsuspecting people on the ship, not least of all those on the Bridge, as the *Queen* angled over into one of the tightest high-speed turns of her career. One can only guess at the chaos in the restaurants where havoc must have been wreaked on beautifully laid tables.

Ivan ('Jack') Horner was on his first trip on the *Lizzie* – a green, junior lubrication engineer in the aft Engine Room. After the ship had left Southampton he came on watch and read the report left on the blackboard by the previous watch.

The Cabin Class swimming pool had, unusually, been filled whilst crossing the Channel and, for safety reasons, it was required that it had to be pumped-out before the *Elizabeth* reached Cherbourg. It was Jack's job to see that this was done.

Unfortunately no one had told the engineer that the steam (that circulated between the pool's base and the structure beneath to warm the water) had also to be turned off.

It was not long before a frantic and almost unintelligible swimming pool attendant telephoned the engine room: 'The swimming pool's blowing up! There goes a tile .... there's another!' as tiles erupted in small explosions from the overheated floor.

A never ending job was the baking of fresh bread and rolls.
The original brick ovens lasted throughout the liner's life.

R. Bruce Grice

In the main kitchen Senior Chef Coward checks on the boiling
of a ham.   *R. Bruce Grice*

Part of a greaser's job was to oil the many plummer blocks that transmitted the thrust of the propeller shafts into the forward or astern motion of the ship.

A few of these blocks were housed in the shaft tunnels extending out of the ship's side, terminating at the propellers. A very cramped space and, if an unwary greaser leant too far over, the rotating shaft would catch him and roll him over.

It was not unknown for the Engine Room to telephone the Bridge for permission to stop one shaft in order to retrieve a stranded – but wiser – greaser!

The more sociable of the engineers always enjoyed a good party whether it was their own or somebody else's.

The pursers usually extended a token invitation to 'one or two engineers' to attend their party but one day somebody in the pursers' department made a mistake and the invitation was addressed to 'The Engineers'.

As a consequence – and once it was known whisky was to be provided as well as beer - the engineers arrived in droves as they came off duty. The party was thus kept going for hours, the whisky arriving by the box!

The engineers' cabins were sited on the Sun Deck forward of the Verandah Grill, a lesson learnt from the *Mary* where accommodation was originally sited near the Engine Room. This had meant that the engineers did not see much sunlight – as well as being disturbed by the noise of the 'shop' when off duty – so additional accommodation was built over the Verandah Grill during an early refit.

Some of the least popular engineers' cabins on the *Elizabeth* were athwart-ships with the amidships expansion joint in the corridor floor outside. When the ship was 'working' during rough weather the joint would noisily creak away with each pitch of the ship's bow, keeping the slumbering engineers within the affected cabins awake.

The engineers' own parties were held in one of their cabins that became legendary (and notorious) – Cabin 52.

For some reason Cabin 52 was larger than most and proved to be ideal for the influx of engineers and guests that the parties attracted.

The ship's musicians were often invited to the gatherings, their music giving the proceedings an extra boost and, sometimes, musically talented members of the Engineering Department would join together to give an impromptu jazz-session.

One particular party in the cabin lasted for almost FOUR days with a change of personnel every few hours as duty called some away and relief brought in new faces or those who were returning for more.

The party came to an abrupt end when the Staff Chief called on the participants '... to pack it in!'

As a postscript, a disgruntled party-goer crept into the Staff's cabin at 4 am when the latter was asleep and activated a fire extinguisher. The doused 'Staff' swore that he heard the sound of fleeing footsteps receding towards a particular cabin. As a result three alleged culprits were marched before the Staff Captain and were later transferred to the *Mary*.

The real culprit, however, remained on the *Lizzie* until he struck again: annoyed by a squeaking segregation gate on the Sports Deck above him he hacksawed the offending item from its hinges and dropped the remains overboard.

He was soon apprehended because when he had collected the hacksaw with which to perpetrate the deed from a tool store he had signed for it in his own name!

A large storeroom also became another popular venue for crew gatherings. The room – normally used to store disassembled coffins – was rigged with coloured lights and other essential trappings and became known as 'The Coffin Club' entry to which was by specially printed membership cards.

Life for the crew on board of course was not a continuous succession of misdemeanours and parties although such incidents do provide many memories for some of the men who served on the *Queen Elizabeth.*

The passengers who filled the ship were, on the whole, unaware of the off-duty activities of the crew and the ship's reputation for efficiency and service remained unblemished. If they did know, then not a few smiles would have been raised.

Misfortune sometimes struck the liner and the crew, too, was not immune. On the morning of Trafalgar Day (21st October) 1953, during a routine lifeboat exercise in Southampton (that required selected lifeboats to be manned, lowered and raised again), number 26 boat was being retrieved from the water when it suddenly broke from its falls. As it fell it capsized, two men were catapulted into the sea and the falling boat collided with boat number 24, injuring the latter's tillerman.

Douglas Warsom, a twenty six year old waiter, dived from boat 24 and bravely rescued those who had fallen into the water. One of the men had received severe injuries and was later awarded £4,000 in compensation.

In spite of potential dangers the crew were always ready to enjoy themselves – even if a little foolhardily.

A young second Hors d'Oeuvrier, Martin Rowland, recalls one such incident that occurred during one of the *QE*'s cruising jaunts to the Caribbean during her twilight years:

Some of the crew had decided they would besport themselves with a little fishing. Attaching a ham to a meat hook which was connected, via a strong line, to a steam winch, their attempt at shark fishing was about to commence over the liner's stern. Before long one of these fearsome creatures was caught and the steam winch strained to haul it in. To prevent its anticipated thrashing on the after deck, a rather slow minded kitchen porter was attached to another rope and lowered over the side. His purpose was 'to clobber the shark with a club' before it could wreak havoc on board!

In their heyday the two *Queen*'s would spend two, three or four days in port during each turnaround. In Southampton this meant time at home with families or friends, but a similar time spent in New York might hang heavily once the excitement of being in that thriving city wore off after a few voyages.

However, many of the crew enjoyed a relationship with the city and its inhabitants. Many New Yorkers were enthraled by someone not only with an English accent but by one who also worked on the great liners.

Theatre, music and visiting American friends (perhaps made while on board) occupied the time of some, while others might be happy in buying $100 suits (ordered one trip and collected the next) that would impress the people at home.

Whilst in New York a crewman might find himself short of cash as, even after an allotment had been paid to his family, he was allowed to take only limited funds ashore.

A good method of obtaining money was to sell a pint of blood to a local hospital. One hospital gave $10 a pint but if the wrong establishment was chosen he would receive only an enamelled flag pin for his trouble.

Money could be made on board even in port. If the chance of winning the crew's own 'Nantucket Sweep' (the 'Nab Sweep' on the English side) was missed-where $1 bought a minute of an hour's estimated time that the ship would pass the sea mark ($1 per half minute in the similar Engine Room "Battery Sweep") – then a steward could act as a guide to eager American sightseers.

With twenty people in such a group each tipping $5 this could be a lucrative pursuit.

Whether or not the company approved was another matter as these guided tours could be expensive to the Line in terms of lost 'souvenirs'.

Apart from illegal dice games played furtively on board (or with dockers on either side of 'The Pond'), other, more imaginative, betting games were played.

One New Year's Eve found the *Queen Elizabeth* in New York so sixteen men joined in a $5-a-head race from the ship to the top of the Empire State Building with the winner taking all.

The crew also had their own benefit club into which anyone on board could pay one shilling (5p) a week. This donation entitled them to two pounds ten shillings (£2.50) a week for up to a year should they be unfortunate enough to be ill for that length of time.

Sports and social activities and interests were also encouraged on board. A special magazine, the '*QE*' was published and intership sports, such as the 'Atlantic Cup' for football, were hotly contested. Underprivileged children in Southampton were entertained during the winter overhaul with tea, American comics and a show, all paid for by the crew.

Whilst in New York some of the crew preferred to visit famous haunts such as 'Jack Dempsey's' or the 'Market Diner', an all- night establishment opposite Pier 90 and long regarded as a favourite of Cunard men.

Engineer Ian Baker recalls enjoying a drink with a friend in the 'Market Diner' when, looking out at the *Lizzie*, they saw that the liner was about to sail.

As they should have been on board they left their drinks, ran across the road, past a security guard and on to the Pier towards the last gangway.

The shouts of the security guard fell on deaf ears but the sound of gunshots and the sensation of bullets flying past them encouraged the two men to fall flat on the ground. The guard was then able to inspect their passes at ease!

Sometimes, as the *Queen Elizabeth*'s propellers started to churn up the murky riverbed ooze of the Hudson, a

Above: The starboard aft engine room platform showing ahead and astern manoeuvring valve control wheels, Bridge telegraph, Chadburn counter (to the left of the officer) and, to the right, the deck where the junior engineers wrote up their logs. *R. Bruce Grice*

Left: A junior engineering officer tops-up one of the plummer blocks that transmitted the thrust of the propeller shaft into motion. *R. Bruce Grice*

body, victim of murder or suicide, would float to the surface. One crewman recalls the gruesome sight of a New York policeman's body so appearing: the murdered man had disappeared several weeks previously.

The hygiene of foreign ships visiting their ports was a prime consideration to the American authorities and they were very conscientious in the performance of their duties.

On each arrival the 'Rat Man', as the crew called him, would arrive on board with his torch and mirror in readiness to inspect the *Elizabeth*'s kitchens. Heavy fines were liable should any food etc. be found under work benches. After one such complaint Cunard were requested that sills should be fitted over the spaces between bench and deck before the liner sailed.

This meant that deck tiling had to be chipped up, the sills fitted and then the tiles relaid.

The liner was also fined if she emitted too much smoke whilst in port. After receiving a vigorous telling-off for such a misdemeanour the Chief Engineer called his men up to his cabin so that he could pass on the admonishment he had received.

After doing so he must have felt sorry for the engineers standing before him, so he offered them a drink. Knowing that their chief was allowed a quota of spirits for which he did not pay, the men from the engine room asked for beer – for which he did! (Sailing across the Atlantic the Engine Room received a haughty call from the Bridge: 'Did you know there is black smoke coming from the funnels?' 'What colour did you expect it to be?' came an irate reply, 'Green?')

Over the years – especially those following the end of the war – there were luxuries and goods obtainable on board the liner or in the States, which were either unobtainable, scarce or far more expensive in the United Kingdom.

Tinned peaches were a luxury in the early days that could be taken ashore when going on leave as a treat for the family; Merchant Navy coupons were also available during the long period of post-war rationing, that enabled a crewman to buy extra warm clothing.

But some were never happy with the basic allowances and found that the only way to get extra cigarettes, nylons, ballpoint pens, etc, into Britain for their friends was to indulge in a little smuggling. Although a practice that could bring instant dismissal, many crew members could not resist the temptation but only a few would try to take it to the extreme.

With fashionable neckties in New York obtainable for $1 for 3; nylons at $6 per dozen pairs (which would sell for 3 guineas in the UK); US cigarettes at $1 per 200 carton which would sell for £1 in some Southampton pubs, the temptation often proved too great.

When the 'Rummage Squad', the Customs and Excise men, came on board with the pilot they would often search places like the Engine Room (the side plate of the steam condenser had to come off on one occasion with its hundreds of bolts having to be undone at first and then re-tightened) before the crew's accommodation was searched.

A couple of engineers wanted to get three thousand cigarettes ashore and decided to wait until they returned from two weeks' leave (as the Queen Elizabeth was laying up for her annual winter overhaul) before they took their 'booty' ashore.

Ninety-nine per cent of the time the liner's forward boiler rooms were used for maintaining in-port services, so the engineers concealed their packages in the after funnel casing.

Unfortunately for them a change in plans brought the after boilers into use, and by the time the two men returned from leave their contraband had been turned into dry brown tubes that crumbled to dust in their hands.

If, after the customs-men's search of the vessel, the crew's contraband was still intact, it had still to be taken through Dock Gate No. 4 where British Transport Police were on duty.

This proved to be less of a problem than it first seemed as a half-crown (12½p) coin concealed within the seaman's pass tendered for inspection ensured that his taxi would be waved through the gate. A lack of the two-and-sixpenny incentive would lead to the taxi and its passenger being thoroughly searched, thus taking up the valuable leave time of those in the taxis queuing behind.

The Southampton City Police got wind of the practice, raided the dock police office and temporarily took over the duties of search themselves. On the day this happened a long queue of taxis carrying crew members going on leave extended from the dock gate back to the ship.

As word of what was happening spread along the immobile rank whatever shipboard store the taxi's occupant might happen to have in his possession was quickly discarded.

Meat from the ship's cold store was a popular 'perk' and, as a result of the unexpected raid, dock workers arriving for work the morning after found the side of the road littered with hastily abandoned turkey legs and hams that were eagerly gathered up.

Anecdotes about the two great Queen liners abound and reflect a way of life that has now disappeared. These few recollections of some of the crew (which does not necessarily mean that all of them indulged in such 'lively' activities – many of them led a more peaceful life punctuated by seeing their families once a fortnight) will hopefully, balance other books which, however excellent, have tended to dwell on the more glamorous shipboard jobs or on stories about the famous passengers – part of the 'cargo' – whom the ship carried.

Although, as previously mentioned, the Queen Elizabeth did not enjoy the same affection that the Cunard men held for the Queen Mary, being described as the 'colder' of the two ships, she was nonetheless a popular ship. The loyalty that she was given by her crew, the lifeblood of any ship, was reflected in the service given to her passengers who patronised the ship in vast numbers time and time again.

In turn the numbers of passengers carried meant enormous profits for the proud steamship company which owned them and the two liners would repay their original investments many times over.

The two Queen's became an establishment, a familiar sight to those who saw them sailing and arriving at their ports of call, a way of life to the crew who sailed them and source of an almost endless supply of increasing profits in the late 1950s to the Cunard Line.

It was a way of life that seemingly had no end and it was this complacency that would be destroyed completely within the next decade.

Chapter Eleven
"In Luck's Way"

The 'Cargo' – the passengers – varied greatly in both status and circumstance. From millionaires to politicians; from film stars to stars of industry; from tourists to students and from emigrants to the occasional stowaway, all wanted a fast or glamorous (or both) ride across the ocean.

Many passengers were loyal to the *Queen* for many years, others might wish to be seen travelling on the biggest ship afloat but the majority wanted a quick and, if they could afford it, comfortable passage to America, France or England.

Some had a long-held desire to travel on 'the' ship of their dreams and foremost amongst these was Her Majesty Queen Elizabeth (later to become the Queen Mother) who had expressed a wish that one day she might sail on the ship she had launched.

Before that day came, however, the Queen would visit the liner with her husband, King George VI. The King had missed the vessel's launch because of the crisis in Europe back in 1938.

On the fine summer's day of July 28th 1948, the Monarch and his consort, accompanied by their younger daughter Princess Margaret Rose, were received on board the flagship of Great Britain's merchant fleet.

The purpose of the royal visit was to enable Her Majesty to present the ship with her personal standard, framed and hung in the Main Restaurant. But the prime reason for the day's visit was for the Queen to unveil a portrait of herself.

Originally vetoing the idea of allowing her portrait to be hung in the ship when the liner was launched, the Queen had now relented and had consented to a painting being commissioned.

The portrait of Queen Elizabeth by Sir Oswald Birley that came to be hung in the Main Lounge.
The University Archives, the University of Liverpool

She had been persuaded to change her mind by her brother, the Hon. David Bowes-Lyon, recently appointed to the Board of the Cunard.

David Bowes-Lyon had previously been shown over the *Elizabeth* by her captain, Commodore Robert Thelwell. During an exchange of views about the various works of art and decor that they saw the captain said: 'You know, of course, that the *Queen Mary* has the big bronze medallion of the Queen Mother' (as Queen Mary was at that time) 'and in a glass case on the main staircase there is her own personal standard? In this ship we have no memento at all.'

David Bowes-Lyon took the hint, had a word with his sister and Sir Oswald Birley was given the commission to paint the portrait that now hung in the First Class Lounge.

To make room for it the large marquetry panel depicting 'The Canterbury Tales' (which had attracted so much acclaim when it first appeared) was re-hung at the head of the Main Hall stairway.

The Queen's '... cherished wish' that she might someday sail on the liner, materialised in October 1954 when, by now Queen Mother since the King's death, she embarked at the beginning of a tour of the United States and Canada.

Arriving on board on the eve of sailing, the Queen Mother's family accompanied and dined with her before making their farewells.

One of the unofficial strikes which plagued the '50s was in progress at that time, so the liner had been backed into the Ocean Dock, stem pointing towards the dock entrance, to enable her to achieve an easy departure should the strikers attempt to disrupt the sailing.

But the liner and her very special passenger had the full co-operation of the tugmen, and she sailed on time

A gala day for the great Cunarder occurred on 28th July 1948 when their Majesties King George V and Queen Elizabeth visited the liner. *Southampton City Museums*

with Commodore Sir Ivan Thompson in command. It was October 21st, yet another Trafalgar Day.

During the crossing the liner encountered rough weather but this did not deter the Queen from making daily tours to various parts of the ship, attending Divine Service on the Sunday and dining either in the Main Restaurant or in the Verandah Grill, the latter restaurant being so exclusive that in normal voyaging the First Class passengers lucky enough to obtain a seat there had to pay a supplement of 3 guineas – £3.15.

En passage to New York the *Queen Elizabeth* passed the east-bound *Queen Mary*. The great excitement that preceded the meeting grew to a crescendo, especially on the *Mary* whose passengers lined her rails watching the other liner with HM's standard fluttering at her masthead. As the two sisters sped towards the mid-ocean encounter, the *Mary*'s passengers first cheered the *Elizabeth* with her royal passenger as they passed and then watched the *Elizabeth* disappear astern as the gap between the two *Queens* of the Atlantic rapidly widened at 70 mph.

The Queen Mother replied to a signal from the *Queen Mary* on which she would be returning to England at the end of her tour:

'I send you my greetings and good wishes to all on board. I hope you get better weather soon.

Elizabeth R.'

In 1953 the two liners transported guests and spectators alike to and from England for the great event of the year, the Coronation of Queen Elizabeth II.

Various celebrations were held on board the *QE* as a salute to the grand occasion, and a special menu was devised that would reflect the royal event. Presented on Monday, June 1st, the dishes had been suitably dubbed with such regal annotations as 'Smoked Salmon Britannia', 'Fillet of Lemon Sole Buckingham', 'Guinea Chicken Clarence House' and 'Sirloin Steak la Reine'.

Coronation Day itself found the *Lizzie* away from the shores of a very Merrie England and docking alongside Pier 90 in New York. But, on the following day, recalled bedroom steward Terry Little, a film of the pageantry and crowning was flown over to the States and shown in another favourite haunt of Cunard men – 'Maxi's San Susie' bar.

Commodore Harry Grattidge also recalled an anecdote that arose a short while after the event, in his book, 'Captain of the *Queens*'.

The Commodore had been present at the Coronation in Westminster Abbey as one of three representatives of the Merchant Service. A month after the crowning he was back on board. The Marquess of Salisbury was travelling and was one of his table guests.

One evening the film 'A Queen is Crowned' was being shown in the ship's cinema and the Marquess, a quiet person who apparently preferred listening rather than talking, asked the Commodore to accompany him to see the film. His main aim was to see how he looked during the ceremony as, in his capacity as Lord President of the Council, he had taken an active part in the noble pageant.

When the two men arrived in the packed cinema the film had already begun so, in the semi-darkness that pervades all cinemas, they edged their way into two seats in the back row.

Commodore Grattidge continued: 'Before long a stifled chuckling became audible. One or two people turned round. All was quiet for a moment or two, then a sudden gurgle. Someone 'shushed' indignantly. This time the gurgling stopped for good, but from time to time there came from the darkness the stifled sounds of a man who knows he must control his mirth whatever the cost. It was Lord Salisbury, overcome by the anguish of his own face as he wrestled with the enormous weight of the Sword of State!'

Amongst many loyal devotees of the two *Queens* were the Duke and Duchess of Windsor. (Their allegiance was later transferred to the American, record-breaking, super-liner *United States* when she appeared on the Atlantic in July 1956, easily grabbing the Blue Ribband from the *Queen Mary* with a speed of 35 knots).

The Duchess was for ever sparklingly gregarious but her husband's moods could vary. Sometimes he was delightfully animated and then his mood could sway in the other direction when he appeared to be inwardly reflecting on what might have been.

One Christmas Eve the Duke descended to the 'Pig and Whistle' where a crew's concert was about to commence. He was greeted with cries of 'Good old Teddy!' and' God Bless the Prince of Wales!' Changing his mind after first asking to play the drums, the Duke decided to address the crew from the makeshift stage, beginning with 'My fellow Englishmen ....' At the finish he sat down with Chief Officer (later Commodore) Donald MacLean and Lord Sefton in a space on a bench made by two burly, dungareed and singleted stokers shifting their positions. The Duke then proffered Royal cigars to those around him. He thoroughly enjoyed the ensuing show – probably of a standard as risque as ever. (Whether or not the famous 'Jane' sang that night is not recorded!)

The start of that particular crossing found the Duke almost escorted off the Bridge as a trespasser on the 'Holy of Holies.' It was not until the Chief Officer (sent by the captain, who had as yet not recognised the interloper's identity, to perform the act of eviction) approached the Duke that he realised who he was. After a few remarks about the weather and a request to be able to stay on the Bridge, the Duke of Windsor was discreetly left alone with his own thoughts, watching the lights of Cherbourg (where he had boarded the liner by tender) recede into the darkening distance of a bitter, sleet-filled night of 21st December 1949.

Many members of international royalty also chose the *Queen Elizabeth* as their means of transport to and from the States.

Ex-King Michael of Rumania, and his mother Queen Helen; Crown Prince Akhito of Japan; Maharajahs with gold buttons studded with diamonds and their fabulously be-jewelled consorts – all preferred the luxury they found on board.

The Sheik of Kuwait travelled with a case containing several gross of gold watches which he liked to give away to those who served him well. Young 17 year old Prince Mohammed Feisal (later crowned King Feisal II of Iran) forgot his camera just before disembarking at Southampton in November 1952. Although he was supposed to have been the first passenger ashore he returned to look for his mislaid property. The ship was dressed overall for the arrival and a regimental band waited for him to disembark.

The band had been instructed to strike up when they saw the first passenger – presumed to be the Prince – appear. It was never ascertained who was the more surprised – the performing bandsmen or the first man actually ashore, none other than Charlie Chaplin!

British Labour politicians including Messrs. Morrison, Bevan and Brown crossed on the *QE* (important Socialists seemed to revel in the luxurious living that the Cunard Company provided, noted Commodore Robert Thelwell) as well as prominent Conservatives such as Sir Anthony Eden, 'Rab' Butler and their wives (Mrs Butler was always knitting, Commodore Grattidge later recalled), Edward Heath and many other figures of politics whether British or Foreign, Left or Right, Communist, Royalist, totalitarian or democrat – all seemed to be 'levelled' by the superb conditions that they found on board.

The Russian diplomat Molotov travelled on the *Queen Elizabeth* on several occasions but his famous – or rather infamous – 'Niets' in the United Nations seemed to mellow into 'Da's' whilst on board. An interpreter travelled with his entourage although he could speak very passable English.

However, Commodore Thelwell seemed to be unaware of this fact, as the feared diplomat had only spoken to him in Russian translated through his interpreter. So when the Commodore arrived at Molotov's suite after accepting an invitation to cocktails, the Russian smilingly greeted him in perfect English. When a surprised and momentarily undiplomatic captain retorted: 'Ah! so you can speak English Mr Molotov!', the smile disappeared from the face of a now wary Russian, and the captain was thankful when he was later called away from the party.

In September 1960, Tito, the late President of Yugoslavia, boarded the liner, which respectfully flew his personal standard at the main-masthead, at Cherbourg where he had arrived in his armoured train. The security surrounding his crossing to a Security Council meeting of the UN infused the trip with a military atmosphere not experienced since the war. Randolph Churchill was also on the ship for that voyage, his earlier chagrin aroused during the *Queen*'s grounding in 1946 apparently having long disappeared.

But not all the *Queen Elizabeth*'s passengers were so seriously minded.

Many of the stars of the world of entertainment performed during a voyage, and their audiences of fellow passengers were encouraged to make a collection – customarily for seamen's charities.

Sophie Tucker, that bubbling mountain of personality and fun, gave a non-stop, three hour performance of songs and monologues during a crossing in 1961. Her audience was left clamouring for more.

In November 1949 Kathleen Ferrier, a singer of a completely different genre, left her audience spellbound by the ethereal quality of her exceptionally beautiful voice. She was followed by Field Marshal Lord Montgomery who gave a short speech in favour of the seamen's charities for which the evening was as usual being held. The proceeds from that evening represented a record to date – £400 collected in an enthusiastic ten minutes!

Actor Phil Silvers – forever remembered for his television role as the scheming, fast talking 'Sergeant Bilko' – gave a performance one evening that equalled the talents of his television character. Asked to perform the duties of auctioneer (selling sweepstake tickets for the time of arrival), he brought Sergeant Bilko's skills of painlessly extracting money from his 'customers' into use. He gradually coaxed up the bids for the favourite ticket through a crescendo of humorous banter, until only two contenders were left in the bidding – Lady Docker and a Texan oilman. When the offers reached £100 Lady Docker decided to turn the bidding to guineas (21/- or £1.05). 'Guineas?' Bilko asked with serious incredulity as his grasp of the financial situation momentarily wavered, 'What kind of money is THAT?'

Phil Silvers was equally at home in the company of the crew. Of Silvers' invitation to the Engineers' Ward Room, engineer Lovell Taylor wrote:

'What a great character old Phil is. He's got this crowd of us round him, including the Chief Engineer, up in the wardroom. He's performing the three-card trick "Find the Lady" for the completely baffled .... Chief Engineer. He just can't pick out the 'queen' card and, what with Phil's

A sparkling *Queen* on a sparkling sea.

The University Archives, the University of Liverpool

slick line of patter, he gets more embarrassed by the minute.

'If the Chief Engineer can't do a simple thing like "Finding the Lady" how do you ever manage to run a ship like this?' he says, 'thats what I'd like to know, how can a dumb guy like you ever run this goddam ship?'

'We all fall about laughing, and the Chief made some lame excuse to get the .... out of there.'

Other personalities were less gregarious. The famed American conductor Stokowski (well-known for conducting the music in Walt Disney's film 'Fantasia') travelled, incognito under his Polish Christian forenames in their anglicised form of 'Antony Stanley,' with his young wife to whom he was most attentive – almost to the point of resenting any steward or bell boy who held her chair or opened a door for her before he had a chance to do so.

Rita Hayworth and Rosalind Russell had also travelled under assumed names when they travelled.

Boarding the liner in New York Charlie Chaplin set out on the start of what was to be a nostalgic visit to his birth place in the East End of London.

Almost half-way across the Atlantic the famed clown received a message from the United States, telling him that his long-standing permit enabling him to live and work in that country had been rescinded.

The anti-American activities committee which had been investigating his (and thousands of other Americans') communist leanings had found that, many years previously, he had donated $100 to the now outlawed party at a time when it was seen to be the only apparent champion against oppression. This small gesture was considered enough to banish him to an enforced exile in Switzerland. (At the

time, Cunard crew members were also asked by the immigration authorities, on each arrival in New York, if they had any communistic tendencies or sympathies. 'I'm a commis' the young waiters would reply, tongue-in-cheek, to questions as to what they were!)

Earl Mountbatten of Burma, always bronzed and fit in spite of the vast amount of work with which he travelled, enjoyed the hospitality of the liner, and Lord Montgomery of Alamein enjoyed a 63rd birthday party given in his honour. Sir Adrian Boult, that most gentle of English orchestral conductors (on board the *Mary* he had conducted the occupants of the Main Restaurant in singing 'Happy Birthday' to Captain Donald Sorrell), travelled as did playwrights Noel Coward and Tennessee Williams.

Sportsmen carried over the years included such boxing champions as Joe Louis, Randolph Turpin and Sugar Ray Robinson.

Organised groups journeyed on the liner and sometimes entertained the passengers; the renowned Vienna Boys Choir sang in the Main Lounge to great acclaim.

Amongst the more unusual passengers was counted one Edgar Foster who booked a return passage in July 1953. Fifty four years of age and a clothing businessman from Birmingham, he had an almost unique hobby – diving from unusual platforms. Was it to celebrate the Coronation that he paid £500 for his round trip in the *Queen Elizabeth* to pursue his self-taught pursuit? Once in New York he balanced on the ship's rail and, to the cheers of his accomplice who had held his legs as he precariously balanced above the murky waters into which he would soon be plummeting, he made his self-gratifying plunge.

157

He also wanted to dive from the *Lizzie*'s Bridge on the liner's return to Southampton, but a shoulder hurt during his dive into the Hudson – and the captain's downright refusal to give him permission – dissuaded him from his ambition. At the end of his voyage he still felt that his fare had been money well-spent!

At the other end of the passenger strata David Stroyman of Brooklyn, Massachusetts, must have – in February 1956 and at 71 years of age – ranked as the oldest stowaway ever to attempt a free passage on the liner.

Hoping to catch some of the *Queen*'s glamour on film the Rank Organisation based a movie musical 'As Long as They're Happy' around the liner in 1954, and in the 1960s two television documentaries were made on board.

The first was produced by the now defunct Southern Television company of Southampton, and was called 'Profile of a Commodore', the position held at that time by Donald MacLean. The documentary was broadcast on Thursday, 9th November 1961.

Another Commodore, Harry Grattidge, had earlier become involved in film making but in an advisory role only, when he became Technical Advisor to the Rank Organisation when the classic *Titanic* film 'A Night To Remember' was made in 1958.

An American television company made the second documentary which revolved around the lives of the captain, chief engineer and chief steward during one voyage.

The *Lizzie* returned to the big screen in 1959, appearing briefly in Columbia's 'The Mouse That Roared'. During the film she was attacked with arrows (sticking into the Bridge above the head of the captain) fired by Peter Sellers and his bunch of chain-mailed soldiers crossing the Atlantic on board the tug tender *Paladin*, *en route* to attack the United States.

Towards the end of the decade that followed, the *Queen Elizabeth* would make a last appearance in one of the exciting series of 'James Bond' movies, 'The Man With the Golden Gun'.

Throughout her career the *Queen* was commanded by men who had reached the pinnacle of their profession. The officers under their command were also highly qualified, with Masters' and Extra-Masters' certificates, but all this skill was needed to navigate the world's largest liner over the world's (at times) roughest ocean.

The North Atlantic Ocean would on occasion delay the *Queen Elizabeth*, sometimes by many hours, through storm, fog, ice and, even in late post-war years, by a drifting mine spotted in the English Channel!

A severe storm could cause damage to both ship and those on board as well as to the timetable. In the latter event some of the lost time could be made up on an eastward crossing by a quick dash across the English Channel between Cherbourg and Southampton – or rather the Nab Tower.

The *Queen* often broke her own records for this short passage making one particularly fast crossing in March 1958, when a time of 2 hours 24 minutes was recorded.

A storm in December 1959 delayed the *QE*'s arrival in Southampton (under the command of George Morris) by 37 hours. A 75 mph gale, during which waves of 50 to 60 feet in height were observed, had been encountered.

During the gale a porthole had been blown in on 'A' deck, flooding a cabin – A94 – and injuring its occupant. Two thousand pieces of crockery and glassware were also broken during the storm.

Amongst those on board were J.D. Goulandris, the Greek shipping magnate, and the British film actress, Margaret Leighton.

On disembarking Miss Leighton told the Southampton Southern Evening Echo:

'It was horrible, but I was terribly impressed with the way the ship rode the storm. It was much more comfortable than I have experienced in other ships in rough weather.'

After a similar gale – but with reputedly even larger waves – earlier in February 1957 (and with Jack Buchanan the film actor on board), the ship apparently '.... rode beautifully because of the stabilisers.'

In the seven years following the entry of both *Queens* entry into post-war service it was found that many passengers – especially women – were terrified of the rough conditions of which the North Atlantic was capable in wintertime.

Convinced that the delays, changes, bumpy and cramped dash offered by pre-jet aircraft was preferable to the 'horrors' of winter sea travel, these 'lost' passengers had to be attracted back to the sea.

Deciding to compete against the wings in the sky, Cunard put plans into action to equip their ships with wings under the ocean by fitting the two mighty *Queens* with Denny-Brown stabilisers.

This equipment had previously been successfully fitted to the much smaller Cunarders *Media* and *Parthia* and it was now time to start the huge conversion jobs on the *Queens* intended, as the publicists said, 'to smooth your way across the Atlantic'. Work started on preparing the *Elizabeth* whilst she was still at sea – fifteen months before the actual fitting of the stabilisers was due to take place.

During this preparation work oil tanks were converted to become stabiliser machinery compartments. Existing machinery was also resited, not an easy task since the liner's designers had used the available space to full advantage.

The fitting of the stabilisers took place during the *Queen Elizabeth*'s 1955 long winter overhaul which began with her dry docking on January 21st, bumping both sides of the dock as she entered it.

Two sets of stabilisers were fitted to the *Queen* with a distance of 150 feet between sets. Originally it had been hoped that one set of larger fins would be sufficient, but the small space available between hull and dock walls precluded this.

John I. Thornycroft, the Southampton firm of shipbuilders and shipfitters, had made full size mock-ups of the equipment to ensure that any foreseeable problems could be overcome well before the work was done. They certainly had a difficult job especially in reorganising the internal layout of the ship in the way of the stabiliser machinery.

The dry dock also only had cranes along one of its walls so the ship's own equipment had to be used in conjunction with the dock facilities to cajole the new equipment from one side of the dock to the other.

The installation work required 5 miles of cable, 12,000

feet of piping, 600 feet of trunking and 4 motors of 80 horsepower each.

Each stabiliser fin had an outreach of 12 feet 6 inches and a width of 7 feet 3 inches. Both sets could be extended and operated independently of the other so that only one set need be operated in a moderate swell.

Operated from the bridge the forward set had a righting moment of 11,500 ton/ft and the after set exerted 14,000 ton/ft. It was calculated that a roll could be reduced by 75% within a very short time.

The *Queen* came out of her longer than usual refit of ten weeks on 23rd March, having spent some time alongside a 'wet' berth after leaving dry dock. The first priority was to test the new installations and this was scheduled for the following weekend.

The trials took the form of a short cruise to the Lizard with several guests boarding the liner on the eve of departure.

Unknown to those peacefully sleeping in their beds that night, an emergency arose in the Engine Room which the engineers struggled to overcome before the rest of the ship awoke.

At 4 am a fuel pump had jammed and the ship suffered a severe loss of power. This resulted in the boilers going out, the level of water in the boilers going down and a loss of steam. All electricity supplies had to be cut to conserve what little steam there was until the jammed fuel pumps could be induced to work, thus gradually bringing back into operation all the vital machinery that had been brought to a halt.

When underway at last, only a moderate swell was encountered so an artificially induced roll was created by operating the stabilisers in reverse, achieved by reversing the response of the gyro control.

Once the liner had developed a roll of sufficient dimension, the gyro control – and hence the stabilisers – were 'normalised' to reduce the motion, which they did quite satisfactorily.

On the first post-refit voyage to New York the stabilisers' designer, Sir William Wallace, travelled with the ship. He later declared himself to be ' .... very satisfied' with the equipment especially as the ship had encountered winds during her eastward run of around 50 miles per hour for a forty-eight hour period. The *Lizzie*'s captain, Commodore Sir Ivan Thompson said that his ship was ' ... as steady as a rock' during the rough weather.

As mentioned earlier the two *Queens* each had two annual overhauls. The summer overhaul was a short one of about one week's duration generally during late July, early August. This consisted of a general smartening up with a coat of paint and carrying out small repairs and maintenance in readiness for the peak, lucrative summer season.

The second – and main – overhaul lasted from five to six weeks during the off-peak winter period and could occur anywhere between late November and early March.

It was during the winter lay-up that a great deal of essential maintenance, survey and testing was done on the liner's hull, machinery, fittings and furnishings in order to keep the ship at the top of the league.

In 1956 the *Queen* appeared from her winter overhaul fitted with 'wings under the water' which helped Cunard promote their 'Smooth Your Way Across the Atlantic' campaign in an endeavour to attract passengers back to winter crossings.

Southern Newspapers plc,
Southampton

The liner spent about three weeks in the King George V dry dock at Southampton, with the remainder of the period being spent alongside a quay on a wet berth. Up to fifteen hundred men swarmed over the ship, untidying what had hitherto been immaculate.

The amount of work to be done was prodigious.

As the water in the dock was pumped out so workmen in punts – attached to the liner by 'wash-lines' – ranged to and fro along the length of the liner as she sat on the dock blocks scrubbing the underwater hull clear of weed and barnacles as the water level fell.

When at last the dock was dry and the liner snug on the blocks, the three sixteen-ton anchors and 330 fathoms of cable were lowered to the dock bottom. Each anchor was then surveyed, cleaned and painted as was every 2 cwt (51 kg) link of the cables that snaked across the dock beneath the sharp, yacht-like bow that towered above.

At each winter overhaul one of the four propeller tail shafts, each weighing 37 tons, would be extracted and surveyed as would the propellers or their bosses (cones).

During the January 1961 winter overhaul a new propeller was fitted to the inner port shaft. Much lighter than the one it replaced, the new propeller was made of a nickel bronze alloy instead of manganese bronze. It proved to be effective at higher speeds (the shaft turning at a few revolutions less as a consequence) but tended to 'shunt' its propeller shaft at lower speeds, with a knocking noise coming from the plummer blocks.

The small door in the rudder was also opened and men would enter its interior to inspect and paint. Once the access panel was re-bolted into position the watertightness of the rudder would be tested with compressed air.

Inlets and outlets, normally underwater, were inspected and the 15,000 square yards of underwater hull was then painted with seven tons of primer and anti-fouling compositions applied by 120 painters. Another large quantity of paint would be used to freshen up those marvellous funnels, the buff masts, the white superstructure and black hull.

While the *Elizabeth* was in dry-dock only one of her boilers was kept fired in order to maintain essential ship services. Fresh water and electricity were supplied, meanwhile, via connections made to the dockside.

Concurrent with the work being carried out on the exterior of the ship, the machinery had also to be inspected and tested. 160,000 boiler tubes (some of which – the upper economiser or pre-heat tubes – were replaced by glass versions in the 1962 refit. This was because the steel variants had to be previously replaced almost yearly due to

disintegration caused by the gases – having reached a low temperature and 'dew point' – releasing sulphuric acid in the tubes which caused them almost to crumble to the touch) were tested and hundreds of feet of oil pipeline carefully checked.

257,000 turbine blades, 30 oil and water tanks, 35 lifts, 30,000 lightbulbs, 750 electric clocks, 600 telephones, 530 electric motors (ranging from 0.25 to 300 horsepower) – all had to be checked, tested, and replaced where necessary, painted where needed, along with a thousand other jobs that had to be done.

The hotel services were also busy during the lay-up stocktaking their hardware and linen.

A lot of logoed Company tableware usually disappeared during the course of each year through the eagerness of souvenir hunters, and the chief stewards had a good deal to account for on their inventories: 54,000 pieces of china and earthenware (including 21,000 plates, 8,500 cups, 7,000 saucers) plus 26,000 pieces of glassware, and 40,000 pieces of silver plate consisting of 10,500 knives, 10,000 forks and 6,750 spoons.

Three and a half thousand items of furniture and equipment were taken ashore for survey, whilst painters and polishers smartened up metalwork and the huge areas of rare veneers.

When the winter lay-up was finally complete a mess usually remained in the crews' 'Working Alley' but, within a day of leaving refit, all had been tidied and cleaned.

Once more the *Queen Elizabeth* was ready to take on what both the North Atlantic and the contemporary, ultra-discerning, travelling public would demand of her.

Sometimes more would be asked of the ship than

A stern view of the *Lizzie* in the King George V dry dock in Southampton during an annual overhaul.   *Author's collection*

would normally be expected but she and her equipment had been designed to withstand almost everything that would come her way.

As has already been noted fog was often one of her greatest adversaries either delaying the liner or putting her into danger.

It was in such thick weather that the *Queen* was approaching Cherbourg, eastbound, in January 1965.

The liner's last incident at the port had occurred in November 1953, when she had sustained a 20 foot buckle in her side plates after bumping into the pier. Her sister had been less fortunate – almost disastrously so – and had gone aground on the Seleine Bank within the harbour confines. Only by sheer luck had she grounded on one of

Before the construction of Southampton's Ocean Terminal building the gangways were lifted between quayside and ship by crane. *The University Archives, the University of Liverpool*

the strongest parts of her hull – otherwise she would have surely broken her back.

But now, on 25th January, the *Queen Elizabeth* under the command of Commodore Frederick Watts – and with pilot Captain Marcel Castel on board – was brought to a halt as the liner approached Cherbourg. Visibility in the thick fog that prevailed ranged from a mile down to zero.

It was low water and the *Queen* started to drift sideways in the oily water, an unnoticed drift that was brought gently to a halt as the liner grounded on a mudbank.

She was there for an anxious half-hour but, as the tide rose, she floated easily off the underwater mound.

She had grounded on her portside fore-end and, on docking in Cherbourg, divers were sent down to inspect her hull. Nothing untoward was found and a similar inspection on her arrival in Southampton also revealed nothing.

Fog had proved to be more troublesome six years earlier on the Stateside of 'The Pond'.

Visibility was down to less than two hundred feet as, on 29th July 1959, the *Queen* left New York.

Her pilot was manually sounding the ship's siren to warn other ships which might be in her vicinity and this intermittent distinctive booming was heard and recognised

by the officers of the United States Line's cargo vessel *American Hunter*.

On the Cunarder engines were stopped and two radar screens (2 mile and 4 mile ranges) were manned. There were several 'targets' on each and, as one target appeared to be closing, the *QE*'s engines were put into reverse.

But it was too late. The 'target', the *American Hunter* (also with engines put astern), found the giant liner crossing her bow, the latter still having a forward motion.

A collision was unavoidable. The cargo ship hit the liner inflicting dents in some plates and a hole below the starboard hawse pipe, (later temporarily repaired with cement on a quick return to New York). The American ship merely suffered a two foot dent.

The *Elizabeth* arrived in Southampton only 24 hours behind schedule.

Five years later the *Queen* had another brush with yet another GI.

She was moored alongside her quay in Southampton when the *General S.B. Buckner* arrived in port on 16th September 1964. Caught by the strong wind, the American ship, still slowly underway, was blown over to the *Queen*'s berth and brushed against the *Elizabeth*'s side. There was no structural damage.

January 1959 saw the *Queen* fogbound on the last leg of an eastward trip. For fifty hours she was delayed – firstly just south of the Nab Tower and then for a long period in Cowes Roads. Her passengers were taken off by the tenders *Paladin*, *Romsey* and *Vecta*.

Fog, collision, storm and grounding are but four of the many hazards that can be encountered at sea but perhaps the most feared is fire.

It had been fire that had caused the premature demise of the fabled *Normandie* and many other fine ships, and so the men of the *Queen Elizabeth* were ever vigilant in protecting their beautiful ship from a similar fate.

However, the *Queen* – like any large town – experienced several fires during her term as Empress of the Atlantic, usually of a minor and easily controllable nature.

What with carbon dioxide blanketing for the holds, baggage rooms etc; pressurised water sprinklers in accommodation and public rooms and a full-time, manned fire station, the *Queen* was as well-protected against fire as she could be under current legislation.

Small fires would break out now and then. For example, the Engine Room fought fires which perhaps started in the pipe lagging, impregnated with the fine oily mist pervading that particular area.

But on three occasions the blazes that arose on board could have had consequences of great magnitude.

The first, as the *Elizabeth* was being converted to her peace time role in 1946, has already been recounted. The second occurred whilst the liner was in dry-dock during her winter overhaul of January 1953.

This fire started at around 8.15 pm in the wardrobe of cabin M93 which, as a result, was badly damaged. Charred remains were taken away for expert investigation but the cause of the fire remained a mystery.

The day after the M93 fire – only a few hours later – the Southampton Fire Brigade was called out for a second

An impressive view of the *Queen Elizabeth* in drydock at Southampton. Spare propellers were usually kept on the dockside by the pumping station at the right-hand side of the dock gate.   *Southern Newspapers plc, Southampton*

time, this time to extinguish a small blaze in a pile of oily rags found in cabin C146.

And for a third time within forty eight hours the Brigade rushed to the ship, this time to find that the alarm had been false.

With the industrial unrest and the very militant 'unionists' who were active in the country at that time, it is still surprising that the first of the fires remains a mystery in view of the subsequent alarms.

Seven years later, in September 1960, a serious fire broke out in the main electrical switchboard (during a westbound voyage in the English Channel) which took a hundred men of the ship's crew three hours to control. Several cabins had to be rebuilt as a result and thirty starboard cabins on three First Class decks remained untenable for the next trip.

Danger in entering and leaving port was ever present and the nearest that the *Queen Elizabeth* came to complete and instantaneous destruction was only narrowly avoided. She had just left Southampton and Commodore Thelwell recalled the event in his book 'I Captained the Big Ships':

'Ten-forty. A tongue of orange flame shot as usual from the high chimney of the Fawley Refinery. The scene was familiar, comforting.

'But as we approached the jetty, a not-so-familiar sight swung into view. Holt [the pilot] and I saw it at the same time.

"My God!" I said, involuntarily.

'Near the jetty a black blob of a tanker lay at anchor, almost athwart the channel and heading westerly into the path of the *Queen Elizabeth*. Further south, a second tanker was attempting to make fast to buoys and sheering easterly in the process.

'Holt snapped out an order at once: "Reduce speed". He waited for a moment until the order was transmitted. "They told me before we sailed that the tankers would be safely berthed and out of our path", said Holt in his quiet voice.

'Those who have served under me in the big ships will concede, I think, that whatever my defects, a tendency to panic is not one: but I confess that at that moment I was near to panic. Pilot Holt was navigating the ship but the responsibility for the safety of the lives of the passengers and crew, and for the safety of the ship itself, was mine alone.

'And I knew, as Holt did, that we were heading for certain disaster with hardly any cards in our hands to play and little to do except wait and pray that our luck would hold.

'For the tankers were loaded with oil. The slightest collision would generate sparks and the tankers would become more lethal than a torpedo discharged into the unprotected belly of the ship I commanded.

' ... I began to think of the orders I would give when the searing explosion took place – assuming that I was still alive to give orders and that there were any officers and seamen left to carry them out. My war experience had not, fortunately, included the sight of a tanker attacked by enemy aircraft, but friends had told me how terrible it could be and I had a picture in my mind of broken bodies, a smashed ship and a sea of blazing oil. It was quite possible that the explosion would be so violent that my gigantic ship would be sent to the bottom of Southampton Water before we could lower any of the boats.

'Whilst these fearful thoughts raced through my mind, I glanced away from the tanker for a few moments. The white, tense faces of the staff captain and chief officer showed that they had seen what the pilot and I had seen. Below us on the decks the passengers strolled about in the sunlight or leaned over the starboard side to gaze in awe at the refinery. The ship was gliding to almost certain destruction yet only a handful of us, of all the souls on board, knew it.

'A quiet voice interrupted my thoughts. 'You know, Captain,' said Pilot Holt, 'this is the sort of situation that can cause a considerable amount of danger.'

'I could not and cannot recall ever hearing such an understatement in my lifetime.

'We both now stared ahead, unable to take our eyes away from the two tankers as we bore down on them.

'Reduce speed – dead slow.'

'I knew as well as Pilot Holt that we dared not reduce speed any more or the rudder would be useless and the ship hopelessly out of control. We had gone to the limit of what we could do in the matter of speed.

'Ease the helm.'

'Only superb steering and luck – especially luck – could now save the ship.

'Port easy. Port more.'

'We had sailed at high water, and the tide was behind us and a still freshening wind would have made it hard to keep the ship on course at the best of times, without additional hazard. Yet Pilot Holt's modulated voice contained no hint of nervousness.

'A hundred yards and we should know our fate.

'Fifty yards.

'Now we were within twenty yards of the leading tanker and we could see her cable across the bow and apparently leading somewhere astern. The two tugs which had been berthing her stood off. The wind blew harder and, in spite of all the pilot could do, caused the ship to drift nearer the tanker.

'Fifteen yards to go – fifteen agonizing yards which could just as well end in death as in life. I could scarcely breathe as the gap between the tanker and the track we were taking narrowed inexorably.

'Ten yards. The crisis was on us and over almost at the same time. The *Queen* was holding to her course.

'I think we're in luck's way this morning, said the quiet voice of Pilot Holt.

'A few more moments and we were safe, though with no more than ten feet to spare. The passengers on the rails, cheering and waving to the tanker's frightened crew, would never know why there was not a wave in return or how close they had been to a terrible death.'

The second tanker was passed by with five hundred feet between the two ships.

The *Queen* sailed on, but the next few years would see a certain change in her fortunes.

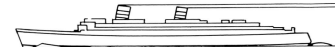

Chapter Twelve
'Lovely to the Last ...'
(Byron)

The years spanning 1947 and 1956 were hugely profitable for Cunard with their ships sometimes carrying 50% of the total North Atlantic traffic. In one year alone this meant a million people travelling by Cunard, representing a record for any company.

The two *Queens* recovered their original building costs by many score and, because of the phenomenal success of their ships, the board of Cunard became complacent about the competition of the propeller-driven aircraft which was never considered a real threat: people would always prefer to cross the ocean by liner and preferably by Cunard!

With the advent of the high-flying jet aircraft, however, all this suddenly and dramatically changed. 1957 proved to be the irreversible turning point when an equal number of people were transported by jet as were carried by ship.

After that fateful year there was a steady change of balance in favour of the jets: thereafter the fortunes of the North Atlantic shipping companies began to change, all experiencing an accelerating decline into the abyss of

oblivion. Instead of the scores of passenger liners operated by dozens of international companies there is now, in the late '80s only one true transatlantic liner left: one that belongs to the first company to start a regular fleet service across the Atlantic in 1840 – the Cunard: sadly, the ship – *Queen Elizabeth 2* – operates the route only in the summer months.

The decline that was yet to come was sensed by Cunard as early as 1957. Although after that date the revenue from the passenger side of the business would begin to fall, the cargo profits would remain buoyant for a while longer; that is, until the advent of container ships – the 'box boats' – each of which could carry the cargo equivalent of several conventional cargo ships but cheaply and more quickly.

But the passenger trade was affected adversely almost immediately and this decline was brought into highlight by the economic performances of the *Queen Mary* and *Queen Elizabeth*. On one eastward trip the number of stewards on

After yet another Atlantic crossing the *Queen Elizabeth* arrives in the Hudson River, giving her passengers the never-to-be-tired-of thrill of the Manhattan skyline.
Queen Elizabeth Historical Society

With her upper decks crowded with passengers enjoying the spectacle the *Queen Elizabeth* steams serenely through the Coronation Fleet Review of 1953.   *Southern Newspapers plc, Southampton*

board the *Lizzie* actually outnumbered their charges!

In spite of the recurrent losses the *Queen Elizabeth* could still carry, on occasion, an almost full complement. In June 1963, for example, over two thousand passengers were carried on one trip. Not bad for a 'dying' service!

In the 'sixties receipts for Cunard were in the region of £22m per year but the passenger carrying business continued to lose money – the £1.9m in 1962, £1.6m in 1964 and £3m in 1965 being the worst losses with lesser, but still severe, losses incurred in the years between.

Drastic surgery of both ships and men would be needed before the company could become, once again, a viable, commercial proposition.

It was not only the declining fortunes of the company's business that threatened the fleet of which the *Queen Elizabeth* was still the flagship. Labour disputes at sea and ashore also menaced, or promised to menace, the liner's scheduled services and on such occasions she was used as a massive pawn – a prime target – in various disputes involving tugmen, dockers (usually supplied by the local ship repairers), longshoremen (in New York) or the crew, either singularly or collectively. These men obviously felt that if they could interrupt either of the *Queens'* schedules then their case would be won.

In November 1948 an early success was scored by strikers. A longshoremen's strike was underway in New York and, as the liner was about to leave Southampton, the *Queen Elizabeth*'s crew 'came out' in sympathy as they regarded the ship's sailing as a 'strike-breaking' strategy.

There then followed a succession of events which continued even after the New York strike had ended. Tides were missed, delays were caused by fogs and a belated strike was called by the catering department.

Food supplies almost became a problem (the *Queen* normally stored in New York). Effluent discharged from the ship accumulated in the dock around her, causing worries about health.

1,000 of the 1,500 who remained of the original 2,200 passengers who had boarded the liner then added their own protests to those of the crew. After fourteen continuous days spent on board they protested that they could not afford to go ashore to stay in hotels etc and subsequently staged their own strike by refusing to leave the ship.

However, on 2nd December, and after sixteen days of strikes and latterly fog, the ship sailed on the same tide as the *Queen Mary* and *Aquitania*, a unique event in the peacetime history of all three vessels.

165

The mid '50s saw some unpleasant scenes as 'peaceful' pickets jostled passengers as well as crew, first at the dock gates and then at the quayside during an unofficial dispute.

In spite of the ugly scenes ashore, the *Queen* managed to sail: not to do so would be unthinkable and, besides, in sailing the strike could be broken.

As the *Elizabeth* pulled away from the Ocean Terminal jeers from the malcontents on the quayside were drowned by a few well-timed blasts on the ship's sirens.

It was felt by some of the long-serving and loyal members of the crew that much of the trouble on board had been caused by a particular young element of the crew. National Service was still in force and the young men of the country were given the choice of either joining one of the forces or serving in the Merchant Navy.

In the section that chose the latter alternative (the pay – plus any tips – provided an income many times that which a National Serviceman could expect), there were a few disruptive types, some of whom unfortunately had joined the Cunard. When dissatisfaction was expressed by the regular crew on matters of limited concern the young 'conscripts', lacking in long-term loyalty, would attempt – by fair means or foul – to exacerbate the situation, sometimes with dubious success.

But these disputes could often highlight the skill of the ship's navigators and engineers.

During strikes, either by dockers in Southampton, by longshoremen in New York or by tugmen, the *Queen* would have to be berthed unaided.

In 1957 the *Elizabeth* docked in her British port with tugs but with only half the usual number of stevedores in attendance; but the greatest feats of docking, unaided by striking tugs, took place in New York and earned the admiration of both mariners and the press.

Commodore Marr recalled the last time that the *Queen Elizabeth* was docked in such circumstances in his most readable autobiography 'The Queens and I'.

The idea was to wait for slack water – that short moment of still water between tides – in the River Hudson (problems were sometimes caused by 'freshlets' or Winter-melt water coming from up-country) and then to pivot the liner's bow either about a lowered anchor cable or about the 'knuckle' at the outer, near corner of the pier.

The ship would then be swung round until she was pointing towards the shore and laying parallel with the pier. The ship was then pulled in using her own hawsers previously taken ashore by row-boat.

Docking a giant ship in such circumstances always attracted a lot of press attention and, although practiced with great precision, was fraught with danger; often several dozen telegraph orders passed between Bridge and Engine Room during the execution of the delicate manoeuvre.

Of all the strikes and disputes that hit the *Elizabeth* the ultimately most catastrophic was the great Seamen's Strike of 1966. The strike brought Britain's merchant marine to a halt. However, great benefits were obtained for the seamen involved but these benefits would be of an unknowingly short term nature for many, as the British merchant navy would soon go into decline.

On 16 May 1966 the *QE* became one of the first major ships affected and the first that would make up a dazzling collection of great British liners in a two-month, strike-enforced lay-up in Southampton.

The strike cost Cunard an estimated £3¾ million through lost revenues, re-scheduling and re-coordinating of sailings, and, with the current losses then being experienced, brought the company's loss for the year to over £6m.

Sir Basil Smallpeice, (Cunard's chairman since November 1965 when he had succeeded Sir John Brocklebank on the latter's retirement through ill-health) decided the time had finally come for the drastic long-delayed surgery that the company so badly needed.

Sir John Brocklebank had, during his chairmanship, started a revolutionary policy of 'new thinking' which not only saw the cancellation of an intended replacement for the mighty *Queens* (a project known as the 'Q3' which later became known as the 'Q4' – the *Queen Elizabeth 2*) but also saw some of the other units of the fleet converted for cruising.

To this end two of Cunard's Canadian service ships, *Ivernia* and *Saxonia*, were converted for cruising in 1962, reappearing as the *Carmania* and *Franconia*. *Sylvania* and *Carinthia* would also be up-dated two years later with improvements being made to their passenger accommodation but with no change in name.

Not only were ships re-located in employment. The shore staff – for so long an almost separate organisation from the sea staff – was trimmed to meet the needs of a much reduced fleet.

Offices, too, were rationalised. Under Sir Basil's chairmanship many were closed, sold or transferred. The company headquarters was transferred from Liverpool to Southampton and many hitherto separated divisions came together under one roof.

Each department of Cunard had from now on to become a profitable, self-supporting unit – and this included the ships.

With the *Carmania* and *Franconia*, (painted in Cunard's cruising green) and with the *Mauretania* similarly employed, the company now had four ships (the *Caronia* being already employed in such a role) sailing the oceans of the world, chasing the sun in a trade that would expand spectacularly over the next two decades.

To meet the growing demand (and to reduce their winter losses) Cunard announced from New York in May 1962 that the *Queen Elizabeth* would be taken off the North Atlantic service for a month during the following winter and sent cruising. She would make three cruises from New York to Nassau and the 1,000 to 1,300 cruise passengers (2,200 were carried on normal voyages) would have their needs looked after by a specially appointed Cruise Director and a team of Social Directresses.

It was also in 1962 that the *Queens'* summer overhaul was dispensed with to effect further economies. As a result the liners would thereafter miss out on their fresh, summer coat of paint which had smartened up their gleaming hulls in readiness for the following high season.

The *Elizabeth* had some internal alterations made during the £450,000 1962 winter overhaul when a new cocktail bar was fitted, replacing the old Cabin Class

The 45 day Great Seamen's Strike of 1966 ended on 1st July 1966 and during that time many great British liners were laid up in idleness. Southampton's Western Docks presented a spectacular sight with (from left to right) *Windsor Castle, Queen Elizabeth, S.A. Vaal, Arcadia, Canberra, Good Hope Castle, Reina del Mar* and *Edinburgh Castle*. The strike accelerated the decline of the British Merchant Marine.
R. Bruce Grice

Lounge. 150 Cabin Class staterooms and cabins were also furnished in new colour schemes, even having fitted carpets in lieu of the old carpet squares.

Sir John Brocklebank, then still chairman, described the *Queens* as 'the best hotels travelling between Southampton and New York' and more conversions were planned to maintain their premier position.

The first cruise of a *Queen* began on 21 February 1963 when the *Queen Elizabeth* made her first trip to the Caribbean since the war.

Sir John Brocklebank decided to cancel his booking for the first cruise, possibly due to the increasingly poor health which would ultimately lead to his resignation in 1965.

Two more cruises were announced for the first season, leaving New York on 28 February and 6 March respectively. The first cruise to Nassau was almost delayed by a tugmen's strike in New York but Commodore Watts undocked the ship without them.

On the liner's return the Commodore had to perform the trickier task of docking the ship, also unaided, which he did successfully. Two subsequent sailings and arrivals were performed under similar circumstances.

If the cruises of the *Elizabeth* proved to be successful, Cunard said, then both *Queens* would be sent cruising during the following season, with the *Queen Mary* cruising out of Southampton to the Atlantic Isles.

In March 1963 an anonymous telephone call to the New York Police warned of a bomb hidden on board the *Lizzie*. In spite of the limited search that was possible (because of the ship's enormous size) by both police and crew, nothing was found. It was probable that the hoax was perpetrated by frustrated 'union' activists.

The *QE* proved to be popular in her new role and as a consequence it was decided to make further interior improvements over the next few overhauls to suit her to the new market.

To this end, during the 1964 winter (January) refit, a new First Class Cocktail Bar was built in place of the under-used Promenade Deck Saloon. This new bar became known as the 'Midship Bar'. Decorated in dark green hide panels and colourful, contrasting furnishings of pink, dark green, gold and that popular colour of the 'Swinging '60s' – orange – the name and style of decor became very popular and would later find a complementary echo in the forthcoming Q4 – the *Queen Elizabeth 2*. A coral pink carpet – which surrounded a central dance floor – lay beneath a lowered ceiling that held aloft a glazed dome.

The same refit also saw two innovative rooms dedicated to teenaged travellers. The Teenagers' Room on the Main Deck was sited in a new structure placed under the new Lido swimming pool (but to the starboard of it) and aft of the old Cabin Lounge, now renamed the Caribbean Room. The Teenagers' Room contained a bowling alley,

The *Queen* berthed opposite to her usual quay. The Red Funnel tug *Vulcan*, also seen in the photograph, had a long and venerable career, having assisted the ill-fated White Star liner *Titanic* depart on her maiden voyage in 1912.

Dearden and Wade – now Thunder and Clayden – of Bournemouth/Queen Elizabeth Historical Society

Arrivals at terminus ports meant a great rush for luggage, porters and taxis. This shows one such arrival in New York.   *The University archives, the University of Liverpool*

A winter arrival in New York. Not only is there ice on the Hudson but the steam from the tugs has frozen on the ship's side.   *The University Archives, the University of Liverpool*

football and car-racing tables, a cold drinks machine and the inevitable juke box.

Amongst the restyling for the new market the Cabin Class Restaurant became the Windsor Restaurant and the Cabin Smoking Room on the Promenade Deck became the Club Room for the new Lido.

The next refit (late 1964) saw soft furnishings fitted in all Main Deck suites.

The crew also benefited in a small way from the gradual, almost piecemeal (officially described as 'progressive') conversions for cruising.

The ship's men usually enjoyed a relaxing pint or two of beer in their off duty hours and a great deal of labour and space had been used in supplying the crew with adequate quantities of good English ale.

So far, 2,400 gallons of beer had been consumed by the crew on each round trip, the beverage being supplied via three to four hundred barrels containing between 5½ to 11 gallons per barrel. To cut down the intensive, unprofitable manpower required to load and unload the barrels, the cellar of the 'Pig and Whistle' was fitted with

nine tanks, each of 360 gallons capacity, in February 1965.

In that same month the Cunard decided that, if the *Queen* was to become completely viable as a cruise ship, large scale alterations had to be put in hand to make her more competitive with her rivals and more attractive to a public that was becoming increasingly aware of the pleasures of cruising, a growth industry that was to herald the resurrection of the giant passenger ship after a period of decline.

The alterations that would be carried out on the *Lizzie* would, it was anticipated in a news bulletin released for publication from the Cunard Building in Liverpool at 3 pm on Thursday 18 March, 'be spread over a four month period.'

Improvements to the liner would include the installation of full air-conditioning in both passenger and crew accommodation to help cope with the tropical climes into which the *Queen* was now being taken. Air-conditioning had hitherto been confined to the public rooms (for the liner's designated North Atlantic role) and the introduction of the system to the crews' accommodation was welcomed as their quarters on the Atlantic run had been, at best, stuffy. As a result of the alteration the *QE* changed from the unpopular ship that she had been (with some of the crew) to 'a much happier ship'.

To supply her with conditioned air, sixty four units were to be dotted about the ship in the vicinity of their associated Thermotanks. The existing Mail Room would be converted to house the refrigeration machinery.

Additional private showers and toilets were planned to be fitted in 250 Cabin-class and Tourist cabins, representing an increase of 230. 50 other rooms, already fitted with a toilet and shower, would also be supplied with a shower. A larger sea-water distillation plant would be installed to produce fresh water that would increase the *Queen*'s cruising range and a new decor would be created in all Tourist cabins which would also be furnished with fitted carpets in bright (but 'tasteful') colours.

The main structural change would involve the construction of a Lido area on the afterend of the Promenade Deck involving the erection of additional steel work extending aft to the Docking Bridge (these new screens would be emulated by the 'Q4') and the installation of an outdoor heated swimming pool as has been mentioned.

The contract for the conversion job – much to the chagrin of Southampton's shipyard unions – was awarded to the liner's original builders, John Brown and Co. (Clydebank) Ltd. The work would be carried out in the new graving dock in the Firth of Clyde which had been recently opened by the then Princess Royal.

The managing director of John Brown, John Rannie (later to be responsible for the building of the *QE2*), said in a news statement that welcomed the order (worth £1.5m):

'We are particularly pleased to receive this well balanced contract, providing work for all trades and ensuring continuity of employment for all our men when the Swedish American liner completes this year. The *Queen Elizabeth* will be in our hands from early next December to early March of next year, the three winter months, and will

During her conversion for cruising the Cunarder was dry-docked in the new facility on the Clyde.

George Outram & Co Ltd, Glasgow

employ on board at the Firth of Clyde Dry Dock, Greenock, over 2,500 men. 2,000 will be from Brown's of Clydebank, the remainder from the Dry Dock Company and the principal sub-contractors for the air conditioning plant, J. & E. Hall and Thermotank Ltd.

'This contract will provide work under good conditions for large numbers of joiners, plumbers, electricians and painters, at a time of year when employment is scarce. We believe it was awarded to us partly because of a satisfactory job done on the *Sylvania* this winter, and partly because the conversion is a large task to be completed in a short time and, having built the ship, we have the necessary data.

'Most of the steel work involved will be done by the Dry Dock Company and the engineering work by John Brown's engineers. We employ close on 6,000 men but could employ another 350, a few vacancies existing in all trades.'

Unfortunately the managing director's optimism would prove to be short-lived. The refit ran out of time with many jobs, especially in the new cabin areas on 'A' and 'C' decks which had not even been started, left undone. These would have to be completed in Southampton or even at sea.

The yard put the delay down to an epidemic of influenza amongst its workforce but Cunard considered that another vessel, three months behind its own schedule, had taken priority over their ship.

It was not only the delay in schedules that worried the Cunard people. Pilfering became a major cause for concern.

Not only did seven hundred brass bolts (amongst other items) intended for securing portholes disappear (apparently these had a "marketable" value in the dock road pubs of one pint for one bolt) but other non-ferrous items were pilfered that would have serious consequences long after the ship had left the Clyde.

With the fitting on board of so many new shower units and toilets – which would bring the *Elizabeth* up to a standard that was becoming expected by American travellers – there was a lot of copper piping about.

Sawn into short lengths this valuable piping could be smuggled out of the yard to become easily saleable scrap metal.

Not just content with taking scrap pieces of pipe, the pilferers would sometimes remove a covering panel concealing newly fitted pipe, scrape the paint to ascertain that it was copper and then drive a nail through to make sure that water was not already flowing through the length.

If the pipe was both copper and dry, then a saleable section would be sawn from it and the covering panel replaced.

As a result when water was later turned on as required (when the ship sailed from New York on her first cruise), cabins and corridors were flooded with water often appearing well away from its source.

Two days after the newly appointed Commodore Geoffrey Marr joined his ship (on March 7th), the liner left drydock on the first of two days of suitably high tides.

The blustery weather of the 9th was worrying but, as gales were forecast for the second day, the 25 knot gusts on the 9th were considered the lesser danger.

After an anxious journey down the Clyde (during which the pilot was convinced that the ship had twice lightly touched the bank because of the wind) the *Queen Elizabeth* reached the Tail O'the Bank where she anchored.

It was here that her reconditioned lifeboats, along with the new motor launches to be used as tenders during cruises, were to be taken on board – they had been left off for the journey downriver to help keep the liner's draught to a minimum. Lengthy attempts to hoist them on board had to be abandoned because of the weather but they were successfully embarked the next day.

Whilst the *Queen Elizabeth* was refitting on the Clyde many old hands who had built the ship took a pride in showing their children – and grandchildren – the beautiful ship that they had helped to create so many years before.

In spite of all the additional work that had been carried out on her the *Queen*'s tonnage had been reduced during the refit to 82,998 tons gross. When she first appeared she had been near 84,000.

So it was with a certain nostalgic regret that the Clyde bade farewell to 'No. 552' as she sailed for Southampton. On board were many of John Brown's men travelling south in an attempt to finish the unaccomplished work. Many hundreds more headed south – by rail – with the same intent.

As the *Queen Elizabeth* sailed south she passed the Island of Bute on her starboard side. As she did so the

At sea in her element the *Queen Elizabeth* makes a marvellous sight in a turbulent sea.

Roger Sherlock collection

Commodore saluted octogenarian William McFarlane, who lived in retirement on the island, with a blast on the ship's whistle. McFarlane had been the shipyard manager in direct charge of building the great liner.

When she sailed from Southampton on Tuesday 29th March, the *Elizabeth* took thirty workmen with her to New York hoping to get the cabins on 'C' deck finished and the new cabins on 'D' deck started, their basic structure as yet un-erected.

On the uncompleted work Sir Basil Smallpeice commented 'It would be unrealistic to pretend that we are not disappointed – contractors and owners alike – that the whole of the work could not be finished on time. Much work had been carried out on time or ahead (of schedule) ...'

As has already been mentioned, shortly after the *Queen Elizabeth* sailed from New York where she had been given an enthusiastic – perhaps almost relieved – welcome, at the beginning of her first post-refit Caribbean cruise, floods occurred (due to the pillaged and damaged copper piping) with water three inches deep in eight cabins forward on 'C' deck. Carpets and curtains were quickly changed in the affected cabins and the rooms dried out: their temporarily displaced occupants returned to them apparently none-the-worse for their experience.

The cruise was nevertheless a great success.

After the cruise the *Queen* returned to the North Atlantic route, making a few crossings before the big strike of 1966. Although suffering heavy losses through the lay-up of their strike-bound fleet the company managed at least to achieve the completion of the cabins on 'D' deck, a task that could have possibly taken six months had the *QE* been at sea.

The strike over, the *Queen* sailed on Saturday 16th July, for the start of a short season of transatlantic voyages.

On 21st September the *QE* started her first long cruise from New York. Gales followed the ship from Bermuda all the way to Lisbon, a call at the Azores was cancelled, a short cruise around the island being undertaken instead. Tangier was also omitted because of the wind and a large sea swell in the harbour, but from Madeira to Dakar and back across the Atlantic to the Caribbean it was sunshine all the way with the storms and the disappointment of ports missed soon being forgotten.

The new air-conditioning had worked well in the recently fitted cabins but the public rooms were stifling and many events were held in the open air. Although when the liner was built the public rooms had been fitted with what had been, at the time, thought of as remarkable air-conditioning, it had been designed to operate on sea temperature, which meant the coolness of the North Atlantic.

But in the tropics, the temperature of the sea rose to 80-90°F and as a result the rooms became almost untenable. However, an adjustment back in Southampton brought the new plants spare capacity into play and the problem was solved. Further extensions to the system were made during the winter overhaul of November 1966.

In October of the same year a tugmen's strike in Southampton found the *Queen* stranded in Cherbourg, unable to reach her home port. Passengers were tendered back to England but a group of stewards who joined the tender in order to reach home to get their cruising whites for the cruise that was to follow were ordered back on the *Lizzie* by the Master-At-Arms as all shore leave had been cancelled.

A nasty situation was averted when the men were allowed to fly home. The company gave an assurance through the union/ship liaison group (the *QE* was the first ship to have such a group, organised after the Seaman's Strike) that such an occurrence would not happen again, as catering, engineering and female staff had walked off the ship in sympathy. (The union liaison group had, amongst other things, negotiated for corned beef to be supplied for the crew as a homely change to the rich food provided. It never reached the crew as apparently the officers and pursers 'commandeered' it!)

The subsequent winter cruises to the West Indies were poorly patronised and, as had already been described, one of the series was cancelled and replaced with an unscheduled North Atlantic voyage.

This also suffered from low bookings and was known as the 'Ghost Ship Voyage'. It was also costly to the company especially through the oil fuel required to maintain the required fast passage.

The short cruises to Nassau from New York took one and a half days each way with a similar length of time being spent ashore. On one cruise a sudden storm hit the area and the *QE* had to sail round to the lee of the island leaving two hundred pleasure seekers stranded ashore to sleep 'rough in a barn'. They returned to the ship the following morning.

The short cruises of that season were followed by another extended cruise to the Mediterranean, the *Queen Elizabeth* sailing on Tuesday February 21st (1967). The liner was scheduled to visit fourteen ports in thirty seven days, arriving back in New York on Thursday March 30th.

The idea was good but the Commodore kept to himself his reservations that it was the wrong time of year for such a long cruise.

A total of fifty-eight shore excursions had been arranged by American Express who had their own office on board (the crew had their own tours arranged for one third the price) ranging from a few hours ashore for $6 to six day extended tours for $416. These latter tours would take the lucky passengers from the ship (anchored off Alexandria) to places such as Cairo, Aswan, Luxor, Jerusalem, Bethlehem, Baalbek, the Dead Sea, Damascus etc. before rejoining the liner at the then lovely city of Beirut.

From Las Palmas and Gibraltar the *Queen* headed towards North Africa but for the second time a half-day call at Tangier was cancelled because of yet another heavy swell. However, the promise of a complete day in Palma on the island of Majorca was well received by the passengers.

Shortly after midnight after leaving Majorca the ship was put around in a heavy sea that had been whipped up by a strong WNW gale. A crew member was reported overboard.

Only a perfunctory search could be carried out because of the weather conditions so, after two hours, a message was sent to other ships requesting them to keep a lookout for the missing man. Apparently he had been depressed, had been drinking heavily and had deliberately jumped overboard.

The *Queen Elizabeth* found the sea conditions at Alexandria too rough to effect any landings. After consulting Cunard in Southampton and obtaining reluctant permission to rearrange the itinerary (and to spend an extra £20,000 in fuel!) Commodore Marr asked the American Express people on board to re-schedule the next few days of tours.

All this resulted in the *Queen* diverting to Athens (which would have come later in the cruise anyway) and then dashing back to Alexandria where the planned complex series of tours could belatedly go ahead.

After three days at Alexandria the *QE* then went on to Beirut (where she picked up her passengers from the extended tours) then headed west to Messina. The call at Rhodes was omitted in order to make up time. Athens had already been visited.

Naples, Cannes, Barcelona, Lisbon and Madeira (where crew members swopped old pairs of shoes for wicker chairs etc bartered from the local 'bum boats') followed before the ship headed once again for New York where she arrived in the afternoon of Thursday 30th March, thus completing a very successful cruise as far as the passengers were concerned.

The Commodore, however, had slipped on a patch of spilt detergent shortly after leaving Madeira and suffered a 'dislocated right ankle, a fractured fibia and a cracked tibia'.

He handed over command to his Staff Captain, George Smith, and it was whilst the Commodore was home on sick leave that the axe fell.

The *Queen Mary* had been scheduled to be phased out in 1968 with the *Queen Elizabeth* carrying on in partnership with the new Q4, for a year at least.

But the letters that were opened concurrently on board both liners on 8th May 1967 said differently. Captain William Law was in command of the *Lizzie* on the poignant occasion. He later told the press 'It will be awful to say good-bye to this magnificent ship. It has been an honour to command her.'

In spite of her recent expensive refit and her gradual progression into profitability the *Queen Elizabeth* was to be withdrawn a year earlier than had been anticipated, just a year after the *Queen Mary*'s retirement.

The news was stunning, not least to Commodore Marr. It had been arranged that he would remain with his flagship until after the introduction of 'Q4' (the *Queen Elizabeth 2*) and run his vessel in conjunction with the 'New Cunarder', providing a vestige of the old two ship service.

Captain 'Bil' Warwick would have command of the new liner.

But the news meant not only the early retirement of the great ship, but also the early retirement of Commodore Marr who would also have to take a proportionate cut in pension!

On the same day the letters were opened on board the two *Queens*, Sir Basil Smallpeice said:

'Although the *Queen Mary*'s retirement next year had long been forecast, it had been hoped that the results of the *QE*'s cruise programme last winter would confirm the viability of the company's plan to keep her in service when the 'Q4' came along in 1969. In the event, the results had been very far from satisfactory. The board's decision to withdraw her and the *QM* is part of the unrelenting process of facing realities in their determination to put the company on to a paying basis.'

Recently introduced legislation by IMCO (International Maritime Commission) also influenced the company's decision. The Americans demanded that the *Queen* be brought up to the new standards of fire-protection which would have to include the fitting of additional fire-sprinklers and the boxing-in of stairways that could otherwise act as deadly draught tunnels in the event of fire.

The work, Cunard estimated, would cost £750,000 but would keep the *QE* on the Atlantic for a few more years running in conjunction with the 'New Cunarder'.

However, the U.S. legislators had another surprise up their sleeve. When Cunard requested that the Americans sent over an inspector to approve the improvement work as it progressed the authorities declined. The Americans wanted the work on the ship completed and then send her over to New York for inspection prior to approval and certification.

This would mean an empty, expensive trip to New York and, if the inspection failed, an equally expensive return trip back to the U.K. for the work that would then be needed to bring the liner up to requirements. Added to this there was also the loss of revenue.

In total, the prospect to Cunard was too daunting and contributed greatly to their decision to dispose of the *Queen*.

As soon as the decision to retire the *Queen* was made public the *QE*'s cruises and Atlantic liner voyages became popular with those who had travelled on and had loved the ship over the length of her career; the ship started to make a profit. On occasion a hand-made 'For Sale' notice would appear on the dockside or through a porthole as crew and passengers tried to make the point that Britain's heroic heritage was about to be auctioned off to the highest bidder.

The *Queen* made a few Atlantic crossings in between her winter cruises but the weather encountered during her northern voyages left her paintwork rather too dishevelled for her cruising role.

By this time special offers were made available in England for people to travel to Cherbourg by regular ferry and then join one of the *Queens* on the short trip to Southampton.

The enthusiastic Channel travellers often had the huge public rooms to themselves when the liner travelled overnight. Daylight brought a dismal view.

Large tarpaulins had been erected over the decking aft of the *Lizzie*'s funnels in an attempt to keep the wood planking free of the smuts that exuded from the less-than-pristine stacks. But grime found its way under the covers, themselves grimy from the falling soot.

The *Queen*, it seemed, was tired and only waiting to go.

Ever since the announcement of her impending redundancy within the future plans of Cunard, the once proud liner seemed ready to slip into oblivion.

Scrapping seemed to provide the obvious, almost humane, answer for exiting the world stage especially after such a magnificently full career. But many thought the *Lizzie* should be preserved in Southampton as the *Mary* had been in Long Beach, California.

The *Queen Mary* had been fortunate in finding a buyer in the form of the City of Long Beach for which port she had left Southampton on October 31st 1967.

In the last years of her own career the *Mary* had cruised from Southampton to the Atlantic Isles just as the *Lizzie* had cruised from New York to the Caribbean.

The two great liners met for the last time when they were both at sea. Just after midnight on 25th September 1967, the *Queens* passed each other in mid Atlantic, the *Queen Mary* en route to Southampton for the last time. Lights illuminating five funnels flashed on and off in a mutual salute as Captain Treasure Jones on the retiring ship and Captain Marr on the *Elizabeth* doffed their caps from their positions on their respective Bridge wings. Within a few short minutes the plans, hopes and successes of three decades came to an end as sirens boomed out across the water, the whole poignant scene witnessed by a few passengers braving the night wind.

Now, in a great blaze of publicity, the *QM* left Southampton on what was billed as 'The Last Great Cruise' which included a passage through the Magellan Straits taking her around the notorious Cape Horn to California.

She is still at Long Beach and, rumourdly after two changes in management, seems likely to continue her life as an entertainment and business complex under the aegis of the Disney empire.

Spurred on by the £1.5 million they had received for the *Mary* the company now looked to get a better price for the second of the 'set', so over the months that followed the announcement of her forthcoming disposal Cunard received many offers for their ageing – but still yacht like and beautiful – flagship that now seemed almost too big for anyone to do anything with.

But the bids came in and, between September 1967, and the following March, Cunard had received serious enquiries from many quarters.

The Japanese wanted her for a marine science museum in time for the 1970 Tokyo World Fair. Honolulu was interested as were the Australians. Mexico wanted her as an attraction in Acapulco where the *Queen Mary* had been well received en-route to Long Beach. Brazil wanted her for a gambling den.

Sir Howard Pitman was interested in the ship for use as a huge emigrant carrier to Australia and even good old Britain said why not keep her for British holiday makers?

Evangelist Dr. Billy Graham offered £2.083 million for her to become a floating Bible School and the United States

Institute of Technology wanted her for a floating university.

Six actual offers for the liner came from approximately one hundred enquiries and on 5th April 1968, Cunard announced the successful bidder.

For $7.75 million (£3.23 million) *Queen Elizabeth* was won by a group of Philadelphian businessmen who planned to moor her off Hog Island in their Pennsylvanian Delaware river. Delivery would take place sometime after the liner had completed her very last cruise on 15th November.

Charles Willard, one of the three men whose company had won the ship, said in the words of a royal suitor:

'We Americans have turned to your great nation so often for inspiration and instruction. We now come to obtain one of your prized possessions. Be sure the *Queen Elizabeth* will be welcomed and cared for in the fashion her long and illustrious career in war and peace warrants.'

In deference to the 'New Cunarder' the liner would be renamed *The Elizabeth*.

But two months later the purchasers with their $25 million plan ran into difficulties one of which (perhaps with hindsight) had been strangely obvious – the Delaware River was not deep enough! Even more strangely, perhaps, Cunard had not sent a representative to check that the Philadelphia site was at all suitable.

Added to this the State of Pennsylvania budget had been so cut that the planned highway to the ship would not be built for at least another four or five years.

However, a new site had been found for the liner – fast becoming a pawn in a giant game of real-estate politics – at Fort Lauderdale in Florida.

Two of the three buyers pose by the liner's binnacle.
Philadelphia Magazine

The *Queen*, meanwhile, carried on sailing almost like 'a cheap store that has huge notices outside which say Final Closing Down Sale more or less permanently displayed' as Geoffrey Marr recalled. He considered that the *Queen Elizabeth*'s retirement had been announced far too early for decency.

The liner's last cruises from New York were successes with the ship sailing to ports which could actually accommodate her. The mis-placed winter North Atlantic voyages that interspersed the cruises were less than well patronised – and the weather tended to spoil the paintwork for cruising. The high speed Atlantic dashes also lost money because of the heavy fuel consumption that was required to maintain express timetables.

Happily the *Queen*'s final summer season was financially successful as many old friends of the ship travelled on a last nostalgic journey.

But her slight turn in fortune came too late to affect any change in the decisions that had emanated from the Cunard Boardroom a few months previously. The 'New thinking' of the Board could not be dissuaded from its course of reform.

The *Queen Elizabeth*'s final season on the Atlantic was uneventful other than for the enthusiasms expressed by her old passengers from the years of peace and war, and who wanted to travel on her for just one last time.

Sailing from Southampton on 12th September the liner carried a large scale model of her successor – the *Queen Elizabeth 2* – at that moment completing her own fitting out on the Clyde.

The *Lizzie* left Southampton at the outset of her last voyage on October 23rd. Sadly this was marred by a tug dispute but the liner managed to make the tide at the Brambles and her sailing was not delayed.

Because of the uncertain financial and organisational condition of the liner's new owners, an announcement was made by Cunard which coincided with the *Queen*'s last sailing from Southampton to New York.

The company stepped in to moderate a worsening situation by more or less taking over the new venture themselves. Injecting $1 million into a new company called 'The Elizabeth (Cunard) Corporation' – of which they would have control with an 85% share – Cunard hoped that their continuing involvement with the *Queen Elizabeth* would reap worthwhile dividends in the years to come.

The three Philadelphians, however, still held a small interest in the company and would lease the ship from Cunard for $2 million a year. They would also have the option of completely taking over the ship after a period of ten years.

Sir Basil Smallpeice for Cunard said that the new agreement would benefit his company considerably. 'Once the project is underway' he told the press 'it should be capable of generating its own finance' adding that the new contract would enable Cunard to retain control of the policy and development of the *Elizabeth* Corporation for as long as Cunard wished.

On board the liner the Commodore told a gathering of four hundred crew members that the company would still be retaining an active interest in the liner's future role after her retirement. The meeting cheered him to a man.

The centre of all of the speculation arrived in New York for the last time on Monday, 28th October, to a series of farewell tributes that would put her home port of Southampton to shame.

Before she sailed on her final departure from her New York home the *Queen Elizabeth* was feted and honoured with both private and official functions being held on board.

The English Speaking Union held a $100-a-head dinner with guests being piped on board by the Glen Eagle Highlanders pipe band.

Mayor John Lindsay boarded the liner on the 30th, sailing day, to bid an official farewell. Presenting the ship with a plaque from the Department of Defence to commemorate the liner's remarkable war service, Mayor Lindsay said 'Today we can say 'The *Queen* is dead, long live the *Queen*' because in three months time the Cunard Steamship Company will bring into New York the splendid new flagship, the *Queen Elizabeth 2*'.

As the crew called 'Last call, all ashore' for the very last time the band played 'Auld Lang Syne' as the crowd of visitors was reluctantly ushered towards the gangway.

So on Wednesday 30th October the *Lizzie* sailed, finally, from New York. Responding with three blasts on her mighty sirens she replied to each of the decorated small craft that tooted their own tributes as they accompanied her, wake-like, on her journey down the River Hudson to the open sea.

Commodore Geoffrey Marr's lasting memory of the event had been received in a letter. Writing on 22nd October, L.W. Douglas, one time American ambassador to the Court of St James (his daughter would be travelling on the last trip on honeymoon), eloquently summed up the worth of the *Queen Elizabeth* and her sister:

'My Dear Commodore Marr:

'On the Eve of the *Queen Elizabeth*'s last voyage to her native shores it is fitting that the people of the Western World should be reminded of the indispensable role that she and her older sister, the *Queen Mary*, played in the last great worldwide convulsion.

'For almost three years, these two Sovereigns of the Seas silently sped across the waters of the North Atlantic, carrying with them more than two million fighting men from this continent to join the soldiers of the English-Speaking world who had fought so gallantly (and were to continue to engage so successfully) the evil forces that Hitler had unleashed on the world.

'In the darkness of the night, each of the great ships would quietly slip into the sheltering harbours of the Clyde or New York and, within less than seventy-two hours, in the greyness of the dawn, or the blackness of midnight, unheralded and unsung, would vanish into the vast spaces of the Atlantic, to run the gauntlet of the hostile German wolfpacks awaiting them. Unescorted, except during the last few miles of each voyage, their speed, and the skilful command of their officers, enabled them successfully to elude the vigilant enemy that would have sent them to the bottom of the ocean.

'Each ship made two round trips a month. During every summer month, when the North Atlantic was less boisterous, together they carried almost 70,000 soldiers to fight for freedom in England and in Europe; during each of the winter months, when the seas were apt to be more turbulent, they lifted almost 62,000 men in uniform to the white cliffs of Southern England.

'There is in history a chain of events that, as the first link is welded, leads on to others. So it is in the case of these two noble ships.

'Had it not been for Sir Percy Bates' determination to cause the *Queens* to be constructed and to slip down their ways into the Clyde; had they not been available to move more than two million American troops across the North Atlantic; had these troops not been assembled in Britain for the cross channel operation 'Overlord' in June of 1944, there would have been no invasion of Normandy, and the 'buzz-bomb' launching pads on the European continent would not have been captured in time to save London from being reduced to a pile of rubble.

'The two great *Queens* thus soldered the chain which was to frustrate Hitler's ambition to obliterate the basic freedoms of the civilized world.

'And so – as you guide the last of the two matchless *Queens* on her final voyage, will you bid her an affectionate and reverent 'ave atque vale' from those in this troubled world who owe so much to their uninterrupted and glorious contribution to the cause of free men, everywhere.

'They have merited a high place on the roster of the world's immortals.

'One generation succeeds another. Soon another *Queen* will replace the one we now salute. She will carry on the unfinished task of binding the Old World closer to the New.

L. W. Douglas'

The Commodore had the text of the letter typed out and pinned on the crews' notice board.

At sea, on Sunday 3rd November, to mark the *Queen Elizabeth*'s final North Atlantic Eastbound crossing, the Commodore held a Farewell Dinner.

After a journey that was remembered as being particularly happy the last night out was understandably a poignant and emotional occasion. At the end of the evening's entertainment as a large a crowd as possible of passengers and crew (including the Commodore) poured onto the dance floor for a heart-felt rendition of that traditional song of farewell by Robert Burns, 'Auld Lang Syne'.

Among the passengers were Lord and Lady Montague of Beaulieu and Jack Frost, journalist and a lifetime devotee of the *Queen*. He had co-authored, with Neil Potter, a magnificent tribute to the liner, 'The Elizabeth', published a few years before in 1965.

Frankie Howerd, the British comedian, was also on board and had entertained the passengers during the trip.

The last crossing was described as ' .... a gala trip .... one of the best crossings we've had' as when, on 4th November 1968, the liner arrived in Southampton coming to the end of the career for which she had been designed.

It was the end of Voyage 495. She had crossed the Atlantic 896 times; she had carried over the years 2,300,000 passengers (excluding her war service) and had steamed 3,472,672 miles in the service of the nation that had so

The Queen Mother, accompanied by Commodore Marr, surveys the ship from the advantage of a Bridge wing.

Commodore Geoffrey Marr chats to H.M. as she wistfully holds the wheel that she held during the liner's trials in 1946. Sir Basil Smallpeice listens in during this final Royal visit to the ship that the Queen Mother had also launched.
Both photos Southern Newspapers plc, Southampton

proudly given the ship her being and had latterly made 31 cruises.

The advent of her last transatlantic arrival in the Hampshire port (an hour late due to bad weather) turned out to be a quiet affair, the occasion lacking the thousands of spectators that the similar arrival of the *Queen Mary* had commanded. The *Lizzie* gave three blasts on her siren.

As the liner pulled alongside Berth 107 in the New (Western) Docks the Commodore on the Bridge became anxious as the prevailing wind tried to blow the *Queen Elizabeth* away from the quay and at the way that a couple of mooring lines were being handled. Picking up his amplified megaphone he roared out 'Heave away for'd!'

Hearing the admonition from above him a wag on a lower bridge front deck recalled Frankie Howerd's referring to the Commodore as a 'god' during a cabaret act during the voyage (the comedian had got Geoffrey Marr's permission 'to take the mickey' out of him) and called out 'Has God spoken?' The tension was broken.

It had been announced earlier that the day following the last arrival, on 6th November, Her Majesty the Queen Mother would visit the liner to pay her own tribute to the Pride of Britain that she had launched thirty years previously.

In readiness for the Royal visit the shoreside paintwork of the liner's superstructure and funnel was scrubbed and cleaned. The omission of a summer overhaul, a stormy North Atlantic and the breakdown of a couple of forced draught fans had given the liner a rather too grubby an appearance.

Internally the woodwork and metalwork was polished until it gleamed. By the time the flower and plant arrangements with which British Rail had decorated the terminal building had found an echo in 'R' Deck Square where the Queen Mother would embark the ship's company had a ship of which they could be justly proud.

Just before noon on the appointed day Her Majesty stepped on board, having arrived from London by train. The Queen Mother was met by Commodore Marr and Staff Captain W. J. Law. She then chatted to the crew members who formed the guard of honour before being taken up to the Midships Bar where senior officers and senior company representatives awaited to be presented.

Lunch followed (Dover Sole followed by Saddle of Southdown Lamb all washed down with Chateau Lafite Rothschild '59 and, the Royal favourite, Batard Montrachet '62), after which Sir Basil Smallpeice presented the Queen Mother with one of the limited edition goblets specially engraved as keepsakes for the crew. In response the Royal guest thanked everybody and made expressions of her close interest in the liner's career as it had gradually unfolded over the years.

The *Queen*'s journey into history was approaching fulfilment but in a way less grand, less magnificent and even less dignified than suited her position.

Geoffrey Marr then conducted the Queen Mother on a tour of the ship during which she met, at her own request, as many of the 'old' Cunard hands as she could. The tour included a visit to the open areas of the Promenade Deck and Bridge where the feathers of Her Majesty's hat blew in the lively breeze of the fading autumnal afternoon of what had been a bright, sunny day.

During the course of the tour the Commodore and his regal guest had discussed her portrait painted by Sir Oswald Birley that hung in the Main Lounge. It was the commissioning of this portrait that had caused so much controversy just after the war, over twenty years previously.

After the Queen Mother had stepped ashore for the very last time the Commodore was able to reflect on the events of the day.

At lunch the Queen Mother had asked him about the future plans for the ship after her arrival in Florida. Her Majesty 'expressed the hope that the end of the liner's life would be in line with the same proud tradition she had maintained in both peace and war'.

Geoffrey Marr, however, was not so hopeful but 'kept my forebodings to myself'.

The beginning of the final act. Almost 'stealing away' the Queen Elizabeth edges away from her final berth. *Cedric Wasser*

His doubts, especially about the future financial security of the ship, had been fuelled by an article he had read in the June edition of the American magazine, 'Philadelphia'.

This reputable publication had been approached in mid-May by Stanton Miller, one of the trio of the successful bidders for the *Queen Elizabeth*, to write an article about the liner's forthcoming arrival in Philadelphia in order to help persuade the City to release more land for car parking; to point out the advantages of having the liner as the city's 'newest landmark' (as a Cunard advert had referred to the ship during the *Queen*'s final season); and to try to rekindle some enthusiasm for the project in the local press.

The 'Philadelphia' editorial stated that it had '... assigned one of our writers to do a piece on the ship and the deal,' but added ominously 'The story he brought back .... was not the story he went after.' The reporter wrote an article that '.... raises more questions than it answers.'

The three business men, brothers Robert and Stanton Miller along with their partner Charles Williard (the three of whom collectively liked to be known as 'C-B-S') '.. were known' the editorial continued, 'to this magazine' from previous investigations.

The Millers were, it was claimed '... closely associated with people to whom this publication is an anathema' referring to the brothers' dealings with the Teamsters Union in various business arrangements that 'smelt' badly of Mafia involvement.

Williard, president of a large electrical contract firm, had been attacked by the magazine a year previously for '.... playing funny games with a free wheeling labor boss.'

It also transpired that two eminently unqualified persons had carried out the 'careful investigations' on behalf of C-B-S to ensure that the planned locale for the

Almost stealing away into the mist on the morning that she left Britain forever the *Queen* was watched by very few spectators. *Author's collection*

Queen's final berthing place in the Delaware River was suitable for the task. These 'experts' failed to show an insufficient depth of water (the river would need expensive dredging); they failed to investigate the possible hazard that could be caused to low-flying aircraft flying to and from Philadelphia's international airport; they failed to note the noise pollution caused by aircraft every few minutes and they failed to report on the pollution caused by odours emanating from the nearby oil-refinery.

The Philadephian trio soon thereafter decided that their

city was not, after all, geared-up for their ambitious venture. Using the lack of roads to connect their site to the main highway as an excuse they decided that perhaps Florida would make a more appropriate site for their acquisition.

Financial difficulties followed as C-B-S found that they were unable to raise the balance of the agreed purchase price for their gigantic piece of floating hardware.

Their hopes, and the hopes of those people who perhaps shared the 'Philadelphia's point of view that their city had within their grasp '... an unparalleled opportunity for them and for the city ..', an opportunity that '... must not be lost ...', were dashed as the prospect of millions of dollars' worth of tourism and conventions faded from view. Philadelphia felt jilted.

However, in New York, Cunard's negotiators still spoke of C-B-S as 'extremely gracious people'!

No wonder the Commodore felt uneasy!

On the evening of 7th November the crew held their own farewell dance in a Southampton ballroom to which Commodore and Mrs. Marr had been invited as guests of honour.

The crew had all contributed to make a presentation to their captain. This took the form of a heavy, solid silver rosebowl inscribed:

'RMS *Queen Elizabeth*, 2nd (sic) November 1968. Presented by the Ships Company on the last voyage to Commodore Geoffrey Marr DSC RD RNR. In appreciation of his unfailing thoughtfulness and his many timely arrivals.'

The 'unfailing thoughtfulness' and 'many timely arrivals' referred to, recalled the Commodore's earnest attempts to dock the *Queen Elizabeth* in Southampton – often ahead of schedule – so that crew members going ashore could catch the last bus or train home to their families or perhaps get to their favourite pub before closing time!

Geoffrey Marr, even now in 1989, still relishes the sentiments expressed with great amusement and still appreciates what had generally been a good and loyal crew.

The day following the dance and presentation saw the *Queen Elizabeth* sailing on her ultimate cruise of farewell. This would take her to Las Palmas and Gibraltar. To the strains of Southampton's Salvation Army band playing the *de-rigeur* 'Auld Lang Syne', she slipped into Southampton Water, the prelude of her commercial swan-song.

The cruise gave a small part of Britain a chance to voice its regret as her passing, a chance that would again put the mother-land to shame.

As the liner left Gibraltar she was escorted by a flotilla of ships of the Royal Navy. Before they turned away for 'Gib' they steamed by and saluted the *Queen* as she gradually built up speed. Jet fighters roared overhead. Geoffrey Marr recalled 'It was a wonderful farewell. The dreadful thought behind it was that it was farewell.'

The *Queen Elizabeth* arrived back at Berth 107 in Southampton Docks an hour late, again because of a high wind, on Friday 15th November. That evening the crew paid off. Some would join the QE2, a few (193) would sail with the *Lizzie* to her new home but the rest found themselves 'on the beach' after many years of loyal service.

On 18th November the last function to be held on board was a dance held for nine hundred serving and ex-officers and for senior local dignitaries. The occasion was over subscribed and, because the ship's company had been dismissed, an outside firm of caterers provided the refreshment. The evening combined regret that the largest liner the world had ever seen was passing from the oceans with a thankful feeling that the ship's life had been well lived.

But the future of the *Queen Elizabeth*, even at this late hour, was still uncertain as she slipped away from England in the early morning fog of a dull 28th November.

As the ship sailed the Commodore's wife, daughter, the ever loyal Jack Frost and a handful of officials had to be landed by tug. The liner had slipped her moorings a little sooner than had been anticipated because only half the usual number of seamen were on board attempting to cope with casting off the mooring lines.

Other than for Southampton's Albion Band the quayside was almost bereft of well-wishers. The *Queen Elizabeth* was almost slinking away under the cover of the fog. Mrs Marr recalled the departure as 'a disgrace'. Her opinion was shared by many who compared the sailing as being diametrically opposite to the grand farewell given to the *Queen Mary*.

Later, Geoffrey Marr wrote badly of the sailing comparing it to the farewells given to the ship in New York and Gibraltar. He described it as '... a British understatement with a vengeance, as though the British world of ships and shiplovers looked the other way until she had gone!'

The other ships that were in Southampton that unhappy morning saluted the *Queen Elizabeth* as she passed by but received no acknowledgement to their respectful signals. A temporary electrical fault had developed with the *Lizzie*'s whistle control gear and she left the port in a silence that only added to the almost furtive feeling of the departure.

As the *Lizzie* made her silent passage through the Solent and Spithead she was cheered by the ship's company of HMS *Hampshire*, one of the Royal Navy's class of guided missile destroyers.

Passing down through the Channel later that evening the homeward-bound cruising Cunarder *Carmania* made her own farewells to her giant sister.

Queen Elizabeth 2, the 'New Cunarder', also sent a message of good wishes for the future success of her predecessor as the former liner underwent her own initially successful trials off the Isle of Arran. A month later disaster would strike the QE2 on her prolonged trials to the Canaries – a disaster that would take many months to resolve and would even cast a shadow on her future role with Cunard.

For the *Queen Elizabeth* steaming towards a new life in Florida it was the end of an honourable, wonderful, prosperous and often glamorous career.

But it was not yet to be the end of the ship that was once RMS *Queen Elizabeth*.

Two aerial studies of the liner show the *Queen Elizabeth* passing by Weston and Netley (above) and Fawley oil refinery (below) as she leaves Southampton Water for the last time. The two photographs graphically show the 'spit and polish' applied to the starboard side of the liner in preparation for the Queen Mother's visit whilst the port side remains stained from her final voyages.

Reproduced by kind permission of FotoFlite, Ashford, Kent

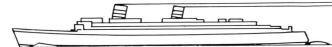

Chapter Thirteen
'... The most Mighty of Pyres ... the Roaring Flames Mingled with Weeping ...'
('Beowulf')

As a postscript, the last years of the liner were far from the honourable time that many had hoped for her but they must be related in order to complete the saga of the ship which had once been the *Queen Elizabeth*.

The first inkling that the officials of the cities of Fort Lauderdale and Hollywood in Broward County, Florida, had that the liner was to be retired in their shared harbour of Port Everglades (instead of Philadelphia) came in January 1968.

Late that month Mayor-Commissioner Edmund R. Burry wrote 'It has come to my notice that there is a possibility of situating the *Queen Elizabeth* in Port Everglades on a permanent basis.

By June, after much discussion and local argument about who would pay for road access to the liner, water supply, sewage, police and fire services, etc, the two cities were still enthusiastic. Commissioner Al Hines wrote to William Skillings, whose public relations firm was doing much of the planning: 'It was encouraging and most flattering for all of Hollywood's city officials to learn this week that the *Queen Elizabeth* will be located at Port Everglades as opposed to the many cities and nations who were interested.

'... thank you for the effort you have expended in keeping excitement at a fever pitch ...'. Director James Beattie of Hollywood's Publicity Department wrote that its advertising advisory board was:

A view of the *Elizabeth* alongside what would become the passenger terminal in Port Everglades. One can only wonder as to her success as a hotel etc had she remained there to enjoy the port's later rise to a premier cruise port.
Peter Walters

'... your proposal would certainly be well received by this community.

'... I am convinced that the placement of this great vessel will benefit us immeasurably.'

The Mayor-Commissioner then went on to envisage the liner '... retaining a British atmosphere ...' and that he would be 'opposed to allowing such a great ship being degraded in any manner.'

'... completely overwhelmed at the decision ..'

Even by the time that the *Elizabeth* was on her last cruise to Gibraltar the two cities still expected that the liner would be with them sometime during the new year. It was fully expected also that Cunard would want much of the conversion work to be done in Britain which would give Broward County ample time to prepare the site and its services.

Under her own steam at last and almost looking her old self, *Seawise University* makes a cautionary call at Rio en-route to Hong Kong.
                                                    Collection of Robert Lenzer, Richardson, Texas

Everybody must have been surprised when it was announced that the liner would be arriving off the Florida coast early in December.

After a ghost-like voyage that took her diagonally across the North Atlantic, the liner arrived off Boco Raton on Saturday 7th December. Dredging had not been completed in Port Everglades so the Commodore was told to cruise the ship down the coast to show the flag, which he did. Slowly sailing as far south as Key Biscayne her progression was watched by thousands of spectators during the day, thrilled by the sight and sound of the magnificent ship, and by many thousands more at night who marvelled at the beauty of a liner bejewelled by hundreds of lights, as others had marvelled before them.

Heading north from Key Biscayne the *Queen Elizabeth* spent the night of 7-8th December steaming around the ocean off Fort Lauderdale, waiting for her triumphant entry into the port early the next morning.

At 11.15 on the morning of the 8th after the ship had berthed, Commodore Marr rang that final, often fatal, order on the Bridge telegraph to the Engine Room:

'Finished with Engines.'

Shortly after arrival the Commodore received a cryptic cable from Captain Storey, Cunard's nautical adviser in Southampton: 'For Commodore Marr in *QE* on arrival. Acts 27 Verse 39 (signed) Storey.'

Looking up the reference quoted in the Holy Bible, the Commodore found the passage 'And when it was day, they knew not the land: but they discovered a certain creek with a shore, into which they were minded, if it were possible, to thrust in the ship.'

It was in this 'certain creek' of Port Everglades that the liner would remain for two years.

Initially response to the presence of the *Elizabeth* – the ship that was the *Queen Elizabeth* – (the prefix *Queen* had been dropped at Cunard's request) was good after the liner opened to the public on 14th February 1969, but finance and local politics soon took a hand.

The old Cunard hands who had been interviewed by Stanton Miller to stay with the ship to act as guides and advisers were later reduced in number from 120 to 30 (mostly engineers who had been retained to assist in running boilers and generators). Some men who had sailed her over had returned home after the ship's arrival. Others would return after the ship's later sale to Queen Ltd.

A few months after the ship's opening, the liner was

again up for sale. Offers came from all over the world: £3 million from a concern wanting to operate the *Elizabeth* between the United Kingdom and Australia; the Charter Travel Club offered £1.7 million and another bid was made by Puerto Rican interests.

The successful bid for the liner came in July when the ship that had been the *Queen Elizabeth* was sold for $8.64 million to Queen Ltd. a subsidiary of Utility Leasings in which the old trio of C-B-S had an interest.

It was whilst under the new ownership that a hurricane warning caused the by then almost deserted ship to be partially scuttled to prevent her, it was feared, tearing away from her berth.

Deserted and by now almost unwanted, the neglected liner, once the pride of Britain's merchant marine, was once more put up for auction. Queen Ltd. was bankrupt with debts of $12 million.

The notice of sale proclaimed that the liner would be offered 'free and clear of liens and encumbrances' whilst the catalogue listed forty lots that would come under the hammer. The sale would be held at the Galt Ocean Mile Hotel, Fort Lauderdale, between 9th and 10th September 1970.

The lots on offer included furniture from crew and passenger areas; radar and compass equipment; liferafts; oil paintings; a tapestry, and many other fittings. The apparel of a great ship would be dispersed piecemeal, unless a single buyer could be found for the entire ship and its contents.

A representative of the Island Navigation Company of Hong Kong made an almost last-minute but successful bid of $3.2 million (£1.33 million). The Island Navigation Company (to be responsible for moving and repairing the ship) was in turn a subsidiary of the giant Orient Overseas Line also of Hong Kong which would be the liner's actual owner and operator. This enormous shipping empire, which contained much well-looked-after second-hand tonnage within its fleet, was owned by Mr C.Y. Tung. Described as a dynamic, jolly, man his interests incorporated tankers, bulk carriers, and car ferries as well as passenger liners.

Mr Tung's plan (he liked to be called 'C.Y.' by his devoted employees) was based on an idea first instigated by U. Thant, Secretary General of the United Nations, that a ship be used for educational purposes whilst spreading goodwill and understanding amongst the nations and between different cultures.

C.Y's plan was ambitious: to convert the world's largest ship into the world's largest floating university (which would be on charter to the Chapman College of Orange, California) and carry eighteen hundred students plus eight hundred cruise passengers in great comfort to destinations bordering the Seven Seas. An initial shake-down maiden cruise around the Pacific would be followed by Round the World Cruises to coincide with American Spring and Autumn terms. (A Chinese crew would help alleviate running costs aggravated by the ever increasing price of oil fuel.) Quite wittily, and using a clever pun on his own name, C.Y. decided to name the new ship after himself – *Seawise University*. When not cruising the *Seawise* would be used as a floating campus in the United States.

But first the liner had to be taken from Point A (Port Everglades) to Point B (Hong Kong). It was first reported that the ship could be towed as far as Singapore where there was a dry dock able to accommodate her (the same she had used during the early days of the Second World War) before carrying on under her own steam to the crown colony off mainland China.

However, it was finally decided to steam her all the way and arrangements were made to ready her for the long journey.

A Chinese crew under Captain William Hsuan and Chief Engineer W. C. Cheng were flown to Florida along with workers from C.Y's own shipyard.

As the *Seawise* – the ship that had been the *Queen Elizabeth* – was larger than anything that the Chinese had experienced before, it was felt prudent to invite experienced advisers to assist with readying the ship for her long journey that would take her more than half-way around the world.

Accordingly Commodore Geoffrey Marr and Chief Engineer Ted Philip received invitations to leave their retirements and fly to Florida to rejoin their old ship, which they were delighted to do.

Preparation for departure was already underway by the time they arrived and Geoffrey Marr, arriving on 18th November, a little later than the engineers, was appalled at the mess that he found on board.

The worst job of all was the problem of ridding the ship of 4,000 tons of oil-contaminated water but this was partly achieved after much effort by the Chinese accompanied by much complaint by the local authorities.

Engines were checked and boilers tested but only six out of the twelve boilers were considered functionable for the long voyage.

During two years of near neglect, deterioration had rapidly set in, especially in the fragile boiler tubes, which substantiated the fears of the dozen or so other English engineer advisers that the best way of getting the ship to Hong Kong would still be to tow her there.

Sailing day inevitably changed from the planned-for date in early December to the date estimated by Geoffrey Marr of February 1971 as 600 boiler tubes had to be changed in the six boilers that would be needed to get the *Seawise* to Hong Kong. Engines, too, were repaired; radar, radio and other navigational aids overhauled; testing was undertaken and approval obtained by classification societies on various pieces of equipment; the ship's bottom was cleaned of growth accumulated since December 1968; lifeboats replaced; cables and anchors retrieved from their beddings on shore (where they had acted as additional moorings) and replaced in cable lockers and hawse pipes; and so on and so on and so on.

The first two repaired boilers were flashed-up on New Year's Eve and engine trials were carried out on 3rd February 1971.

At last the day of sailing could be decided. After several days of gales, a lull coinciding with a suitable day-time tide was chosen – Wednesday 10th February.

The day was similar to the one that saw the *Elizabeth* arrive in Port Everglades but with one difference. The *Seawise* was now comparatively underpowered and manned by an inexperienced crew and, should anything amiss occur, the liner would become 'the biggest dam' cork that Port Everglades had ever seen!' as Commodore Marr told the press, much to C. Y. Tung's concern as the statement immediately increased the insurance premiums on the ship!

The *Seawise University* left unmourned from her resting place alongside the undeveloped berths 24 and 25 in Port Everglades. The berths were in the passenger area of the docks and were sited at the southern end of the harbour just inside the busy entrance to the Intracoastal Waterway. The berths had been temporary as it had been planned to move the ship later to a permanent berth further down the waterway. On board the ship as she left the harbour that had welcomed her with so much rapture twenty six long months previously was Port Commissioner W. Phil McConaghey who was making a short trip before disembarking onto one of the accompanying tugs.

The Commissioner, elected to office after the liner's arrival at the Florida port, had been appalled at the slackness of the commercial and leasing agreements that he had inherited from the previous administration.

Quite rightly he reappraised the confused situation and found it to be drastically wanting. Unhappily, especially as he admired the *Elizabeth*, he took his remedying measures to the extreme and, using a helpless 84,000 ton ship as a scapegoat, the symbol of all the ills caused by local mismanagement and political squabbling, became determined to rid the port of her.

Before the *Seawise* even left her berth a message was received by the Bridge that one of the six operational boilers had developed leaks in its tubes during the preceding night and was thus unoperational.

By the time the liner had been taken from the mouth of the Intracoastal Waterway and turned in the harbour of Port Everglades to face towards the 300 foot entrance, another boiler went out of action. Fate, as well as Florida, now seemed to turn her back on the former Queen of the Seas.

Technically the liner did not now have enough power to manoeuvre, should the need arise, but she did have enough momentum – plus the aid of tugs – to carry her through the entrance opening. Advisor Commodore Marr had telephoned his counterpart, Ted Philip, in the Engine Room just before the second boiler blew 'We are committed to the channel now. See that they give her everything they can!' This timely order ensured that the liner just managed to gain enough way to glide through into the open sea without slewing around at the harbour mouth in the 15 knot wind that was blowing.

The fall-off in power also prevented the ship that had been the *Queen Elizabeth* from manoeuvring once out in the open sea. She could not now provide a lee for the tug that came bucking alongside to take off the pilot and her civic passenger.

At least one person on the liner thought that almost poetic justice would be done if the man, who had done so much to rid the port of the hapless liner and send her into a second exile, was pitched into the sea by the giantess from which he was now disembarking!

The next day as the ship proceeded south there was a massive loss of feed water in No. 4 Boiler Room but this was corrected by the British advisers and soon an excess of water was being produced.

But luck again took a downward turn as a serious fire in No. 4 Boiler Room broke out just after 9 am on Saturday 13 February. An hour later the fire had been brought under control but one of the boilers was found to be badly damaged.

Captain Hsuan decided to signal for a tug. Meanwhile the liner drifted helplessly at the mercy of the winds and currents. At night a white light rigged fore and aft and two red lights on the foremast warned other ships that the *Seawise University* was not under control.

The Norwegian cruise liner *Starward* approached the wallowing leviathan just before Sunday midnight, playing on the darkened liner with her brash, bright searchlights. An offer of assistance by the Norwegians was declined by Captain Hsuan as he waited for the tug.

The salvage tug *Rescue* arrived on the following Tuesday as the liner completed her drift down through the Windward Passage between the Scylla and Charybidas of the Caribbean – Fidel Castro's communist Cuba on one side and 'Papa Doc' Duvalier's voodoo-ridden Haiti on the other.

It had been intended to tow the old Cunarder to Jamaica but again wind and tide thwarted the plan. The second choice of Curacao was also abandoned and the small Dutch island, Aruba, was chosen. Situated a few miles off the northern Venezuelan coast, the island had extensive oil-orientated facilities and would make a suitable base for repairs.

But to gain the island a second tug had been summoned and together the two small craft laboriously towed their charge, trailing a quarter of a mile astern, on her Odyssean journey across the Caribbean.

On arrival off Aruba the pilot ordered her to anchor but, after the tugs had left her and before anyone could realise, she had been brought to a halt some way off the planned anchoring ground.

A wind blew up and the *Seawise University* drifted, dragging her anchor, out to deep water.

The trailing anchor bedded itself into an offshore sandbank. Another tug, the *Schelde* out of Oranjestad in Aruba, came out and towed the liner off the relatively safe anchorage of the sandbank and then, under the pretext of having engine trouble herself, cast the *Seawise* adrift and helpless in deeper water hoping, it seemed, to return later to claim salvage.

After enquiries by C.Y. Tung's representatives the *Schelde*, now in harbour, suddenly became free of any problems and, with another tug, *Los Cocos*, towed the *Seawise* to another haven where the liner put down two anchors, six miles from Oranjestad.

Men, boiler tubes and other equipment were flown to Aruba to hasten the liner's repair. C.Y. Tung visited the ship in person and ordered the Boiler and Engine Rooms to be thoroughly cleaned and painted. By the time the two chief advisers returned from a short leave in England they found that the Old Lady was almost her old self.

After seventy-four days spent in a pleasant climate (although with a choppy sea) the British contingent felt that, at long last, the old *Lizzie* was being given a new lease of life. She sailed from Aruba bound for Curacao under her own, now certain, power, lifting her bows to the ocean's swell.

Fresh water and fuel oil were taken on at Curacao and another similar stop was made at Port of Spain on Trinidad.

Speeds varied between a discreet 7 and 11 knots, with the latter speed using 300 tons of bunkers per day.

The British contingent wished that she could be 'opened up' but Captain Hsuan decided to play safe. Also, rather than steam directly for Capetown, he diverted his ship to Rio de Janeiro where she arrived in the early dawn of Sunday 30th May to an interested welcome.

A fortnight later the *Seawise University* arrived to a warm reception in an otherwise windy Capetown which left Geoffrey Marr thinking that the ship would always be welcomed there during her future world cruises.

As the *Seawise* crossed the Indian Ocean, steadily rising and falling to a swell that had other ships dipping their bows in showers of spray, the old Cunard hands were reminded (other than for the speed being made) of the halcyon days on the North Atlantic when the liner was the *Queen Elizabeth*.

A call at Singapore on 7th July brought forth a splendid welcome by aircraft of the RAF but the publicity was kept low-key as her new owners wanted her to be properly welcomed there when she was finally restored, pristine in her new paintwork. (At that time it was anticipated that her hitherto black hull would be painted a light grey, her superstructure would remain white and her funnels painted in Orient Oversea's orange with an applied plum blossom motif.)

The *Seawise University* arrived in Hong Kong after being '... the slowest boat to China' but her performance was such that she arrived early and had to steam around the harbour at slow speed to kill almost a day.

However, on Thursday 15th July the liner was given an early morning welcome by helicopters, a fire boat display and a multitude of small craft bustling around her.

This time the Queen was home and about to embark on a new lease of life.

Gradually, over the next few months C.Y. Tung's great ship was reconditioned and converted into the ship of his dreams. The IMCO fire-fighting standards (that Cunard were not able to afford) were incorporated, bringing the liner into line with the stringent standards that the Americans especially – with all their bitter experiences of years gone by – demanded of foreign vessels.

Two thousand men were shipped out daily to the vessel that was undergoing a gigantic renovation exercise equalling the liner's immediate post-war conversion from troop-ship to passenger liner on the Clyde in 1946.

By the New Year of 1972 the *Seawise University* floated resplendent in her new livery of white hull and orange funnels, the legend 'Orient Overseas Line' proudly emblazoned along each side of the hull below the Bridge and level with the Main Deck. All twelve boilers had been reconditioned and her four engines thoroughly overhauled. Dry docking in Japan would shortly follow to check, clean and paint her underwater hull and fittings.

Hope sparkled in the clear sunshine of Sunday 9th January. About 540 workmen were left on board, many of the usual 2,000 who were kept busy on the conversion work having already gone ashore for lunch. The ship's catering staff busied themselves preparing for a reception to be hosted that day by C.H. Tung, C.Y's son.

About 11.30 that morning a lone yachtsman, indulging in the pleasures of the harbour and of the day, looked over to the huge, white liner and, to his consternation, saw flames flickering from what appeared to be a pile of rubbish dumped by an open door in the ship's side.

On board, too, other fires were discovered – three at least had started almost simultaneously (there could have been many more) – and these quickly spread, fanned and carried by the ample supply of air coming into the liner through the openings in the hull.

As the ship's fire-fighting crew struggled to control one of the blazes (they were unaware of the existence of the others), the remainder of the crew and the party guests who had already arrived on board hurriedly abandoned ship, some sliding down hawsers to escape the rapidly spreading flames.

Nearing completion as a university cruise ship, the *Seawise University* made a sparkling sight in Hong Kong harbour. The plum-leaf motifs have not yet been attached to her funnels.
John Havers

A whole hour passed after the first cry of 'Fire' before fire-fighting tugs arrived at the scene and started pumping a part of Hong Kong's harbour into the ship, thousands of gallons of water that fell onto the upperworks of the burning ship that had been the *Queen Elizabeth*.

Dense smoke billowed from along the length of the liner as the fire spread, drifting in clouds across to the island city. As the fire took hold, feeding on woodwork, carpets and furniture, and as rare veneers and marquetry blistered, peeled and briefly fed the conflagration within the ship, explosions racked the liner. Her newly-painted hull blistered and flared as the paint pulled away from the influence of the heat within.

After four hours the liner was left to burn herself out, abandoned by those who had wept as they had struggled to save her. By now the weight of water pumped on board

'The Most Mighty of Pyres ...'. Smoke billows across Hong Kong harbour in the early stages of the fire, the liner's hull, as yet relatively unscorched.

Collection of Robert Lenzer, Richardson, Texas

by the fire-fighting tugs had caused the liner to list; water started to pour through the open doors near to the water-line.

By midnight of that awful day the fire had burnt through five decks and the liner had developed a list of 17°. Her starboard side was red hot with much of the paintwork completely burnt, exposing the charred steel plates of the dead hull.

Not only had the Chinese inherited the largest liner in the world they had also inherited the spectre of the *Normandie* as the *Seawise University* started a slow and unstoppable capsize.

Twenty-four hours after the discovery of the fires the old *Queen* was resting at an acute angle on the harbour bottom, her upperworks and bridge collapsed inwardly if they had not disintegrated, her funnels blackened, her masts contorted. The fire would burn for another day.

Back in England Geoffrey Marr had by this time learnt with horror that his 'darling' was burning and making headlines worldwide.

At 6.45 on the morning of 10th January the Commodore was annoyed to be awakened by the jingling of the telephone. His annoyance soon disappeared as he answered the instrument.

It was John Timpson of the BBC. Had the Commodore heard that his last Command had just capsized in Hong Kong harbour and did the Commodore want to make any comment?

Almost at a loss Geoffrey Marr recalled Noel Mostert's words which he quoted as an epitaph, ending:

'..... no tanker, no matter what its size, could ever convey the visual impact of these two magnificent ships, especially when seen at speed, flinging aside the North Atlantic in huge combers, their whole line one of power and splendour: oceanic palaces of magnificent proportions'.

John Timpson said simply, quietly:
'Who could follow that?'

The retired Commodore had thought that, as the liner had been four times as large as anything the Chinese had owned before, they were afraid of the ship. At least the Cunard people had become accustomed to leviathans in progressive stages.

He also considered that, as so much money had been expended on the old *Lizzie*'s refit, arson could be the only cause. The Court of Inquiry held later backed up his assessment.

The *Queen* was dead, but the problem now existed that she was an eyesore and a hazard.

A year later she was still there, still rusting. On the first anniversary of the ship's destruction her one time commander, Sir Ivan Thompson, joined a small group of men in a memorial service at the end of Pier 90 in New York. The old *Lizzie* was still missed, still remembered with affection by those who had known her.

She also found fleeting fame as she slept forever. Ian Fleming's famous spy James Bond found British secret headquarters built into the listing liner in the film 'The Man With the Golden Gun'. But that was about as far as romance would touch the old liner as she was laid-out in Hong Kong.

Oil gradually seeped from ruptured fuel tanks and an inflated boom was floated around the rusting hulk to contain it. Two years later 3,000 tons of the stuff would be pumped out at a cost of £140,000 as C.Y. was pressed to move the wreck.

It would have taken millions to salvage and rebuild the liner so in December 1974 the owners decided, sadly and reluctantly, to scrap her.

A month later a memorial to the ship was unveiled by Mayor Lindsay outside Orient Oversea's New York offices in Water Street. Made of granite the memorial contained two eighteen inch letters, 'Q' and 'E', from the liner's name along with carved copies of letters from the Queen Mother and the Secretary General of the United Nations.

The rest of the hull was cut or blown into sections of up to 250 tons each and, in all, 45,000 tons of metal were lifted from the wreck, much of it destined to become reinforcing bars in Hong Kong's changing skyline.

The heat of the fire had also fused glass from porthole lights into their surrounding brass frames and seven hundred pounds of this unusual material was purchased by the Parker Pen Company. As a result a limited, numbered edition of beautiful green/gold, almost sparkling, fountain pens were produced one of which, resplendent in a mahogany casket, was presented to Commodore Marr.

The Korean scrappers, under the guidance of a British engineer, decently buried the remains of the wreck in the sand of the harbour bottom, hoping that they had given the Old Lady a respectful burial.

But even her remains may now not be allowed to rest in peace, as it was hoped, forever.

In a letter to the nautical magazine 'Ships Monthly' (August 1989) Bernard Young of New South Wales, Australia, concluded a letter concerning Hong Kong '... Stonecutters Island, the site of ... wreck of ... *Queen Elizabeth*. Although no longer visible, a large part of the wreck still lies on the sea bed and I understand it is causing some problems for the designers of a proposed new tunnel

Scorched with collapsed steelwork, the *Seawise University* sits dangerously in the water, her lower cargo ports level with the sea. *Queen Elizabeth Historical Society*

near there. Poor old *Lizzie*, or what is left of her, lies in the way and they have to decide whether to go round her or blow her up.'

'To see thy beauty fade ...
Lovely to the last,
Extinguished, not decayed.'
(Byron)

Almost 35 years from the laying of her keel the old *Queen Elizabeth* reaches an undignified end, a charred, rusting hulk thousands of miles from the land that gave her being.
Terry Little

Looking forward over the bow on *Queen Elizabeth* taken a year before her withdrawal by Cunard. June 1967.

W. J. Windebank, courtesy of Barry J. Eagles

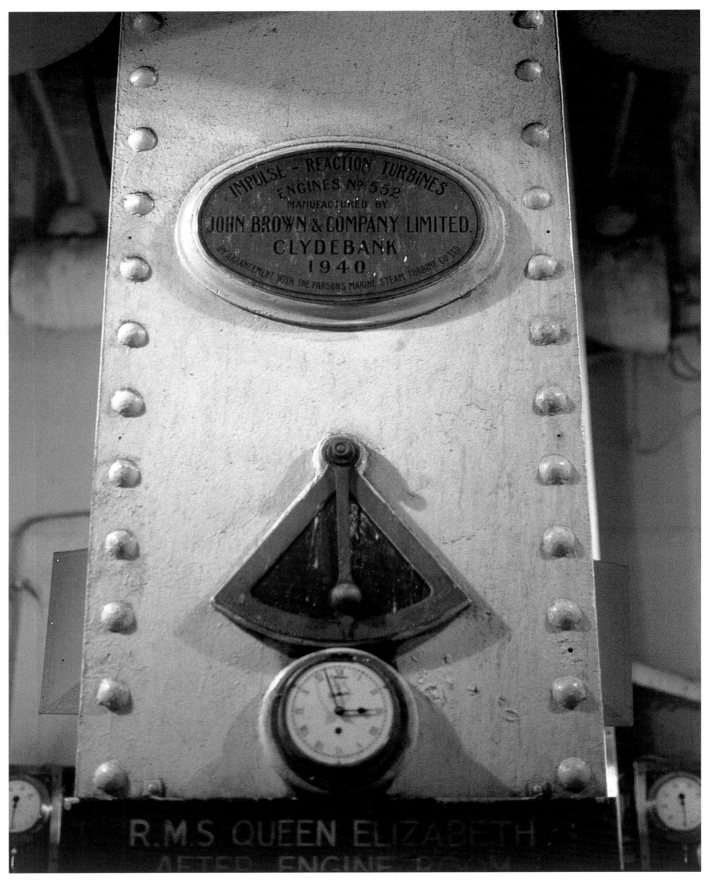

The Engine Room platform on the *Lizzie* in June 1964. The builder's brass nameplate is clearly visible.

W. J. Windebank, courtesy of Barry J. Eagles

Above: Seen off Hythe on arrival, the *Queen Elizabeth* is escorted through Southampton Water by attendant tugs. August 1965.
Below: The liner at her berth in Southampton Docks. Her towering superstructure is shown to advantage in this view.

Both, W. J. Windebank, courtesy of Barry J. Eagles

Acknowledgements

The preparation of a ship biography - even a brief one such as this - would not be possible without the help of people directly involved in building, sailing or travelling in the ship concerned. I am indebted, therefore, to those so involved and who so freely gave of their time and of their memories of the *Queen Elizabeth*.

I am particularly grateful to Commodore Geoffrey Marr DSC, RD, RNR (ret'd) for his recollections, for writing the Foreword and for allowing me the honour of dedicating the book to his late wife.

To the Commodore I also extend to a second vote of thanks for reading through the typed manuscript and to Captain Peter Jackson and Kippy Robinson of Hamble for performing a similarly onerous task, although mine is the final responsibility for any errors and omissions.

The anecdotes and recollections that I have collected can only scratch the surface of an apparent wealth of stories, but I hope that I hav e given a flavour of the life on board a great liner through the stories presented. Two other special sources must also not go unacclaimed: firstly Sam Campbell who patiently answered my detailed questions on his own involvement in the building of 'No. 552' and, secondly, Harold Philpot of Ararat, Virginia. Harold is courageously and single - handedly building a museum (RMS Queen Elizabeth Historical Society, Route 1, Box 217 Ararat, Virginia 24053, U.S.A.) dedicated solely to the great ship. To his great enthusiasm and encouragement I owe a great deal.

Many others helped to fill in the gaps with information, photographs and artefacts. I am very mindful of their invaluable contributions and thank them all, including: Peter Ashton; Ian Baker; Stewart Bale Ltd; Len Betts; Peter Boyd-Smith of 'Cobwebs' (Oceanliner Memorabilia) Southampton; George Boyd; Frank O.Braynard of Sea Cliff, New York; the late Len Brown; Simone Clarke; James Collins; Harley Crossley; Cunard Line Limited; William Doig; John Eaton; Jill Fackerell; Eric Flounders; Fotoflite, Ashford, Kent; George Gardner; University of Glasgow Archives; Paul Gosling; Les Gough; Thomas Gough; Bob Bruce Grice; Charles Haas; Charles Harrison of Nairobi; John Havers; Ivan 'Jack' Horner; Imperial War Museum; Norman Jackman; Jim Jone; Tim Jone; Baroness Patricia de Kerbrech; Phyllis Larkin; Sylvia Lee; Robert G. Lenzer of Richardson, Texas; Terry Little ex Cunarder and enthusiast, of 'Oysters' Wine Bar, Southsea; University of Liverpool; Jill MacCullum; the late Mrs Geoffrey Marr; Nicola Massey; Bill Miller of Jersey City, N. J.; William Miller; William H. Mitchell; Captain John Moffatt; Dennis Money; Frieda Moody; Denis Morrell; Nigh's of Ventnor (Mr Denis); George Outram Ltd.; Nigel Overton; Red Funnel Steamers; Philip Rentell; C. P. Richards; Martin Rowland; Gary Smith; Mrs Isobel Sorrell; Southampton City Museums; Southern Evening Echo; Ian Sparshatt; P. E. Spriggs; Lovell H. G. Taylor; Alma Topen; Cedric Wasser: Peter Walters; Captain G. D. Williams; Rodney Wise; and George Wolseley.

At a special luncheon held on board *Queen Elizabeth 2* to commemorate the 50th anniversary of the launch of the "old" *Lizzie*, Her Majesty Queen Elizabeth, the Queen Mother, dined with ex-captains of the three *Queens* as well as those currently in command of *QE2*.

Southern Newspapers plc, Southampton

Bibliography

Should the reader require further details of the career of RMS *Queen Elizabeth* then I can particularly recommend, from the list below, the books by Stevens, Winchester, Potter and Frost, Konings and - of course! - Miller and Hutchings.

The recent 'Destiny's Daughter' by Russell Galbraith is also recommended for its detailed look into the subsequent tale of the *Queen Elizabeth* following her sale - a period that I have only lightly touched upon as she was technically no longer the subject of this book.

Commodore Geoffrey Marr's 'The Queens and I', although rare and out of print, is also eminently readable. Let us hope that it will eventually be re-published.

Bisset, Sir James - Commodore (Angus & Robertson, 1961)

Bonsor, N.R.P. - North Atlantic Seaway (David & Charles, 1975)

Braynard, Frank and Miller, William H. - Fifty Famous Liners (Patrick Stephens Ltd, 1982) Cunard S.S. Co - The Cunarders 1840 - 1969 (Peter Barker Publishing Ltd, 1982)

Galbraith, Russell - Destiny's Daughter (Mainstream Publishing, 1988)

Grattidge, Capt. H. - Captain Of The Queens (Oldbourne, 1956)

Hutchings, David F. - QE2 - A Ship For All Seasons (Kingfisher Railway Productions, 1988)

Hutchings, David F. - Queen Mary - 50 Years Of Splendour (Kingfisher Railway Productions, 1986)

Hyde, Francis E. - Cunard And The North Atlantic 1840 - 1973 (The Macmillan Press Ltd, 1975)

Kludas, Arnold - Great Passenger Ships Of The World, Vol.4: 1936 - 1950 (Patrick Stephens Ltd, 1977)

Lacey, Robert - The Queens Of The North Atlantic (Sidgwick & Jackson, 1973)

Maclean, Commodore Donald - Queens' Company (Hutchinson, 1965)

Mcguire, Joseph B. - The Sea My Surgery (Heinemann, 1957)

Marr, Commodore Geoffrey - The Queens And I (Adlard Coles Limited, 1973)

Miller, William H. - Transatlantic Liners 1945 - 1980 (David & Charles, 1981)

Miller, William H. - Great Cruise Ships And Ocean Liners (Dover Publishing Inc., 1988)

Miller, William H. and Hutchings, David F. - Transatlantic Liners At War - The Story of The Queens (David & Charles, 1985) Rentell, Philip - Historic Cunard Liners (Atlantic Transport Publishers, 1986)

Smallpeice, Sir Basil - Of Comets And Queens (Airlife, 1981)

Southampton City Council - The Queens (Harvey Barton - St. Stephens Publications, 1969)

Stevens, Leonard A. - The Elizabeth, Passage Of A Queen (George Allen & Unwin, 1967)

Thelwell, Commodore Robert G. - I Captained The Big Ships (Arthur Barker, 1961)

Winchester, Clarence - The Queen Elizabeth (Winchester, 1947)

I acknowledge and thank many of the above authors and publishers for some of the quotations used.

Periodicals and newspapers also referred to:

The Daily Telegraph, The Times, Southern Evening Echo, New York Times, The Miami News, The Miami Herald, Fort Lauderdale News, Sun-sentinel, Broward County, Philadelphia Magazine, Ships Monthly, Sea Breezes, Shipbuilding & Shipping Record.

July 1952 and the *United States* passes the Prince's Green at Cowes on her approach to Southampton after taking the Blue Riband on her maiden voyage. The *Queen Elizabeth*, having left Southampton an hour previously, prepares to pass the US liner in the difficult bend of the Solent channel.

By kind permission of Nigh's

QE2 - A Ship For All Seasons

Foreword

By Captain Robin A. Woodall. RD★, RNR Retíd., HCMM, FJMU. (Captain [Retired] RMS Queen Elizabeth 2)

It had always been my ambition to go to sea. As a small boy living in London during the Second World War I used to enjoy looking at books of the sea, especially at those that included the great liners of that era, and thinking: 'That is what I want to do - go to sea in those ships'. I little thought then that one day I would fulfil that ambition. I have been very fortunate in realising this small boy's dream and have served in many of Cunard's famous passenger ships, including *Queen Elizabeth 2* for fourteen years of my forty-four years at sea, and feel very honoured to have been given command of that great ship from 1987 up to my retirement in 1994. So it gives me great pleasure to have been asked to write the Foreword for this updated and revised edition of 'QE2 - A Ship For All Seasons'.

The author is a great 'Cunardphile' and has written many excellent books on various ships of the Cunard Line and this new edition of his book on *QE2* is no exception. A fine 'potted history' - warts and all! - of what is arguably the greatest ship in the world.

Now thirty-five years on from the laying of her keel, this book catalogues her career right from her conception and through her many and varied changes. It also shows that she has always had the aim of pleasing her passengers - be it in peace or war.

Long may it continue, and I look forward to a third edition of this book in the years to come as her remarkable history is by no means over!

Captain Robin Woodall, Hoylake, Merseyside

Introduction

Like a regal matron that, in elegantly accepting the ageing process that comes to us all in bidding farewell to the slim, sleek looks of our youth, so the *Queen Elizabeth 2* has entered the fourth decade of her career having matured with an ease and grace that belies her years. Conceived with the future in mind by men of vision who swam against the tide of traditional thinking in ship design, the *QE2* was soundly built to be versatile.

Achieving her destiny admirably, this great liner has now caught up with the future that had been anticipated for her (and thickening about her waist in the process!) and she has been extensively refitted to enable her to compete with much younger ships for years to come. Whether plying the vigorous waters of the North Atlantic between the Old and New Worlds in the summer season or sailing to exotic ports in the winter, the *Queen Elizabeth 2* is, indeed, 'A Ship For All Seasons'.

Widely regarded today as the most famous ship sailing in the world, the *QE2* creates enormous interest wherever she goes and in whatever she does. So popular is this ship that a huge new Cunarder is being planned to emulate her success on the Atlantic run.

The purpose of the updated edition of this book - as with its predecessor - is to provide an historical background - whilst including some of the events that have befallen her - as to why and how the *QE2* was built; how she has adapted to change; what she has achieved; - and what she has survived!

Enjoy the book - enjoy the ship

David F. Hutchings   Lee-on-The Solent, Hampshire 2002

Dedication

To the memories of my parents whose love of the ships both great and small that passed through the waters of The Solent proved too infectious for me to resist.

Left: QE2 receives a salute from Concorde. From Lloyds List 27th October 2003, "CUNARD flagship *Queen Elizabeth 2* bid its own special farewell to Concorde on Friday as the supersonic aircraft passed over the ship on the Atlantic for the last time.
"From one British icon to another. *QE2* and Concorde have been an improbable, unique and successful transatlantic partnership for the past 20 years. We are sorry to see you go", ran the message sent by the *QE2*'s master Captain Ray Heath to the captain of Concorde.
Photo taken in 1990 by R. Bruce Grice

Contents

Chapter One
A Ship For All Seasons 194
Chapter Two
Do or Die 197
Chapter Three
Building for the Future 200
Chapter Four
Fourteen to One 206
Chapter Five
The Element of Risk 211
Chapter Six
Trials and Triumph 220
Chapter Seven
The Best 226
Chapter Eight
Royal Approval 228
Chapter Nine
Serenity, Security and Storm 232
Chapter Ten
Echoes of War 238
Chapter Eleven
The Brightest Star on the Ocean 249
Chapter Twelve
A Second Career 259
Chapter Thirteen
Propellers to the Fore 263
Chapter Fourteen
Anniversaries and Accolades 267
Chapter Fifteen
A Cruise of Celebration 269
Chapter Sixteen
An Anniversary Fit for a Queen 272
Chapter Seventeen
Rescues and Remembrance 274
Chapter Eighteen
Rumours and Rocks 277
Chapter Nineteen
Towards a Third Decade 282
Chapter Twenty
D-Day and Disappointments 285
Chapter Twenty One
Transmutation to Magnificence 291
Chapter Twenty Two
Storms Abating and Arising 300
Chapter Twenty Three
Sailing On 303
Chapter Twenty Four
For Sale - Or Good For Thirty Years? 310

Chapter One

A Ship for All Seasons

Cunard's mighty *Queen* liners were growing old.
From the years preceding the Second World War the *Queen Mary* – and the *Queen Elizabeth* since – had plied the North Atlantic between Europe and North America with a regularity and luxury that had brought full passenger lists and huge profits to the Cunard Steamship Company.

That is until 1957. In that year the numbers of passengers travelling by sea began to dwindle, the new jet airliners cutting the transatlantic journey from a crossing of four days by ship to just a few hours by air. That particularly fateful year proved to be the fulcrum of the fortunes of many shipping companies as the proportion of passengers being carried by air and sea reached 'evens'. From then on the scale of numbers being carried weighed heavily in favour of the airlines. Over the next decade many ocean liner companies would cease to exist as profits and passengers (especially the tourist and businessman) took to the air, preferring the quicker, time and money-saving passage that came with the aircraft, flying above the bad weather of winter.

Cunard had anticipated that they would eventually have to replace their two beloved *Queen* superliners (these had been the realisation of a long cherished dream to operate a weekly trans-atlantic service with just two express liners). Accordingly, by the late 'fifties, the line had drawn plans for replacements, but the planned ships would be on a 'like-for-like' basis, albeit built with updated technology. Within the company's board of directors there was a hard-core of traditionalists who believed that the aircraft presented no more than a temporary setback to the institution that was Cunard: passengers would always prefer to travel by sea!

The proposed ships would continue the usual North Atlantic trade and be designed purely for the route. No consideration was entertained that the ships might go cruising during the unprofitable winter months when the prospect of a rough crossing on the notoriously wintery Atlantic, the roughest ocean in the world at that time of year, deterred many a prospective traveller. As passengers sometimes struggled to maintain a footing 'Getting there is half the fun!', Cunard's famous slogan, ceased to have much meaning at that time of year.

By 1959 the designs were advanced far enough for Cunard to approach the Government for financial assistance to enable the company to proceed with their new project. As before with the *Queen Mary* and *Queen Elizabeth* a loan was to be sought which

Leaving Southampton's Ocean Terminal is the magnificent *Queen Elizabeth*. This prima donna of the Atlantic gave her name to the 'New Cunarder'.
Southampton City Museums

Right: Sir John Brocklebank, chairman of Cunard, shakes hands with Sir Matthew Slattery, chairman of BOAC, after signing the BOAC-Cunard agreement on 6th June 1962. Sir Basil Smallpeice (right) was at the time, managing director of BOAC, little realising his future intimate involvement with Cunard. *British Airways*

Above: A VC10 at London Airport (now Heathrow) proudly shows off its new BOAC-Cunard logo. The lettering of each company's name seems to be in proportion to the number of shares held by each! *British Airways*

would similarly be fully repaid, thus making the new ships unique amongst their peers of other nations in being self-sufficient in their operation rather than being subsidised.

The Government, in its turn, formed a committee in September 1959 led by Lord Chandos to consider Cunard's application. After due investigation, two 75,000 ton ships were recommended with speeds of 30 knots and carrying 2,270 passengers.

Soon after the Chandos Committee was formed Cunard's chairman, Colonel Denis Bates, died and Sir John Brocklebank was appointed as his successor.

During the early years of his chairmanship Sir John resurrected an idea that had originally been formulated in the early 'thirties by the then chairman, Sir Percy Bates, to put Cunard into the air business. Subsequently, in 1959, Cunard bought Eagle Airways. In 1960 Cunard – Eagle, as the line would be known, applied for a licence to fly the Atlantic to New York and at the same time purchased two Boeing aircraft to show their determination. The licence was granted, then revoked after an appeal by BOAC.

Although Cunard carried on its air operations from the United Kingdom to Bermuda (and from there to New York etc)

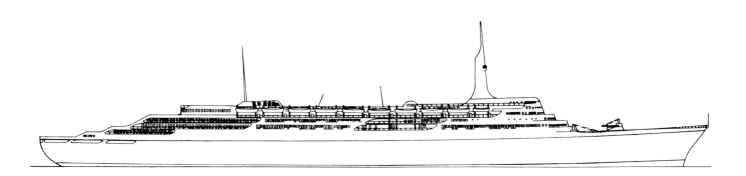

A drawing of 31st March 1961 shows a proposal for the Q3 project. The funnel configuration has not yet been decided but one could assume that it might have been similar to the John Brown-built Swedish liner *Kungsholm* that was launched in 1965.

Based on a drawing supplied by Liverpool University

the company finally came to an arrangement with BOAC in June 1962 and BOAC–Cunard was formed, with the shipping company holding a 30 per cent interest.

Perhaps the Government seeing Cunard spend £8.5 million on this new enterprise had second thoughts as the Chandos Committee now recommended that the company should be granted a loan for the building of only one new ship, designated 'Q3', and that she should be designed solely as a three class North Atlantic express liner. A loan of £17 million, at a low rate of interest, would be made available against the £28 million (maximum) that the new ship would be expected to cost. Many of the younger directors were still unhappy about the type of ship that was being selected and they found an ally in Sir John Brocklebank.

Sir John reappraised the whole situation – dwindling passenger numbers, increasing losses, potential actual cost of the Q3 by the time of building – and took a momentous decision and cancelled the new liner. He later described the decision to build her as a 'disaster'.

A fresh look was taken at the company's requirements and at the advances that had been made in the arts and technologies of shipbuilding, in propulsion machinery and in materials available to the shipbuilder. The new ship, Sir John Brocklebank stated, would not be an updated version of the two existing *Queens* nor would it be a re-working of the Q3 idea.

Sir John liked to refer to the new project as 'The New Cunarder' but the ship soon became known as the 'Q4'. Spike Milligan, that most zany of British comics, parodied the nomenclature theme for a television comedy series – 'Q6'. Other 'Qs' in this popular series followed thereafter.

The initial concept for 'The New Cunarder' was for the 27 and 12 boilers of the *Queen Mary* and *Queen Elizabeth* respectively, and their four propellers each, to be replaced in the Q4 by four boilers and two propellers. Modern engines etc had enabled an almost equal amount of power to be obtained from a smaller installation. Enough fuel would also be carried to last a complete round North Atlantic voyage at an average speed of 28.5 knots. 2,000 passengers, in three classes, would be carried in maximum safety with a corresponding reliability of service. Rooms, too, would be flexible in as much as they could be changed from one class to another, ideal for when cruising.

58,000 gross tons would be contained within the 960 foot hull and a beam of 104 feet would enable the liner to pass through the Panama and Suez Canals with just 18 inches clearance on either side of the former. This, with the ability to produce her own fresh water (the old *Queens* could carry enough only for a few days), would open up the world to the new ship.

The dual role of North Atlantic liner sailing and tropical ocean cruising became increasingly attractive to Cunard.

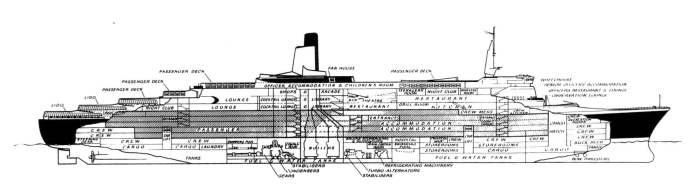

Q4 – the new 58,000 ton CUNARDER

Advance publicity for No. 736 shows how the liner would be divided, although classes have not been designated. *Cunard*

Chapter Two

Do or Die

Under the relatively short chairmanship of Sir John Brocklebank with his policy of 'new thinking', Cunard diversified its passenger operations.

Although Cunard was still carrying more passengers than any other shipping company, their transatlantic passenger service was developing into an ever increasing loss-maker and it was decided to send some of the other passenger ships in the fleet cruising. The only full-time cruise ship that Cunard operated was the luxurious *Caronia*, popularly known as 'The Dollar Princess' or 'The Green Goddess' because of the three shades of light green in which her hull was painted.

Cunard had also made a study of other Atlantic liners that had been sent cruising during the winter months as an alternative to running with that season's associated reductions in patronage on the northern ocean. The magnificent *France* of the French Line was studied in depth as was the US Lines' *United States*.

Ultimately two of the Cunard's Canadian service ships, *Saxonia* and *Ivernia*, were sent to John Brown's shipbuilding yard in Scotland for extensive rebuilding to convert them into cruise-ships. This was done in 1962, the liners reappearing as the *Carmania* and *Franconia*. The lessons learnt from this pair were of great practical benefit when the facilities and materials to be incorporated in the Q4 were being considered.

The experience in building a third sister, the *Sylvania*, of 1955 had also been of use. Plastic piping, plastic baths, lightweight furniture and specially developed, deeper than usual, girders (which had holes cut into them to enable easy passage of piping and electrical cables) had been used to facilitate the saving of weight and these ideas were to be used to advantage ten years later.

The *Mauretania* too went cruising and, then, in 1963 the mighty *Queens* found winter employment in this lucrative and expanding market. Their great prestige ensured that they were popular in their new roles, although their draughts of 38 feet and beams of 118 feet precluded their access to the harbours of many ports that they visited. Consequently they had to anchor offshore from these prohibited havens, ferrying passengers ashore by their own ship's boats.

It was planned that the Q4 should have a greatly reduced beam and draught in comparison to her predecessors: this was to be made possible by stringent weight saving through the careful use of lighter materials in her construction that had been made available from the very latest advances in technology. Thus the ports made inaccessible to her predecessors would be opened to the new ship, enabling her to moor alongside jetties in sheltered waters and allowing her passengers to disembark directly from ship to shore in comfort.

Cruising from New York, the *Elizabeth* sailed to the Bahamas and sometimes crossed the Atlantic to visit various ports in the Mediterranean. On this side of 'The Pond' the *Mary* sailed from Southampton, rolling her way through the Bay of Biscay with her stabilisers retracted (to conserve fuel en-route) to the Canaries, Lisbon and Gibraltar.

During one flying visit to the *Mary*, whilst she was calling at Cannes during 1966, Sir Basil Smallpeice paid a visit to his counterpart of the French Line who was on board the *France*, anchored a short way from the British ship. From this visit stemmed the idea of operating the 'Lizzie', and later the Q4, in mutual co-operation with the *France* instead of in competition. It was also planned that the *Mary* and *Elizabeth* should be kept in service until 1968 and 1969 respectively before withdrawing them. The 'Lizzie' would be kept on the route for a year longer than the *Mary* in order to provide the Q4 with a running mate. Commodore Geoffrey Marr was to keep the *Elizabeth* as his flagship with the captaincy of the Q4 passing to William ('Bil with one 'l' ') Warwick who would also stand by 'The New Cunarder' whilst she was being built.

But in 1966, because of its passenger fleet losses of the previous few years (only slightly alleviated in the early years of the decade by the more healthy revenue derived from the profits of its cargo operations before they, too, declined), Cunard's financial position deteriorated even further. This, combined with a £4 million loss caused by the lengthy seaman's strike of that year, forced the company to once more reappraise its position. An innovation for the company occurred with a switch to containerisation when Cunard joined, in December 1966, the Atlantic Container Line which saved the cargo business by its resultant profitability.

Sir Basil Smallpeice had by this time taken over the helm of the company and he proceeded to take the policy of Sir John Brocklebank's 'New thinking' to its brilliantly successful – albeit extremely unpopular at the time – conclusion. By re-thinking the new policies he arrived at the conclusion that ships should not merely be used as a means of getting from 'A' to 'B' but should be used as part of the journey, a hotel that took its passengers to places whilst, meanwhile, enjoying themselves during the passage.

Perhaps spurred on by shrewd observations from senior staff such as the fleet's newly appointed Commodore, Geoffrey Marr, who pointed out that the shore staff and offices had not

Carinthia and *Caronia* (The 'Green Goddess'), the last Cunard ships to go before 'Q4' came into service.　　　　*Norman Jackman*

The *Queen Mary*, the epitome of the ocean liner, leaves Southampton for a final cruise before her ultimate sailing on 31st October 1967 *enroute* to preservation and a whole new career in Long Beach, California.
Southampton City Museums

been trimmed to match the needs of the fleet and that in many instances posts and functions were excessively overmanned, Sir Basil put further economies into practice, convinced that to be a viable proposition the company had 'to do or die'.

Older ships and those not converted for cruising were sold (after the sale of the *Caronia* in May 1968 only the *Carmania* and *Franconia* were left); the main passenger office was moved from Liverpool to Southampton (March 1967); offices in many towns were shut and sold and Cunard's interest in BOAC–Cunard were bought back by BOAC, realising a handsome profit for the shipping company.

But the heaviest decision of all came as a blow to Britain generally: the beloved *Queens* were to be retired one year earlier than had been anticipated.

The *Mary* was withdrawn first on 20th September 1967. On board the old liner Captain John Treasure Jones, himself facing his own retirement, toasted a portrait of the 'New Cunarder' that was being launched in Scotland that day; on the 22nd the liner left New York for the last time after due honours had been paid to her by the city's Mayor, leaving behind a sadness and a void in the city that has never since been filled.

Everyone was losing 'their' *Queen*. As the three-funnelled Atlantic liner headed towards home, and a continuation of her destiny, she passed the *Queen Elizabeth* for the last time just after midnight in mid-Atlantic on September 25th. The sister ships bade a poignant, final farewell to each other with their mighty whistles as their illuminated funnels flashed on and off.

The *Mary* had been sold for £1.25 million to the City of Long Beach and, after a final short cruise from Southampton, sailed for her new home on October 31st, via Cape Horn, where she was refurbished as the 'Hotel Queen Mary', being rebuilt in some areas as an attraction centre. Well looked-after, she is still there – a legacy of art deco and luxury from the days when the sea track was the only highway between Europe and the USA.

A different fate awaited the *Queen Elizabeth*, however. It had been intended to sail her in conjunction with the Q4 for at least a year after the latter ship's introduction into service but a combination of Cunard's financial circumstances exacerbated by the seamens' strike and the partnership between the *Queen* and the *France*, which could be carried over to the new ship, caused her premature demise.

Sold to a somewhat 'shady' American consortium she left Southampton in circumstances very different from the emotive but affectionate farewell given to the *Mary*: it seemed as if she was being banished, sailing almost furtively, in the early morning fog. It had been planned to keep her in Philadelphia but she languished for two years, gradually rotting, at Port Everglades near Fort Lauderdale in Florida. After this interlude of despair she was again offered for sale and found a buyer in C.Y. Tung of Hong Kong.

Sailing from Florida in August of 1970 she was renamed *Seawise University*, undergoing conversion to a cruising university in Hong Kong.

Before she even once sailed in her new role she caught fire in several places at once and, after blazing for several days, rolled over and died. As in the mid-60s Cunard had spent $4m converting her for cuising and installing fire prevention standards to US regulations it was considered that the cause of destruction had been sabotage. A sad ending to the world's finest and largest ship, a symbol of Britain's post war recovery in the days of austerity and rationing.

Throughout this financially and emotionally complex period with its cut-backs at sea and the closure, sale or transfer of shore offices the main aims of the stringent rationalisation were carefully nurtured until they reached fruition with the survival of Cunard and the tangible result of the 'new thinking' – the planning and building of the most versatile liner that the world had yet seen.

On 19th August 1964 the Cunard line invited five shipbuilders to tender for the construction of the 'New Cunarder' and by 30th November the bids had been returned. Within one month the final choice had been made and the contract to build Q4 was awarded to the John Brown shipyard of Clydebank (the former builders of the *Queen Mary* and *Queen Elizabeth*) as their tender of £25,427,000 was the best received.

Just after 3pm, on 30th December within the augustly solid surroundings of the Bank of England, Sir John Brocklebank (then still chairman of the steamship company) and Lord Aberconway, chairman of John Brown and Company (Clydebank) Limited, signed the contract.

The initial contract called for a twin screw ship of 28.5 knots (less speed would be required for cruising), with four boilers and catering for the American, as well as the traditional, demand for three classes. One boiler was dispensed with during a later cost-cutting exercise and, in order to cut down on kitchen logistics and to provide an easier operating environment for cruising (when the ship would become one class), the ship sensibly also became a two-class vessel. These changes were decided upon even whilst the ship was building, an early indication of the design's versatility.

Cunard, it seemed, was set fair on a course for recovery and all bade well for the future – once the ship was completed.

But there were still shoals ahead.

Within the solid walls of the Bank of England on 30th December 1964, Sir John Brocklebank (for Cunard) and Lord Aberconway (for John Brown, Clydebank) sign the building contract for Q4 - the 'New Cunarder'.*Cunard*

Chapter Three

Building for the Future

July 2nd 1965 dawned a beautiful, bright day over the expectant shipyard of John Brown and Company Limited. The keel of No. 736, the shipyard's order-book number for the 'New Cunarder', was due to be laid on the short length of wooden blocks that would eventually be extended down to the water's edge along the length of No. 4 slipway, the birthplace of many a Cunard ship, including the two mighty *Queens*. She was to be Cunard's 172nd ship and her keel laying was to take place just two days before the 125th anniversary of the company's founding by Samuel Cunard of Halifax, Nova Scotia.

From this neat row of blocks extended six baulks of timber placed horizontally at right angles to, and erected level with, the top of the blocks. To one side of the building blocks a prefabricated section of the new ship's keel and double bottom rested on these baulks and other temporary blocks waiting to be ceremoniously slid into place.

John Rannie, the managing director of the shipyard whose crowning achievement the Q4 would be (he would be retiring when the ship was finally handed over to Cunard), had stipulated that the prefabricated section being built in the workshops should weigh forty tons. This would be within the combined lifting capabilities of two tower cranes adjoining the slip which, with the aid of a powerful winch fixed to the concrete base of a long vanished derrick crane, would lift and pull the keel section into place.

At least, that was the plan.

Lady Aberconway, the wife of John Brown's chairman, had agreed to perform the ceremony and various reporters had been invited along to witness the occasion. At the appointed time the cranes took the strain of the steel section and the winch commenced to take in the slack on the wire cables. Unfortunately the cranes were designed to lift their maximum load of 20 tons each in a vertical direction and not at the angle induced by the pull on the winch.

After moving slightly the keel section refused to move any further which placed an enormous strain on the winch. Consequently, as the winch continued to pull in its cable, the entire concrete block into which it was fixed started a process of being extracted from the earth, dried out during recent fine weather.

The ceremony thus came to a hasty and slightly undignified halt and the pressmen were quickly ushered into the Model Room where they were liberally entertained.

The recalcitrant keel section was quietly eased into position onto the building blocks on the following Monday, 5th July, by a carefully chosen gang of men who had delayed their start of the local 'Clydebank Fair'; the shipyard was normally closed-down during the fortnight of this annual holiday.

After an initial public embarrasment, the keel of No. 736 was quietly slid into place on Monday 5th July 1967. *Boyd Haining*

Even before the contract had been signed an air of confidence that the company would be given the contract to build Q4 had existed within the boardroom of John Brown's. This confidence, almost mounting to an assumption, was based on the Company's record of building many previous famous Cunarders such as the *Lusitania*, *Aquitania* and, of course, the *Queen Mary* and *Queen Elizabeth*. The prevailing confidence even extended to the pronouncement of an early delivery date for the completed 'New Cunarder': one which would have unhappy consequences.

During the months preceding the laying of the first few symbolic tons of the new 736, a mass of work had already taken place. Calculations, drawings, estimates and planning, the preparation of network charts (showing in a numerical and time form what job had to be done, in which order and when – in

Many funnel designs were considered and tested at John Brown's. Here some of the designs are shown together.
University of Liverpool, Cunard Archives

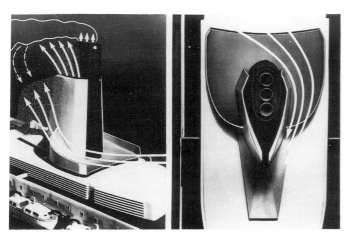

The liner's novel funnel design, shown here on a large model, with added arrows graphically showing the wind direction induced by the wind-scoop and casing. *University of Liverpool, Cunard Archives*

order to avoid 'bottlenecks' and hold-ups) had all been started. The advance ordering of much material had also gone ahead and the basic design principles had been established. These latter criteria would not be changed, whatever else was, and included positions of support pillars, bulkheads and, most importantly, the location of engines. This was determined as being just aft of amidships (for stability and strength): in turn this dictated funnel location which, being placed almost amidships, allowed the development of a dual purpose series of terraced decks, cascading down through five decks towards the stern, providing shelter during North Atlantic passages and offering delightful sun-traps whilst cruising.

Heading Cunard's design team were their naval architect, Dan Wallace, and technical director, marine engineer Tom Kameen. Dan Wallace had served his apprenticeship in the esteemed shipyard to which he now returned, finding himself senior to those who had once been his peers.

John Brown's own prestigious but secretive design office was led by the yard's technical director, John Stark, who also had responsibility for the yard's experimental tank in which were tested differing hull models of the new liner until one had been perfected. On the forefoot of the ship a 'bulb' would be fitted; this bulbous bow would 'punch a hole' in the water ahead of the ship thereby cutting down water resistance on the hull – and also cut down the fuel bills. The traditional bow wave, beloved of all marine artists, would disappear, robbing Q4 of her 'bone in the teeth' when she was underway.

Cunard's naval architect, Dan Wallace (right), discusses a point of the Q4's design. *University of Liverpool, Cunard Archives*

From the initial laying of the keel the erection of steelwork on No. 4 slip went on at a steady pace. Extra men were taken on when necessary and if they did not hold any documentary evidence that they were competent at their trade then they were given a test task.

To maintain an adequate supply of steel sections (such as angle-bar and tee-bar) the steel mills in the vicinity of Clydebank would give advance notice of their rolling dates of particular sections to the drawing office so that sufficient time could be allowed for ordering. Weekly co-ordinating visits by John Brown's commercial manager to the mills also ensured that a flow of information was maintained.

Aluminium alloy was to be used in great quantities in the construction of the superstructure once the steel hull had been completed. 1,100 tons, the largest amount (including some of the biggest plates) ever used on a British liner, were to be supplied by Alcan who organised a special training centre within the yard. The trained welders were also periodically checked for standards of workmanship which thus remained high throughout the building of the ship.

Above: Several differing models of the Q4's hull were built and tested in John Brown's towing tank. One model is shown being put through its paces in simulated rough weather conditions.
University of Liverpool, Cunard Archives.

Left: 1,100 tons of aluminium was to be used in the liner's superstructure and much of it was prefabricated in the shipyard's workshops.
University of Liverpool, Cunard Archives

A workshop for the preparation of the aluminium plates (of which many were delivered in ready-to-use sizes) was specially dedicated for this purpose having its floor treated with a special sealant to prevent any foreign particles affecting the metal. As soon as the aluminium was prepared and welded into prefabricated units it was primed with a special anti-corrosion paint and this remained superbly effective throughout construction.

The use of aluminium (along with other innovative weight saving design features) had enabled the design team to reduce the liner's draught by several feet than if steel had been used in the superstructure. It also enabled the number of decks to be increased from 12 in the old *Queens* to 13 in the Q4.

The addition of an extra passenger deck more than compensated for the limits on length and beam that had been imposed by the planned usage of the Panama and Suez Canals. This additional deck had also been made possible by the reduction of 6 to 9 inches in the heights of other decks by running electrical cables, piping and ventilation trunking over main passageways and bathrooms where a lower headroom was acceptable. Cunard's engineering staff had also managed to save a creditable 3 feet in the height of the machinery spaces.

Lloyd's ship surveyors were also keenly interested in the superstructure as it was to be regarded as part of the ship's strength structure. Accordingly, expansion joints (the narrow, protected transverse 'gaps' in the uppermost deck of a ship that allowed the superstructure to 'work' in heavy weather when the main hull bends) were omitted.

To prevent any corrosive electrolytic interaction between the steel of the hull and the aluminium superstructure a careful bonding method had to be utilised. A special epoxy compound was spread along the joints between the two metals and then steel rivets were used for the final connection.

Left: Surrounded by a web of scaffolding, the curved stem and bulbous bow already display their elegant curves.   *Boyd Haining*

Below: Partially built from prefabricated sections, these deck houses on the boat deck will soon accommodate the Double Up Room, shops and theatre balcony.   *University of Liverpool, Cunard Archives*

The various weight saving exercises proved to be a worthwhile – and potentially profitable – operation but it also affected the centre of gravity which, as a consequence, had to be lowered. The usual method of remedying this problem would have been to add, in the Q4's case, 750 tons of otherwise useless ballast to the bottom of the ship. But the designers ingeniously did away with the use of this dead weight and instead turned it to advantage.

Their solution was to increase certain steel plate thicknesses in areas where greater than usual wear (or corrosion) could be reasonably expected to occur, such as in the lower most structure in way of machinery and the fore part of hull, strengthening it against ice. Increasing the weight of steel work within the double bottom by constructing more closely subdivided double bottom cells also added to the ship's strength.

Of the many thousands of items that were to be fitted into the hull of No. 736, many had to be made specially for the liner.

The propulsion machinery – boilers, turbines, gearboxes, condensers and propeller shafts – and much ancilliary machinery was made by John Brown Engineering (Clydebank) Limited but built under licences from the respective designers or developers. Much of the machinery had been conceived in its original form in the years succeeding 1954 when the idea of replacements for the *Mary* and *Elizabeth* were first mooted, culminating in the ill-fated Q3 project. The Q3 designs were resurrected and modified until the machinery for the Q4 was finally chosen. Reliability, simplicity and efficiency were to be the watchwords.

Twenty seven boilers in the *Queen Mary* and twelve in the *Queen Elizabeth* had given 160,000 shaft horse power to four propellers (40,000 shp each) to give a service speed of 28.5 knots.

Left: With launching cradle in place and with new paint gleaming, the bow of the 'Q4' towers above the slipway.
University of Liverpool, Cunard Archives

Below: One of the two 19-foot six-bladed propellers, each weighing 31 tons 13 cwt (32,157 hg), poised above the tidal Clyde. Each of these propellers would absorb 55,000 shp to give a service speed the same as the old Cunard *Queens*. *University of Liverpool, Cunard Archives*

Advances in marine engineering had been such that the Q4 was to have four watertube boilers which would deliver 120,000 shp giving the same speed from only two propellers. The propeller manufacturers, Stone Manganese Marine of Greenwich, were concerned at the amount of power that each of their products would have to absorb and were greatly relieved when, because of economies, the four boilers were reduced to three. 110,000 shp would now be produced, giving the same service speed.

The boilers were of Foster Wheeler ESD II design and, at 278 tons each, were the largest ever constructed for a marine installation. Steam was produced at 850 pounds per square inch at a temperature of 950°F (later rising to 1,000°F).

The steam was fed into two sets of turbines (double reduction, double helical, dual tandem gearing) which were built to a design by Pametrada Limited. Pametrada or, to give its proper title, Parsons Marine Engineering Turbine Research and Development Association (supported by shipbuilding and various marine turbine engineering firms) was the successor to the firm founded by the inventor of the turbine, Sir Charles Parsons.

The magazine 'Engineering' described the turbines: 'Each set is a two-cylinder unit, in which the flow from the high-pressure turbine feeds one double-flow low-pressure turbine, exhausting into an underslung condenser. The turbines are connected to the main shaft by a dual tandem arrangement of double helical gears'.

Amongst many companies that produced other machinery for various purposes AEI built three turbine-generators which would produce the ship's life forces, steam and electricity, for the various ship's services. Many years later AEI, as part of the GEC group, would have a further major involvement in the life of the liner.

However, to ensure that the maximum, most efficient use was obtained from the available machinery space, a scale model was made showing the positions of every pipe and piece of gear.

The 'New Cunarder', like her predecessors before her, loomed over her surroundings during her building. Because she was practically all-welded the traditional sounds of rivetting no longer sent their staccato rhythms out over Clydebank.

There was a quietness in the town, a silent overture to the coming years of change.

One of the many items contracted-out to smaller firms. Here one of the propeller cones is about to leave Southampton-based Hardingham Pressure Vessels Ltd. for Glasgow. *Roger Hardingham*

Two sets of stabilisers were built into No. 736 enabling, amongst other things, the restaurants to be carried higher in the ship. *Boyd Haining*

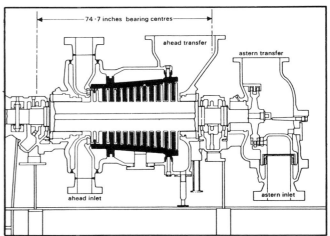

Diagram showing the high pressure ahead turbine and astern turbine. Because of the high temperatures involved, stainless iron blades were used. *Engineering Magazine*

Chapter Four

Fourteen to One

Yard No. 736 rested sleek and serene on the stocks of Slip Number 4.

Her Majesty, Queen Elizabeth II, had graciously consented to launch the new liner and for many weeks previous to the chosen day a great deal of conjecture surrounded the possible name of the new ship.

Many suggestions had been put forward: *Princess Anne, Queen of Britain, British Queen, Queen Victoria* (a name previously mooted for the subsequently named *Queen Mary*), *Britannia* (Cunard's first ship), *Prince Charles, New Britain, John F. Kennedy* and *Churchill* were amongst the more serious contenders that found varying odds in the betting shops.

Perhaps it was because one *Queen Elizabeth* was still in service that that particular name did not attract much attention for the new ship. Odds of 14 to 1 were offered. Her Majesty's own name (although Queen Elizabeth II of England she was yet Queen Elizabeth I of Scotland) did not figure high in the betting stakes.

Even at this eleventh hour before the launch there had been anxious moments in the higher echelons of Cunard. A loss of £3.5 million had just been announced on the passenger ship operations and, to aggravate matters even more, an increase in the cost of Q4 was expected to be in the region of £4 million. (A final price of £29,091,000 would eventually be agreed in later months).

The £17.6 million loan that the company had secured from the Government was clearly not going to be enough, so Sir Basil Smallpeice met Sir Harold Lever, Financial Secretary to the Treasury, on September 13th, just one week before the launch date.

The result announced on the 14th was an increase of the original loan to £24 million and the day was saved. The £24 million was later reduced by £4 million when Cunard found that the full amount was not eventually needed. This was because the sales of the *Carinthia, Sylvania, Queen Elizabeth* and *Caronia* in 1968 realised £7 million. This would leave, other than Q4, only two ships in service, the *Carmania* and *Franconia*, and the three ships would be marketed by the newly-formed Cunard Line Limited.

So, not only did Cunard still have a business that they were once in danger of losing but they had a new ship and a new hope for the future, all won by so much drastic economic surgery of ships and men.

Q4 almost ready for launching as seen from the Clyde.

Steam and Sail

Her Majesty The Queen, HRH Prince Philip, The Duke of Edinburgh, and John Brown's Shipyard Director, George Parker, pause during a tour of the slip prior to the launching of No. 736. Sir Basil Smallpeice, Chairman of Cunard, stands to the left.

University of Liverpool, Cunard Archives

The mood of a revived Cunard seemed to be reflected by the sunshine that greeted the Queen on her arrival at Clydebank on 20th September 1967.

The launch of the 'New Cunarder', like the launches of her illustrious predecessors, had occupied the talk of the people of the upper reaches of the Clyde for many a day, and thousands flocked to the yard or to the fields on the opposite side of the Clyde, to view the proceedings.

The weather was made ideal by a light westerly wind which helped to ensure that the required depth of water would be available at the end of the standing ways in good time for the launch. Wind of another 5 knots would have presented a problem, however.

Stewards were posted at various points within the viewing compounds and at various danger points such as at cranes where individuals could be deterred from climbing them to obtain a better view.

Princess Margaret (she had previously opened an exhibition of the Q4's specially designed fitments at the Design Centre) had arrived in Glasgow on the eve of the launch, touring the launch slipway the following day. Her early appearance increased the odds on the selection of her name for the liner.

John Brown's managing director, John Rannie, greeted the Queen on her arrival, outshining Sir Basil Smallpeice and his own chairman, Lord Aberconway, as her host. After introducing Her Majesty to various leading figures involved with Q4, John Rannie accompanied the Queen on her tour to inspect the launching trigger which she would soon be remotely activating.

The launching party then ascended to the platform at the very bow of the ship, against which the bottle of champagne would shortly be splitting and frothing.

Continuing the traditions of the launching ceremony the Queen was handed an envelope containing a sheet of paper on which was written the long-kept secret – the proposed name of the new liner. (The written reminder of the ship's name had become a considered necessity ever since an august personage had forgotten the name of the ship to be launched!) A similar envelope had been deposited in the safe at Cunard's New York office, just in case of a breakdown in communications. Her Majesty refused the proferred envelope. 'I won't be needing that!' she joked, then spoke clearly into the microphones: 'I name this ship *Queen Elizabeth the Second*. May God bless her and all who sail in her'. It was 2:28pm.

A great roar went up from several thousand throats as the Queen cut the ribbon, using the same gold scissors that her mother and grandmother had previously used in the performance of launching their Royal namesakes, releasing the christening wine that stiffly swung its way to destruction. A button was then pressed that electrically released the launching trigger that kept a last land-locked hold on the mighty hull.

The Queen, the first reigning British monarch to launch a liner, had used her intuition to name the ship. The envelope that she had refused – and the one in New York – had contained the name *Queen Elizabeth*.

After the launch Sir Basil Smallpeice consulted with the Queen's Private Secretary Sir (later Lord) Michael Adeane and it was decided that the suffix 'Second' would be written as the Arabic '2', and not as the Roman 'II'.

This was done for several reasons. Firstly, it was good publicity; secondly, only battleships had carried a reigning monarch's Romanic suffix, thirdly, the ship was to be the second ship to bear the name *Queen Elizabeth*, a nice deference to both the Queen and the Queen Mother after whom the first *Lizzie* had been named as Queen Consort; and, fourthly – and perhaps most importantly – the Queen was still, in fact, only Queen Elizabeth I of Scotland and to name the ship with 'II' would have been an insult to the people of the country that had now produced a fitting successor to the Queens *Mary* and *Elizabeth*.

As the last wedges retaining the ship on the slip were knocked away, the ship seemed to stick on the well-greased standing ways and only to the trained eye did she apparently move. A voice shouted, 'Give her a push!' and George Parker, the shipyard director, stepped forward and jokingly did so! Slowly at first, then with an ever increasing momentum, the *QE2* slid over tons of tallow towards her fast-approaching element.

Bundles of drag chains, weighing hundreds of tons in total (which had lain neatly alongside the launching ways, attached to the hull cables and later-to-be-removed eye bolts) gradually moved into rattling, clanking motion as the ship pulled them with her towards the specially-dredged River Clyde. The purpose of these bundles was to slow the ship down as she entered the water on this the first, short – but most dangerous – journey of her life, and to prevent her ramming the opposite bank of the river with her stern.

As the new *Queen* touched the water a perfectly timed anchor-formation of aircraft from the appropriately designated No. 736 Squadron of the Fleet Air Arm flew overhead.

The many hundreds of people in the fields opposite the shipyard had been warned by the police that the expected mini-tidal wave generated by the liner's entry into the water would

Above: Just minutes before the launch. The Q4 stands proud and ready on No. 4 slipway.
University of Liverpool, Cunard Archives

Left: At 2.30 pm on 20th September 1967 No. 736 is launched by Her Majesty Queen Elizabeth II. The liner would now be known as *Queen Elizabeth 2*, the *QE2*. A crowd of thousands watch as the liner takes to the water for the first time.
University of Liverpool, Cunard Archives.

Nearing completion, the liner is freshly painted and almost ready for launching. *Boyd Haining*

A trip to the fields on the opposite side of the Clyde to the shipyard always proved a worthwhile journey. Shipbuilding and agriculture are indelibly intertwined in this evocative photograph. *Boyd Haining*

From the opposite bank of the Clyde the *QE2* is seen to advantage as she makes contact with the water.
University of Liverpool, Cunard Archives.

probably flood the edge of the fields in which they stood. But once the launch was over the crowd moved forward to watch the 'New Cunarder', the *QE2*, as she was taken into care by tugs. Ushered towards the fitting-out jetty which would be her home for several months to follow, she would here take on the apparel appropriate for the world's newest *Queen*.

Meanwhile the official launch party headed towards the specially refurbished Mould Loft where a champagne afternoon tea had been arranged. A luncheon had been precluded because of the time of the launch and by the Royal party's programme.

Boyd Haining, then shipyard manager, remembers the tea as 'a delightful affair consisting of dainty sandwiches in variety, and gooey cakes and gateaux. Toasts were taken in champagne selected by Aberconway, knowing HM's taste. The champagne was a heady one – Krug Privee Curee, demi-sec, vintage 1961'.

In his chairman's post-launch speech Lord Aberconway voiced what would in effect be the beginning of the end of John Brown's shipyard as an independent entity. He said that the *QE2* would be the last ship of note of which it could be said 'she was a John Brown ship'. Economics were again at work.

He continued:

'We have announced, with our friends and neighbours on the upper Clyde, that we intend to merge our shipbuilding interests. Without question this would be to the advantage of shipbuilding on the Clyde, of continued employment on the river, and of the country's economy. But it does carry with it the consequence that there will pass from the scene of shipbuilding the name of John Brown, a name which (though I should not say it) is second to none in fame and repute. This yard will go on, playing a major part in a wider shipbuilding setting, and will contribute its skills and traditions to the new organisation of which it will be part. Many great ships will be built and fitted out at Clydebank in the years to come, to the same standards as in the last seventy 'John Brown' years; they will be worthy successors to the *Queen Mary*, the *Queen Elizabeth* and the *Queen Elizabeth the Second*.'

The Queen, in her speech, said:

'I particularly welcome the opportunity you have given me to launch this splendid successor to those two famous Cunarders *Queen Mary* and *Queen Elizabeth*. I suppose these two ships were better known and loved, both in peace and war, by all of us living in these islands, than any other merchantman in our history. I have always had a special affection for them because they were named after my grandmother and my mother, and it does not seem so very long ago that I was present with my sister when my mother launched the *Queen Elizabeth*.

Every great enterprise has an element of risk and uncertainty about it, and I am sure no-one can predict the future career of the new Cunarder. I am equally certain that, in the experienced and capable hands of the Cunard company, she will stand the best chance of a happy and profitable lifetime.'

The element of risk and uncertainty of which the Queen spoke would be realised sooner than any of those present could predict.

Of the proposed, and hopefully beneficial, amalgamation of the upper Clyde shipyards the Queen remarked:

'We have all read, with a touch of nostalgia, that the name of John Brown is to disappear from the list of great shipbuilders. However, this does not mean that the very special skill and spirit of this yard will be lost to Clydeside or to British shipbuilding. In wishing the *Queen Elizabeth the Second* a long life and good fortune on all her voyages, I add my best wishes for success and prosperity to the new consortium of Clydeside shipbuilders.'

Instead of the usual piece of jewellery the Queen was then presented with a new motor launch for the Royal Yacht *Britannia*. 'I suppose we ought to paint it in Cunard colours and call it *John Brown*!' said Her Majesty. 'Why not paint it brown and call it *Cunard*!' retorted a wit at the top table.'

Within a very short time, under the recommendations of the Geddes Committee, John Brown would become the Clydebank division of Upper Clyde Shipbuilders. It would be under the regime of this new consortium under the chairmanship of Tony Hepper but with John Rannie still in direct control of the *QE2* project, that the liner would be finished.

Chapter Five

The Element of Risk

The liner lay berthed alongside the fitting out jetty, her empty compartments soon to be transformed into carpeted rooms of luxury or hygienically tiled storerooms and kitchens.

But meanwhile she contained a bustle of men and machines. Cables lay like black snakes along the decks or hanging down from overhead and the shouts and calls of the skilled workforce filled the corridors, rooms and machinery spaces as they went about their myriad tasks.

Fitting, inspecting and testing carried on, day in, day out until, part by part, the *QE2* metamorphosed from what appeared to be chaos to the casual viewer, to a unity of practical beauty.

The *QE2* was to be a showpiece for Great Britain, for her country's art, design and engineering skills, not only now in the late 1960s but in the decades to follow. Her decor had not only to be modern but futuristic; it had to anticipate tastes for years to come – an almost impossible task for the designers involved.

But it was done.

In the past the interior decoration had almost been left to chance and a hotchpotch of styles were used that, as a whole, sometimes lacked unity.

Sometimes a chairman's wife might be given the task of choosing materials; in large ships renowned architects, more used to designing country mansions, were also appointed and the resultant decor in the ships' lounges and restaurants would reflect the lavish days of Imperial Rome, Classical Greece or elegant, timbered English mansions. The sea outside was almost deliberately forgotten.

The *Queen Mary* had perfectly reflected the art of the 1930s in her Art-Deco, architectural interiors (her 'Ocean Liner' style becoming more popularly known as 'Odeon') but these had soon dated. The *Queen Elizabeth* became the symbol of British post-war recovery and great things were done with the available materials. But she too, partially reflected pre-war design and was stylishly and architecturally luxurious.

Safely berthed alongside the fitting-out jetty, the *QE2* takes on the appareil of a luxury liner, still surrounded by the bustle of the shipyard.
Scottish Record Office

QE2 would be everything inside and out. She would reflect the art and technology of the 1960s whilst being timeless. She would also have a carefully built-in versatility rather than built-in architecture that would enable her to change to reflect new tastes and styles.

The style of the 'Swinging 1960s' that had made Britain the leader in world design and fashion, along with the bright, colour awareness which had been distilled and matured from the early 1960s, all helped to create the feel of the QE2. To ensure that the best in design was made available to Cunard the Council of Industrial Design was consulted.

Lady Brocklebank, wife of Cunard's chairman at the time when Q4's contract was signed, had originally been appointed to lead a team of designers. Her wide experience of travel, of ships and hotels ('I know what people like and dislike' she once said) made her admirably qualified for the post.

Lady Brocklebank disappeared from the scene upon the retirement through ill-health of her husband but not before she had appointed James Gardner as co-ordinator for the whole design.

James Gardner (he had designed the successful 'Britain Can Make It' exhibition at the end of the war) was 60 and had become a scholarship student at Chiswick School of Art at the age of 12! His remit was to balance the design of the ship and his main responsibility lay with the aesthetics of the liner's external appearance.

Because of Gardner's other work commitments, Dennis Lennon became joint co-ordinator and together they gave the QE2 a balance of design. Everything was to be attractive but practical. There would not be one 'gimmick' on the ship and the two men would work closely with Dan Wallace, Cunard's naval architect, whose own team designed the structural layout of the ship often considering the needs of the interior designers in their work. The design team came from Britain, Canada and Australia.

From the earliest days of the Q4's construction, highly detailed mock-ups of various cabins had been built in the shipyard and these were constantly visited by design team members and many changes were affected. Passengers preferred beds to bunks

Mr. James Gardner had overall responsibility for the 'New Cunarder's' interior design and exterior appearance.

Shipbuilding & Shipping Record

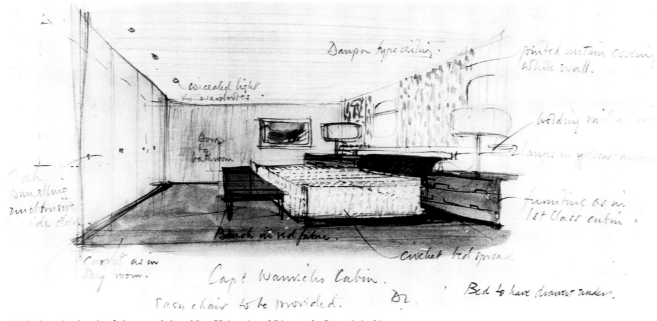

A designer's sketch of the captain's cabin. *University of Liverpool, Cunard Archives*

'Real' wood was used in several areas on the liner, such as in passenger furniture and decorative veneers and this photograph shows the Signal Deck being laid with teak planking.

Architectural Press

Fitting out alongside the jetty at John Brown's Clydebank shipyard. Here the funnel had already been fitted.

George Gardner

Above: A view of the Double Room, looking forward, from the top of the sweeping stainless steel and glass stairway. In later refits, amongst other changes, the upper lounge (the Double Up) would be given over as an extension of the shopping services.

University of Liverpool, Cunard Archives

Left: One of the majority of cabins that have a porthole. Compact and comfortable - luxury at sea available to everyone.

University of Liverpool, Cunard Archives.

Below: The space-age circular midships lobby. This would act as a lounge during voyages but would be the first class reception area whilst in harbour.

University of Liverpool, Cunard Archives

Part of the main kitchen on Quarter Deck as built. This kitchen would serve the Britannia Restaurant on the Upper Deck above it, the Columbia Restaurant aft on the same deck level as the kitchen and the Grill Room. *University of Liverpool, Cunard Archives*

and a great proportion of the rooms (the word 'cabin' was dropped) were so fitted. Bath and showers were fitted more widely in rooms than ever before.

Because of the advanced planning of the rooms about ninety had been completed on board by the time the ship was launched.

During the building of the liner it was decided – after much difference of opinion – that a two-class ship would be more advantageous than a three class vessel (especially for conversion to cruising when she would become, to all intents and purposes, a one class ship). The existence of the mock-up cabins ensured that no real difficulties occurred because of this change of direction. The opportunity to change to two classes arose when delays in the building occurred: Cunard turned these to their advantage. One major disadvantage of the delays was that the 1968 Summer season on the North Atlantic would be lost.

Extra space was also made available by the resultant reduction in the number of public rooms and associated services. By one brilliant stroke two lounges (tourist and cabin) on adjacent decks were made into one, two decks high, with the upper lounge providing a lounge balcony overlooking the lower. The two decks were connected with a stainless steel and glass stairway, cascading from one deck level to the next. This brilliant joining of the two lounges became the 20,000 square foot Double Room, one of the largest rooms afloat.

Two restaurants instead of three, and one kitchen to serve both, were to be raised from the traditional position of such rooms in earlier ships. The Verandah Grills in the earlier *Queens* had been popular, even in rough weather, because they were high in the ship and had large windows with sea-views. The other restaurants on the older ships were sited low down in the hull in order to reduce motion during stormy weather; (but they still remained un-patronised in such condition).

It was therefore decided to raise the restaurants in the *QE2* to the superstructure. The use of aluminium and the installation of stabilisers during building enabled the extra weight to be carried higher in the ship and both rooms were extended to the ship's side. Large windows built near to deck level gave wonderful views of the sea.

The kitchen, too, was raised for easy access to the restaurants, one aft and the other on the deck directly above the kitchen. Large windows were not needed in the kitchen so portholes were retained. One problem was noted by Jim Jone as he looked over the ship, as so many Cunard sea-going personnel did, to offer the benefit of his experience. In the *Mary* and the *Elizabeth* the kitchens, being low in those ships, had a garbage shute which opened to the sea through the bottom of the ship and down which rubbish could be jettisoned. There was no such shute on the *QE2* so garbage would have to be bagged and manually thrown overboard. That is, until a special door was cut into the side of the ship, disguised behind the large 'U' of the red CUNARD logo painted on the superstructure at the fore end of Quarter Deck.

One of the most elegant rooms afloat. Michael Inchbald's 'Queens Room' was decorated in white and silver and could be used for a variety of purposes.

Philip Rentell

Many of the layouts of public rooms and cabins had been created by the carefully selected group of designers with their designs co-ordinated by James Gardner and Dennis Lennon.

Some remarkably pleasant rooms were created and many designs were discarded along the way. Natural lighting was to be used as far as possible to take advantage of the large windows. The public rooms could be extended to the ship's side at night by utilizing what would be promenade space during the day.

As James Gardner was busy with the exterior styling of the ship Dennis Lennon carried on with some of the interior designs. Amongst his work were the Britannia Restaurant, the Queen's Grill (the successor to the popular Verandah Grills on the previous *Queen* liners where, on the payment of a supplement, passengers could enjoy an exclusivity denied to other passengers), the Theatre Bar (in shades of red) and the Midship's Bar (dark, mostly in greens).

The enormous Double Room (the balcony known as the Double Up, the lower deck the Double Down) was created by Jon Bannenberg and decorated with a red carpet and plum coloured suede walls. Bannenberg also did the Card Room in various greens and the swimming pool, on Six Deck, with its round changing rooms.

The classic Queen's Rooms, one of the most beautiful rooms ever to go to sea with its trumpet like columns, was finished in white and silver with a walnut veneered wall at one end which looked more substantial than suggested by its construction. A bust of the Queen, by Oscar Nemon, was set into a recess in this wall. Carpets and curtains gave a splash of colour in reds, honey

and lemon patterns. Its designer, Michael Inchbald, also designed the Quarter Deck library, furnished with chairs of green leather, brown tweed sofas and other chairs of black hide and brass.

Don Wallace, Cunard's naval architect, designed the Midships Lobby with its twenty-six foot diameter recess. This lobby with its dark blue leather walls, would act as a reception area in port and as a lounge whilst at sea. Curved green sofas bordered the recess.

The superb 500-seat theatre could also be used as a conference hall or as a church as well as a cinema. Gaby Schreiber wanted different moods to suit different occasions by varying the colour of the lighting. She also designed several of the delux suites.

Some of these original rooms have long since disappeared, their spaces being used for other functions. Amongst those lost were two night clubs.

The first, the Q4 Room, was designed by David Hicks, the son-in-law of Earl Mountbatten of Burma. The walls were of grey flannel and as a night club the tables had black cloths laid on them in the evening. In the day time, however, the room could be put to other uses and the table cloths were changed to ones of red and pink, providing a brighter mood.

The other night club, the 736 Room, was the creation of Stefan Buzas who also designed the London Gallery. The 736 Room could also be changed from its night time purpose and become a bar and discotheque during the day.

Theo Crosby's Observation Bar (also known as the Look Out), with its forward views of the sea, was panelled in cedar veneer. This was the only public room with such a view and has now sadly been put to another use and denied to passengers.

Amongst many other works of art on board three tapestries that faced the entrance of the Columbia Restaurant were noteworthy. These depicted the building and launch of the *QE2* and were designed by the Canadian, Helen Banynina.

Statues, model ships, paintings and many other works of art would decorate the ship. The crockery and glassware, with its special *QE2* logo, was also carefully chosen and soon became targets for souvenir hunters.

Amidst all this luxury and comfort the safety of her future passengers had not been forgotten and was ensured by many lifesaving and safety features.

There were twenty ship's boats, placed ten on either side of the liner. Two class 'A' 27-foot emergency boats, painted red, were located at the fore ends of the boat deck. Four class 'B' motor launches and eight class 'B' lifeboats were all 36 feet long; the six 40-foot cruise launches could take sixty people ashore or act as lifeboats for 80 if necessary.

Sixty-two Beaufort inflatable life rafts could each take 25 persons. In all, the life saving equipment could accommodate well above the complement of the liner. 3,200 Hart-Imco life jackets were also provided.

The fireproofing of the liner also featured strongly in the technical press.

Cunard had been given a choice of either adopting the American method of using as little inflammable material as possible or the British concept of supplying adequate water sprinklers and an inert gas smothering system where electrical and other water sensitive equipment was in use. They opted to use both.

To comply with the acceptance of the American regulations a reduction in the use of natural woods was implemented, although the use of this most comfortable of mediums still appeared to figure strongly in the decor and furnishing of passenger areas.

This was done by using thin 1.5mm veneers of natural wood fixed onto backings of compressed, asbestos-based sheeting called 'Marinite'. Real wood furniture was also used, especially in passenger rooms.

In all 2,000,000 square feet of 'Marinite' was used on board the ship and it was often faced with wood or plastic. The Formica company produced several patterns of textured decorative laminates, all of which had been specially designed by the designers of the various rooms and these were bonded to the 'Marinite'.

The perilous effects of working with asbestos were just beginning to be recognized and the legislation that was being introduced to protect those shaping the material had to be fully complied with.

The joiners' unions had a field day and the management found themselves with a major headache.

The 'Marinite' was produced in 8 × 4 feet sheets which were delivered to a specially fitted-out part of the joiners' workshop. The cutting and drilling machines were fitted with vacuum extractors and the men issued with protective clothing. Those working the 'Marinite' were also sent for regular and frequent chest x-rays. Off-cuts and dust from the material were carefully gathered, bagged and buried in a disused quarry on the outskirts of Glasgow. This procedure was carried out once a week.

To double the shipbuilder's responsibilities towards the health and safety of its workers a similar procedure had to be carried out on board the ship where the material was often necessarily cut for final fitting.

Sometimes even after the panelling had been fitted it had to be taken down for further work to be carried out on the systems

concealed behind it. Usually, being fragile, it broke and had to be replaced. The workmen did not mind – it was continuing employment for them as it prolonged the job which, in turn, contributed to the delay in completing the ship.

'Marinite' was used as a fireproof ceiling too. Instead of being hidden by 'Formica' it was concealed beneath ribbed and polished aluminium or cedar planking.

As in many work places where 'attractive' items are being used a certain amount of pilferage occurred. This is called 'squirreling' on the Clyde and the *QE2* proved vulnerable to it.

To the shipyard the amount of 'squirreling' that took place was normal but to the Cunard staff seconded to the ship it was worrying. 'They are stealing an entire ocean liner and there is very little we can do about it', police officers told Chief Officer Bob Arnott.

Brass porthole fittings found ready exchange for a pint of the local ale in the pubs of Clydebank and Glasgow; short lengths of copper piping (often cut into length even after being installed on the ship) were easily smuggled out of the yard. One local house was raided and was found to be furnished almost entirely in 'squirreled' *QE2* material!

Light bulbs, light fittings, curtains, equipment from lifeboats, almost everything was marketable.

One of the worst cases was shown to a bedroom steward who had travelled north to view his new domain. The first class

Even with two 36-foot motor launches in place on the starboard side, the *QE2* is still far from complete. Note the small radial crane temporarily fitted aft on the Upper Deck. *Scottish Record Office*

HRH Prince Charles joined the *QE2* for her short trip down the Clyde from the shipyard to the drydock. Prince Charles is seen talking to Captain Bil Warwick and Sir Basil Smallpeice.

QE2, arranged for the ship to be opened to the public of Clydebank during the evenings. A long standing tradition would thus be maintained. (Similar 'open-evenings' were also held later at Greenock.)

One of hundreds who visited the liner, Lilian Gibson, remembers that a specific route around the ship had been laid out. This was not only for the visitors to admire the spaciousness and vastness (as well as noting the occasional incompleteness) of the ship but it was also for the benefit of the shipyard who wanted to steer their guests away from the unfinished areas which were 'a shambles'.

Visitors were still coming to the ship on the eve of departure and a namesake of the shipyard, John (T.) Brown, recalls joiners and other tradesmen still working in the passenger cabins in an effort to get as much 'work completed as possible. It seemed to him that 'there was still a long way to go'.

By 8 o'clock on the morning of 19th November 1968 Prince Charles was on board the *QE2* as she was readied for her first and final departure from the town that had brought her into being. A special holiday had been declared for the local townsfolk.

From the cold, dark, early hours of the morning great crowds had travelled by all means of transport to line the fields

Watched by thousands who had waited patiently in the early morning chill, the *QE2* sedately leaves her birthplace shortly after 8 am on 19th November 1968.

reception area, the Midships Lobby, had been fitted with a beautiful carpet. It was there one evening at the end of the day shift: the next morning a large square of it had disappeared – cut out of the centre of the round recessed area. 'We won't come here again' a dismayed Cunard manager, referring to the yard, told the bedroom steward as they walked away from the scene.

Still, in spite of these irritations the *Queen* was fitted with £3 million worth of luxury. More irritatingly her completion date was put back.

To hurry the yard along Cunard announced that His Royal Highness Prince Charles would be at Clydebank to sail with the liner on the short journey down river to Greenock. Here, at Inchgreen, the *QE2* would be dry-docked to have the remains of her launch gear removed and to have her bottom plates cleaned and painted.

For the week before departure John Rannie, now Upper Clyde Shipbuilder's Clydebank director in direct charge of the

and shores alongside the River Clyde. Between Clydebank and Greenock an air of excitement and expectancy hung in the fresh morning air as each person patiently waited to watch the regal procession of the new gleaming liner.

John T. Brown came to watch the spectacle as he had done so on other departures. But he felt that the *QE2* was something special, and he brought along his cine camera, as well as his ordinary one, to record the event.

Captain Warwick was on board his brand new charge as she progressed down the river. He allowed the youthful Prince Charles the thrill of sounding the *QE2's* siren for the first time as the liner left Clydebank.

HRH had also been given a guided tour of the ship but, like the visitors before him, had been steered away from the unfinished areas.

The *Queen* passed round the bend at Dalmuir where the *Queen Mary*, caught by the breeze 35 years earlier, slewed round

Accompanied by her tugs, the *QE2* steams down the Clyde and to the start of her trials.   *University of Liverpool, Cunard Archives*

Once at Greenock she was carefully inched into the dry-dock and would remain there for a week, having work and inspections carried out on her underwater hull. Her rudder, internally, was maintenance free. Unlike her mighty antecedents, which had doors in their rudders for maintenance access, hers was filled with plastic foam.

The *QE2* was several months behind schedule but Cunard still hoped to have her ready for the lucrative summer season of the following year and had arranged a series of 'mini-maiden' voyages in the form of short cruises to prelude her maiden voyage proper to New York.

Each day hundreds of workmen were transported to Greenock from Glasgow and Clydebank to work on the unfinished cabins at the fore end of the ship. Feeding these men was a mammoth task but a local catering firm, who specialised in providing a service for ships going on trials, managed most efficiently.

She was due to sail on a comprehensive trial to the tropics, testing amongst other things, her air conditioning. But firstly, technical trials had to be carried out in the Irish Sea.

So, on 26th November she left Greenock for these preliminary trials which would allow a normal working-up procedure of the gearing. She achieved 164 revolutions per minute.

On 29th November the beloved *Lizzie* sailed from Southampton en-route for Florida, eventual re-sale three years later and ultimate destruction in the far-off waters of Hong Kong. The *Queen Elizabeth the Second* was the successor to a glorious precedent.

The following day, the 30th, the trials of the *QE2* finished unexpectedly. Oil fuel had contaminated the steam and feed system via the oil burner supply system and the liner had to return to Greenock. She was again dry-docked for a lengthy cleaning and decontamination period.

Her main trials to the Canaries were postponed. She had been due to sail on 4th December but, because of the unwanted extra work, this was postponed.

Cleaning completed, she left for a second trial on 17th December, finishing on the 20th. Speed had been increased to 177 r.p.m. and her full potential of 110,000 s.h.p. had been developed. She was vibration free and a new sailing date for her main trials was set for the 23rd.

Everybody was happy.

and had grounded for a few seconds, completely blocking the Clyde and causing great concern, and earning herself a place in Lloyd's daily casualty list!

Bob Arnott, later to become captain of the *Queen*, was on board as her first-ever chief officer and, as such, had been 'standing by' the liner since just after her launch. He now stood aft, in charge of the mooring lines and tow ropes.

The *Queen Elizabeth 2* steamed 10 miles down the river at a speed of around 6 knots leaving a Clydebank suddenly made empty by her departure.

As she left Clydebank John T. Brown caught a bus and raced to Greenock. He was fortunate enough to arrive in time to witness the liner's arrival there.

Off the Scottish island of Arran, the *Queen* was put through her paces. Her bulbous bow enabled her to achieve a creditable 29 knots without the tell-tale white bow wave that was usual when the old *Queens* were travelling at speed.   *University of Liverpool, Cunard Archives*

Chapter Six

Trials and Triumph

By the end of 1968 prospects had begun to look brighter for Cunard as the grievous losses of previous years turned into profit. But this was only after complex and careful husbandry of financial resources and what Commodore Marr later described as 'the sale of Cunard'. By the end of the 'rescue' of Cunard only two ships were left at sea with Q4 on the stocks.

With fewer ships to operate, employees on shore as well as at sea had found themselves without a job, the unfortunate casualties of a hard-won victory. An especially bitter pill to swallow after, in many cases, years of loyal service to the company.

QE2, the symbol in steel of Cunard's retreat from the precipice of collapse, had had her main sea trials postponed until Monday 23rd December. The company then had to quickly arrange for some of its employees to act as guinea-pigs (less colourfully known as 'stiffs' to the crew!) for the trip. The first of the 'mini-maiden voyages' that had been scheduled for the new ship was to have been a Christmas charity cruise in aid of Cancer Research. As this was cancelled due to the delay in the completion of the ship a generous contribution would be later made to the charity by Cunard.

Hurriedly, Christmases were rearranged in many households as five-hundred passengers, consisting of employees and their families, headed towards Greenock.

The trials were to be sea trials in every sense of the word and the passengers had been instructed to order anything from the menus in order to test the kitchens and the ship's novel hotel department.

This was to help 'hone-up' the organisation on board as the trial was intended to be a dress rehearsal for the liner's commercial debut, a mini-maiden voyage to be taken as a cruise due to start on 10th January 1969. This in turn, would be a prelude to the maiden voyage proper leaving Southampton on the 17th for New York. A fourth 'maiden-voyage' was also scheduled for 1st February, leaving New York for the West Indies – an early test of the fabulous liner's duel-role.

Many of the crew had transferred to the new ship from the *Queen Elizabeth* and travelled north to Scotland on a freezing overnight train. These circumstances gave some of them a foreboding for the future.

On trials off the Scottish coast, the *QE2* performed superbly. She is seen here executing a turning circle.

University of Liverpool, Cunard Archives

Two fine examples of Britain's maritime engineering: one built for peace, the other for defence. QE2 passes a 'Resolution' class nuclear powered submarine. *University of Liverpool, Cunard Archives*

Because the new *Queen* would be away from Britain for long periods of time during cruises, the crew found that they had been given neat, two-berthed cabins instead of the old dormitory style rooms that had held from twelve to twenty men. Their new dining arrangements also ensured that they would not have to eat almost where they stood as had been the case in the past. The officers also found themselves in tastefully decorated rooms.

The provisions of smaller rooms for the crew was all very pleasant but it would eventually help to destroy the sense of community (that had come from the occupancy of the old dormitories) and which had induced such fierce pride in individual ships.

The standard of food, too, was altered. Surprisingly though, the standard of choice but not of quality for the men went, if anything, down! This was at the men's own instigation, their opinions being represented by chief steward Jimmy Smith. In the old ships the stewards, for example, had to eat what the passengers were offered; but it was all very well having superb roasts, steak, fowl, etc for dinner every day but that, it was pointed out, was not how the men ate when at home. How about steak and kidney pudding, tripe and onions or Irish stew? Home cooking was what was wanted. The company concurred.

Novel design was the hallmark of the *QE2* and this extended to the hotel staff's uniforms. Stewards were given beige jackets ('like a bush jacket!') and white polo neck jumpers. Some expected to find 'The Thoughts of Chairman Mao' tucked away

in the breast pocket! The new uniforms looked smart and were fine if the wearer was slim, but worn on torsos that were sometimes over fond of food or perhaps a few pints of good English Ale the new design 'looked . . . awful', as one bedroom steward put it. The uniforms would be changed within a year.

The new hotel organisation on board the *QE2* caused other problems for the crew. In the past passengers were served with tea and biscuits in their cabin before going for breakfast in the main restaurants; but now they could order breakfast in their rooms. This meant a double trip to a cabin: one to pick up a checked off breakfast menu and another to deliver the meal. Twice the walking!

Most of the 'teething problems' caused by the new concepts were soon sorted out at staff level but a more serious problem would soon be facing the ship herself.

For the shake-down cruise to the Canaries the shipyard had embarked two-hundred men. Mainly consisting of joiners, plumbers and electricians as well as shipyard and engineering workshop staff, it was hoped that they could complete the unfinished work in the cabins at the fore end of the ship. Upper Clyde Shipbuilder's (Clydebank) director in charge of the *QE2*, John Rannie, embarked with his wife.

Far from luxuriating in their surroundings the passengers had to earn their keep. There was still a lot of cleaning and washing down of walls to be done and the embarked Cunard staff set-to to do what they could to get the liner ship-shape.

All was going well until ten o'clock on Tuesday 24th December – Christmas Eve.

Down in the Turbine Room a small-bore pipe on a pressure gauge sited over the starboard h.p. turbine fractured, spilling oil over the ahead and astern turbine, and over the differential expansion indicator which then gave a warning, apparently due to flooding with oil.

At the same time vibration was noticed to be coming from the turbine and it was at first thought that this was due to the cold oil that was being spilt onto a hot part of the machinery.

Speed was reduced on the starboard engine as an attempt was made to account for the continuing vibration.

By 3.35 in the afternoon the vibration increased severely and the turbine was stopped. The port engine was slowed to 60 r.p.m.

The starboard h.p. turbine was inspected and this examination continued until 8.30 on Christmas morning. Two hours later the starboard engine was re-started until both engines were achieving 150 r.p.m.

This speed was maintained until 4.15 on Boxing Day morning when the errant turbine once again started to vibrate. Reduce speed was ordered once more until, twenty-four hours later, the turbine was stopped altogether and allowed to cool. Just before breakfast the turbine was again started; the vibration was still there but it was not so strong as it had been.

The problems were far from over as it was now the turn of the port side machinery to malfunction. By the early evening the vibration had increased. At 8.30 on the morning of the 28th the bridge ordered speed to be reduced as the ship was approaching her anchorage off the Canary Isles where she stopped with engines on 'Stand by'.

Just after 5 o'clock that afternoon, the *QE2* weighed anchors to proceed to Las Palmas but, as she got underway, a bumping noise was heard coming from the starboard turbine followed by a grinding crunch. After this the turbine ran vibration free, the ship reaching Las Palmas three hours later where she anchored at 8.25pm.

Immediately on anchoring Sir Basil Smallpeice and Anthony Hepper came on board having previously flown out from the UK. A meeting that would last for eight hours was then held in the Card Room with Tom Kameen, Cunard's technical director, reporting that John Brown Engineering did not yet know what had caused the damage let alone how to cure it.

Angus Gibson, one of the John Brown tradesmen on board, wrote home from Las Palmas: 'There has been trouble with the engines for the past two days. I don't think we will be getting ashore. We are only stopping for a couple of hours. The weather is quite good but not a lot of sunshine. We are working most of the time so there is not much time for relaxing. There is not much to do anyway except go to the pictures. If all goes well we should be docking at Southampton on Wednesday 1st January . . .'

The letter posted on board the *QE2* bore an ironic 'Acceptance Trials' cancellation mark.

Sir Basil Smallpeice kept the ship's company informed of events over the tannoy. Members of the press had also embarked at Las Palmas and they now sent, fortunately, mostly sympathetic and often enthusiastic reports home.

That evening John Rannie spoke to his men at dinner and asked them if they would be willing to work for another seven days at Southampton after their arrival there.

On the following day, Saturday, 'J.R.' sent a radio message to his shipyard manager, Boyd Haining, telling him that a turbine had broken down and that the ship was at anchor. The fault was major and could not be rectified at sea. To bring the ship back to the Clyde was just not practical: Southampton was the nearest suitable port.

Boyd Haining was also instructed to contact Geoffrey Moss, managing director of Cammel Laird's at Birkenhead, with a view to leasing their submarine/trials accommodation ship the *Cammel Laird*.

The shipyard manager was invited to inspect the vessel and his heart sank when he subsequently saw the result of many months of neglect. However, Geoffrey Moss recalled some men from their Christmas holidays and the vessel, the ex-Irish Sea ferry *Royal Ulsterman*, was made habitable. The *Cammel Laird* tied up at the Ocean Terminal at Southampton a day and a half

before the great Cunarder arrived at her new home for the first time (which was also her port of registration). (All the other great Cunarder's had been registered at Liverpool although they had used Southampton for many years.)

It took *QE2* three days to limp home, arriving in Southampton on January 2nd, one day later than had been anticipated. Sadly, the day before, a ship's hotel officer, George Boyle, had collapsed and died.

The planned reception for the ship that had been organised by Cunard was cancelled as the company said that it would not be 'the splendid arrival it should have been'. A launch to carry officials; hundreds of inflated balloons; the Hampshire Police Band; all were cancelled.

However, the Sotonians felt differently and they warmly welcomed 'their' new ship that would replace the former *Queens* in their hearts. The Mayor and other city officials welcomed the ship on behalf of the city and a feeling of celebration pervaded the ship and town.

John Rannie slipped quietly ashore, returning to Clydebank to complete the paperwork for the ship's completion and handing over. He was not to board the liner again for many years.

As Boyd Haining reached the top of the gang-way he was greeted by Bert Farrimond, personnel director of UCS, with the words: 'Now I know how Mafeking felt'! Boyd Haining's first job – he was responsible for personnel matters for the Clydebank division as well as being shipyard manager – was to pacify the Scottish workforce and to get their problems sorted out.

The 'Bankies' were eager to get home and many were still suffering from 'having celebrated rather too well over the festive season' (Hogmanay having occurred a few hours previously). The secretaries on board could not cope with the clamour for travel warrants or for money, hence the greeting given to the personnel manager on his arrival.

Over the next few days the situation was eased, as the workmen went home on leave and fresh men arrived from Scotland. On their arrival they found that accommodation had been arranged for them around the city; the *Cammel Laird* had

Captain 'Bil' Warwick surveys the river ahead of his liner as he takes her to sea for the first time.   *Architectural Press*

met with initial disapproval as being too cramped, especially after the men now on leave had experienced the luxury of the *QE2* whilst on trials. Berthing on the smaller vessel was later reduced by half.

More men were also flown down from UCS (Clydebank) as the turbine breakdown had provided an ideal opportunity to at last finish the uncompleted cabins. The engineering difficulties thus proved to be 'an enormous blessing in disguise' for the ship-building department as all publicity now fell on the turbine troubles and attention was diverted from the unfinished state of the accommodation.

Vosper Thornycroft sent in local squads of platers, welders and caulkers to assist with the work and daily meetings were held between shop stewards of both shipyards presided over by the shipyard manager of UCS. Fourteen-hundred men were soon to be working on the liner.

Daily meetings were also held between Cunard (headed by Sir Basil Smallpeice) and Upper Clyde Shipbuilders, represented by Tony Hepper and John Brown's technical director, John Stark.

Cunard had refused to accept the ship of course and at one time even considered selling her. Sir Basil even put forward ideas that, whilst laid-up, the ship should be hired out for private functions to help make her pay.

Relations between the two companies became increasingly strained; at one point they became so strained that Cunard decided to withdraw the facility of providing lunch time coffee and sandwiches for all staff. The shipping company had just cause to be angry. All sailings (six altogether, losing £2 million) had had to be cancelled starting with the maiden voyage, and an expensive advertising and marketing campaign written off. The crew, so painstakingly trained, had to be retained throughout the repair period and many were sent home on full pay.

By this time many heated debates had taken place in the House of Commons. David Price, Member of Parliament for the Southampton district of Eastleigh, made a plea on January 24th: 'At this moment the clear priority is for the *QE2* to be completed successfully and speedily and nothing should be said or done that would divert those concerned from fulfilling that purpose'.

During the early part of January the immediate priority of repairing the damaged turbines had been put in hand. On the *QE2's* arrival in Southampton the covers had been removed and the turbines visually inspected.

The immediately visual evidence of damage to the starboard turbine was that hundreds of blades had been stripped from the main body of the rotor hub. A complete circle of blades at No. 9 stage and several from stage 10 had been carried away and lay at the base of the casing. On further inspection cracking could be seen at the bases, or roots, of other blades. In the starboard turbine the damage was less extensive, seven blades had gone from stage 9 and there was some cracking in stages 8 and 10.

The rotors were taken out, boxed and flown back to John Brown Engineering Ltd. on 6th January, leaving the turbine room looking like 'a flour mill' after the insulated cladding had been stripped off.

A thorough investigation to assess the causes of the damage and to make recommendations that would obviate their re-occurrence was set in motion. The investigating team worked under the leadership of Sir Arnold Lindley, President of the Institute of Mechanical Engineers, and their findings were published in an important paper (by Messrs. Coats and Fleeting) that was read to the Institute of Marine Engineers.

It was found that the blade roots, which were square, did not expand as much as could be expected and that the steam supply nozzles, used to deliver steam on to the blades, were of below standard quality. There were also too many of these nozzles.

The badly damaged starboard high-pressure turbine rotor. The extent of the damage to the 9th and 10th stages of blades can be clearly seen. *Shipbuilding and Shipping Record*

The resultant vibration and resonances that were induced in the blades proved to be too much and as one cracked and sheared it took away its immediate neighbour until masses of blades had been torn from the rotor.

The remedy was to provide new blades with strengthened roots and to 'tie' them together with a continuous length of one eighth of an inch stainless steel wire welded between all blades of each stage, thus providing a stiffness and a resistance to resonance.

Sir Basil Smallpeice thought that such a basic fault that had caused the damage should have been found during test-bed trials and blamed John Brown Engineering. Pametrada, the turbine's designers, had gone out of business under the Geddes committee recommendations that had streamlined so much of Britain's shipbuilding and marine engineering industry.

The port turbine rotor arrived back at Southampton by road and arrived at Vospers for inspection on the evening of Saturday 1st March.

With the arrival of the starboard rotor imminent, Sir Basil Smallpeice announced that the maiden voyage of the *QE2* was scheduled for 2nd May with proving trials first taking place, and there was no foreseeable reason why Cunard should not take delivery by the second half of April. He said that by then her accommodation would be 100% complete and there would be no doubt about the reliability of her engines: 'QE2 will more than fulfil the promises made to her prospective passengers as to her performance.' He added: 'She will be the most superb example of the shipbuilders craft the world has yet seen.' Taking another chance to market the liner Sir Basil finished: 'QE2 is certainly a new place to visit between New York and London or Paris!'

The North Atlantic was almost finished as a highway between Europe and the USA. During January there was only one sailing from Southampton by a transatlantic liner. The German *Bremen* of North German Lloyd had the windfall of taking the passengers originally intended for the *QE2's* postponed maiden voyage of 17th January. She had also picked up the passengers who should have sailed on the now strike-bound *United States* – the holder of the out-moded Blue Riband – the fastest liner that the world had seen.

Cunard's vision of a ship for all seasons was about to be vindicated.

A typical study of the *QE2* in the Ocean Dock, Southampton, alongside the now demolished Ocean Terminal.   *Norman Jackman*

Photographed amidst the splendour of a Norweigean Fjord, the *QE2* serenely glides through the unruffled waters.   *Cunard*

Above and below: The first arrival of the *QE2* in Southampton was far from the splendid arrival it should have been as the ship limped in at slow speed. Fortunately the press was sympathetic.   *Both, R. Bruce Grice*

Chapter Seven

The Best

The refurbished turbines were reinstalled and the ship-builders assured Cunard that the liner would be completed two weeks ahead of the revised estimated schedule.

When all was ready in the engine room, QE2 was put through her basin trials. These consisted of various engine trials undertaken whilst the liner was tied up alongside the Ocean Terminal. To test the reliability of the main machinery overspeed tests were carried out which involved the disconnection of the propeller shafts from the engines and running the latter at higher speeds than could be expected in the normal operation of the ship.

The basin trials were happily successful. The next test would be to take the ship on a short series of trials in the English Channel, off the southern coast of Hampshire and Dorset.

So, after three months delay, at 7 o'clock in the evening of Monday 24th March the QE2 sailed at last leaving Southampton for the first time, under the command of Captain Warwick and with Jack Holt on board as pilot. Amongst those on board were two men with a keen interest in the outcome of the short sea-trials – Sir George Gardiner, chairman of John Brown Engineering and Sir Arnold Lindley, President of the Institute of Mechanical Engineers. They were looking forward to the tests with 'cautious optimism'.

The liner anchored for the night off the Nab light-tower in the eastern approaches to Spithead and the next day compass trials were undertaken. A speed of 18 knots was also achieved.

The 'swingiest fashion show ever staged' took place on board whilst the liner was underway and five-hundred press-men were embarked to record events.

As the passengers sat down to lunch the American superliner *United States* sailed by. As she did so one man was reported, perhaps apocryphally, as saying: 'There goes the world's fastest liner.' His companion came back with 'but not the best'! The latter's retort would soon be echoed by many.

Anchoring each evening off the coast the QE2 was put through full speed trials during the day. She also did a crash stop in which she came to halt in seven minutes, travelling one-and-a-half miles in doing so. Going astern she reached a speed of fourteen knots, sustaining this speed for a lengthy period.

Back in Southampton on the 27th the QE2 entered the King George V dry dock in the Western (also known as the New) Docks at 7.30 in the evening. It was the building of this very dock, the largest in the world when it was opened in 1933, that had finally persuaded Cunard to use Southampton as its British terminus for the *Queen Mary* when she was being built.

Unusually it would be from the flooded dry-dock that the new *Queen* would sail on her previously interrupted shakedown cruise to the tropics to test her air-conditioning.

During the day of 30th March seven-hundred invited passengers boarded the liner; in the early evening several members of the hotel staff walked off the ship. They were protesting about what they felt was excessive vibration in about ten cabins on Five Deck caused when the liner was travelling at her normal service speed of 28 knots.

The company promised to investigate the complaint (two months later, after further complaints, the worst affected cabins were turned into staff offices whilst others were fitted with extra insulation) and the crew re-boarded the liner. The *Queen* sailed at 9.30pm.

During the first few days of April the *Queen Elizabeth 2* proved her worth. Her passengers were more than happy with both their accommodation and the service. The engines – especially the turbines – performed superbly. Averaging a speed of 30 knots the liner, on occasion, reached more than 32.5 knots.

After reaching the coast of Senegal at about 15° latitude north of the Equator (where the passengers stayed cool in their air-conditioned paradise whilst the air temperature outside reached 90°F) the liner turned north to steam around the Canary Islands before heading once again for Southampton. She arrived back in the port on the 7th.

The next day Sir Basil Smallpeice held a press conference and declared himself 'highly satisfied' with the liner. Although she had lost an estimated £3 million because of her unhappy start,

The sheer grace of the liner's forward hull can be judged from this quayside photograph, taken as the ship safely reached Southampton after her disastrous trials. *University of Liverpool, Cunard Archives*

Slowly edged into her berth, the new *Queen* prepares for many weeks of battling between owner's and builders.   *R. Bruce Grice*

Sir Basil stated 'she is being handed over to us in a better condition than I ever thought possible at one time'.

Sir Arnold Lindley was also happy with the remedial work that had been carried out on the turbines: 'I think we can regard the trouble with the turbines now as something in the past', but Upper Clyde Shipbuilders wanted to satisfy themselves that this was so. They announced that they were hoping to hand the ship over to Cunard on the 18th of the month but would first open up the turbine casings for a final inspection.

At a private lunch on board on the 14th April Sir Basil Smallpeice, his deputy chairman Lord Mancroft, Cunard's managing director John Whitworth and Anthony Hepper, chairman of UCS, entertained three-hundred VIPs including the top civic dignitaries of Southampton; representatives of the port, shipping and commercial interests; the lone, world circumnavigating yachtsman Sir Alec and his wife Lady Rose; and the last captains of the two great deposed *Queens* – Geoffrey Marr and John Treasure Jones.

It was announced that Her Majesty Queen Elizabeth II would visit the liner that she had launched twenty months earlier on the day before the maiden voyage proper, May 1st.

As previously stated the liner was to be handed over to the Cunard Line by her builders on Friday 18th March, but the official ceremony did not take place on board the ship: Unusually it took place in an office many miles away in London and occurred one hour later than originally announced.

At the same time, 1.15pm, in Southampton, the liner gave a three blast greeting on her whistle as the builder's flag was lowered and the scarlet flag of Cunard with its rampant golden lion clutching a globe was raised in its place.

The ship, at long last, belonged to Cunard.

A captain of *QE2* talks with a captain of industry. Bill Warwick chats with Sir Basil Smallpeice, the one man to whom Cunard would owe its survival.   *University of Liverpool, Cunard Archives*

Chapter Eight

Royal Approval

The *Queen Elizabeth 2* was due to depart on her first voyage with fare-paying passengers, leaving Southampton on Tuesday 22nd April 1969. This would be in the form of a short cruise to Las Palmas in the Canary Islands, and was billed as the first 'mini maiden voyage' of the new liner.

Amongst the hundreds of activities taking place that would prepare the liner for her commercial debut was the consecration of the shipboard Jewish Synagogue, designed by Professor Mischa Black, and performed by Chief Rabbi Dr Jakobovits. Professor Black had declined the offer of utilising the old synagogue of the *Queen Mary* in the new ship as he considered the *Mary's* synagogue as being 'not in keeping with the modern trends of the Jewish faith'.

At 4.45 in the afternoon of the appointed day, the *Queen* sailed to the sounds of a military bank playing on the quayside as a mass of balloons was released. Hundreds of spectators watched as the liner was gently eased in Southampton Water by tugs gaily dressed overall with flags that stiffly fluttered in the prevailing gusty wind.

The cruise would last eight days and in its course would encompass the discovery and disembarkation (to a pilot cutter) of a stowaway, the christening of little James Clifton and the death of a fifty-one year old male passenger.

Arriving back in Southampton on Wednesday 30th April, the liner was prepared for her Royal visitors who would be inspecting the ship the next day. Her Majesty the Queen would be following the royal precedents set by her grandmother and mother when they had visited their mighty namesakes on the eves of their maiden voyages.

The Queen and the Duke of Edinburgh duly arrived the next morning at 11.50 am and stayed on board for two and a half hours, touring the ship with Captain William Warwick and Staff Captain George Smith who acted as guides.

Amongst the many fittings in which the Queen showed great interest were the navigational aids on the bridge. She also admired a figurehead of Britannia (the name of Samuel Cunard's first pioneer transatlantic paddle steamer) in the Britannia Restaurant. The figure, carved in yellow pine, had been presented by Lloyds of London. This 'wooden maiden' had lost her fingertips after a particularly lively party on board a few weeks earlier!

Lunch was taken in the Grill Room with the guests sitting at tables of four. The Queen sat with the captain, Sir Basil Smallpeice and the Vice-Lieutenant of Hampshire, Lord Malmesbury, lunching on melon ball cocktails, cold Avon salmon, mayonnaise, new potatoes and a green salad; strawberries and cream followed; a 1962 Montrachet was served. The Queen would later compliment the executive chef, Mr Townshend, on the meal and its serving.

After lunch the royal party walked through the lovely Queen's Room (this room had been flooded with oil during fitting out; an act of vandalism, it was rumoured, to delay the final departure from the Clyde). Lord Mancroft, Cunard's chief of marketing, pointed out to Her Majesty the bust of herself sculpted by Oscar Nemon. Although it was only a painted plaster cast, the Queen was interested to see it in the position that the actual casting would finally occupy.

Sir Basil Smallpeice recalled the conversation: 'You are putting it here, are you?' the Queen asked, 'How did he manage to finish it so soon?', Lord Mancroft explained that it was only a plaster copy. The Queen then described her seven sittings for the sculptor and how each time Oscar Nemon had been dissatisfied with his work. The Queen continued, quoting Nemon: 'That's no good' he says, and wrenches my head off!' whereupon the Queen twisted a clawed hand above a clenched fist to give demonstration of the sculptor's action, much to the delight of onlookers.

Before she left the ship the Queen remarked about the excellent condition of the vessel and expressed her hope for a happy maiden voyage that would be starting on the following day, and for a subsequently successful career for the liner.

The euphoria of the royal visit was replaced the next day by that of the *QE2's* departure for New York on her long delayed maiden voyage. The original maiden voyage to New York, that should have started on the 17th January, would have taken a circuitous route taking thirteen days via the Canaries and the Caribbean; a mixture of cruise and North Atlantic ferry voyage combining the two roles that had been designed into the ship.

Rain in the morning had failed to dampen the excitement that prevailed in Southampton and many vantage points both within and outside of the docks were occupied by people in their thousands.

Fourteen hundred passengers had been booked for this premier voyage; some people were only taking the short channel

The Oscar Nemon bust of Her Majesty Queen Elizabeth II which adorns a small alcove at the forward end of the lovely Queen's Room. The bust was altered in colouring from copper green to gold during a recent refit.
Philip Rentell

A very dismal 2nd May 1969 witnessed the *Queen's* maiden departure for New York. A good crowd still attended the event. *Southern Newspapers*

trip, but six hundred others were making the complete round voyage, obviously considering that the chance to attend this party-of-a-lifetime was too good to miss! The ship also carried nine hundred and six crew in all departments.

The liner had been scheduled to leave the Ocean Terminal at 12.30, but because of a delay caused by the handling of the baggage she was a quarter of an hour late in getting away.

The Hampshire Police Band had entertained the crowd of well-wishers on the quayside as well as those lining the railings of the liner's boat deck but, as she pulled away, trumpeters from the band of the Royal Corps of Transport played a specially composed fanfare 'Cunard Queen'.

Hundreds of brightly coloured balloons bespeckled the sky as Buccaneer jets of the Fleet Air Arm flew overhead. Arms waved as the thin paper streamers thrown from the high decks of the liner broke, the last tenuous link between ship and shore.

A bevy of small craft awaited the liner in the main stream, and tugs used their fire-fighting equipment to send plumes of water high into the air in joyous salute.

A little later as the *QE2* passed the jetties at the Fawley oil refinery, the tankers berthed there added their throaty greetings. The *Queen* responded with her siren.

Turning to port off Cowes on the Isle of Wight – always a vantage point from which to watch the comings and goings of the great liners – the *QE2* headed towards Le Havre, her next port of call.

The French harbour was delighted at being chosen as the European port of call for the new Cunarder. Up until now Cherbourg had had the honour of serving the previous *Queen's*

and a huge crowd had turned out to greet her as she docked on schedule.

The liner was handled through the agencies of the French Line (Compagnie General Transatlantique) as Cunard had since closed its own agency in France. It was a nice extension to the co-operation that would exist between the *France* and the *QE2*. It was also actually CGT who had given preference to Le Havre on behalf of Cunard.

During the two hours that the liner stayed in Le Havre one hundred passengers disembarked to return to the UK, the European passengers embarked and then the *Queen* was off – destination New York.

The maiden voyage was unhappily marred by the death of a sixty-one year old steward, 'Jack' Sharp, and his remains were committed to the sea as the liner came to a temporary halt in mid-Atlantic.

New York had prepared a welcome to outdo the departure from Southampton. Mayor John Lindsay had declared 7th May, as *'Queen Elizabeth the Second* Day' and, with a group of civic dignitaries, boarded the liner in the Lower Bay.

Bathed in sunshine and escorted ahead by the US Coast Guard cutter (which had brought out the mayor and his party) and a US destroyer astern, the *Queen* sedately approached the famous Manhatten skyline, the water around her continually churned white by the accompanying fleet of pleasure craft, tugs and river ferries.

Bob Arnott recalled a patriotic thrill derived from 'a gigantic sea and air display of twin triumphs in British design, advanced technology and engineering skills' when a 'jump-jet

Greeted by an enthusiastic crowd, (which would become typical all over the world as the Queen took to cruising), the liner arrives at Southampton assisted by tugs.   *Architectural Press*

(Harrier) hovered at each extremity of the bridge as we entered the harbour'. This surge of patriotism would find a home in many British hearts in the years to come when the ship would be welcomed in many foreign ports.

The *QE2* docked at Cunard's New York terminus, Pier 92, in the North River at just after 3 pm.

The after decks of the *QE2* provided a cascading sun trap for the passengers. Each of the aluminium framed verandah windows had been individually manufactured to suit the bevel and sheer of the ship's lines. These decks would be changed to suit a variety of purposes in future years.
                                                                          Cunard

The City's Mayor, John Lindsay, said that the ship would 'continue the Cunard tradition of sailing great ships into this, the greatest port in the world, for decades to come'. Thousands of people were entertained on board the new ship as she became the 'in' place in New York with socialites and politicians of many countries counted amongst the guests enjoying the British hospitality.

The New Yorkers, like the Sotonians in Britain, had been surprised at the *QE2's* appearance. Her all enclosed superstructure gave away the comforts of an air-conditioned interior, but the funnel was the strikingly different feature of the ship. Gone was the traditional Cunard funnel of carmine red with two or three narrow horizontal black bands and a broad black top; in its place was a device that was almost a sculpture. A black pipe, protruding from a white casing, surmounted by a soot and smoke deflecting windscoop that was white on the outside but painted in 'Cunard red' on the inside. The terraced decks aft of the funnel cascaded to the stern providing both shelter and sun trap; the hull itself also broke from the traditional black, being painted in charcoal grey to the contemporary British Standard of BS-9-028.

The company shade of red was also echoed in the name of CUNARD painted on either side of the forward superstructure. Deck-house sides along the boat deck, and also the bridge front, had been painted in light khaki to give additional depth. In the styling of the liner's exterior, James Gardner had done his job well.

Visitors on board were also surprised at the spaciousness of the vessel. Compared to the space allotted to each passenger on the old *Queens* each passenger now had fifty per cent more deck area. Combined with her modern decor the liner presented an almost revolutionary appearance; she was a superb blend of good and practical design.

Counted amongst the twelve hundred passengers on the return leg of this, the first voyage, was one of the principle guests at the official New York reception, Lord Louis Mountbatten.

A few days after her arrival back in Southampton Lord Louis sent an autographed photograph of himself to the officers' wardroom to 'update' the one of himself that had graced a similar position in the old *Queen Elizabeth*.

With a total complement of 2,025 the *Queen's* early voyages were somewhat underbooked, but that was put down to the season. West bound traffic was particularly under-patronised in the early days for, when the *QE2* returned to Southampton, she was scheduled to carry only seven hundred on the next trip to New York.

Amongst these were two well known personalities. The Southampton newspaper, the 'Echo', reported Peter Sellers as saying, 'it's nice to have the time to take a little rest on board. You get a little tired jetting it everywhere'.

As almost an accolade to the modern image of the *QE2* Ringo Starr, the drummer of the phenomenally popular music group the 'Beatles', was also travelling: 'It's rather like a splendid hotel – better than you get at Scarborough!'

The *Queen* sailed on her second westbound voyage on Friday 16th May, at 12.30 pm.

Outward bound through Spithead she passed through the assembled, multi-national fleet of NATO which the Queen was reviewing (making it an unique occasion as reigning British monarchs had only ever reviewed British fleets) from the Royal Yacht *Britannia*.

The liner blew her loyal greeting as she drew abreast of the Royal Yacht, Captain Warwick signalled: 'Captain Warwick and the ship's company of the *Queen Elizabeth 2* with their humble duty send their best wishes and hope that Her Majesty will have an enjoyable day reviewing the NATO Fleet'.

The after verandah decks provided a sheltered meeting place - weather permitting.

Architectural Press

A group of celebrities boarded the liner for her delayed trial cruise to Dakar and the Canaries. *University of Liverpool, Cunard Archives*

Her Majesty replied: 'I am grateful for your signal. I send you and all on board my best wishes. Bon voyage. Elizabeth R.'

The Royal interest in the liner was continued on the ship's next arrival in Southampton. On Thursday 29th May His Royal Highness Prince Philip Duke of Edinburgh paid a lone visit to the ship to present awards on behalf of the Council of Industrial Design.

Many weeks earlier when it was suggested that the awards should be presented in surroundings that epitomised the spirit of the occasion the Duke himself suggested the *QE2*.

Gaby Schreiber's theatre was chosen as the venue for the presentation of the eighteen trophies. The Duke toured the liner visiting passenger and crew areas, as well as control rooms and kitchens. He backed up his selection of venue by saying that '. . . the ship represented the culmination of the work of a great many designers in a great many fields'.

Throughout the summer of 1969 the *QE2* showed her paces and proved her worth. It would, it was realised, take time to make an impression on the source of her main market, the Americans, but meanwhile the liner put Cunard back into the realms of viability.

She proved herself worthy of the faith that had been so painstakingly placed in her. In the first six months of operation between her maiden voyage and the end of her eleventh round voyage in September, she realized a profit of £1,674,000. The plug in the drain on Cunard's resources had become a foundation on which to build for the future.

Chapter Nine

Serenity, Security and Storm

To relate each and every voyage of the *QE2* and to chronicle every incident that has befallen the liner would be beyond the capabilities of this book.

However, be it sufficient to say that the *Queen*, like so many other ships before her, usually remains out of the news as long as she performs what is asked of her: the quiet and efficient performance of her scheduled voyaging.

Safe navigation and the careful maintenance of her fiercely demanding timetable has ensured that the liner has continued the Cunard Line's enviable reputation of never losing a life during peacetime operations.

Incidents are bound to happen, of course, when a ship – such as the *QE2* – annually sails so many thousands of miles. It is usually the occurrence of such incidents that brings the *QE2* into the headlines but often these events are a result of outside influences or because of accidents happening to other vessels in which the Cunarder becomes involved, through her responding to calls for assistance.

Sea lanes, like their land-based counterparts, are safe so long as their users observe specific laws and rules. Imprudent navigation on the part of other ships may, on the rare occasion, put the *QE2's* navigators to the test, especially at the 'junctions' of popular cruise ports where ships of many flags converge – sometimes too speedily!

Like most highways, those of the sea can occasionally produce a sudden drama and one ship may call on another to assist her in her distress.

The big chance of the *QE2* came on 8th January 1972.

Whilst cruising in the Caribbean the French Line's handsome *Antilles*, white hulled with the company's deep red funnel with its black top, was sailing in the vicinity of the island of Mustique, the passengers being given a closer look at the scenery.

In spite of frantic warnings from local inhabitants the ship sailed in rather too closely and struck an uncharted reef. Her oil tanks ruptured and oil spilled into the surrounding tropical seas and, worst of all, into the liner's own engine room where it ignited.

Soon the liner was ablaze and the six hundred and thirty five people on board gave the vessel up to the flames and abandoned ship. One of the ships within capable reach of the stricken *Antilles* was the *QE2*, herself on a cruise to the exotic islands of the Caribbean. Still under the command of Bil Warwick, the liner weighed anchor from her stopover point in St. Lucia and sped towards the scene of disaster.

On arriving at the location at 10.30 pm, the *Queen* found the night sky lit in a pulsating dome of dull red by the blazing French vessel. By now the *Antilles* passengers had been transferred to the island by their ships boats and it was from here that the *QE2* picked up over three hundred survivors. Initially it was thought that many had perished but these people had been picked up by other ships from another local island.

QE2 sailed at 5:30 am and later landed her rescued at Barbados. Amongst the many messages of congratulation that Captain Warwick received was one forwarded by Cunard from the President of Compagnie General Transatlantique (the French Line) and passed on to the ship by an equally grateful Sir Basil Smallpeice: 'I want to thank you for the assistance which has been afforded to us by Cunard in the accident which struck our liner *Antilles*. Please convey to the captain of the *QE2* our deep appreciation for taking onboard passengers which our crew had evacuated and put on Mustique Island.'

Fire is the most feared of all the fates that can befall a ship at sea. For centuries many fine ships – including such maritime jewels as the *Henri Grace À Dieu* of Henry VIII, Charles I's carved and gilded *Sovereign of the Seas* and the impeccable *Normandie* – have blazed to total ruin and ways had been sought to at least control, if not obviate, the fiery nightmare that might occur.

The *QE2* had been built to be as fire-proof a ship as possible, at the time of building conforming not only to current and potential British legislation but also to American. Fire-resistant materials and superior automatic fire extinguishing and detection equipment make the *Queen* one of the safest ships to have been built. Trained fire patrols in harbour or dry-dock ensure that the unhappy fate that befell the beautiful *Normandie* does not reoccur.

Even so, the liner has not been entirely immune from fire but these have been quickly and efficiently dealt with.

A particular engine room blaze in 1976 left the *Queen* without the use of one boiler and she limped back into Southampton with the lower white casing of her statuesque funnel blackened. The effected boiler had to be replaced by dry-docking the liner by cutting an access hole in her side to remove the damaged machinery and install its replacement. Similar damage to an

The external evidence of the blaze in which one crew member was injured in 1976.   *Southern Newspapers*

older ship would, perhaps, have resulted in its premature scrapping.

Fire when unchecked, can destroy even the best of Man's creations whether afloat or on land but the main cause of wanton and deliberate destruction is often Man himself.

One occasion arose during the eventful early years of the *QE2's* career and was one which would seriously affect the liner's future security arrangements – including her public accessability.

It all began in New York, May 1972. Of many evening classes being held at various locations in that bustlingly cosmopolitan city was one particular English class at Hunter College in Manhatten. A pupil of the class, Miss Barbara Shelvey, had written a short story based on a shipboard bomb scare of a previous year and Miss Shelvey's own uneventful voyage on the *QE2*.

The action of her story took place on board the Cunarder and involved two main characters who had booked passage. One character was a Mrs. Garth, terminally ill with cancer, and the other an ex-convict who found no joy in life. Their plan was to hijack the liner by holding-up the captain on the bridge at gun point and then commit a jewel robbery prior to escaping in one of the ship's launches.

Because of Miss Shalvey's shyness the evening class teacher, Professor Philip Freund, read the short story to the rest of the class. Only five students were present in the class that evening and one remarked on Miss Shalvey's 'fantastic imagination'.

A few hours after the reading a telephone call was received at Cunard's New York office, taken by Charles Dixon, Vice President finance and operations of the company's American organisation.

The caller said that unless a ransom of $350,000 was paid in ten and twenty dollar bills two accomplices, one terminally ill with cancer, and at that moment on board the *QE2*, would detonate six explosive devices, depth charges, concealed within the ship.

The FBI was called and Cunard alerted the Ministry of Defence and Scotland Yard in London. Money was obtained with which to pay the ransom in New York whilst, in England, the RAF readied two aircraft: a Hercules which would fly out a bomb disposal team and a second aircraft, a Nimrod, which would be used for communications.

The military bomb-disposal team consisted of four men – Captain Robert Williams, Sergeant Clifford Oliver, Lieutenant Richard Clifford and Corporal Thomas Jones. Together the men represented the Special Air Service (SAS) and the Special Boat Service (SBS) of the Royal Marines.

The liner had been en-route for Cherbourg (the *QE2* had reverted to using this traditional Cunard port instead of Le Havre in early May) and Southampton, but had hove-to in mid-Atlantic to embark the military parachutists. On board for Voyage 84 were 1,438 passengers including the conductor, Leopold Stokowski, and Mr George Kelly, Uncle of Princess Grace of Monaco. It was May 18th.

Captain William Law had previously arranged a search of the ship and informed the passengers of what was happening. Generally they remained calm, but one or two women, who could not apparently stand the suspense, were visibly upset.

Excited passengers lined the ship's rails to watch as the four parachutists appeared, dropping from beneath the low cloud base into the sea at the liner's starboard bow. A ship's launch under the new command of Junior First Officer Robin Woodall (later to be a captain of Cunard's Caribbean cruise-ships and later relief Captain of the *QE2*) picked up the men and brought them to the ship. After the first officer had introduced their leader, Captain Williams, to Captain Law on the bridge the army com-

mander reached inside his wetsuit and produced a copy of that day's newspaper which he presented to an astonished skipper.

The military men then conducted a search of strategic points in the passenger accommodation, baggage storage rooms etc.

About an hour after the disposal team had boarded the rumours started: 'They have found two bombs already in Two Deck baggage area!', a stewardess excitedly told crew-member Barney Gallagher and his work-mate.

The bomb scare proved, as was suspected, to be without foundation and nothing was found.

The Manhattan evening class professor had, by now, heard the news of the bomb scare and realized the close similarity between his pupil's story and fact. He telephoned the police and the next day a New York show salesman, Joseph Lindisi, was arrested. He was later sentenced to twenty years imprisonment pending a psychiatric examination.

Although the whole affair had been a hoax Cunard had gained valuable first hand experience in anti-terrorist security, and ship-board security was subsequently tightened. No longer would the casual visitor be able to stroll around the ship whilst in port – and out went the traditional 'Bon Voyage' parties held by passengers in their cabins for those friends being left behind.

But as one very relieved American passenger said after the dramatic mid-Atlantic meeting between ship and security forces: 'It was very comforting to think that Britain can still reach out.'

Although deliberately induced harm has been guarded against (more than it had been in the air) the ship is, as are most types of transport, still prone to the whims of nature.

'WNA' is a marking on a vessel's load-line which indicates a special condition: Winter North Atlantic. The designers of the *QE2* did away with winter on the North Atlantic for their ship as it was planned that the ship should go cruising during this inhospitable Atlantic season. Although the *QE2* can still encounter storms on this ocean information given by modern navigational aids and computers can enable the bad weather –

May 1972 saw British military parachutists jumping into the sea near a stopped *QE2*. A bomb hoax had started a full-scale exercise which still has its echoes in the continuing security arrangements today. *Cunard*

and sometimes, in early Spring, ice – to be avoided by sailing around the affected area.

But when inclement weather is unavoidable then the force of the sea, which man can only ignore at his peril, can often leave its mark.

In April 1972, the month before the bomb hoax, one particularly severe storm lasted for several days and the *Queen* arrived in Southampton 36 hours late.

The six hundred passengers were presented with bouquets upon disembarking, leaving behind them pianos, crockery and glassware smashed by the effects of the turbulent ocean.

Captain Mortimer Hehir also presented a signed 'Storm Certificate' to everyone on board:

This is to record that on her North Atlantic voyage leaving New York on the 16 April 1972, for Southampton, England, *RMS Queen Elizabeth 2*, of 65,863 gross tons encountered exceptionally severe weather in position Latitude 42° 18' North, Longitude 55° 52' West.

During this storm, winds reached speeds in excess of 100 mph. Combined with heavy swell, waves were encountered of 50 feet in height.

This weather caused even the *Queen Elizabeth 2*, with her exceptional size and sea-keeping qualities, to lie hove to for 21½ hours between 17th and 19th April 1972, until the storm abated.

I commend all passengers in sharing this unique experience with great cheerfulness and calm.'

Mortimer Hehir
Captain

The 'uniqueness' of this particular storm was spoilt in September 1978, when Captain Douglas Ridley encountered similar severe weather which damaged the liner's fore peak railings.

The ship's size and ability to weather most seas was proven when the liner went to the rescue of a yacht, crippled in a Mediterranean storm during the season of the Mistral.

A northerly gale was blowing on 25th September 1974 when, as the *QE2* cut her way through the heavy swell of the

---

QUEEN ELIZABETH 2

STORM CERTIFICATE

This is to record that on her North Atlantic voyage, leaving New York on the 16th April 1972, for Southampton, England, RMS QUEEN ELIZABETH 2, of 65,863 gross tons, encountered exceptionally severe weather in position Latitude 42°18' North, Longitude 55°52' West.

During this storm, winds reached speeds in excess of 100mph. Combined with a heavy swell, waves were encountered of 50 feet in height.

This weather caused even the QUEEN ELIZABETH 2, with her exceptional size and sea-keeping qualities, to lie hove to for 21½ hours between 17th and 19th April 1972, until the storm abated.

I commend all passengers in sharing this unique experience with great cheerfulness and calm.

Captain

An early spring crossing of the *QE2* in April 1972 met a late severe gale. The captain had this special certificate issued to commemorate the event. Passengers were also given bouquets as they disembarked.

T.S. Gough

Mediterranean between Naples and Barcelona, distress rockets were seen at 3 am. Responding promptly to the call for help and in order to avoid causing further damage to the French yacht *Stephanie*, which was in immediate danger of sinking, Captain Peter Jackson stopped his liner some way off and allowed her to drift over to the stricken vessel, thus giving her a lee in which the six survivors could be rescued from almost certain death. The flare that the captain had seen had been their last but one.

The liner then gave warning of the wreckage to other ships in the area and the next day the US cruiser *Little Rock* of the US 6th Fleet confirmed that they had sunk the remains of the yacht.

Peter Jackson was later received by the Chairman of Lloyds of London in recognition of his masterly navigation and humanity. From other authorities came silence, a strange reward indeed for such a notable action.

Danger lurks not only on the surface of the sea but also under it, waiting for the unaware navigator.

The *QE2* had gone to the rescue when an unchartered reef had caused the total constructive loss of the *Antilles* and it would be, ironically, an incorrectly chartered reef that would cause enough damage to the *QE2* to warrant her dry docking for repairs.

This happened during a Caribbean cruise when the liner was manoeuvring in the 'swinging' ground at Nassau prior to sailing. As the liner's bow turned, her underwater bulbous bow collided with a coral reef, was holed and the liner had to proceed to New York, the remainder of the cruise being cancelled.

Captain Hehir was held responsible but on the 28th January 1976, the liner's next call at the port, Staff Captain Peter Jackson, along with first Officers Sturge and Warwick and members of the ship's sub-aqua diving club took a boat and set off to investigate the reef.

To the exoneration of their captain they found, by the use of sextant readings and landmarks, that the reef had been incorrectly charted: instead of running practically straight it had two 50 foot 'headlands' and on one of these, which projected from the charted line, was found evidence of the *QE2's* collision. A marker buoy was also found to be incorrectly moored (being 130 feet away from its recorded position) and the two errors combined confounded the ship's navigators' assumption that the safe water that they had reason to expect was not there.

It is usually the *Queen's* involvement in dramatic events that ensure her of a headline and general public interest, but to the thousands who travel on the *QE2* it is the trouble-free ferry voyages across the Atlantic or her cruising to places of interest that evoke the happy memory of ports visited and sights seen.

Her winter cruising days started with forays to the Caribbean from New York but, by 1975, these had developed into full World Cruising. The *QE2* has now completed either one of these cruises or else a comprehensive Pacific cruise each year and many new and exotic ports have been added to her itinerary for the delight of her passengers.

She broke new ground for Western liners by cruising to China in 1975. On her popular visits to Hong Kong the *Queen* often takes advantage of an economic cosmetic treatment when local painters swarm over bamboo scaffolding, erected precariously on small boats bobbing around the ship, giving her hull a smart new coat of paint.

The liner's transition of the Panama Canal is always popular, with passengers crowding the rails to witness the event. The largest ship to pass through the canal, the *QE2* also pays the highest fees but the savings in fuel costs by doing so far outweighs the longer passage south. However, the *QE2* is due to round the Horn in a special South American cruise in 1989 following in the wake of the *Queen Mary* when she passed Cape Horn en route to her final destination at Long Beach in 1967.

Attended by 'mules' on the rail tracks to either side of the lock, the *QE2's* 105-foot beam (still in her post-Falklands livery) is eased through the lock-gates whilst transiting the Panama Canal. (Her maiden passage through the canal was in 1979). An expensive journey of a few hours cuts out an even more expensive alternative voyage of rounding the Horn.   *Captain Borland courtesy of Southampton City Museums*

From Southampton the liner cruises to the Atlantic Isles, the Iberian Peninsula and to the Mediterranean. North Cape cruises, too, are extremely popular with the liner dwarfed by the magnificently spectacular scenery of the Norwegian Fjords as she steams in sheltered deep water between sheer mountain cliffs, cascading with pine forests and waterfalls.

During the course of the *QE2's* World Cruises her passengers have many options open to them. One of these is to join the ship for only part of the voyage and the experiences gained from such a journey can be most enriching. Owing to the cessation of the majority of the old-style, regular liner voyages a part of the *Queen's* cruise can be used as a substitute, making a visit to friends or relations that much more rewarding. Passengers can join *QE2* anywhere in the world by plane and in recent years the ship has enjoyed a unique distinction in being paired with that superb product of Anglo French co-operation, Concorde.

The list of islands visited in the Pacific – Tonga, Tahiti, Fiji, the Society Islands where one can see fish swimming in the coral from glass-bottomed boats – seems endless. Dancing to Joe Loss and other bands, discos, midnight buffets, patriotic departures from New Zealand and the gala firework welcomes in Australia (which make the British amongst the passengers proud to be British) all make world cruising in the *QE2* so popular with many people often repeating their bookings. Wry British humour on board, whilst appreciated by compatriots – 'Watch out for the bump!' as the liner crosses the Equator – can leave other passengers worried!

During one Pacific cruise of the *Queen* in the early 1980s, Alan Whicker, the television presenter of 'Whickers World', based

one of his series around the liner. This proved to be very unpopular with the crew as it encroached on their private relaxation and gave, perhaps, a one-sided view of life on board – and on shore. Many people, including passengers, refused to take part in the glossy documentary.

The *Queen Elizabeth 2* is an extremely popular visitor to Japan, her arrivals there drawing crowds to the quayside numbered in thousands. Yokohama, especially, gives the liner a rapturous welcome, so much so that the city has chartered – at a reported fee of £14 million, the ship for 'Yokohama Exotic Showcase '89' which will commemorate the 130th Anniversary of the Port and the centenary of the municipality of the city. The charter will extend from March until September 1989 and will last for seventy-two days.

One particular charter was surrounded by a extraordinarily high-level of security that was, fortunately, never brought into action.

The *Queen Elizabeth 2* sailed not only into New York, in early April 1973, from a Caribbean Cruise but into the start of an intense security exercise.

The liner had been chartered by Assured Travel of Worcester, Massachusetts, run by Mr Oscar Rudnik. He had conceived the idea of chartering the *QE2* to take travellers to Israel to join in the celebrations of the Twenty Fifth Anniversary of that State's founding.

Cunard had anticipated carrying twelve hundred passengers each way but that would turn out to be the final total number for the entire voyage. Mr Rudnik had hoped to recoup his subsequent losses by using the liner as an hotel whilst she was in Israel,

Above: The *QE2* at anchor in one of the many exotic harbours that she visits during the course of her annual cruising itinary. An anchor was lost during a westbound Atlantic crossing and, in doing so, punched a six-inch hole in the Fore Peak Tank. Speed was reduced to 24 knots and the ship was diverted to Boston, Mass, where the ship was ballasted to bring the damaged area above water. A plate was welded over the hole until more permanent repairs could be made during a later dry-docking. The anchor was never replaced.

Cunard

Left: Leaving New York in the early 1980s, this photograph shows the build-up of penthouses on the Signal Deck just behind the Bridge.

Cunard

but permission to do so was refused by the Israeli government.

However, the *QE2* sailed into an even tighter security net when she arrived in Southampton on April 11th. Her dock was sealed off, passes were required and scrutinised and frogmen patrolled the water around the stationary liner. Lorries were searched as they delivered stores.

Captain William Law went on sick leave with a strained back and his relief captain, Mortimer Hehir, took over. The crew each demanded £50 danger money for the voyage plus four years wages should they fall victim to Arab terrorists during the voyage.

Questions were asked in Parliament ('Who was paying for the Civil and Military security?' 'Cunard.') and the passengers (mostly American Jews who had saved for this 'trip of a lifetime') arrived in Southampton in coaches accompanied by police escorts. Fifteen men with Israeli passports reportedly boarded the ship at Southampton as did members of the SAS who would keep a low profile during the voyage guarding strategic points, such as the bridge, and keeping their conversation to the minimum with the crew with whom they came into contact. Ten members of the crew having Irish connections were put ashore in fear that they might identify the SAS men to unfriendly Irish agents. Cunard's own security people reportedly placed dummy bomb-like objects at various points around the ship which, using a percussion cap, made a loud bang if moved. The astute crew found and reported each device and, as instructed, not one of the devices was touched.

Crowds once again lined the shores of Southampton Water as the *QE2* sailed on Sunday 15th April.

Her next port of call was Lisbon in Portugal. The security conscious Portuguese closed the Salazar Bridge whilst the *Queen* passed beneath it and the security surrounding Rochas Quay reflected the Portuguese watch against hi-jacking, ever intense since their own liner, the *Santa Maria*, was taken over by an anti-governmental faction several years before.

Sailing on, the *QE2* passed through the Straits of Gibraltar. Here, the fabrications that emmanated from the media during this 'non-event' of a danger cruise were in evidence. A radio reporter, broadcasting 'live', described naval craft coming out from 'Gib' and steaming in line ahead and astern of the liner in glorious sunshine. The ship's radio officer, listening to this report, went on deck. The 'glorious sunshine' was murk and nothing could be seen of the navy! Unhappily, this standard of reporting existed throughout the cruise and dismayed many of the crew.

The liner passed north of Malta and Crete thus avoiding the North African coast. This was done, the captain was reported as saying, to avoid the unintended provocation of the anti-Israeli North African Arab nations who might think that 'we are thumbing our noses at them'.

The liner sailed through most of the Mediterranean to Ashod in blackout. Her arrival at that port angered many Orthodox Jews as it occurred on a Saturday.

David Ben Gurion visited the ship before she left for Haifa, where she stayed for a few days, later returning to the new deep water berth at Ashod. Strict security surrounded the ship at all times with passes being thoroughly scrutinised both at the dock gate and at the ship; troops continuously patrolled the dockside and fast patrol craft were in evidence out in the open sea. Anti-personnel devices were detonated in the harbour at night around the floodlit ship in order to deter unfriendly divers.

The *Queen* spent just over two weeks in Israel before returning to Southampton, where the security exercise was repeated, on Sunday 13th May.

The whole charter may have passed into the realms of 'just another cruise' but for a startling revelation made one year later.

The late President Sadat of Egypt was being interviewed on the BBC television current affairs programme 'Panorama'. In it he said that he was awoken in the early hours one morning by a telephone call. The caller asked for confirmation of orders issued by President Gaddafi of Libya with whom Egypt was sharing a political and military alliance under a temporary unification of the two countries.

President Sadat rescinded the orders immediately when he found out what they were. Gaddafi had ordered an Egyptian submarine to go and sink the *QE2*!

The *QE2* once unwittingly aided the deadly aims of terrorism when, on October 20th, 1971, the liner called in at Cobh in Southern Ireland. After she had sailed, six suitcases were found unclaimed on the quayside and a burly Irishman attempted to lift them. Unable to do so because of their weight he alerted the authorities and subsequently a cache of arms intended for the IRA was discovered.

The story was continued three years later when, after a long police investigation, a gunfight took place in the unlikely setting of Southampton. It all ended with the arrest of Gabriel Megahey, a quiet Irishman, one time stevedore and Cunard crewman, — but the head of the IRA unit in the Hampshire city.

Adventure for the *QE2* there has been, but the great majority of her journeys are safe and happy voyages. Apart from charters — including one from New York to inaugurate the new deep water oil terminal at Come-by-Chance in Canada when John Rannie (the managing director of the ship's builders) travelled on the liner that he had built for the first time since her disastrous trials — the ship sails on special or inaugural trips to many ports that welcome her as an honoured guest. Some of these ports are subsequently used as frequent ports of call such as Boston which the liner visited for the first time in 1971.

The vessel was the centre of attention in her American home town of New York when, watched by millions, she opened the festivities surrounding the Hundredth Birthday celebrations of the Statue of Liberty in 1987.

In May 1982, the city of Philadelphia on the Delaware river welcomed the ship for the first time. (*QE2* has visited this port on many occasions since, including one arrival detoured from New York when, at the end of a special trip to celebrate the Fiftieth Anniversary of the *Queen Mary's* maiden voyage, she diverted there to avoid ice in the Atlantic).

The first visit was as part of the celebrations surrounding the city's 300th anniversary of its founding by William Penn. During their stay in the 'City of Brotherly Love' thousands of paying guests were entertained and fed on board the liner, helping to pay for the ship's stay there; the ship's restaurants ran an almost non-stop service.

The visit was a great success and many Philadelphians took the opportunity to sail with her back to Southampton.

It was during this voyage that the curtain rose on the most dramatic episode in the *QE2's* history.

The requirements of Cunard and peaceful commerce would soon be laid aside in favour of the needs of the *Queen's* country.

Chapter Ten

Echoes of War

'Often whole divisions at a time were moved by each ship. Vital decisions depended on their ability continuously to elude the enemy, and without their aid the day of victory must unquestionably have been postponed . . .' These words, written after the end of the Second World War by Winston Churchill, referred to the work done by the *Queen Mary* and *Queen Elizabeth* in safely transporting thousands upon thousands of Allied troops to the war zone. Towards the end of that conflict each ship was carrying fifteen thousand GI's on each trip from New York.

Churchill estimated that their joint contribution to the Allied effort shortened the war by at least a year.

No-one ever thought that Britain would have to call on the services of the last of the country's Atlantic liners to act in a similar capacity, but the unthinkable was about to become reality.

Captain Peter Jackson had been enjoying the last few days of his leave at his home near Southampton and was due to take the *QE2* over from his relief captain, Alex Hutcheson, for her next trip – a cruise to the Mediterranean.

It had been six weeks since the Argentinians had landed on South Georgia on Friday 19th March 1982, and almost a month since the Argentinian army had invaded the Falkland Islands, those specks of British Colonialism claimed by the Argentinians as their 'Malvinas'.

A week after the invasion the requisitioned Peninsular and Oriental liner *Canberra* had sailed south as a troopship, carrying 3 Commando Brigade, and it was 'on the cards' that the *QE2* might also be called-up to join 'Operation Corporate'. But Cunard continued to scoff at any such idea.

So far Peter Jackson had received no word at his home that anything was about to happen to his ship, except that she was a little late and would not be berthing until about midnight. So it was with great surprise that the captain listened to the BBC One o'clock News on Monday 3rd May. The *QE2* had finally been requisitioned by HM Government to transport three thousand troops to the Falklands.

The news, too, came as a surprise to those on board the ship. Many heard the same BBC news that had surprised Captain Jackson, others remained in ignorance – including the relief captain, Alex Hutcheson! The first that he heard of the requisitioning was when the BBC telephoned him for confirmation.

First Officer Philip Rentell and some friends were on their way to lunch. Bumping into one of the liner's nursing staff they were asked if they had heard the news and their initial state of shock lasted throughout their lunchtime.

Just as the liner was approaching The Lizard, Captain Hutcheson made a broadcast to passengers and confirmed initial reports. As he finished, the sound of cheering could be heard coming from various parts of the ship.

The liner docked with her port side against the Queen Elizabeth II quay in Southampton at two minutes past midnight on the morning of 4th May, the passengers disembarking between 9 and 10.30 am after breakfast.

Following her call-up the Cunarder was quickly converted into Her Majesty's troopship *Queen Elizabeth 2*. Her forward heli-pad is here being fitted after previously being prefabricated by Vosper Thornycroft's shipyard.

Len Betts

One of *QE2*'s officers studying the girder supports to the aft heli-pad sprouting from the after swimming pools, the area on the liner capable of supporting great weights.   *Southern Newspapers*

Weighed down with luggage, troops of 1st Battalion, the 7th Duke of Wellington's Own Gurkha's Rifles prepare to board *QE2*.
                    Southern Newspapers

4 pm Wednesday 12th May and *QE2* leaves Southampton carrying 3,000 troops of 5 Infantry Brigade.   *Southern Newspapers*

By 8 o'clock that morning the Ministry of Defence was already at work. Chief Officer Ron Warwick (son of the *QE2's* first ever captain) and Phil Rentell accompanied a naval representative as the latter made quick decisions on how to turn the liner into an aircraft carrier. The ship's officers were horrified to hear him say 'oh yes, I think we can chop this lot off here', referring to the verandah windows aft, and also making a suggestion that the swimming pool should be filled with cement to take the weight of a forest of red-leaded, steel flight-deck supports which would bear the load of landing helicopters.

The upper aluminium superstructure, being constructed for lightness and maximum passenger use, was not sufficiently strong enough to take the weight of the proposed 'heli-pads' so the highest steel deck was chosen to take the feet of the new supports. Quarter Deck suited the bill and the heli-pads were eventually built level with the next highest deck, forward in front of the bridge-front hatch and aft level with One Deck.

Captain Jackson arrived on board at 10 am only to find his cabin already full of Cunard officials, including Executive Captain Douglas Ridley, and people from the Department of Trade, Lloyds and Royal Naval and military personnel.

That evening at 10 pm the liner was turned starboard side to the quay. It was not until 10.30 on the morning of Thursday 6th May, that an increasingly unhappy Captain Jackson heard via a 'phone call from Ralph Bahna, chairman of Cunard, that he would be actually sailing as Master of the *QE2*. As he was not in the Royal Naval Reserve the liner would continue to fly the Red Ensign of the Merchant Service, thus indicating that the ship was of a non-combatant status.

In turn the captain telephoned his wife to tell her the news. He now felt that he could get his teeth 'into this project with some enthusiasm'.

That day saw the start of the work to prepare the ship for her future role as the decks were stripped in the areas that would accommodate the heli-pads.

Much furniture, paintings, sculptures, ship models and fruit machines had already gone ashore along with stores, such as the caviar, that would not be required on the voyage. Military stores flowed in the opposite direction although ammunition would not be loaded until the 9th.

Meetings were held every day both on board and in London as the conversion was satisfactorily progressed. On Saturday 8th Captain Jackson took Ralph Bahna around the ship to show him the 'general devastation and new construction'. The captain considered his chairman to be 'in a state of shock for a while'!

Over the next few days the ship took on a more orderly appearance as she prepared to take on her hundreds of expected guests. Carpets which could not be taken ashore were covered in hardboard sheeting fixed together with black tape. The names of troops were later marked on the hardboard flooring outside the cabins that they were to occupy.

Workmen from Vosper Thornycroft's shipyard worked around the clock to get the ship ready. Prefabricated heli-pads that had been constructed in advance in the plate shops of the yard were now transported to the docks. Here they were lifted onto the liner and welded into place, huge table tops on many legs made of vertical 'I' bar girders.

First Officer Phil Rentell was also a lieutenant in the R.N.R. and, on the *QE2's* arrival in Southampton, had gone home to Sutton Coldfield to collect his uniform. He had volunteered for the Falklands trip and had been asked by Douglas Ridley, himself a senior officer in the R.N.R., to travel south acting as a liaison officer between the ship and the naval party.

A Royal Naval preparation party came on board on the eve of departure to ensure that everything was ready for the troops' embarkation the following day.

On the morning of sailing, Wednesday 12th May, Captain Jackson arrived on board early at 6.30 am only to find that troop embarkation had already started. A 'Heads of Department' meeting had been arranged for 9.15 am with Ralph Bahna and Bernard Crisp in attendance; at 10.30 am a navigation and flying operations briefing session was held on the bridge. Peter Jackson had already studied charts of the port to be visited enroute for oil and water (Freetown in Sierra Leone) and had decided that there would be a sufficient depth of water for the *QE2* to go alongside the QEII quay in the container terminal there.

As the morning melted into the afternoon troops that made up 5 Infantry Brigade still continued to ascend the gangways, entering into a world of barely concealed luxury that would be their barracks for the days to come.

Each of the units that boarded had a band or piper to play them aboard. The Gurkhas created the biggest stir – their priest blessing them as they boarded – weighed down with back-packs almost as big as the fearsome soldiers that bore them. The Gurkhas would be berthed low in the ship where they would be less vulnerable to the sea-sickness to which they were prone.

By early afternoon Royal Naval Party 1980, Headquarters Land Forces Falklands Islands and 5 Infantry Brigade were all on board, eagerly seeking their cabins or improvised dormitories before going back on deck to watch the excitement of departure.

A large crowd had gathered on the quayside and bands played cheerily. Television cameras relayed the occasion in complete contrast to the secrecy that surrounded the similar trooping movements of the *Queen Mary* and *Queen Eliabeth* to and from the Clyde during the Second World War.

The world knew where the *QE2* was going and what she was carrying. The world knew that Prime Minister Margaret Thatcher meant business!

It had seemed that all the top 'Brass' wanted to come to see both the ship and the troops before the departure and the quayside alongside the ship took on the appearance of a heli-port. Lord Victor Matthews, head of Trafalgar House, arrived on board at 12.30 am. The culmination to the flow of visitors came when John Nott, the British Minister of Defence, visited the ship, moving quickly amongst the troops so that he could not be asked any awkward questions.

Although the world outside was in a patriotically festive mood Captain Jackson had not yet had his share of worries for the day.

As the afternoon built up to a crescendo of fervour, the Captain received a message at 2 pm that all was not well in the engine room. One boiler had been shut down for maintenance, and now a second boiler had developed a massive leak in its supply of distilled water, 20 tons an hour, which could not be traced.

It was essential for publicity purposes that the ship should sail on time – even on the one boiler remaining in service. So, at 1545 hrs – with Captain Peter Driver on board as pilot, a force 4 to 5 wind blowing from the south east and with three tugs made fast forward and two aft – 'Stand By Engines' was rung on the ship's telegraph.

At 1603 hrs all mooring wires and ropes had been released and the liner headed up-river, there to turn in the stream before heading down towards the Isle of Wight.

Two tugs let-go by the Brambles buoy, two others let-go a little later leaving the little *Albert* alone at the bow to give the underpowered *Queen* extra manoeuvreability should she need it. She was achieving forty revolutions which gave her a speed of seven knots.

Around half past five, two 'Sea King' helicopters arrived, their pilots skilfully testing the turbulence created by the forward motion of the liner and landed on the after flight deck.

Using an improvised swimming pool made of wood and canvas on the forward heli-pad the troops celebrated the tradition of the 'Crossing of the Line' ceremony.   *Imperial War Museum*

The *Albert* released her charge at 6 pm as the *QE2* headed eastwards towards the Nab light tower.

Captain Driver disembarked onto the pilot launch at 8 pm just as the liner had the Nab on her starboard beam.

The *QE2* would anchor overnight 3 miles south of the Nab and away from the gaze of shore based sightseers. During her stay there the Admiralty tug *Bustler* came out from Portsmouth with various additional stores in the early hours of the morning.

At 8 am on Thursday Peter Jackson was advised by the engine room that the ship would be ready to sail at 9 am. The source of the distilled water leak had been detected: a valve had simply been left open! During the next hour all lifeboats were tested and swung out and the engines, too, were checked. At 9.20 the anchor was hauled up and, fifteen minutes later, the *QE2* was underway.

The troops were put through their first lifeboat drill. It proved to be quite chaotic but many lessons were learnt and subsequent drills proved to be more proficient. Because of the lower deck on which they were accommodated the Gurkhas would have to ascend several decks to their lifeboat stations. So, in case an emergency should take place and the ship was darkened, these Nepalese warriors practiced finding their way blindfolded!

Because of the vast distances to be travelled the *QE2* would need to have her oil supplies replenished at sea whilst underway. To this end an oil pipeline had been fitted on Two Deck which would take the oil to the tanks.

To practice the art of Replenishment-at-Sea (RAS-sing as it was colloquially known) the liner was due to redezvous with the Royal Fleet Auxiliary vessel *Grey Rover* later that afternoon.

Before then, however, two patients had to be flown off the ship by helicopter to the nearest hospital. As the liner was due south of The Lizard this happened to be Treliske Hospital in Truro, Cornwall. One patient had a torn Achilles tendon and the other had suspected appendicitis which turned out to be meningitis. Unfortunately this patient later died.

The huge Double Down Room became the troops' mess.   *Southern Newspapers*

Above: QE2 in Cumberland Bay, South Georgia, with the cross-decking of troops clearly in progress. The wintery conditions are very apparent in this rare colour view.
Captain Peter Jackson

Left: Only occasionally did a helicopter use the forward heli-pad. Trying to land at the same speed of the ship and having a 65,000 ton hotel approaching at 27 knots was a daunting prospect for many a helicopter pilot.
Captain Peter Jackson

However, the ship's nurse who accompanied the men, Jane Yelland, thoroughly enjoyed her flight and took the opportunity to relieve the hospital of as many newspapers that she could find for the benefit of the men on board the troopship *QE2*.

The *QE2* met with *Grey Rover* on schedule, a line was passed and in one minute a token ton of oil pumped from the tanker to the liner. The pipe was then blown through to clear it and the ships parted. The whole operation was a success and had only taken three quarters of an hour.

On the Friday, with the ship doing 24 knots on two boilers, Captain Jackson gave written instructions to the Chief Engineer for the passage to Freetown and Ascension. This would necessitate the use of all three boilers so efforts were increased to get the third boiler 'on-line'.

In the days that followed, the troops set themselves training tasks. Stripping down and reassembling small-arms, jogging around the deck – each unit had its own allocated time, and woe betide anyone who infringed it! – attending various lectures, or practicing firing small arms over the ship's side. Black garbage bags, full of rubbish and which were normally discharged at night,

Jokingly known as 'paraffin pigeons' to the ship's crew, the helicopters practiced using the heli-pads in readiness for *QE2's* arrival in South Georgia.   *Brian Atkinson*

After conducting the Sunday church services, Captain Peter Jackson (right) got himself 'fully booted and spurred' in flying kit and was taken on a flight around his ship.   *Courtesy of Captain Peter Jackson*

were thrown overboard and used as targets. Greater care had to be taken with live ammunition as the ship's officers complained that the railings were being shot through in several places!

The captain and officers swapped their blue uniforms for 'whites' on the 15th as the *Queen* approached warmer waters. Also, on this day, the third boiler was brought into action and so a good reserve of speed became available.

Helicopter exercises were carried on daily. After conducting the Church Service on the first Sunday at sea, Captain Jackson attired himself in full flying kit, joined a helicopter, and took the opportunity to take some photographs of his ship from the air and to investigate a Russian Intelligence Gathering Auxiliary 'posing as a trawler'. His verdict on the flight? – 'What a wonderful experience'!

During the captain's absence, his ship was technically (as well as physically!) without a master, so Peter Jackson officially handed over the command of the liner to his relief, Alex Hutcheson.

That evening the captain joined the Gurkhas for dinner. It was their eightieth birthday and he received a lethal Kukri as a gift.

Of the actual ship's crew six hundred and fifty had volunteered to go south. The stewards were told that they would not really be needed as the army units would provide their own messing arrangements. However, many stewards did go, some of them with experience from the previous war on board the old *Queens*, and served in the officers' messes.

The crew were later to be thanked by 5 Brigade's commanding officer, Brigadier Wilson, when he said that both he and his troops had the greatest respect for them. They (the crew), he said, had volunteered whereas he and the troops had had to go to the war zone. It was, after all, their job.

At 8 am on the 18th, the bridge gave the engine room one and a half hours notice of arrival at Freetown, Sierra Leone, where they would take on fuel and water.

Two pilots boarded the ship. Although their presence was compulsory and they wore masses of gold braid on their white uniforms (plus a pair of thick heeled, bright green shoes on the feet of one of them) Captain Jackson took the ship alongside the quay himself, as he was informed by the pilots that masters usually bethed their own ships in that port!

The liner took on 1,867 tonnes of oil, completing the operation three hours earlier than had been expected, and sailed at 11 pm. Meanwhile, First Officer Phil Rentell, along with many others, busied himself in 'that old tropical tradition of watching a film on deck'! The pilots were dropped off as soon as possible as the *QE2* headed for Ascension Island.

The Equator had also been crossed and the troops had rigged an improvised swimming pool for the 'Crossing the Line' ceremony which had been extended to anyone in the vicinity of the pool, a foul smelling concoction being liberally dispensed.

The 19th brought with it the Doldrums with flat calms suddenly lashed by torrential rains and fierce, sudden squalls. Orders were received that the liner should keep 50 miles away from Ascension and that helicopters would ferry stores and personnel between the island and the ship.

Thursday 20th May marked the Christian festival of Ascension Day. On this day, in 1501, Ascension Island was discovered by the Portuguese João de Nova and now, in 1982, the *QE2* appropriately arrived at her position fifty miles to the west of the island in the early afternoon. But before she arrived another ship was sighted. Captain Jackson turned the *QE2* towards it only to find it was another Russian AIG, the *Primorye*. If he had been informed of its presence the captain felt that he could have avoided the unwanted meeting. An RAF Nimrod also reported an Argentinian ship, the *Chubut*, in the vicinity.

By three o'clock *HMS Dumbarton Castle*, normally a fishery/oil rig protection vessel, was stationed off the liner's starboard side and two helicopters transferred stores from the naval ship to the giant Cunarder.

This completed, the liner steamed to and fro off the island during the night (with an improvised black-out in force) waiting for the arrival of Major General Jeremy Moore and two hundred of his General Staff, who were flying out from the UK that night, plus additional troops and stores all of which would be shipped the next day.

Strict black-out would be imposed south of Ascension and templates for different sized windows and portholes had meanwhile been made, black plastic sheeting being cut to the various shapes. These were then taped to the hundreds of windows and portholes and Phil Rentell, acting under the instructions of Captain James of Royal Navy Party 1980, checked the results of his supervision by flying around the ship at night in a helicopter. The ship, as Captain James said, had been turned from 'the brightest star on the ocean, to the darkest'.

One unfortunate side effect of the black-out arrangements was to raise the internal temperature of the liner quite considerably, the black-out creating a greenhouse effect with the plastic wrinkling from the increased temperature.

Captain Jackson went onto the bridge at 11 pm and noted '. . . a frightening sight, to see this ship belting along at 27 knots on a black night and without a light showing'.

A rendezvous had been arranged by the higher command for Cunard's *Atlantic Causeway* to transfer various stores to the *QE2* on the 22nd. Unfortunately nobody had told the *Causeway* of the intended rendezvous and the ship initially (1 am) refused to identify herself. Eventually the container vessel asked the troopship, 'for what reason do we have the pleasure of this visit?'

The two ships steamed in company, still in the vicinity of Ascension Island, and helicopter transfer of stores started at 7 am, finishing about three hours later.

The *Queen* soon left the *Atlantic Causeway* (the sister ship to the *Atlantic Conveyor* that would be sunk three days later by the Argentinians) and Ascension far behind as she increased speed on completion of her tasks and she soon left Ascension far behind.

That night black-out was rigorously enforced, navigation lights and radars were switched off, and the ship became electronically silent: the latter precaution to deny a homing signal to enemy missiles. Navigation would now rely on the 'Mark 1 eyeball'!

As the *Queen* headed south it was initially thought that she would effect a rendezvous with the *Nordic* and *Baltic* ferries between South Georgia and the Falklands.

Alex Hutcheson took the Church Service on Sunday 23rd as the captain had, like many others on board, gone down with the 'flu' and had retired early.

Exercising of all kinds still continued with special attention being given to life saving and its associated appliances.

The regimental evenings that had been held ceased as the *Queen* approached the war zone. These unit dinners had been great fun with speeches and presentations, but the regimental bands playing within the confines of the Theatre Bar or the Q4 Bar provided a sound that had to be heard to be believed!

By the 25th the *QE2* had sailed far enough south of the Equator to meet the approaching winter chill of the Southern Hemisphere. Once again the officers changed uniform, returning to wearing their warmer 'blues'.

Browning automatic guns were placed on the mounting platforms that had been constructed on each bridge wing during the voyage down and Blowpipe missiles were fitted around the funnel. The *Queen* was now in a very small way, prepared for what she might meet.

The ship was by now heading towards a rendezvous with the battle scarred County Class destroyer *HMS Antrim* in a position ninety miles north of South Georgia.

During the night of 26-27th May the radar was switched on, briefly, every thirty minutes and at 11 pm two stationary 'targets' were seen on the screen, five miles to port. Icebergs!

Captain Jackson was called at half past two in the morning. It was flat calm and many targets were seen on the radar screen (the captain later wrote: 'No way could it be a fishing fleet!') and the ship was put on Ice Routine. At one time more than a hundred bergs could be seen in the illuminated sweep of the radar arm and the captain ordered a reduction in speed as the *QE2* weaved around the ice: '. . . don't want to be the *Titanic* of the South Atlantic' he wrote, '. . . never have I known such a harrowing experience'.

The reduction in speed meant a late meeting with *HMS Antrim* but the delay had been justified. Morning light showed thick fog, becoming patchy, and a radar check at 11 am indicated *Antrim* to be nineteen miles away.

Three quarters of an hour later the two ships had stopped within one mile of each other, and the transfer of Major General Moore, Brigadier Wilson and their staffs commenced.

On the first full day at sea *QE2* rendezvoused with RFA *Grey Rover* to rehearse 'Replenishment at Sea'. A token ton of oil was taken on board from the oiler to prove that the operation could be successfully accomplished. *Captain Peter Jackson*

Whilst sailing off Ascension the *QE2* received Major General Jeremy Moore who arrived from the island by Chinook helicopter.
Captain Peter Jackson

Arriving at South Georgia the *QE2* began to 'cross deck' her cargo of troops by requisitioned trawlers and 'VERT-REP' stores by helicopter.
Imperial War Museum

The sea was undulating in a long swell and although the senior officers, 'cross-decked' by helicopter, other troops had to transfer by ship's boats.

The swell caused a great strain on the bed plates of the Cunarder's davits and at least one was damaged. The troops had to jump to get on to the *Antrim* and in doing so one soldier broke a leg.

The transfer operations were over by 1.40 pm and the *QE2* sailed on, still amidst patchy fog and ice. The temperature at noon had been 3°C. Hundreds of icebergs had been visible since the rising sun had bathed them in changing colours of red and gold, until their 'tablecloths' of fog had cascaded over their sides to eventually obscure them. The numbers of icebergs had decreased as *Antrim* was closed but steadily increased once again as the *QE2* left the rendezvous position. One particular berg was reported as being three hundred feet high and a mile long!

Black darkness fell at 5 pm and, just after 6 pm, South Georgia was visible on the radar. The Right Whale Rocks were discerned and half an hour later two shackles of starboard anchor cable were let out. These hung, suspended from the hawse pipe into the deep water, in readiness for the final anchoring. If all the required shackles were paid out at once the force would have torn the cable clench out of the chain locker structure and the anchor lost.

The anchor was finally let go just after seven in the evening as the liner entered Cumberland Bay. Philip Rentell was in charge of the mooring party and from his position on the prow of the ship could not see the bridge in the prevailing murk, even though lights were now on. Ten shackles of cable were let out in a shower of sparks and rust. Only two were left in the locker by the time the cable brake took its hold, bringing to a halt the heart-stopping rattle that exuded from the liner's hawse pipes.

Canberra had been waiting impatiently for the *QE2* for several hours in the confines of the bay. The rust-streaked P&O liner had seen much action in Falkland Sound and her crew were becoming veterans of the sudden air attack. The liner had on board survivors from the sunken *HMS Ardent* and would transfer these to the *QE2*. The latter ship would in turn transfer, by boat and helicopter, her cargo of troops and stores.

The requisitioned trawler *Cordella* came alongside at 9.20 pm and left for the *Canberra* with the first batch of troops just after 11 pm.

Just before midnight *HMS Leeds Castle*, the *Cordella* and the Admiralty tug *Typhoon* came alongside to take off the last troops for the night, operations ceasing until morning as the combined perils of darkness and black-out made safe navigation and working imprudent.

From one captain to another.   *Courtesy of Captain Peter Jackson*

To Captain Peter Jackson with Many thanks
from all in ENDURANCE   Nick Barker.

From six o'clock on the morning of Friday 28th May baggage, stores and troops were once more transferred to the waiting ships, either by sea or by air. The sea transport consisted of the *QE2's* lifeboats, the trawlers *Cordella*, *Junella*, *Northella*, *Farnella* and *Pict* (collectively known in naval parlance – along with other requisitioned ships including the *QE2* – as STUFT, or Ships Taken Up From Trade). The air transport was by many lifts by the helicopters, their operation being called 'Vertical Replenishment', or VERT-REP.

As well as the *Canberra*, the North Sea ferry *Norland* was also waiting for troops. *HMS Endurance*, the British Ice Patrol ship, was also in Cumberland Bay, maintaining a naval presence.

Canberra sailed at 10.30 pm after taking on hundreds of soldiers and the *QE2's* Sea King helicopters, in turn transferring the survivors of *HMS Ardent* to the care available on the *QE2*. *Norland* had similarly brought men from the sunken frigate *Antelope*. Work continued throughout the night and at four in the morning snow began to fall, covering the *QE2* in a thin white sheet. This, and the presence of patchy but dense fog caused the captain to remark 'what a climate!'.

Saturday, a Cunard cargo ship, the *Saxonia*, arrived for cargo and the Royal Fleet auxiliary *Stromness* brought yet more survivors, this time from the Type 42 destroyer *HMS Coventry*. The *Stromness* would afterwards take on the ammunition for which *Canberra* did not have time to wait.

The *QE2* had not remained immune from damage during her stay in South Georgia, but fortunately this had not been suffered as a result of the conflict. The platform lifts that descended from the boat deck to the sea were damaged by trawlers coming too heavily alongside and more davit bed plates were cracked during boat retrieval operations. The day before a badly corroded pipe in Seven Deck swimming pool had burst causing a widespread flood, damaging the Sauna, darkroom, working alleyway, crew quarters and the laundry.

During the day icebergs drifted into the entrance of Cumberland Bay and then, as if realising that their presence created an anathema, drifted out again onto the wanton highway of the wintry South Atlantic.

A group of crew members were taken ashore for a look around the derelict whaling station of Grytviken. Captain Jackson

The *QE2* steamed slowly up the English Channel to ensure that her meeting with the Royal Yacht *Britannia*, carrying Her Majesty, The Queen Mother, happened on time. With survivors from *HMS Coventry* on the forward heli-pad, *HMS's Ardent* and *Antelope's* survivors aft and the *QE2's* own company on the Boat Deck the liner exchanged greetings with the Royal Yacht.   *Courtesy of Captain Peter Jackson*

was to have gone ashore with them but changed his mind: on his late visit to the bridge on the previous evening he had noticed that the barometer had started to fall so he was now anxious to get the last of the troops off his ship before the promised deterioration in the weather set in, an harbinger of the fast approaching winter.

By four o'clock in the afternoon a north westerly gale was making conditions hazardous: the last sixty men disembarked into the trawlers which were having problems in mooring safely without breaking their ropes. *Junella* was to be the last ship alongside, taking off stores and as soon as she left, at 5.30 pm, the *QE2* started to weigh anchor.

Passing by Banff Point fifteen minutes later the liner increased speed to 18 knots.

Two hours later *QE2* was again in the icefield but, with judicious navigation, she emerged safely at 10 pm;

Lifeboat practice was held on Sunday but the warship survivors were initially unhappy about congregating in the liner's aluminium superstructure, but their fears were allayed by the supervising officers.

Monday was a very uncomfortable day at sea and only the forward set of stabilisers was used. Two drums of hydrochloric acid broke loose in Two Deck baggage room and the chief officer was sent to get them under control.

Just under nine hundred tons of fuel oil were left in the tanks by Tuesday, enough only for a day and a half's steaming.

To replenish the ship, arrangements were made to rendez-vous with the *RFA Bayleaf* and the two ships met in the late afternoon.

The sea was too rough to allow the operation to commence and as it would soon be dark the *Bayleaf* took up an overnight station astern of the *QE2*.

The RFA drifted away from the *Queen* during the night and it was not until nine the next morning that a line was transferred between ships and the refuelling commenced. When the oiling had been completed by 6.30 nearly four thousand tons of top grade admiralty oil had been given to the *QE2*. The operation (carried out in a westerly Force 7 with an accompanying rough sea – although the sky was bright but cloudy) had finished just in time as the chaffing caused by the two ships' movements had caused the connections on the *Queen* to be worn to a point of danger.

In the early evening the captain received a message to say that the *QE2* was to proceed to Southampton and at 7 pm Captain James R.N. told the crew. Many were disappointed as they had anticipated that the *Queen* would put the survivors ashore at Ascension and then return to the war zone. The news was not released in Britain until 6th June, by which time the liner had left the danger zone after stopping off at Ascension.

After their various ordeals the survivors from HM Ships *Ardent*, *Antelope* and *Coventry* relaxed in the free days at sea taking benefit, as many other people do, from the refreshing regime of a sea cruise. Gradually their spirits picked up and eventually they organised a bawdy 'Sod's Opera' which they performed in the Double Down Room to popular acclaim.

Ascension was reached on 4th June, and *HMS Dumbarton Castle* once again met the liner. The *QE2* was once more on her way by 6 pm after a three hour stay during which time the *Dumbarton Castle* had taken off personnel including six SAS men who had survived a helicopter crash on the South American mainland. A public landing in Southampton would have been against the interests of their security.

By now it was known that the Queen Mother wished to greet the *QE2* as the liner returned to the United Kingdom on Friday 11th June.

The naval survivors possessed only the clothes that they were rescued in or had been given by the liner's company. So flying stations were sounded and a helicopter flew off the ship as she steamed near Mount's Bay, Cornwall, on 10th June.

New uniforms were brought out to the ship (plus a liberal supply of fresh Cornish pasties!) and both naval and civilian personnel readied themselves for their royal reception.

Several visitors were flown out to the ship on the bright Friday morning of the *QE2's* homecoming.

At seven in the morning forty newsmen arrived on the ship followed at eight by Admiral Sir John Fieldhouse and Lord Matthews and half-an-hour later by Ralph Bahna. The pilot, Captain Driver, came aboard at 8.48 am.

A message was received from the Royal Yacht *Britannia* from which H.M. The Queen Mother would welcome the ship:

'Captain P. Jackson.

I am pleased to welcome you back as *Queen Elizabeth 2* returns to home waters, after your tour of duty in the South Atlantic. The exploits of your own ship's company and the deeds of valour of those who served in *Antelope*, *Coventry* and *Ardent* have been acclaimed throughout the land, and I am proud to add my personal tribute.

Elizabeth Regina, Queen Mother.'

Captain Jackson replied immediately:

'Please convey to Her Majesty Queen Elizabeth, the Queen Mother, our thanks for her kind message. Cunard's *Queen Elizabeth 2* is proud to have been of service to Her Majesty's Forces.

Jackson. Master QE2.'

The *QE2* passed the famous Needles lighthouse on the western tip of the Isle of Wight at 9 am. Fifteen minutes later, after passing between Yarmouth and Hurst Castle, the Royal Yacht *Britannia* was abeam and, as the liner steamed by the Royal Yacht, the figure of the Queen Mother could be seen, dressed in pale blue, on its after deck. The *QE2's* company and the warship survivors gave three cheers and the liner blew her siren in salute.

From the *QE2* to the Royal Yacht:

'Please convey to Her Majesty Queen Elizabeth with humble duty the Master, Officers and ratings of the Royal and Merchant Navies embarked in *QE2*, join in offering their loyal greetings.'

The *QE2* was almost home. Surrounded by small craft, buzzed by light aircraft and watched by thousands lining the Solent and other vantage points she progressed in state past Calshot, then by the tankers at Fawley which, once again, blew their own greetings. She slowly sailed up Southampton Water to the Queen Elizabeth II terminal in Southampton Docks.

From the quay a sea of faces watched the liner, many looking for loved ones, and banners held high bore messages of greeting. The *QE2* was turned in mid-stream by her tugs and at mid-day came to rest, port side along the jetty.

After steaming 14,967 miles and consuming 10,287 tonnes of fuel, the *Queen* was home!

Elizabeth R

Luncheon
on the occasion of the visit of
Her Majesty Queen Elizabeth,
The Queen Mother,
on board Queen Elizabeth 2
to unveil the South Atlantic Plaque,
2nd December 1982

Host: The Lord Matthews

Wines

Batard Montrachet 1980
(Moillard)

Chateau Gruaud Larose 1966
Second Growth St Julien

Luncheon

Coquille of Fresh Lobster

Roast Saddle of Southdown Lamb

Fresh Broccoli Spears,
Parisienne Potatoes

Fresh Pear, Liqueur Sauce

Petits Fours

Selection of
English Cheeses with Celery

Coffee

Her Majesty Queen Elizabeth the Queen Mother signed Captain Jackson's menu after a very special luncheon held on board.
Courtesy of Captain Peter Jackson

Chapter Eleven

The Brightest Star on the Ocean

Following her trooping duties in the South Atlantic the *Queen Elizabeth 2* had to be refurbished, reconverting and renovating her once again to 'the brightest star on the ocean'.

Before disembarking at South Georgia the troops had cleaned the ship as best they could, removing marks where boots had scuffed the bulkheads and so on. But the helipads had to be removed at Southampton, and Cunard took the opportunity to re-style some of the rooms.

The work of converting the liner to a troopship had taken a mere eight days but this would now take nine weeks to put right. *QE2* spent much of the time in the King George V dry dock in Southampton prior to being berthed alongside a quay in the New Dock, receiving the final touches there.

She emerged from the refit ready for her first post Falklands sailing on 14th August with a pleasant alteration to her appearance. Her funnel casing that had previously been painted white now reappeared in the traditional Cunard colours of red with two, eight inch black stripes, the inner tubular casing providing the black top. Each of these bands was made up of two widths of four inch tape, soon to be flapping in the Atlantic breeze.

But the immediate impact to the eye was in the colouring of the hull. The dark, almost black, charcoal grey had been over painted with a light 'pebble' grey. Apparently so painted on the instructions of Lord Matthews, chairman of Cunard. The paint scheme proved to be unpractical as well as unpopular, soon displaying scuff marks from the nudging bows of New York tugs and unsightly streaks of rust that dribbled down the vessel's sides from portholes and anchor hawse pipes.

The liner thankfully reverted to her original hull colour of charcoal grey a few months later. To the ship-lover she then almost wore the traditional colours of the old Cunard ships and more than ever deserved, through livery and action, the title of *Queen*.

Internally, changes had been effected to maintain the *QE2's* position as leader amongst cruise ships. The Six Deck swimming pool became part of a prestigious 'Golden Door' fitness complex, expensive to use on shore but freely available to the ship's passengers. The exclusive Queen's Grill was enlarged, as was the Casino, and a start was made on the creation of a Club Lido on the aft area of Quarter Deck. This lido would be completed in Germany during an extensive refit in late 1983 when a Magrodome, a retractable glazed sun-roof devised by MaeGregor-Navire (a company familiar with special hatch covers), was fitted over the first class swimming pool making the area habitable during even the early and late Atlantic seasons.

Many bands, large and small, professional and amateur, often entertain the *QE2's* passengers from the quayside. The Highbury Area Band from Portsmouth play the *Queen* away shortly after her return from the Falklands.
Steve Dymock

It was during this particular refit that the aft verandah windows were substantially altered and new, large capacity enclosed luxury motor boats, carried on heavy davits, were fitted at the aft end of the boat deck.

The *QE2's* built-in ability to accept change has been proven on several occasions, the design of her internal spaces lending themselves to alterations in function or arrangement.

Amongst the many changes that have been effected over the years the early alterations were the ones that would cause most comment as, during the course of the work, some of the orignal rooms disappeared making way for new.

The London Gallery, once used as a display area for British art, eventually became the Computer Learning Centre. Once American restrictions on casinos had been lifted the spaces occupied by the Upper Deck Library and the Port Foyer found themselves amalgamated into one in 1972 to cater for the new demand. The Lookout Bar, the only public room to have had a forward looking view, was unfortunately sacrificed to become a kitchen for the new blue and white Queen's Grill, (latterly a casino but formerly the 736 Club which had been described as 'noteworthy' by the shipping press), that would cater for the occupants of the newly fitted luxury penthouses.

These penthouses were fitted in three stages and in three countries, over a period of fifteen years. The preparation for the fitting of the first of these luxury rooms took place whilst the liner was still at sea in early 1972 in readiness for when the *QE2* would be taken out of service in October for her first major refit.

The prefabricated aluminium blocks of luxury cabins (which included the Queen Anne and Trafalgar suites in which the occupants had the distinction of being able to go upstairs to bed) were fitted in two halves, port and starboard. During the same refit other luxury cabins were built on Boat Deck sites previously occupied by shops and store rooms, and the old Grill Room became part of an enlarged Columbia Restaurant. The Britannia Restaurant underwent a change of name and re-appeared as Tables of the World. In 1987 the restaurant underwent another change becoming the Mauretania Restaurant.

The second smaller block of rooms, sited immediately aft of the mast, was fitted in Bayonne, New Jersey, in 1977, resulting in the Queen Mary and Queen Elizabeth Suites. The third block, aft of the first and forward of the funnel, was fitted in the most recent reconstruction in Germany in 1987.

The £2 million refit of 1972 also saw other major changes carried out, the principle work being the reconstruction of the Main Kitchen to one of a highly sophisticated American design. Minor bulkheads were erected, new tiled floors laid, stainless steel fittings and old ovens were replaced and new windows cut during the course of the work. The addition of the new windows spotlighted a serious problem in the reconstruction work. The daylight that now filled the new kitchen shone through a fine, powdery mist. Much to the horror of the workforce, this was found to emanate from the American insulating sheeting being used which, unbeknown to the men using it, was asbestos based, the necessary precautions not having been taken - until then!

Because of the difficulties in fitting out the American kitchen, the seven week refit took rather longer than had been anticipated, the liner finally leaving Southampton two and a half days late. To Cunard's annoyance Vosper Thornycroft had not given notice of the delay until ten hours before the original time of sailing. However, the ruffled relationship between the two companies was soon smoothed and Cunard admitted to being delighted with the work.

Because of all the work carried out on the passenger areas the gross tonnage of the liner has risen over the years. When the ship was still being built it was expected that she would be 58,000

gross tons but, after the restructuring of classes during building, she appeared at 65,862 tons.

The liner, after many modifications, is now 67,139 gross tons and although larger purpose built, light draught cruise ships have been, or are planned to be, constructed, she is still one of the largest true transatlantic liners ever to have been built.

The run-up to the notable changes that were effected to the *Queen Elizabeth 2* in 1972 had their beginnings in the latter half of 1971 when a great change happened to Cunard itself. In spite of a poor financial year in 1970 Cunard was doing well but, due to various factors, the company found itself at the centre of a takeover bid.

The successful bidder from several contenders, buying the company for £26 million, was Trafalgar House. Already owners of civil engineering concerns, hotels and industrial activities (amongst many others) the company would add Cunard to its list of hotel interests.

Victor Matthews became the new chairman of Cunard and Sir Basil Smallpeice transferred to the board of Trafalgar House. He remained there for five months after the last board meeting of Cunard was held as an independant company, on 25th August 1971.

Sir Basil found that, after rescuing Cunard from near collapse, he could no longer effectively assist the company in his new position and 'let myself quietly over the side and went ashore. . . . . with sadness in my heart. . . .'

Since the early years QE2 has enjoyed Royal patronage and in September 1988 will be the venue of a special lunch which will be attended by H.M. The Queen Mother. This will be to mark the 50th anniversary of the launch of H.M.'s illustrious namesake, the first *Queen Elizabeth*, on 27th September 1938 and amongst the honoured guests, both at the lunch and subsequent commemorative voyage, will be the liner's last captain, Geoffrey Marr.

The Queen Mother was previously on board in May 1986, meeting retired Cunard employees and passengers who had sailed on the *Queen Mary's* maiden voyage fifty years earlier. The liner had then sailed on a voyage to commemorate the debut of that remarkable ship, Britain's best loved liner, carrying along with the veterans from that premier trip the *Mary's* last skipper, Captain John Treasure Jones.

After the *QE2's* return from the Falklands the Queen Mother expressed a wish to visit the liner that she had greeted on its return from active service. This she did in December 1982 and took the opportunity to unveil a plaque on which was engraved the message that she had sent to Captain Jackson welcoming him, the ship and the ship's company and passengers back to the United Kingdom.

Three weeks after the liner's reintroduction into service after the Falklands episode the *QE2* broke down off Falmouth. It was one more in a series of engine breakdowns that were becoming both increasingly expensive and worrying to Cunard.

One of the more dramatic breakdowns had occurred in 1974 whilst the *QE2* was on a south-bound cruise from New York. The causes reflected an incident that had called a halt to her technical trials from Greenock in 1968.

The liner had left New York for a cruise to Bermuda on the evening of Saturday 30th March 1974 with 1, 648 passengers on board, including almost 800 senior citizens, and 1,041 crew.

As soon as she was out into the open waters of the Atlantic she ran into rough weather, rough enough to prevent the pilot from being landed. Speed had to be maintained; to decrease it would have nullified the effect of the ship's stabilisers.

Conditions were very much the same on the following day and the captain, Peter Jackson, cancelled the obligatory life-boat

With the twin towers of the World Trade Center dominating a receding Manhattan skyline the *QE2* heads for the open sea. *Cunard*

drill, the prevailing conditions making it dangerous for the passengers, especially the elderly, to try to reach the Boat Deck.

Captain Jackson also made a broadcast (his maxim was 'always keep passengers informed', and to tell them: 'If you hear rumours, ask whether the perpetrator had got it from the captain!') and advised the passengers to stay in their cabins. To this end he took the unusual step of cancelling the Sunday divine service due to be held in the Theatre.

During the evening, as the liner travelled further south, the weather moderated. It was hoped to hold the cancelled boat drill the next day.

These plans were rudely shattered when, at four o'clock the next morning (1st April), the ship came to a standstill in the water.

The captain was told that, because two pipes (one oil, one boiler feed water) had been wrongly connected, oil had contaminated the boiler feed water - water which has to be extremely pure, four parts in a million.

Fortunately by now the weather had calmed and the engineers set to in cleaning the system, working hard all day. The captain made many telephone calls to Cunard and once again cancelled the delayed boat drill considering that, under the current circumstances, it would have an unnecessarily negative psychological effect on the passengers - especially the elderly.

The liner continued to drift and the telephoned remedial action suggested by Cunard's technical department in London was effective for only half an hour.

By Tuesday morning the liner had reached a position of 29° 26′N, 68°06′, approximately 275 miles south west of Bermuda.

Oil was still contaminating the port boiler and there was at least another ten hours of cleaning to do. Because of the situation much of the liner's hotel services had been shut down; the air-conditioning was shut off; the lifts were not operating (these were essential for the old folk); refrigeration had been switched off, the kitchens ceased to fully function and lighting was kept to a bare minimum. But it was the cessation of the operation of

Threading her way through the 1977 NATO Fleet Review the *QE2* provided an elegant splash of colour amongst the various shades of grey of the parading warships. *Southern Newspapers*

the desalination plant that supplied the ship's hotel services' fresh water (there was only five days supply left much of which would be used to flush through the contaminated machinery) that caused the greatest concern.

The captain knew that the nearest available large tug was 600 miles away so he put a suggestion to Cunard.

As a result of the captain's recommendations, which were approved by Cunard, the Norwegian cruise liner *Sea Venture* was sent to assist the *Queen*.

For this to happen special dispensations had to be sought from both British and Norwegian authorities. The *Sea Venture* was licensed to carry 600, only a fraction of the *QE2's* complement, but arrangements were made to cover any discrepancies both in legal and amenity aspects. In the end, the *Venture* was sanctioned to carry an extra 1,000 passengers.

The white Norwegian knight in the form of the *Sea Venture* arrived on the scene at three in the morning of 3rd April, ready to assist the distressed *Queen*.

The one way transfer between ships (almost anticipating the movements occurring during the Falklands campaign) started at 4 am with life jackets and twenty life-rafts from the *QE2* going over to the Norwegian ship to bring the *Venture's* life-saving capability up to legal requirements.

Essential stores followed and, at 7.30 am, the first passengers descended the forward and aft starboard accommodation ladders to board the waiting launches that had been lowered from both liners.

By 3.50 in the afternoon the last of the passengers had disembarked from the *QE2* and an hour later the liner had recovered her boats. The *Sea Venture's* launches continued to transfer stores and baggage until 5.40 am when she hoisted her boats from the sea, sailing for Bermuda ten minutes later.

A total of 1,654 people had been transferred during one of the most unusual operations ever carried out at sea. This number, incidentally, included six crew members who would help with the disembarkation at Bermuda.

The next day two tugs, *Elizabeth Moran* and *Joan Moran*, arrived at 2.13 pm and, seventy five minutes later, started the tow.

As the *Queen* and her entourage approached Bermuda the pilot boarded and two more tugs, *Bermudian* and *Faithful*, came to assist in the liners' passage through the Narrows to Murray's Anchorage.

Here the boilers were purged and the *QE2* was able to sail for New York at 16 knots using two boilers.

After further work at Todd's shipyard the *QE2* sailed for Southampton, still only on two boilers but achieving 24 knots. The voyage home took six days instead of the usual five.

On the liner's initial technical trials from Greenock in 1968 her engines had performed well; her pilot described her as 'handling like a motor car'.

But from the breakdown of the turbines during the ensuing full-scale trials to the Canaries to the breakdown off Falmouth, Cornwall, just after her return to service after the Falklands the engines and boilers have proved expensive to maintain. Many spare parts have had to be specially made by hand and this costly maintenance, along with the astronomic increases in oil fuel prices since the ship was built and high manning costs, caused the Cunard Line to appraise the future of the *QE2*.

They came to a momentous decision.

The *Queen*, if she was to be economically viable and if she was to continue to sail for another twenty years, would have to be re-engined.

Although extremely expensive this would be far cheaper than building a new, similar vessel.

After the initial decision was made a meeting was held in Southampton in mid 1983 to which various contenders from ship-building and engineering firms were invited. Each firm then submitted ideas and tenders for the forthcoming mammoth conversion with Cunard placing the contract with their final choice - the German shipyard of Lloyd Werft in Bremerhaven.

This yard had converted the giant ex-French transatlantic liner *France* into the Norwegian cruiseship *Norway* during the winter of 1979; the yard had also done previous work on the *QE2* including the fitting of the retractable Magrodome and the fitting of a new bulbous bow.

Cunard had for several years favoured foreign yards for the refits of their flagships. British yards had for a long time been shedding expensive manpower and were therefore able in recent years to perform only the lesser tasks in ship repair and maintenance. Unions and public bodies took this export work as a snub to Britain but Cunard had, in between, spent £millions in the U.K. in keeping the liner at sea.

British firms would, on this occasion too, be awarded many of the major sub-contracts that would emanate from the forthcoming conversion. Foremost amongst these would be firms belonging to the giant General Electric Company (GEC). It was part of this company, that under its original title of Associated Electrical Industries (AEI) that had built much of the *QE2's* original electrical machinery, such as the three turbine generators then the largest afloat.

It now fell to AEI's successor, GEC Large Machines Limited of Rugby, to build the two 350 ton, 44 megawatt electric propulsion motors, as the liner was to be converted from steam to diesel-electric propulsion. GEC Turbine Generators Limited, Stafford, would build nine electric generators and the company's Industrial Controls division, also at Rugby, would provide the synchro convertors that would start the motors and provide the slow speed operation of the ship. The engine control room console would be supplied by GEC Electrical Projects who would also co-ordinate all the company's efforts.

The turbine generators would be fitted alongside their power source, nine MAN-B&W diesels, which would be fitted five in the after engine room and four in the forward. The work of installing diesels, associated machinery, fuel treatment plant, generators and motors, would be likened to open heart surgery.

The contract to convert the *QE2* was signed on 24th October 1985 which gave Lloyd Werft almost a year in which to organise their own subcontractors - there were fifty major ones - and to advance their own preparations for the conversion.

QE2 arrived in Southampton for the last time as a steamship on October 25th before leaving for Bremerhaven. Cunard's magnificent flagship arrived at the German shipyard on 27th October 1986 and the carefully planned work began immediately.

The first major job was to strip out the boilers, turbines and other redundant machinery. This was done by removing the funnel and using the emptied shaft below as a passageway - both for removing scrap material and installing the new machinery.

Great care was taken in the removal of the old equipment and, because of the presence of asbestos in the insulation, a delay in the work was caused. This was undesirable as Lloyd Werft were liable to pay penalties for any delays by the day.

Eckart Knoth, chairman of Lloyd Werft, described the stripping-out process as being 'like hell'. By the time it was complete 4,700 tons of scrapped turbines, boilers, pipes and other broken organs of the *Queen* lay on the quayside, dominated by the comparatively still pristine - but to be modified - funnel.

The emptied machinery spaces appeared cavernous with heavy-lift trucks being dwarfed by the surroundings in which they now incongruously moved.

When the liner was being built in Scotland, twenty years previously, a scale model of the engine room had been made to show the location of each and every piece of equipment and pipe.

Looking very forlorn the *Queen* sits in the Kaiserdock II dry dock, Bremerhaven, whilst her engine room, interior, propellers and new penthouse suites are gutted, refurbished and fitted. The P & O liner *Canberra* came in during the *QE2's* stay for a refit, although less extensive, of her own.
Lloyd Werft, Bremerhaven

Similarly, now, a model was made of the new layout and many problems were ironed out well beforehand.

The first major items of machinery to be installed were the British-made electric propulsion motors, shipped to Germany in sections and reassembled at the shipyard, which were carefully lowered through the temporary hatchway and slid aft.

A large floating crane, HEBE 2, performed all the heavy lifting tasks, her lifting capacity of 750 tons being more than adequate for the weights of the *QE2's* machinery.

Then came the nine, four-stroke, nine cylinder diesel engines which were also lowered and slid into place on their seatings in the ultimately unmanned engine rooms.

One of the mini MAN-B&W 9L 58/64 diesel engines on its test bed in Augsburg. *MAN-B&W*

A complete electrical generator shown prior to its packing and shipment to Germany. *GEC Turbine Generators Limited*

Top: Reappearing slightly 'thickened about the waist' after her major 1987 refit, the *QE2* was ready for her third decade in service.
Cedric Wasser

Left: The Queen's Room as it appeared in 1987. The original chairs which had reflected the trumpet-like columns have been replaced by cubic armchairs in soft, brown leather, perhaps less pleasing to the eye than their predecessors. *Cunard*

Below left: The refurbished swimming pool on One Deck Lido boasts a vivid Cunard lion in mosaic tiles. *Cunard*

Below right: The refurbished spectacular Columbia Restaurant with its 750 seat capacity. *Cunard*

Top: The Double Down Room was one of the public rooms to be dramatically altered in the 1987 refit and was renamed the Grand Lounge. The old stainless steel stairway has gone (the new one is sited at the opposite end of the room) and shops have encroached even further into the upper (Double Up) lounge area.   *Cunard*

Centre left: A white piano with a glass top and surrounding glass bar provided the focal point in the new (1987) Yacht Club bar (ex Double Down Bar) on the Upper Deck.   *Cunard*

Centre right: This view illustrates the plush conditions in the cabins that awaited first class passengers.   *Cunard*

Right: The corridor of the new suites fitted in Bremerhaven by Lloyd Werft. This view was generally only seen by those few privileged to travel in this exclusive accommodation.   *Cunard*

The nine engines, MAN-B&W L58/64 (ie, the cylinders were 580 millimetres in diameter and the pistons moved through a 640 millimetre stroke) were named Alpha, Bravo, Charlie etc. up to number 9 which was India.

Part of the contract stipulated that the liner should achieve 28.5 knots on 85% of the engine power and that there should be no increase in vibration over that induced by the now displaced machinery.

To overcome any vibration problem the engines were mounted on layered rubber resilient mounts, placed at an angle to the engine seats, which would keep vibration to an absolute minimum.

With her old, smooth-running steam turbines the *QE2*, at 28.5 knots, had used six hundred tons of oil fuel a day, thus burning up 120,000 tons per year (at £100 per ton). With her new engines consumption would hopefully be reduced to 270 tons a day.

The waste heat from the machinery would also be put to good use. It would be utilised to heat accommodation, to pre-heat the thick oil fuel, provide steam to the various hotel services and help to produce one thousand tons of fresh water a day from the sea via four Serck vacuum evaporators. Another 450 tons per day would be produced from the sea by Reverse Osmosis Plant equipment that had also provided additional fresh water on the Falklands 'cruise'.

The ability to produce more than enough fresh water would enable the liner to reduce her fresh water tankage by 40%.

At the 'business end' of all the propulsion machinery were the two propellers which had to absorb the enormous power produced by the nine diesels.

The QE2 has always remained the largest, most powerful twin screw vessel in the world. Stone Manganese Marine, the manufacturers of her original six (fixed) bladed, 5791 millimetre diameter propellers had insisted that 110000 shp was the maximum that two propellers could absorb.

Now 130,000 shp was required to be absorbed and the Dutch firm of LIPS, of Drunen, had designed propellers with five blades each. But these blades were controllable, they could

be turned remotely on their bosses. This meant that the special astern machinery that was required with fixed blade propellers could be dispensed with as, by turning the controlled blades sufficiently, the liner could be halted and then sent astern whilst the propellers still rotated in the same direction.

The propellers would also be operated at only two speeds - 144 revolutions per minute for speeds above 18 knots and 72 revolutions for those below. The controlled pitch of the blades would do the rest, enabling the liner to go from 34 knots ahead to 19 knots astern.

The propeller blades were also 'skewed' - scimitar shaped - to cut down the effects of cavitation and to reduce the propeller induced vibration on the hull.

The new 5,800 millimetre diameter propellers were to be augmented by recently developed (but long theorised) pseudo-propellers called Grim wheels (named after their professor inventor). At 6.7 metres diameter they were larger than the propellers, had seven slender uniquely shaped blades (or vanes) and freely rotated at about one third of the CPPs' speed.

Their purpose was to absorb the waste thrust lost from the propellers. This was absorbed by the turbine like inner part of the vane and converted into thrust by the vane tip which thus acted like a second propeller. A worthwhile increase in efficiency of almost 4% was expected by the use of these wheels.

The old 32 ton, manganese bronze propellers were sold off. One would be retained as a dockland exhibit in England but its partner was scheduled to become the basis of two and a half thousand sets of high quality golf clubs!

Whilst the *Queen Elizabeth 2* was having a new heart installed into her very depths the shipyard was also restyling much of her accommodation, both passenger and crew. A study of the deck plans contained within this book will indicate the changes that have been made in these areas between the liner's building and major conversion in 1987.

The manning of the liner would also change under Cunard's new plans. The all British crew were given the chance of either contracting their labour or else accept a 'golden handshake' and hand their jobs over to other, perhaps foreign,

Shipshape once again the engine room is ready for business!
Cunard

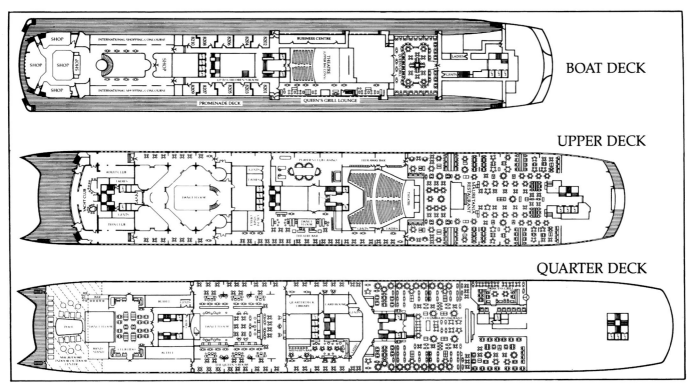

The main passenger decks as they appeared after their 1987 re-arrangement. It is interesting to compare these layouts with those from the time when the 963 foot long liner was built (see inside back cover).

Cunard

BOAT DECK

UPPER DECK

QUARTER DECK

contractors. In spite of union protests that the men would be selling British jobs of which they were only 'temporary custodians', the liner now boasts a multi-national crew in line with other major cruise liners.

Suffice it to say that the whole conversion cost Cunard in excess of £92million, a price that was much cheaper than building an equivalent new ship. Of the cost £2 million alone went to restyling the Tables of the World - originally the Britannia - restaurant. Renamed in honour of the *Mauretania* (Cunard's venerable, record breaking and most loved liner of 1907) the restaurant displays an oversize painting of that liner leaving the shipyard as well as beautifully framed photographs taken on board and of her building and a magnificent model of the old four funnelled liner stands in a glass case for all to admire.

After an absence of many years in an ocean liner restaurant dancing has been re-introduced with the provision of dance floor facilities in both Columbia (another early Cunard transatlantic paddlesteamer) and Mauretania restaurants.

With the expenditure of 1,700,000 man-hours the biggest merchantship conversion ever undertaken was almost complete.

Trials had to be run in the North Sea to test the unification of the whole. These lasted from April 8th until the 22nd. Fuel consumption was as hoped for as were the speeds attained. The maximum speed achieved of 33.8 knots left many, including Cunard (in spite of historical precedents), wondering whether the liner would now contend for the legendary Blue Ribband still held by the American liner *United Stated*.

Testing the new power plant had taken the ship, travelling at full speed, 3 minutes 38 seconds to come to a halt in just over a mile! A further twelve minutes and she was going astern at 19 knots!

Vibration, too, was measurably down in the public rooms although it remained at a similar level as before in the aft sections of the ship.

Work continued during the trials in the hotel areas of the ship in an attempt to finish the uncompleted tasks before the liner left the shipyard. In spite of the frantic efforts workmen would travel with the ship to New York in an attempt to clear the backlog of unfinished work that still needed to be completed in cabins and to plumbing and air conditioning.

The shipyard handed over the *QE2* to her owners on 25th April during a ceremony held on board. Eckart Knoth (chairman), Dieter Haake (managing director) and Werner Luken (project manager for the *QE2*) represented Lloyd Werft whilst Cunard's Ralph Bahna (president and managing director), Alan Kennedy (chairman) and project manager, Mike Novak - not to mention Captain Lawrence Portet - could look on a difficult job well done. The project had not been without its heartaches and moments of apprehension but the company was glad to have its ship back in good order, retrieved from the mess, noise and disorder that degrades the loveliest of ships when in shipyard hands.

Sir Nigel Broackes, chairman of Trafalgar House, was also present at the ceremony amongst the five hundred distinguished guests. He had hosted a party on board the evening before.

Lloyd Werft presented the *QE2* with a special gift - a large, embossed leather marinescape that had originally hung in the First Class Smoking Room of the four funnelled, German record breaker *Kaiser Wilhelm der Grosse* of 1897.

For their part Cunard presented a cheque to the shipyard's welfare fund. In appreciation of the business that the shipping line had brought to his city, the Mayor of Bremerhaven gave a mahogany boxed compass to a smiling Ralph Bahna.

At last the time came for the liner to leave the shipyard that had instilled her with an invigorated hope for the future. She carried with her on her trip across the North Sea many special guests - and also several hundred shipyard workers frantically trying to finish those jobs which were left uncompleted in order to get the ship away from the shipyard in time.

Above: In mid-July 1987 the *QE2* enters the King Geroge V dry dock in Southampton to have the remaining vanes cut off the Grim wheel bosses.
Roger Hardingham

Below: One of the propeller bosses with remains of the grim wheels still attached is lifted away from the ship.

Chapter Twelve

A Second Career

The *Queen Elizabeth 2's* re-entry into service as almost a new ship called for a special, singular honour - a second maiden voyage - and the first day of the revitalised commercial life of the *QE2*, Wednesday 29th April, 1987, started in a most auspicious way.

The Cunard had arranged for several hundred of Southampton's most deserving children to board the ship to make a short commemorative trip down Southampton Water to an anchorage in the confines of The Solent that lay between the Hampshire coast and the northern shores of the Isle of Wight.

There a special guest, Her Royal Highness Diana, Princess of Wales, would join the liner arriving by launch from the yachting town of Cowes on the nearby island. She then travelled with the children on their return journey to Southampton, chatting with many of them *en-route*. The wooded shores of Hampshire and its New Forest must have slipped by the ship almost unnoticed.

The *en-fête* vessel was over-flown by two Harrier Jump Jets of the Royal Air Force and, on reaching the River Test where she would berth alongside the Queen Elizabeth II Terminal, the *Queen Elizabeth 2* was greeted by her contemporary co-masterpiece of British engineering, the supersonic Concorde. The delta winged aircraft saluted in its fly-past both the magnificent ship below and those on board her. Both liner and aircraft had co-operated on many an occasion in symbiotic ventures bringing together the offer of a dream-voyage of a lifetime to those wishing to commemorate, perhaps, a special event with a spectacular journey.

After the children had disembarked the ship was prepared in readiness to embark the passengers and their luggage in readiness for the liners departure on her "Second Maiden Voyage". Just after seven o'clock in the chill of a late April evening the liner motored (for she was no longer a steamship) down Southampton Water being passed, as on many occasions before, by one of the red and white hydrofoils that operate between Southampton and the Isle of Wight. During this and subsequent immediate post-refit voyages - and as is usually expected on a "new" ships entry into service - teething troubles were experienced due, to a great extent, to a modern insistence that a ships essential husbandry and maintenance should be kept subservient to the "bottom line" of a balance sheet. But because this particular sailing had been surrounded by so much publicity, the ship had to sail - ready internally or not.

To mark the final days of the QE2 as a steamship several ex-skippers met on board. Included in this picture are Captain 'Bil' Warwick (right), Mortimer Hehir, Peter Jackson and Bob Arnott (third, fourth and fifth from right). *Southern Newspapers*

In the lower swinging ground off the QEII Terminal the *Queen Elizabeth 2*, assisted by tugs, arrives from Bremehaven in 1987. The two large tenders aft on her boat deck would later be removed.

R. Bruce-Grice

Caught up in the resultant dilemma several passengers had justifiable cause to complain during the *Queen's* first few inaugural voyages. Plumbing problems (including floods, strange happenings in toilets as well as showers not functioning); air-conditioning failing in public rooms; uncontrollable heating and even water that dripped onto diners in the prestigious Queen's Grill. The unfinished state of some staterooms and the inexperience of an almost new hotel staff led to many a passenger voicing disquiet. Compensations were subsequently paid to both passengers and crew for the discomforts experienced in all affected areas.

On a cruise to Madeira and Tenerife following the second maiden voyage two hundred passengers had their bookings cancelled. These passengers had paid for accommodation on 5-Deck but the restructuring of this deck was still mostly incomplete and those cabins that were available had been allocated to workmen embarked to complete the unfinished work remaining from the major refit. The resultant refunds and compensation were costly, Cunard paying out around £100,000 as a result.

The new propulsion machinery deep within the ship was also not without its problems. During an early post-refit cruise (Southampton depart 20th July 1987, six days from £590) she limped into Gibraltar on only one propeller. As part of the ensuing repairs a half-ton electrical coil had to be

flown out to "Gib" from the UK for fitting to one of the main electrical generators. One of the scheduled subsequent Portugese ports of call, at Praia da Rocha on the Algarve, had to be cancelled as the *QE2* sailed back to Southampton, where she arrived one day late at a mere 18 knots. However, according to Cunard, the passengers had enjoyed their extra, albeit enforced, day at sea.

But, as on previous occasions - as well as on occasions yet to come - the complaints were fortunately overcome by results and receded into a memory of past regrets as the liner resettled into her annual round of cruises and line voyages.

Soon, Douglas Ward, author of the respected "Berlitz Complete Handbook to Cruising" and editor of "Cruise Digest Reports", was able to summarise the contemporary impact of the renovated liner: "*QE2* is now the most perfectly integrated passenger ship afloat. She has no equal - for no other ship can cross the Atlantic like the *Queen* - or provide such facilities and style for cruising."

"She is, quite simply, the worlds finest ship and the last of the true express ocean liners."

"Without doubt, the most magnificent ship in the world. And very, very British."

The "Britishness" of the *QE2* had gradually become recognized as one of her most saleable assets - even considering that a proportion of her crewing had been given over to non-British staff. Not only was prestigious

Britishness for sale but Cunard were beginning to realise that the nostalgic style of the old liners also had a marketable value but over the next few years art-deco - the "Ocean Liner" style of the 1930s - and the history of the Cunard Line itself began to make a well-received appearance on board during various refits.

In 1986, as previously mentioned, the British aspect of the liner was in danger of being lost forever. In order to run the vessel in an increasingly competitive market Cunard had to run its flagship in an equally competitive way. Accordingly, this meant employing crew at relative rates and therefore the company had to review its crewing policies. The "new" image of the liner after her major refit provided such an opportunity for such changes of personnel.

Consequently, the British hotel staff found that they had a fight on their hands. The National Union of Seamen became involved and at a meeting of its *QE2* members in Southampton, under the chairmanship of Sam McCluskie and with the parliamentary representation of John Prescott (himself an ex-Cunarder and NUS official), the 800 crew members voted for their future. The ballot was carried at about 600 to 50 in favour of accepting Cunard's terms with 130 members declining to vote on advice from the NUS. This pay-off represented a "golden handshake" of one years salary per man plus £900 for each year of service. In some individual cases payments of £40,000 were made and would, in total, cost Cunard a total in excess of £14-million.

Under the new manning arrangements around forty different nationalities became employed on the ship, although the majority of crew remained British, sub-contracting their labour through staffing agencies such as the Columbia Ship Management of Cyprus. But the ship had been "de-unionised", reportedly resulting in a greater flexibility in working hours. As an added spin-off it was also felt that the ship was being run to a higher standard and was actually a happier ship once the changes had been made and accepted and, at a later date, when the technical departments - the engine and deck departments - followed suit, the *QE2* became a better ship than ever with resultant increases in the quality of maintenance both externally as well as internally.

During the height of the industrial unrest, Cunard threatened to move the liners home port from Southampton, possibly to a new terminal in Cherbourg. Fortunately, this plan dissolved as the discontent subsided and the new working arrangements became implemented.

However, before her next cruise to Lisbon departing on May 30th, the *Queen* undertook one transatlantic "cruise" (the current euphemism for the traditional transatlantic line voyage) with each leg of the twelve day voyage taking six days (four complete days and five nights at sea). The eastbound trip proved, however, to be more than could be expected at that time of year as an unpleasant surprise lay in wait for the *Queen Elizabeth 2*. One of the worst storms encountered by the vessel at that season hit the ship with forty-foot waves driven by winds of fifty miles an hour. The liner was battered for more than fifteen hours during which time the passengers were advised to remain in their cabins. Amongst the £50,000 of damage caused during the ordeal four windows high upon the vessel had been broken by the heavy seas and two grand pianos had been destroyed. The ship arrived in Southampton several hours behind schedule.

Top: The elegant lines of classical design in the *QE2* are demonstrated in this study of the gently curving steel front of her Bridge set against the straight lines of wood decking and distant horizon, all accentuated by the contrast of light and shade.   *Cunard*

Left: A striking view of *QE2* from the air as she cruises past the Needles, Isle of Wight, *en route* to the Atlantic.

Two transatlantics followed a West Indies cruise that had terminated in New York on 4th July. In between each transatlantic the *QE2* was dry-docked in the mighty King George V Graving Dock (originally built for the fabled *Queen Mary*) in Southampton. During her 30-hour overnight stay in the dock (9th-10th July) the remains of the Grim Wheels were removed and replaced by conventional propeller cones. The stubs of these "wheels" had originally comprised seven vanes mounted on a central hub, carefully designed to absorb some of the thrust lost from the controllable pitch propellers that had replaced the vessels 1969 - designed fixed-pitched propellers. Increased speeds - with a slight hope of taking the prestigious Blue Ribband of the North Atlantic - and efficiencies in saving up to £1,000 per day in the fuel bill had eagerly been anticipated at the time of fitting and during the trials that followed. On removal the vanes stubs were retained for analysis by metallurgists from Messrs. Lips. A later offer by these manufacturers to replace the Wheels would be declined by Cunard's technical staff.

Whilst still in place the Grim Wheel stubs had adversly affected the comfort of the crew and of passengers berthed aft by creating vibration and the CPP propellers, which had been designed to run with the Grims, did not alleviate the vibration experienced after the stubs removal to any noticeable extent. Consequently, twelve passenger cabins would remain untenable until a new set of propellers could be designed, manufactured and fitted.

Because of the dry-docking *QE2* missed her 11.30am sailing on 10th July by a few hours but she was able to make up this lost time and returned to schedule by reducing the time of her next turn-around in Southampton (that proceeded her cruise to Gibraltar) to a mere six hours.

August saw the retirement of Captain Lawrence Portet, a tall but private man, who had seen the liners transition from steamship to motorship. His place as Senior Captain was taken by Captain Alan Bennell, a dashing, gregarious man who would prove to be very popular with both crew and passengers. Above all, his love for the ship now under his command was evident to those with whom he came in contact.

A new era had definitely started in the career of *Queen Elizabeth 2*.

The *QE2* glides between the Isle of Wight (with Cowes in the distance) and the Hampshire shore at Stokes Bay near Gosport in the foreground. There are many photographic opportunities in the approaches to Southampton Water.   *Author*

Chapter Thirteen

Propellers to the Fore!

The end of 1987 also saw the end of one of the old propellers that had been removed during the *QE2*'s big refit. Of the original, 19-foot diameter, six-bladed design, the 32 ton propellers had been purchased by Messrs. Sandhill (Bullion) Ltd., of Leeds who planned to cut one of them into manageable pieces within Southampton docks prior to transporting the scrap to the Birkenhead factory of Stone Manganese (the propellers had been fashioned in their London works) for smelting. The resultant smaller, cast ingots would then be taken to St. Andrews, the Mecca of British golf, where they would be formed into 750 sets of golf clubs that would be available to American, European and Japanese golfers at around £700 to £1,000 per set. The second propeller would last until mid-1990 when it would be taken, whole, to St. Andrews where it was put on display during the British Open Golf Championship. Afterwards it followed the same fate as its twin being transformed by Messrs. Sandhill Swilken of St. Andrews into the "Q2 Putter Royale", later sold for £170 each (Duty Free!) on board the liner.

Before the old year was out the *Queen* made a pre-Christmas sunshine cruise to West Africa calling in at Lisbon, Gibraltar, Tenerife, Dakar in Senegal, the Cape Verde Islands and Madeira prior to returning to Southampton on 12th December.

Arriving at Tenerife on 3rd December during this cruise the *Queen* decided to make her mark - or rather Tenerife made its mark on the *Queen*! - as, whilst entering Santa Cruz, she came in rather too quickly and bumped the quay wall, buckling one of her hull plates to a depth of nine inches. Delayed in the port for 24 hours a temporary replacement plate was patched over the damaged area before the ship continued with her cruise. A permanent repair would be made during her August 1988 refit in Germany.

The *Queen Elizabeth 2*'s first major sortie as a motorship came during what was billed as "The 1988 Maiden Voyage Across the World", but in effect took her from New York (departing 13th January, 1988) through the Panama Canal to destinations in and around the Pacific and Indian Oceans.

Calls were made at Fort Lauderdale, Acapulco, Los Angeles, at various islands in the South Pacific and ports in New Zealand and Australia where the ship became officially involved with the latter's Bicentennial celebrations. Then it was on to islands in the Indian Ocean, through to East Africa before heading eastwards to Southeast Asia and Hong Kong. Up to here various shorter segments of the cruise had been

advertised as being available to those other than the full cruise passengers but from Hong Kong to China, Japan, north Pacific islands and back to LA prior to visiting destinations in the Caribbean, it would appear from the itinerary that only the full voyage passengers were embarked until the liner reached Fort Lauderdale where fly-cruise passengers once again joined her. The *QE2* arrived back in New York on 29th April.

It was whilst the ship was cruising the islands of the South Pacific that an announcement was made that the liner would be chartered in 1989 by a group of Japanese businessmen in a deal eventually to be worth almost £20-million to Cunard. Lasting for a staggering 72 days the ship would be moored at Yokohama as an important part of that citys 150th Anniversary celebrations being used for commercial exhibitions and conferences as well as for hotel purposes. The Japanese ranked amongst the greatest admirers of the great ship, ranking her in their affections for all things that reflected the best in British quality.

The 32-day round South America cruise that had been scheduled for the period now to be taken up by the forthcoming charter was cancelled as were various shorter cruises planned for the Los Angeles/Pacific area.

Towards the end of the Pacific and Indian Ocean cruise in late April, a further enquiry was received, again by the ardent Japanese, concerning a second, even longer charter. This time the city of Osaka wanted the ship for a six months charter for use as part of that citys planned World Exposition in 1989. A fee of £50-million was rumoured.

The admiration of the Japanese for the *QE2* was being translated into healthy returns for the Cunard.

Meanwhile, the *Queen Elizabeth 2* arrived in Southampton at 5pm on 4th May for a rare overnight stay. Before she sailed on the 5th an unusual press call was

In a shower of flame and flying sparks from a burner's torch one of the discarded propellers is cut into pieces ready for the furnace and ultimate transformation into sets of unique golf clubs.
Southern Newspapers

organised by the British Post Office. A special 26-pence postage stamp had been produced commemorating the fiftieth anniversary of the launch of the *QE2*'s namesake, the legendary 83,676 gross ton *Queen Elizabeth* - the "Old Lizzie" as she had been affectionately known to decades of crew and travellers.

To launch the new stamp Relief Captain Robin Woodall, along with British television personality Jimmy Saville (a devoted *QE2* fan and traveller) and retired Cunard Commodore Geoffrey Marr (one-time captain of the *Queen Elizabeth*) stood around on the cold, windswept quayside waiting for the press to complete their work. Both elderly and infirm on his legs, Commodore Marr found the experience to be particularly gruelling.

30th June saw the *Queen* arriving in Southampton with a most unusual item on her manifest. In her hold she carried a steel coffin which contained the remains of renowned Hungarian-born composer Bela Bartok, writer of such atonal compositions as "Bluebeard's Castle" and "Music For Strings, Percussion and Celesta". Having emigrated to the United States in 1940 he was being returned to his beloved city of Budapest for a state funeral 43 years after his death.

Otherwise the summer season progressed uneventfully for the *QE2* until it was time for an unscheduled overhaul. This took place in Germany where she arrived on 1st August after an incredible four-and-a-half hour turnaround in Southampton, a ten day transatlantic having been cancelled to enable the work to be done. Amongst the work to be undertaken was the replacement of the hull plate previously damaged in Tenerife, the overhaul of the ships stabilisers and the removal of the controllable pitch propellers that had been designed to work with the deposed Grim Wheels and which were now, as a consequence, out of balance. The replacement propellers (also controllable pitch and provided under the terms of the Grim Wheel guarantee by Lips) would hopefully alleviate the vibration problems that had been plaguing the after end of the ship ever since the disintegration of the revolutionary, vaned appendages.

The hope for the new propellers proved to be well-founded as, when the ship was sent on her post-refit trials,

the crew asked why their ship was apparently going so slowly. One can only imagine Captain Bennell's amusement when he told his men that the *QE2* had been achieving 31 knots! The lack of the vibration so accustomed to over the past few months had lulled the men into a false sense of speed! Captain Bennell later told reporters that the Bremerhaven trip had also been used by the SAS to practice their specialist units expertise in overcoming maritime hijackers.

September, 1988, brought yet another accolade to the *Queen Elizabeth 2* when she achieved her two-millionth mile, doing so in half the time that the old *Queen Elizabeth* had taken.

It was also in September that retired Commodore Geoffrey Marr was invited to sail on the ship in order to talk to the passengers about his time in command of the *Queen Elizabeth* and of the time that he was with her in an advisory capacity during her last voyage when she had been renamed *Seawise University*. As such she had been taken from her interrupted retirement in Fort Lauderdale, Florida, to Hong Kong where, during the last days of her conversion to a floating university, she had caught fire and capsized - completely destroyed.

However, the Commodore decided that he was now too infirm to make the special trip to New York that would celebrate the fiftieth anniversary of the launch of his beloved *Queen Elizabeth* that had occurred on 27th September, 1938. Besides, he said, he wanted his old passengers to remember him as he had been - strolling the decks with his greatcoat swirling about him - and not as an old man.

In his stead the current author was invited to speak and the trip, Voyage 682, departing from Southampton on 29th September, proved to be a memorable one not only for the commemorative events that were scheduled to take place on board but also for the surprise unscheduled events that were added onto the crossing - courtesy of Nature.

These started as the sea became steadily unsettled during the evening of the second day out until a Force 8 to 9 gale, the first of two such gales encountered in the course of the voyage, gave the ship a heavy pitch as she ploughed westwards.

A visit to the Bridge during the late evening of the first storm showed the huge waves, phosphorescent in the faint light of the ship, breaking either side of the plunging bow before, broken into huge clouds of spray, the seas cascaded aft towards the Bridge front where built-in wind deflectors took the spray vertically up behind the Bridge wings, creating dimly illuminated ghostly green curtains. Within the cabins the movement of the ship was also felt as the ship slowly and steadily rolled to either

Captain Robin Woodall (left), retired Cunard Commodore Geoffrey Marr (right) and an as always exuberant Jimmy Saville help to launch a postage stamp bearing an image of the never-to-be-forgotten *Queen Elizabeth*.

Southern Newspapers

side, each roll being checked with a slight judder as the stabilisers took charge and corrected the liners' sideways motion. The thinly veneered panels lining the cabin's bulkheads gently creaked with each movement.

Two such storms should have been enough for one crossing of the Atlantic. On the fourth day out an announcement, broadcast during breakfast, advised the passengers that the *QE2* was approaching the Grand Banks (off Newfoundland, Nova Scotia) and that aquatic and airborne wildlife could possibly be seen as might a few fishing boats but, as the ship was .."well South of the normal ice area...", there was no chance of any ice being encountered.

A mid-morning visit to the Bridge was made, during which dolphins and a herd of Right whales were seen along to starboard, was interrupted by the author's wife: "What's that white thing on the horizon?"

"Probably a fishing boat, madam."

"Looks too white to be a fishing boat to me - looks more like ice."

At this binoculars were raised -- "My God! It is ice! Call the Captain!"

Captain Bennell soon made his appearance and was transfixed by the first ice that he had seen on the Atlantic for thirty years - and which the radar had failed to detect - on the horizon. He made an announcement over the ship's broadcast system and, as passengers flocked to the Boat Deck rails, said mischievously "I bet that's mucked up a few lectures!"

Changing course the *Queen Elizabeth 2* was navigated to within half a mile of the iceberg and, even at that distance, the cold emanating from its mass could be felt. A bank of mist surmounting its peak slowly undulated and, in doing so, gave the appearance that the berg was continuously changing shape. The swell of the sea around the base of the iceberg was eerily discoloured a pale green, illuminated by the light that was reflected from the submerged bulk of the 'berg.

Soon, the ice was receding astern and the excitement was over as the liner resumed her course. On the next voyage Captain Bennell would take his ship towards the by-now well-charted, slow-moving iceberg to show it off to his passengers. From the time that it was seen it was nick-named by the officers on the Bridge as "Benny's Berg" in honour of their Captain!

Much of this particular voyage was being recorded by a publishers photographer, Ian Burney, and his pictures would appear in a book co-authored by the ships First Officer, Peter Moxom. Their combined effort, "From the Bridge - QE2 Cunard's Flagship", would provide a fascinating account of the internal workings and organisation of the ship. The captions to some of the photographs gave rise to concern in high places as, although they reflected the banter that occurs in many a workplace, they were perhaps unsuitable for publication!

The last quarter of 1988 seemed to be intermittently plagued with high winds. On 6th October, when sailing from Southampton at the outset of a nine-day cruise to Ibiza, Cannes, Barcelona, Gibraltar, and Lisbon (nine days from £925) the *Queen* was caught by winds gusting up to 72mph. She had just rounded the long finger of Calshot Spit that, with its ancient castle built in the time of Henry VIII to protect the entrance to Southampton Water, juts out from the New Forest and separates Southampton Water from The Solent where, after making the turn to port to go around the submerged Brambles Bank, the wind caught the ship and pushed her bow to starboard towards the Lepe shore.

After her 1999 refit - and after the debut of the blockbuster movie 'Titanic' - the *Queen* was given traditional wooden deck chairs on which pampered passengers could soak up both sun and sea air.

Author

Because of the apparent risk and as an inward bound containership, the 50,000 ton *Benavon*, was also in the area Captain Bennell ordered the ship to go astern to avoid running out of the channel. With her new engines responding immediately, the liner went astern at 8 knots until she had recovered her position and then everything continued as normal. The event received what was considered to be unwarranted coverage by the press and reports of "...a near collision.." were unfounded.

Most of November was spent cruising the Caribbean with Captain Woodall in command, sailing the waters that he had recently left after having spent ten years there, to join the *Queen Elizabeth 2* as Relief Captain.

Although due to return to New York the liner made one of her intermittent diversions to Boston, Massachusetts, and it was from here that she sailed on the night of 21st November, heading for Southampton.

Captain Woodall recalled that a NNW gale Force 8 was blowing as the ship sailed from the New England port and that this wind had increased to Force 9 on the 22nd. The wind then veered round to WNW the next day, increasing to Force 10 with a big sea running. The direction of the ship was changed on occasion to make it slightly easier for the passengers as she was producing some nasty rolls. After a couple of days the wind went round to the South so, for a while, the ship was ahead of the wind and it was a little more comfortable.

However, two days later the wind direction changed yet again, this time coming over the bow from an East by South direction. The ship had to slow down again to 9 knots and was thus thirty hours late in arriving in Southampton. Another damaged piano, broken crockery, buckled rails on the foc'sle and scattered furniture were some of the "victims" of the four day storm. At the storms height the sound of it could be heard over the ship-to-shore radio in the United Kingdom!

Captain Woodall would later say that, although it was a very nasty storm, worse ones were later to be experienced, confirming his own suspicions that the weather is changing on the North Atlantic with both stronger winds and seas bigger than encountered before.

A cruise to West Africa and the Atlantic isles was followed by a short, four day jaunt from 11th to 14th December around the English Channel calling in at Cherbourg, hopefully creating a taste for a longer cruise to many of those on board.

Arrival back in Southampton, 14th December, meant the arrival of a very special visitor. Her Majesty Queen Elizabeth, the Queen Mother, boarded the liner along with three hundred other specially invited guests including retired Commodores Donald McLean and Geoffrey Marr and Captain John Treasure Jones. The royal visit brought to a head the celebrations that had been held to commemorate the launching of the *Queen Elizabeth* that Her Majesty had named and christened in 1938.

In her speech about the old ship that had borne her name, the Queen Mother said :

"....Throughout the years that followed the *Queen*

Elizabeth was a symbol of so much pride in our country."

"...For me and for many who travelled in her it was a sad day in November 1968 when the *Queen Elizabeth* sailed from Southampton for the last time, leaving a legacy of memories."

She continued: "I am sure it is a name that will live on in history, just like *Golden Hind*, *Victory* and *Cutty Sark*."

Her Majesty then made reference to the ship in which she now spoke: "Like her predecessor the *Queen Elizabeth 2* is a fine ambassador for this country."

The *QE2* spent Christmas in the Caribbean with Christmas Day in Barbados and New Years Day in Fort Lauderdale. A shorter cruise in the same waters followed that ended in New York on 13th January, 1989.

During her Pacific cruise at the beginning of March the *Queen* was buffeted by a severe storm with forty foot waves that lasted for six hours as she sailed between Tahiti and New Zealand. As damage occured to both ship and those on board (forty one passengers and crew had suffered minor injuries) Captain Bennell was furious that he had not been told of these adverse conditions, which with sufficient warning, could have been avoided by prudent navigation. The New Zealand weather bureau later said that their lack of warning was indicative of governmental cut-backs in their service.

It was then time for the first of the two Japanese charters that would take place that year.

A *Queen Mary* anniversary on board saw many retired Cunard captains return to their old command. Left to right (standing) Commodore Douglas Ridley, current Captain Laurence Portet and Captain Bob Arnott. Seated (l to r) Captains John Treasure Jones, 'Bil' Warwick, William Law and Mortimer Heier. Having retired with his beloved *Queen Mary*, Captain Jones was the only captain present not to have been master of the *QE2*.

Southern Newspapers

Chapter Fourteen

Anniversaries and Accolades

1989 was to prove to be an important and profitable year for the Cunard.

The first of the Japanese charters took the *Queen Elizabeth 2* to the city of Yokohama which was celebrating its 130th Anniversary in which the *Queen* was to play an important part. Commencing 27th March the ship would remain berthed alongside her pier at the citys passenger terminal.

A consortium of Japanese companies had chartered the ship for £250,000 a day and it was hoped that this money would be recouped by using the ship as an hotel at £1,690 a night for a suite and for companies to use her for corporate entertaining at £600,000 per day. Both hotel and corporate bookings were eventually well below those estimated. A charge was made to those just wanting to look over the vessel (on-board sales figures exceeded the estimate) and a smaller fee was levied on those thousands just wanting to walk alongside her on the quayside to look at the ship that they considered to be an icon of British quality! Signs and staff on board were changed to Japanese for the term of the charter.

The liner was also licensed for weddings and twenty couples decided to take advantage of this opportunity although the Captain did not perform the ceremonies! The ship's shops and facilities were all open and a programme of entertainments kept the visitors amused. But, in spite of the report that 69,000 Japanese had stayed on board and that 180,000 people had made day visits (at almost £60 for three hours, including lunch) to the ship, the charter still made a loss for the charterers but it was considered to be part of a "learning curve". If the venture had not completely been a commercial success for the Japanese it certainly had been one in an operational sense.

Captain Woodall later said that Cunard had learnt a lot about the Japanese and that they, in turn, had learnt a lot on how to run a big ship. It all ended with both sides respecting each other socially as well as commercially.

Both the Captain and his wife had thoroughly enjoyed themselves on their day sorties from the ship: "The Japanese people were terribly kind and awfully helpful - they couldn't do enough for us - and generous to a fault."

"Wherever my wife and I went we were recognised because we had been on television...and being 6 foot 4

inches and a Westerner in Japan makes one stand out to a certain extent! ....People would come up and talk to us - total strangers - just to ask about the ship and our life on board."

The Captain's overiding impression of Japan ("...a fascinating country...") - "Traffic jams!!..There's an awful lot of cars in an awful small space!"

After seventy-two days in Yokohama the *Queen Elizabeth 2* sailed on 4th June and returned to Southampton, where she arrived at the beginning of July.

Once home, it would not be long before the *QE2* was again making national headlines - but this time they were of the scandal-making variety.

Environmental issues were rightly becoming a concern of major international importance and any infringement brought forth the wrath of nations upon the perpertrators head. In this instance it was the unfortunate lot of the *QE2* to be caught, literally in the act!

Provision had been made on the liner in her early days to dump bagged rubbish over the side but, with the adaption of garbage compressors and the introduction of legislation to protect the seas of the world and its wildlife, this practice was rightly no longer acceptable, unless the waste had been rendered into an an easily dispersable bio-degradable slurry prior to disposal.

The long, sleek bow of the *Queen Elizabeth 2* is seen to advantage in this dockside shot at Southampton.   *Peter Seden*

A damning video was made by two young crew members whilst in the Caribbean in late June showing other crew members dumping black plastic bags of garbage over the stern under the cover of darkness and the video was sent to a national newspaper.

Captain Bennell later explained that the ship had had several thousands of pounds spent in upgrading her garbage disposal by using environmentally friendly methods and that the release of the video was the first he had heard of the illicit dumping.

October brought two items of satisfying news for Cunard and Trafalgar House. Firstly the Round Britain Cruise that would preceed the celebrations commemorating the 150th Anniversary of the Cunard Line in 1990 was sold out and, secondly, it was disclosed that the new diesel-electric propulsion system was using one-third less oil-fuel and, as a result, was saving the company around £7-million a year in fuel bills!

In November, prior to her second charter in Japan, the *Queen Elizabeth 2* was given a short refit in Southampton, a rare occurence in recent years. Work included surveys on boilers and structure; machinery overhauls; overhauling lifeboats and checks on other lifesaving equipment; and refurbishing passenger areas and accommodation that included new carpets and upholstery.

The *Queen* was passed to the charter group just before Christmas on her arrival in Honolulu and ultimately arrived in Osaka on 28th December at the outset of an incredible 180-day stay. During this time she would perform similar functions to those that she performed in Yokohama but would also make ten short cruises as part of her itininary. She would be in Japan during the Spring - an important time in that country - and would be an essential part of World Exposition 1990. A similar fee to that received in Yokohama, £250,000 a day, was being paid for the charter, netting nearly £50-million for Cunard!

The charter continued until 4th June when the *QE2* sailed from Osaka to be later handed back to Cunard's charge in Honolulu, Hawaii. From here she made a five day cruise, starting 19th June, including calls at Lahaina and Kona, both in the Hawaiian Islands, and then a transpacific to Ensenada on the north-west coast of Mexico.

Transferring to San Diego a 13-day trip brought her from the US Westcoast through the Panama Canal, finally arriving in New York on 7th July, Independence Day having been spent at sea between St. Thomas and Ft. Lauderdale. A transatlantic return to Southampton brought her back to New York on 17th July in readiness for one of the most prestigious cruises of her career to date.

Whilst the ship had been on charter in Japan, it was announced in January that her home port of Southampton would be bestowing the Freedom of the City on both the

Queen Elizabeth 2 and her crew in the months to come. On making the announcement the Leader of the City Council described the *Queen Elizabeth 2* as "...a vessel that is very much alive and promoting the present and future of our city...across the world."

On 17th July QE2 departed New York on the outset of a trip that would celebrate 150 years of the Cunard Line. Samuel Cunard's paddle steamer *Britannia* had been the first of his steamers to cross the Atlantic in 1840 leaving Liverpool on 4th July, arriving in Halifax, Nova Scotia, twelve-and-a-half days later, and finally reaching Boston where she was accorded a very warm welcome after a total passage from England of 14 days 8 hours.

It was essential that the *Queen* should arrive in the United Kingdom on time and to ensure that this was done the QE2, under the command of Captain Robin Woodall, achieved her fastest ever eastbound crossing of the Atlantic at an average speed of 30.16 knots and she arrived in British waters in 4 days, 6 hours and 57 minutes.

Shortly after the liner's arrival in the Hampshire port on 22nd July her Captain, on behalf of his ship and her crew, was ceremoniously presented with the Freedom of the City of Southampton, the towns highest honour, by the city's Mayor and Port Admiral, Councillor Mary Key. Never before had the honour been bestowed on so many people at the same time. Captain Woodall recalled that the Freedom meant that he could drive his sheep through the city's ancient Bargate!

From Southampton on 23rd July the *Queen Elizabeth 2* sailed on a 6-day, celebratory cruise that would take her in triumph around the British Isles.

Captain Robin Woodall receives the Freedom of the City of Southampton on behalf of the ship and her crew from the City's Mayor and Port Admiral, Mrs. Mary Key.
Southern Newspapers

Chapter Fifteen

A Cruise of Celebration

During the *Queen Elizabeth 2*'s very special "Cunard - 150 Years" cruise it seemed that all the country wanted to catch a glimpse of the worlds most famous liner as her reception in all of her ports of call was beyond the wildest dreams of those on board for this extra-gala occasion.

The liner would make a different port on each day of the cruise, beginning with Cobh (Cove) on Monday, 23rd July, 1990. Her arrival in the Irish port was scheduled for 7.30am and, as the liner came in past Roches Point and into the beautiful Cork Harbour, she was given a wonderful reception and was soon surrounded by dozens of yachts and other craft. Thousands upon thousands of people could be seen on the surrouding hills and headlands and great numbers of people could be seen around the city and St. Colemans Cathedral as the *Queen* approached her dock. Captain Woodall thought that the berthing position was a very narrow and small space in which to manoeuvre such a big ship but the weather was being kind with a calm sea .

The Trafalgar House "Dauphin 2" helicopter, piloted by Captain David Warren, had been embarked on the liner to fly dignitaries and press on and off the liner, and the ship's Captain was very proud of the fact that his vessel had been turned into "...a great, big aircraft carrier..." for the occasion of the cruise.

The Irish Republican Premier, Mr Charles Haughey, came on board and the *Queen Elizabeth 2* was guided into a new cargo terminal, at Ringaskiddy, which was being inaugurated by the *QE2*'s arrival. Units of the Irish Navy escorted the liner to her berth, the navy's commodore being on board the Cunarder.

The *QE2* sailed that evening at 7pm to the accompaniment of exploding fireworks and with the sky colourfully speckled with hundreds of balloons. Because of the later hour, there were also more people about to witness her departure, the surrounding hills blackened with the assembled crowds.

During the trip across the Atlantic there had been many special entertainments on board including the

wonderful orchestra of The Academy of St. Martins-in-the-Fields. Peter Duchin and His Orchestra had played for the 150th Anniversary Ball and for the Round Britain Cruise Lester Lanin and His Orchestra played for the Royal and Grand Masked Balls and other special dances. The famed Royal Philharmonic Orchestra, under the baton of Andre Previn, would join the ship in Scotland.

The gala cruise progressed in triumph to perhaps the most important destination of the voyage - the Port of Liverpool from where the Cunard Lines story had originally begun in 1840.

Captain Robin Woodall had a special affection for this seaport as he lived on the Wirral, the prominatory opposite the Cheshire city.

The *Queen Elizabeth 2* was expected to be in the River Mersey in the morning of Tuesday, 24th July so the day had to start early for those on board. As the ship approached Anglesey at around six o'clock she steamed in close to pass near to the South Stack and, as the Holyhead lifeboat and a mass of small-craft came out to greet the liner, those on the ship who were already up and about could already see a lot of people on the shore and cliffs looking seawards towards them.

The *QE2* then steamed (even after her conversion to a motorship it is still hard to not use references to steam!) towards the Bar Light marking the mouth of the Mersey where she waited for sufficient water to enable her to safely pass over the sandbar that guards the entrance to Liverpools great river.

Once enough water was beneath her she started to move up the river. It was a beautiful, sunny day with a brisk South-east breeze and the *Queen* progressed in state on the flood tide towards the maritime city where an anticipated half-million people were expected to greet the liner.

Captain Woodall recalled the emotion of the moment: "I remember that the first inkling that I got of the massive crowds that would be there was looking at the shore at Crosby. I thought, well - that's funny! It looks black and it should be nice golden sands over at Crosby. And then I saw the sun glinting off literally hundreds of cars ...looking at it through the binoculars I could see that it was literally black with people! Amazing! And then.....as we closed into the river...looking at New Brighton (it, too, was) absolutely solid with people". Millions of people had been anticipated to see the ship arrive and it appeared that this estimate had been achieved!

The "embarked air", the Trafalgar House helicopter, was again busy bringing the mayors of Liverpool, The Wirral and Birkenhead out to the liner whilst members of the press joined the civic dignitaries on the Bridge to view the unfolding spectacle before them as the great ship progressed up the Mersey.

QE2 is berthed at Cobh during her triumphant call into the Irish Port as part of Cunard's 150th Anniversary celebratory cruise around the British Isles in 1990.   *Richard Weiss*

With Liverpool's famous waterfront providing a fitting backdrop the *QE2* arrives in the River Mersey, at one time Cunard's home port.

Cedric Wasser

As *Queen Elizabeth 2* came abreast of the Pierhead (she was scheduled to be there at noon) with its magnificent vista of the three famous landmark buildings of the Royal Liver Building, the Cunard Building and the offices of the Liverpool Docks and Harbour Board. She dropped anchor and swung round with the flood tide. As the ship came to anchor ten thousand red and blue balloons were released from One Deck Lido from beneath an opening Magrodome to celebrate the *Queen Elizabeth 2*'s inaugural visit to the first home of the Cunard Line.

It was hoped that it was going to be a safe mooring but, in the prevailing weather, the anchor started to drag and, as a consequence, the Captain and the Liverpool pilot had to stay on the Bridge for much of the day. The main engines were kept running to maintain

'....and she shall have headlines wherever she goes!'

Richard Weiss

manouevrability and tugs were kept "buttoned" on to the ship to hold her in those disappointing conditions. It was only when the tide started to ebb and the wind dropped did the liner lay at all well.

As a result Staff Captain Ron Bolton had to go ashore to represent Captain Woodall and perform various civic functions in his stead. These included the unveiling of a bronze bust of Samuel Cunard in the magnificent Merseyside Maritime Museum and attending the dedication of some plaques that had been found in the cellars of the Cunard Building. These latter tablets, listing those Cunard employees who had given their lives in the two World Wars, had recently been installed in St. Nicholas's Church, the Liverpudlian parish church, and were now being dedicated by the Canon of St. Nicholas, the Reverend Nicholas Frayling.

Although the *Queen Elizabeth 2* (with Beatles' recordings playing aft) was due to depart Liverpool at 7pm the Captain recalled that it was nearer to eleven in the evening before she left - and Liverpool once again made the occasion a memorable one. The anchor was weighed in readiness and, as the ship lay stemming the ebb tide, tugs held the ship firm as a magnificent firework display ("One of the best that I have ever seen - anywhere," said the Captain) put on by the Mersey Docks and Harbour Board lit up the evening sky. Then, at the final bang of the final rocket, the *QE2* got underway as members of the crew sang "Ferry 'Cross the Mersey".

As the liner sounded her siren she started to move down the river, again accompanied by hundreds of small craft. Both shores, as passenger Richard Weiss recalled, were "....lit

The liner prepares to depart the Clyde for the next leg of her Anniversary Cruise which took her to the French Port of Cherbourg. Many well-wishers were able to get a view from the water by boarding specially hired vessels based in the area.   *Roger Hardingham*

up by a billion flashbulbs..." as the watching mass of people attempted to capture the moment on film.

A remarkable day in the memory of tens of thousands of people.

The next day saw the *Queen Elizabeth 2* in the esturial waters of the Clyde where, for so long just known both as "Q4" and the "New Cunarder", she had been built a few miles upstream at Clydebank at the renowned shipyard of John Brown, later part of Upper Clyde Shipbuilders, and from which she had sailed twenty two years previously.

The crowds here were not so numerous as they had been on the Mersey but there was still a good enough gathering to see the liner arrive passing Cloch Point and sail on towards Greenock. Again, the embarked helicopter was busy flying local dignitaries and the press to the ship. The *QE2's* draught was too great to allow her to go any further upstream than Greenock so she took a mooring alongside the container terminal, the only berth that could accommodate her.

The security around the ship was such that would-be sightseers could not get near her but invited groups, such as pensioners from John Brown's, went on board to have a look around. With these and other visitors the ship soon became very busy. Most of the passengers had been sent ashore on coach tours to make room for the guests!

The weather had been kind to the *QE2* during the course of this Anniversary Cruise and she departed the Clyde in glorious late afternoon sunshine accompanied, again, by hundreds of small craft. These were soon left behind as the *Queen* picked-up speed, leaving as her sole companion that other proud product of the Clyde, the paddle steamer

Waverley, which kept up with the Cunarder for a wee while longer.

Sailing at speed southwards overnight through the Irish Sea and onwards into the English Channel the liner arrived at Cherbourg just after midday on 26th July. The spell of good weather that had been with the *Queen* thus far throughout the cruise was beginning to break and she arrived at the French port with a strong easterly wind blowing.

Assisted by the prevailing wind, the liner came in a little too quickly and, even with the French pilot on board, did, as her captain described it, a "...destroyer approach..." and made a "...controlled crash..." alongside the jetty. A French naval band played the ship in as she arrived.

By midnight, sailing time, the wind had dropped and the *Queen Elizabeth 2* made a more dignified exit in the by-now calm waters.

At this point Captain Woodall formally handed the command of the ship to Relief Captain Ron Warwick whose father, "Bil" Warwick, had stood-by the ship whilst she was being built and then took her on her maiden voyage. This doubling-up of captains was necessary because the presence of Captain Woodall would be required for the official Anniversary celebrations and ceremonials planned for the next twenty four hours.

Chapter Sixteen

An Anniversary Fit For a Queen

The cold, overcast morning of Friday 27th July, 1990, was sullen with a threat of rain in the air. The Solent was in one of its unseasonable grey moods but this mood was fortunately not reflected by the atmosphere that prevailed on the water.

From Cherbourg *Queen Elizabeth 2* arrived at her position at the end of Voyage 749 at around 8.45am and anchored in her alloted position. Fifteen minutes later the containership *Atlantic Conveyor*, 58,438 tons and built in 1985 to replace her namesake that had been sunk during the 1982 Falklands conflict, took up her designated place (originally alloted to the *Vistafjord*) to the south-east of her fleet-mate and, after another similar period, the graceful, five-star *Vistafjord* (bought by the Cunard in 1983 from Norwegian Cruise Lines - although British built - she still retained her original grey hull) anchored, for some reason late, astern of the "box boat". The presence of these three ships represented perhaps the most famous shipping line in the world - the Cunard and the impending presence of Royal guests indicated the esteem in which the Line was held. An icon of the British Mercantile Marine, if not a national treasure.

Seven small vessels had also arrived at their Review positions and moored in line ahead, parallel to and to the north-west of the three huge ships. Amongst this secondary line were sailing craft (including the three year old sail training vessel constructed for the disabled, *Lord Nelson*, which included a mast donated by contributions from passengers and crew of the *QE2*) and auxiliary naval ships. By 9.15am the assemblage was complete.

Meanwhile, all around the area of the anchorage, dozens of private yachts and motor boats, as well as excursion vessels from nearby Portsmouth Harbour and Southampton, jostled for the best positions from which to witness the unfolding spectacle that surrounded them.

Having left Portsmouth Harbour at 9.25am the Royal Squadron soon appeared as the Royal Yacht *Britannia*, with Her Majesty Queen Elizabeth II and His Royal Highness The Duke of Edinburgh on board, came up astern to the port side of *Queen Elizabeth 2*. The Monarch aboard the Royal Yacht was preceded, as of tradition, by a Trinity House Vessel, the *Patricia*, and followed by Her Majesty's Ship *Broadsword*. Cheering passed over the waters from those on board the fleet to be reviewed.

The squadron passed the anchored ships before turning 180 degrees to progress past the portsides of the anchored Cunarders. The passengers on board the two liners lining the Boatdecks of their ships were again encouraged to give "Three cheers for Her Majesty, The Queen", Her Majesty, dressed in light blue, and her husband, HRH The Duke of Edinburgh, being clearly seen on the after deck of the graceful and, as always, impeccable *Britannia*.

The squadron then turned around the stern of the *Vistafjord* and sailed between the main and secondary lines of moored vessels. Meanwhile, the first of two aerial tributes flew overhead as the elegant airliner "Concorde" made an appearance followed by a Britannia Airways Boeing 767, a heavy-lift "Belfast" and a Boeing 747 of Virgin Airways.

As the Royal Yacht anchored ahead of the reviewed fleet at 11.20am a second fly pass occurred, comprising of "Sea King", "Lynx" and "Dauphin" helicopters and a "Sea Harrier" jump-jet.

The Royal Barge was lowered from its parent vessel and, accompanied by police and naval launches, was soon churning the choppy waters of The Solent towards the lowered, portside accommodation ladder of the *Queen Elizabeth 2*, approaching the liner from around her stern.

The Royal party embarked *Queen Elizabeth 2* at noon, being greeted on the ship by Captain Woodall (who had made a dash down from the Bridge), Sir Nigel Broackes, Eric Parker and Bernard Crisp, Cunard's UK director. Introductions were then made to the Chief Engineer, Steve Hare; Staff Chief Engineer John Tomlins; Hotel Manager John Duffy and Staff Captain Ron Bolton. As the Sovereign was now on board, her Standard was broken-out from the masthead.

A reception followed in the Queen's Room where Her Majesty met Captain and Mrs Alan Bennell. Captain Bennell was still officially Master of *Queen Elizabeth 2* but had been suffering from poor health and had been ashore on sick-leave for some time.

As the Queen came down the stairway to the Grand Lounge she was greeted by a fanfare

During the Anniversary Review HM The Queen and HRH The Duke of Edinburgh responded to cheers and applause from those on board the assembled ships. *Richard Weiss*

The Royal party was then escorted to the Bridge where the Queen and the Duke of Edinburgh were introduced to Relief Captain Ron Warwick who was conning the ship and both royal personages showed great interest in the activity around them.

3.40pm - and the *Queen Elizabeth 2* berthed at the Queen Elizabeth II Terminal at Southampton's Dock Head. Captain Woodall escorted his royal guests to the gangway before handing them into the care of the Lord Lieutenant of Hampshire.

A most significant and memorable day, indeed week, in the career of the *Queen Elizabeth 2* drew to a successful close (complete with a Cunard marquee on the Town Quay and more fireworks) as she lay at her berth in the River Test with the *Vistafjord* astern of her as a companion. The larger ship would sail the next day, Saturday 28th July, for New York on a transatlantic crossing, her third of four celebratory 150th Anniversary Cruises.

Above: On boarding the liner Her Majesty Queen Elizabeth II unveiled a plaque to commemorate the event. The Queen would then travel the 20 miles to Southampton on board the ship, the first ever such trip that she had made since she had launched the vessel in 1967.
Cunard

Right: A good study showing the great width of *Queen Elizabeth 2*, alongside at Cobh, Ireland on 23rd July 1990. Later, in 1994, there would be various modifications to her stern arrangements.
Richard Weiss

played by The Royal Philharmonic Orchestra. Her Majesty then unveiled a plaque to commemorate her visit to the ship on this important anniversary.

During the luncheon that followed the other vessels that had taken part in the review had dispersed leaving the *QE2* the last to leave the anchorage, doing so at 1.45pm. Again led by the *THV Patricia* the Cunarder made her way through The Solent and up Southampton Water towards Southampton. Remarkably, this would be the first time that Her Majesty The Queen had sailed in the liner that she had launched 27 years earlier.

After lunch Captain Woodall escorted the Queen through the various public rooms of his ship and Her Majesty seemed to enjoy the whole ocassion. Passengers, corralled by red-rope restraints, lined the royal route through the vessel, having previously being given coloured coded tickets by Cruise Director Peter Longley's staff which indicated in which part of the liner they should wait.

Chapter Seventeen

Rescues and Remembrance

A short two-night party jaunt, New York to New York, was followed by a couple of transatlantics (the voyage ending in Southampton on 9th August, 1990, marking the liners 500th scheduled North Atlantic crossing) which, in turn, were followed by a cruise to the Norwegian fjords from Southampton before returning to New York for the fourth of the 150th Anniversary cruises.

However, before the final celebratory cruise could take place the cruise to the fjords caused some excitement which was created by the adverse weather conditions experienced *en-route* to Bergen. The following is an extract from the ship's Logbook from midday on 20th August:

"1200 Wind NW Force 9. Barometer 1007.1 and falling. High bow sea, steep beam swell. Rolling and pitching. Moderately overcast. Spraying overall.

"1235 Mayday message received by automatic radio receiver on Bridge.

"1257 Confirmation message received from radio, Denmark, stating that Norwegian oil drilling platform *West Gamma* (LFQX [call sign])situated in the Gorm oil field, Danish Sector, and eight miles from pumping station *Bravo 11*, was in distress. Rig helicopter landing platform and some lifesaving appliances were destroyed.

Rig was adrift with 49 persons on board and requested assistance.

"1250 *QE2* reported present position and offered assistance.

"1300 Estimated position oil rig Latitude 55°23' N, Longitude 04°46' E and drifting 115° at 5 knots.

"1335 Telephone contact made with Farsund radio and *QE2* requested to proceed to area and to act as on-scene resue commander.

"1346 *QE2* alters course to 067° and proceeds at full speed to distress area approximately 47 miles away.

"1348 Captain (Ronald Warwick) makes broadcast to passengers informing them of the situation......

"1415 Helicopter landing area on board *QE2* cleared and prepared for landing operations. Radio communications link established.

"1420 Further situation report made to passengers by Captain.

"1441 Report received from Danish rescue co-ordinating centre that helicopters were hovering over oil rig and that conditions were beginning to look more stable.

"1500 Updated distress position received.

"1505 Communications received from Denmark that the crew did not wish to leave *West Gamma*. One helicopter remaining on scene. *QE2* requested to still proceed to area.

"1535 Wind NW, Force 9; visibility 3.3. miles.

"1539 Situation report made to Cunard Line, New York.

"1540 Tug reported to be on scene.

"1600 Rescue vessel *Esbjerg Omega* reported on scene. Weather - wind NW, Force 9; barometer 1023,3(sic)mb and falling. High seas, moderate to high swell, overcast with drizzle.

"1605 Rig *West Gamma* sighted.

"1610 Situation report made to passengers.

A panoramic view of the New York waterfront as *QE2* backs out from her berth into the Hudson River prior to her transatlantic crossing to cruise around Ireland and Great Britain.   *Richard Weiss*

"1615 *QE2* reduced speed and manoeuvres near rig.

"1623 *QE2* communicates with *Esbjerg Omega* and is informed that crew do not wish to be evacuated from *West Gamma*. *QE2* is released by *West Gamma* and resumes passage to Bergen.

"1624 Situation report made to passengers.

"2000 Weather - wind NW, Force 9 to 10; barometer 1001.5mb and steady; rough bow sea and heavy swell; overcast with rain".

After midnight the miserable weather began to moderate and the *QE2* increased her cruising speed to arrive at Bergen practically on schedule. However, news reached the ship that the rig *West Gamma* had eventually capsized and that the crew had sought refuge in the sea from where they were rescued. One of the boats being used in the rescue had capsized but happily no lives were lost.

The *Queen Elizabeth 2* seemed to come through the ordeal in the North Sea unscathed although a casualty occurred in the Mauretania Restaurant where the large model of the venerable four-funnelled liner (after which the restaurant had been named) fell over in its case snapping funnels, masts and rigging. The model would later be sent ashore for repair by Southampton model-maker, John Lindsay, before being returned to the ship where it still remains. The broken pieces of mast were expertly pinned together rather than a new mast being made.

The final, fourth cruise of the Cunard 150th celebration series started with a 1st September sailing from New York and consisted of a four-night round trip to Boston and Halifax, Nova Scotia, returning to New York on 5th September. This cruise commemorated the ports of call used by Samuel Cunard's first paddle steamer, the 1,135 ton *Britannia*, on her maiden voyage in 1840 which inaugurated the Cunard Line's remarkable one hundred and fifty years of service on the North Atlantic.

September brought some unhappy news when it was announced that the former Master of the *Queen Elizabeth 2*, Captain Alan Bennell, who had relinquished his post earlier in the year, had died on the 19th at the age of 58 from mesothelioma, a cancer caused by asbestos. A memorial service held in Southampton was followed by the scattering of the Captain's ashes by his wife at sea from his beloved *QE2*. Both services were officiated by Bishop Harold Robinson of New York.

The remainder of 1990 was spent cruising to the Atlantic Isles, to the Caribbean or voyaging the North Atlantic.

On many sailings the *QE2* would carry not only those wishing to cruise as individuals but also groups and organisations making block bookings, wanting to make a special occasion even more so.

One such cruise catered for the Young Presidents' Organisation, an exclusive group of the most wealthy, young American corporate presidents (including the US Presidents son, George Bush junior, himself to become a future US President). The cruise chosen was one in October, 1990, sailing to the Canary Islands and calling at Lisbon in Portugal on the return to Southampton. Here, for the two day trip to the United Kingdom, South Africas then President F. W. de Klerk and his wife joined the liner for a double purpose: to address the YPO and to travel to England for talks with Prime Minister Margaret Thatcher.

On arrival at Southampton Captain Woodall - who had found President de Klerk (who was bravely in the process of dismantling the insiduous system of Apartheid in his country) to be a most "...charming gentleman...a man of vision.." - escorted "F.W." off the ship to waiting helicopters on the dockside. Protesters tried to rush the President but, unflinchingly, he continued on to the aircraft whilst his security men dealt with any problems.

Two weeks refit at Lloydwerft's yard in Germany started on 2nd December, the ship returning to Southampton on 16th December. During this refit several cabins were upgraded and a new grill, the Princess Grill Starboard, was created to serve them.

New Year's Eve 1991 found the liner at sea between St. Maarten and St. Thomas during a 14-day Caribbean cruise. A shorter cruise to the same waters followed until her World Cruise, "New York to New York", started on 15th

January. The cruise was hurriedly reorganised *en-route* as, because of the advent of the Gulf War, the *Queen's* transition of the Suez Canal and subsequent cruise through the Mediterranean were cancelled, a detour being made around Africa via Durban, Cape Town, Walvis Bay, Freetown, Dakar, Tenerife and Gibraltar. Her call into Lisbon brought the Cunarder back into her schedule.

1991 was otherwise a relatively quiet year for the *Queen Elizabeth 2* as she carried out her demanding schedule without too much in the way of untoward events - undoubtedly the way that her operators would wish!

But, as usual, the *Queen* did not stay out of the headlines for very long!

Another royal event occurred on board on 15th June when HRH Prince Edward hosted a party on board to mark the 35th anniversary of his father's, HRH The Duke of Edinburgh, Award Scheme (of which the Prince was chairman of the Awards Special Projects Group) which promoted and encouraged enthusiasm in young people from all walks of life.

A special train was chartered from London to bring the eight hundred and sixty guests, paying £280 for a pair of tickets for the Royal Gala, down to Southampton. A seven-course dinner was enjoyed and the revelling continued until the early hours of the morning and, because of the lateness of the *de-rigeur* fireworks (11.30pm), several complaints were received from the local populace! An early 4am breakfast was served on the ship before the party-goers were dispatched back to London, many of them sleeping on the homeward train! Considerable amounts of money had been raised during the Gala for The Duke of Edinburgh's Award Scheme, including monies from raffle tickets that had been sold at £10 each. It was not disclosed at what times the Duke or the Prince had left their own party!

The Autumn brought another unpleasant episode into the *QE2's* routine when she arrived in England on 3rd August. Because of reduced profit margins caused by the Gulf War and the recession in its various operations Trafalgar House had announced that the remaining British ratings on the *QE2* were to be laid off and, once again, cheaper foreign labour employed in their place.

Union officials of the National Union of Rail, Maritime and Transport Workers were incensed that one hundred and fifty deck and engine room ratings were to be dismissed and the union's Executive Officer, Sam McCluskie, threatened to write to HM The Queen to request her to take away the liner's royal appellation. The Palace said that it was a matter for Cunard who, in turn, said that they were employing Third World staff to do menial tasks that European staff refused to do (and at about one third the cost!) The ships staff would still be about 70% European including many Britons.

In the Houses of Parliament the Shadow Transport Secretary, John Prescott, wrote to Prime Minister John Major requesting him to intervene in the dispute: "The *QE2* was the jewel in the crown of the British merchant fleet - the safest, fastest and most luxurious liner in the world and we are giving it to foreign labour!"

Eventually, by the end of the month, an agreement was reached with the British ratings who had been dismissed

HRH Prince Edward is presented to distinguished members of the ship's staff by a beaming Captain John Burton-Hall during a special function held on board the ship.

Eric Flounders/Cunard

being given packages that included a year's salary plus an additional £1,500 for each year served.

Sailing back into more peaceful waters, the *QE2* left New York in early September to make a short cruise up the eastern seaboard. On board on this occasion was a party from Titanic International, one of the American groups of *Titanic* enthusiasts which, during the course of the short trip, befriended the Captain who allowed them to fly the red, swallow-tail burgee bearing a five-pointed white star from the ship's mainmast for a short while. This had been the house flag of the old White Star Line, owners of the ill-fated liner, and which had almagamated with Cunard in the 1930's to become the Cunard-White Star Line. However, it had been a long time since the red and white burgee had been flown from any of the company's ships. The White Star flag that had been kept in the *QE2's* Flag Locker had disappeared several years previously only to reappear in a Southampton memorabilia shop!

The group, including 83-year old *Titanic* survivor Louise Pope (nee-Kink), were on their way to Halifax, Nova Scotia, where many of the victims from the *Titanic* tragedy had been buried after the recovery of their bodies from the sea in 1912. Several so far anonymous graves had been identified by the Society, the members of which were on their way to rededicate the graves in an officially recognised ceremony.

When he heard of their intentions, Captain Robin

During the transition of crew from mainly British to foreign employees John Prescott MP traveled to Southampton to address the Union members of the crew. The Executive Officer of the National Union of Rail, Maritime and Transport Workers, Sam McCluskie, sits to the Member of Parliament's right.

Southern Newspapers

Woodall contacted Cunard and received permission to his request that he represent the company at the forthcoming ceremony as one of the company's ships, the *Carpathia*, had rescued survivors a few hours after the wreck. Permission was readily given.

With ocean-going yachts completing the 1993-94 Round-The-World Southampton to Southampton Whitbread yacht race the *QE2* made a splendid addition to an already spectacular sight as she sailed up through Southampton Water. Ahead of her is the maxi-ketch *New Zealand Endeavour*, skippered by Grant Dalton, the ultimate winner of the grueling race.

Colin M. Baxter

Chapter Eighteen

Rumours and Rocks

The year 1992 started off well with another successful World Cruise being completed and a varying programme of cruises from both Southampton and New York had been planned for the *Queen Elizabeth 2* over the rest of the year.

Shortly after her arrival from the World Cruise the *QE2* was the venue for another anniversary. This time it was ten years since the Falklands War had been fought and, to commemorate the event, Margaret Thatcher, British Prime Minister at the time, was to be guest of honour on the ship that had acted as a troop transport during the conflict.

So, on 10th May, the former Prime Minister - along with Brigadier General Sir Jeremy Moore (commander of the land forces in the Falklands); Captain Peter Jackson who had commanded the liner on her perilous journey to the war zone and three hundred other guests boarded the ship as she lay alongside the Queen Elizabeth II Terminal in Southampton.

A six-course luncheon was enjoyed and after Sir Nigel Broackes, Chairman of Trafalgar House, had toasted "Her Majesty's Armed Forces and the Merchant Navy" Margaret Thatcher (described by a ship's officer as "...a very formidable lady...did not suffer fools gladly...very determined and forthright...") made a response in which she both praised the role played by *Queen Elizabeth 2* and described the time that the Falklands incident turned into war as the "....worst night of my life!"

A few days after Sir Nigel's brave toast there were rumours that Trafalgar House were proposing to sell the Cunard. The rumours, denied by the holding company, were soon to be confirmed as Trafalgar House declared a fall in profits and announced that they had decided to concentrate on construction and engineering.

In June the ship made a call into Torbay for a few hours where she anchored to officiate at the start of the annual yachting "Triangle Race", becoming the biggest "Committee Boat" ever! Passengers did not go ashore although local civic dignitaries came out to the ship for a reception to celebrate the towns bicentenary.

Carrying on as usual *Queen Elizabeth 2* had been scheduled to make a transatlantic from Southampton on 29th July prior to a cruise to Bermuda from New York. Returning in reverse order the ship would arrive back in Southampton fifteen days later.

However, the Bermuda leg of the cruise was cancelled due an unexpected refusal by the Bermudan authorities to grant the required licences and the vessel was therefore re-scheduled to again make a north-about cruise up the eastern seaboard of the North American continent. Sailing from New York on 3rd August, the ship made calls at Bar Harbour; St. Johns, Newfoundland; Halifax, Nova Scotia and Marthas Vineyard before returning to New York to resume her schedule with her advertised sailing to Southampton on 13th August. Cunard's initial disappointment over the cancellation of the Bermudan visit must have been short-lived as, with 1,824 passengers on board, the ship was almost full.

The cruise had been reasonably uneventful as the liner started on the last part of her trip back to New York. Having

Followed by Captain Robin Woodall (left) and Relief Captain Ron Warwick, Margaret Thatcher visited the *QE2* on the 10th Anniversary of the Falklands Crisis during which time Mrs Thatcher had been Prime Minister.   *Cunard*

anchored off Oak Bluffs, her final port of call for this cruise, on the north-east tip of the island of Marthas Vineyard the vessel weighed anchor just after 8.45pm, a little later than had been planned, on the fine, clear, moonlit evening of 7th August. A southerly breeze of 5 to 10 knots was blowing but, as the ship's speed gradually increased, the apparent on-board wind speed also increased as it combined with her own forward motion.

Taking a sight on Nobska Point (nearby to Woods Hole and its Oceanographic Institute) on the coast of the mainland to the north-west the liner turned to port on a course of 237° to sail on a slightly varying course through Vineyard Sound to the east of the island.

The *QE2* continued in a south-west direction, navigated by Second Officer of the Watch John McKie with Captain Robin Woodall and the Staff Captain also on the Bridge. An experienced US pilot, Captain John F. Hadley, had previously taken over the con of the ship from Captain Woodall. It was assumed by the Pilot that he would follow the same route to exit the Sound that he had used when he took the ship in when arriving earlier that day. He later changed his mind.

The Pilot had earlier told the Captain of the position where he wanted to disembark from the liner and, to get to this position from the southern end of Vineyard Sound, two courses had been worked out: one by the ship's Navigator and the other by the Pilot who kept his course in his mind. Neither knew of the others intentions.

At 9.20pm, shortly after passing Woods Hole, the ship's speed was gradually brought up to nearly 25 knots from the earlier 17.5 knots as the Captain did not want a late arrival in New York after the delayed departure from Oak Bluffs. The Pilot, knowing of the Captain's eagerness to arrive at New York on schedule, readily agreed to the increase of speed.

Towards the southern end of Vineyard Sound was a marker buoy known simply as "NA" and which lay about two miles Southwest of Nashawena Island. Here, at 9.40pm, the course of the QE2 was slightly altered to starboard to follow the Pilot's intended route to his disembarkation point.

About four miles further on from the "NA" marker the QE2 again changed course, this time to port. None of those on the Bridge were unduly concerned and did not see any cause to express their thoughts to each other until the Second Officer realised, after making a projected plot from the course required by the Pilot (and as indicated on the radar) that the ship would be sailing over the Sow and Pigs Reef that extended out from Cuttyhunk Island. The officer told the Captain of his findings who then, wishing to go South of the shoal, discussed the situation with the Pilot.

The Pilot aquiesced and the ship was turned to the Southwest, about half-a-mile before the Pilot's own planned point of turn that would take the ship over the 7 to 9-fathom neck of the shoal.

There were several shoals in the vicinity and these had been indicated by hatching on the relevant chart by the Navigator before the cruise to highlight their presence. But crucially, the hatching on one such patch had not been transferred onto the adjacent chart which was now being used on the Bridge.

If this patch of hatching had been transferred it would have drawn the busy attention of those on the Bridge to the shallow, but adequate, depth of water over the varying 7 to 9-fathom shoal and it would have also had indicated a small peak of even shallower water of 6-fathoms 3-feet (39 feet) plus - the Captain had evidently thought - 2-feet of tide (it was later suggested that there may have been in fact only 6-inches of tide at the time) to the South of the Southern-most tip of the Sow and Pigs Reef. The Pilot knew that this reduced depth of water existed in this area but he also knew that even there the shoal still had sufficient depth of water to allow the minimum of just over the 40-feet that he had stipulated for the safety of the ship which was drawing 32-feet 4-inches forward and 31-feet 4-inches aft. The charts being used were based on information gathered fifty years previously - rather surprising as the Woods Hole Oceanographic Institute was only a few miles away!

A few minutes before 10pm the Queen Elizabeth 2 had reached a point approximately 3.5 miles SSW of Cuttyhunk

Island and was about to pass over the southern tip of the shoaling seabed as she prepared to skirt the main areas of the reefs.

Many of the passengers on board QE2 were taking a late dinner when, at two minutes before ten o'clock a noticeable vibration pulsated throughout the ship which was quickly followed by a second, more violent sensation. A group of waiters serenading an anniversary couple evidently did not falter in their song and, according to reports, the band played on in the best tradition! The engines began to slow.

The Queen Elizabeth 2 began to lose way as her Captain ordered the controllable pitch propellers to be feathered to zero pitch. On the Bridge three thoughts in quick succession sped through Captain Woodall's mind as he ordered the ship to stop after the second vibration: "My first thought was that it was a catastrophic machinery failure; an engine broken loose or a propeller come off!" The last thing that he thought of was of the liner going aground as his previous glances at the chart had shown adequate water beneath his ship. A return to the navigational documents that mariners rely on still made the Captain momentarily disbelieve that his ship had impacted with the bottom.

A call to the Engine Control Room quickly dispelt any idea of a mechanical breakdown as the propeller shafts were still turning at 144rpm (although the controllable pitch propellers had had their forward thrust zero-ed) and the First Officer on the Bridge dismissed any idea that the ship had been involved in a collision. As the grounding of the liner seemed to be the only plausible explanation left the Captain ordered that the engineers should sound the double bottom tanks for any evidence of flooding.

The senior officers of the ship had by now arrived on the Bridge and the Chief Officer was sent on a tour to inspect all compartments that might be affected for signs of damage. Several minutes after the two vibrations had alerted both passengers and crew that something had happened to the ship, and on the Captain's instruction, the Staff Captain made an announcement over the ship's broadcast system explaining that the liner had passed through shallow water and that the vibrations that she had experienced had been caused by "Shallow Water Effect". In the later American official report on the grounding the officer was reported by the passengers as saying: "Ladies and Gentlemen, we seem to have struck an unidentified underwater object. There is no apparent damage to the vessel and no cause for concern; the ship is perfectly safe". At least, Captain Woodall was one of those in command of the ship who, over the years, felt it prudent to keep his passengers aware of what was happening around them. In some previous cases the lack of such information had been the cause of much concern and many complaints.

The Queen Elizabeth 2's gradual loss of headway also meant that she had lost steerageway (ie insufficient rate of forward movement to respond to her rudder) and was

QE2 hit the headlines after hitting the rocks! Oil containment booms can be seen streaming out astern.

therefore drifting. Captain Woodall ordered "Slow ahead" until the liner achieved a manouevrable speed of 4 knots.

Initial damage assessment showed that a sounding pipe to No 1 Saltwater double-bottom ballast tank had been fractured and water was gushing into the forward Tunnel space. A tapered, damage control wooden plug was forced into the pipe to arrest the flow before the floodwater in the tank could be pumped out.

The previously empty No 10 fuel oil overflow tank in the double bottom had also filled and an officer was sent aft to see whether any traces of residue oil were contaminating the ship's wake. The discovered seepage was reported to the US Coast Guard when a further report was made, the initial report being made forty minutes after the grounding.

A cofferdam, (between Nos 13, 14 and 15 freshwater d.b. tanks - the latter two later found to be contaminated by seawater - and Nos 8, 9 and 10 fuel oil tanks) was also found to be full. The tank top at the bottom of No 3 Hold was discovered to be buckled, possibly from the pressure of the air being compressed by the ingress of water and a damage control team was sent to wedge sturdy wooden shoring between the deck and deckhead in an attempt to prevent any likelihood of the tank-top rupturing under the tremendous pressure with a subsequent flooding of the compartment above.

Meanwhile, at 8.55pm, the Coast Guard had ordered the *Queen Elizabeth 2* to proceed to an anchorage in Rhode Island Sound, almost 11.5 miles west-southwest of Gay Head, the southerly point on Marthas Vineyard, and 20 miles southeast of Newport, Rhode Island. No 11 boat, one of the ship's passenger launches, was launched to check for oil leaks (the presence of which could be smelled) and the Master informed the passengers that the ship had actually grounded and that she would remain anchored at least until morning. Some passengers retired to the bars as, undoubtedly, the drinks were on Cunard that night!

Just after 2am the Coast Guard vessel *Bittersweet* arrived on site and Coastguards boarded the vessel. Because the ship was carrying 923,454 gallons of oil fuel, of which there was a danger of 38,500 gallons leaking, the Coastguards prudently ordered one of their cutters to rig an oil containment boom from amidships on one side of the QE2, around her stern to amidships on the other side. The oil in doubt was secured when it was pumped into another tank.

Shortly after the grounding the US Coast Guard requested that a nurse be sent out from the shore to subject the Captain, First Officer and the Pilot to drug and alcohol tests as required under American law. (After testing the samples in Salt Lake City it was reported that only low levels of caffeine had been found!) The other three watchkeepers on the Bridge were not tested until later as they were, by then, too busy assisting in ferrying passengers ashore.

It had been decided that the passengers would have to be disembarked and, after divers had carried out an underwater survey of the QE2's hull at the request of Cunard, five hundred and fifty five passengers boarded a small passenger vessel, the *Schamonci*, and taken to nearby Newport. The vessel only made one trip and, because no other such vessels were available, Captain Woodall sought permission to take his ship closer in to Newport. The request was granted and the *Queen Elizabeth 2* moved to another

anchorage, mooring about 0.7 mile north of Brenton Reef Light.

The liner was now able to use four of her own lifeboats (Numbers 9 to 12) and also her own tenders, *Alpha* and *Beta*, to tranship passengers ashore. Two local ferries, *Viking Queen* and *Spirit of Newport*, also helped in the disembarkation process and by 2.20am on 9th August all passengers were safely ashore, including veteran film actor George Kennedy, Tom Clancy (author of "The Hunt For Red October") and British Member of Parliament Neville Trotter. Passengers were then bussed or entrained to New York. A Cunard official nicely described the evacuation of the liner as a termination of the voyage rather than an abandonment of the ship.

The oil protection boom was removed (the ship had mercifully only lost an estimated 30 gallons of oil) and prior to the QE2 weighing anchor and, in the company of a Coast Guard cutter and two tugs, sailed for Boston, Massachusetts, at around 8 knots. She arrived there after a nine hour and twenty-six minute journey to be dry-docked for survey and, as it turned out to be, temporary repairs.

The *Queen Elizabeth 2* was drydocked at the South Boston yard of the General Ship Corporation and the previously surveyed damage to her hull was confirmed once the dock was pumped dry.

The damage was extensive. Extending over a length of 400 feet aft from the bulbous bow the collision damage covered a width of 80 feet over the keel and either side of it and consisted of indents - some up to 240 feet in length and 14 inches deep - gouges and fractures. Twenty inner bottom tanks - mostly empty or carrying fresh water - had been damaged to some extent although one, No 10, an empty fuel tank, was the only tank to have leaked a small amount of oil residue at the time. The fractures in way of some of the indents were from 10 to 70 feet long and a 32 foot length of the port bilge keel had been severely damaged during the grounding.

Internally some of the transverse floors and longitudinals (both structurally important upright "walls" that comprise a ships cellular double bottom) were damaged by buckling and only in No 3 cargo hold was the deck bulging inboard, possibly as a result of the flooding.

The site of the grounding on Sow and Pigs Reef was also located and surveyed. The 1939 sounding of 6 fathoms 3 feet was found to be dangerously reduced by the presence of rocks that had stood up to 2.8 feet proud of the seabed. Signs of contact were evident as traces of red anti-fouling paint and shavings of steel (on analysis found to match those

A powerful impression of the 'business end' of the ship as she rests in a floating dock.

Cunard

Above left: The *QE2* was urgently dry-docked in Boston, Massachusetts, where the enormous scale of the underwater damage could be ascertained. *Above right:* The *Queen* suffered massive damage to her hull that lesser ships might not have survived. Curiously, Cunard were reluctant to release information about the incident.

Photographs courtesy of George J.G. Wolseley

materials from the *QE2*) were found on several of the rocks which had either been moved bodily horizontally, compressed into the seafloor or partially pulled out of the seabed by almost a foot.

The resultant reduction in the depth of water over the shoal had been exacerbated by the *Queen* as she passed overhead. This had been due to an effect known as "Squat" which is caused by a ship moving through shallow water and displacing more water than would be the case in deeper seas. Although the ships draught remains unaffected the clearance between keel and seabed is reduced according to the speed at which the vessel is moving. In the case of *QE2* it had been thought that she would squat around 3-feet at 10 knots and this, because of the lack of such information provided on board, was probably the figure that was in mind before the time of grounding.

The Captain's own estimate of the squat value was in the region of 18 inches to 2-feet as he later conducted trials over "...a level and well chartered channel...." (at the entrance to the US Navy yard at Newport News) at varying speeds up to 25-knots whilst observing the depths of water under his ship.

However, she had been travelling at nearly 25 knots over an "uphill" seabed which would increase the effect of squatting and subsequently, at that speed, the squat was calculated to be in the region of at least 6.5 feet. No wonder that the ship had "run out of water"! By her grounding *Queen Elizabeth 2* had almost continued a family tradition by following her illustrious predecessors: *Queen Mary* had grounded in Cherbourg harbour in 1949; *Queen Elizabeth* was stuck on a sandbank off Calshot in 1947 and the four-funnelled *Aquitania* had grounded on another sandbank in The Solent in 1935!

It had initially been hoped to complete the repairs at Boston but it became apparent that the rundown of the industry in that city over the years had deprived it of sufficient staff and resources to do the complete job. Many shipyard workers who had been unemployed found at least

three weeks work on the ship, even completing the temporary repairs ten days ahead of schedule. The time-scale factor along with the non-availability of the correct grade of steel led to the Captain, Cunard, Lloyds Classification Society, the British Department of Transport and the US Coast Guards making a conscious decision to transfer the ship to another yard and, as a result, put out invitations to tender for the work.

The Boston yard had done a good job - as Captain Woodall said later: "The quality of the work...was excellent". Leaving Boston on 1st September the ship sailed for the German shipyard of Blohm + Voss in Hamburg.

To smooth the *Queen Elizabeth 2*'s passage across the Atlantic advice had been sought from the British Meteorological Office in Bracknell in order to avoid those sea and wind conditions that the ship might best avoid. The advised route was straight across and, because of the good weather - a moderate sea and a moderate swell - and the excellent repair job that had been made in Boston, the ship was able to safely sail eastwards at 24 knots.

On arrival in Hamburg the liner was lifted in a floating dock and full repairs were undertaken. Strangely, Cunard seemed to be reluctant about talking publicly about the

High and dry in Blohm + Voss' floating dock in Hamburg, permanent repairs were made to the *Queen*.

Southampton gave a jubilant and thankful welcome to its heroine as the *QE2* returned from Germany after hull repairs to the damage caused by her grounding. Here the *Queen* has just passed the power station at Calshot and the Fawley oil-refinery. The Solent and the shores of the Isle of Wight recede into the distance. Repairs had cost £8m and lost revenue of nearly $50m.   *Southern Newspapers*

accident although in their ship they certainly had something to be proud of. Any lesser vessel could possibly have become a total loss after such punishment; but their *Queen* had survived her ordeal and remained as popular as ever.

Two investigations were subsequently held, one by the British Marine Accident Branch of the Department of Transport whilst the *QE2* was en-route for Boston and the other in the United States by the National Transportation Safety Board on the ship's arrival in the Massachusetts port. Their conclusions and recommendations were quite similar, concentrating on the provision of more information on squat; improvements in Bridge conferences between pilots and masters; the current value of charts of other nations; safety (passengers who had joined *QE2* in Halifax were not given a comprehensive briefing or an emergency drill); and the Americans also wanted a tightening-up of their own toxicology testing procedures. In spite of the American reports strict tone, the President of the Court of Inquiry said that he wished to comment on the "....professionalism and outstanding ability of all the personnel on *Queen Elizabeth*

2..." and that the crew had "...reacted favourably .." and that he had "...no criticism of their actions whatsoever".

Several cruises had been cancelled as a result of the accident and the total cost to Cunard and their insurers - taking into account compensatory travel vouchers issued to the passengers of the terminated cruise, the Boston repairs, full repairs in Germany and the loss of income through seven cancelled cruises (ten thousand refunds had to made) - was reported to be in the region of at least £30 million. To add to their troubles Trafalgar House were fighting off a bid from financial giant HongKong Land, a 32 per cent associate of the Jardine Group.

On completion of the extensive repairs *Queen Elizabeth 2* arrived back in her home port of Southampton to a heroines welcome on 3rd October. Three tugs met her at Calshot and, with water plumes cascading skywards in greeting, escorted her in well-earned triumph up through Southampton Water, many Sotonians turning out to welcome her home at the end of yet another chapter in her remarkable life.

Chapter Nineteen

Towards a Third Decade

During the *Queen Elizabeth 2*'s absence from Southampton a local group of business men, councillors and authors had encouraged shipping giant Sea Containers to put in a bid for the veteran Cunard liner *Queen Mary*, then in retirement at Long Beach but up for sale. A £15-million bid was put forward under the aegis of "Project *Queen Mary*". Proposals included using the old Cunarder as an overnight hotel for the *QE2* after shipping passengers from London on the prestigious Orient Express. The ship was eventually taken off the market and the bid was withdrawn.

However, the plans had awoken the local government to the fact that there was not an example of the type of ship that had helped Southampton to prosper so the city fathers put forward a proposal to berth *Queen Elizabeth 2* alongside Mayflower Park once she was retired by Cunard. This plan, too, would come to nought as Cunard was not ready to relinquish their prized asset just at the moment!

Queen Elizabeth 2 started her first post-repair cruise on 4th October, the day after arriving back in Southampton from Hamburg - an eight-day, Sunday-to-Sunday cruise to Spain, Portugal and Gibraltar. Strangely, it was called a "Western Mediterranean Cruise" and special discounts were offered to those who were celebrating wedding anniversaries. One special couple on the cruise were Sunnie and Jackie Mann. Jackie Mann, still looking frail after his lengthy ordeal as an hostage in Beirut, boarded the liner in a wheelchair. A series of other cruises by or around the Iberian Peninsula or down the western coast of the United States completed her 1992 schedule but was punctuated by a £4.5-million refit in Germany from 28th November to 14th December. The refit saw the replacement of one of the engines and the addition of new carpeting. Two purple and gold carpets bearing the ships famous intials surrounded by laurel leaves supported by a ribbon bearing the legend "Cunard" were fitted. As passengers did not perhaps need reminding that they were on the most famous ship in the world these somewhat overstated carpets were mercifully removed in a later refit. The year finished with a 21-day Christmas and Caribbean cruise.

The start of the New Year saw Sir Nigel Broackes ousted as chairman of Trafalgar House, being replaced by Alan Clements just before HongKong Land eventually won their fight for control of Trafalgar House. Under the new

The *Queen* rounds East Cowes off Osborne Bay in 1993.   *Author*

management Cunard briefly expanded their fleet by making purchases of "second-hand" but excellent tonnage which did not exactly give the impression of a united, co-ordinated fleet.

Queen Elizabeth 2 had arrived back in New York on 3rd January and had sailed the same day on her 1993 World Cruise entitled "Historical Wonders and Vibrant Cities". From New York the ship would make calls in the Caribbean, the east coast of South America and then Port Stanley in the Falkland Islands although she did not actually visit this area during the war of 1982. For this part of the cruise Captain Peter Jackson (who had commanded the *QE2* during the crisis) embarked at Rio De Janeiro to talk to the passengers of his experiences at the time.

The *Queen* then sailed around Cape Horn and up the South American west coast to Los Angeles before making a circumnavigation of the Pacific, returning through the Panama Canal to New York and then to Southampton, arriving there on 22nd April. During her absence the RAC had awarded the *Queen Elizabeth 2* their Five Star designation, an accolade normally only given to the finest hotels ashore.

In June 1953 a very young and beautiful Queen Elizabeth II had ascended the Throne of Great Britain and its Commonwealth and, to celebrate the fortieth anniversary of her Coronation, her youngest son, HRH Prince Edward, again looked to the ship (that his mother had launched) on which to hold another gala event.

The Prince joined the liner via helicopter being greeted on the *QE2*'s flight pad by Captain John Burton-Hall. The Prince toured the ship and mingled with the passengers boarding for a "Northern Capitals Cruise" to Edinburgh, Stavanger, Oslo and Copenhagen.

Also on board was a BBC Television film crew plus the main actors from the popular series "Keeping Up Appearances" as a Christmas Special was to be filmed during the course of the cruise. Talented actress Patricia Routledge was in character as the formidable "Hyacinth Bucket" and sat to the Prince's left at lunch with Mrs Burton-Hall to his right. Lord Patrick Lichfield, too, was embarked on this Coronation Anniversary cruise to present lectures on the British Monarchy.

Prince Edward was later taken off *Queen Elizabeth 2* by helicopter whilst the ship was at sea off Cornwall.

The *QE2* spent the rest of the summer uneventfully carrying out her schedule of cruises on either side of the Atlantic interspersed with transatlantic voyages. A 9-day cruise, "Land of the Midnight Sun", was carried out in July, the liner's route to the North Cape and ports along the way reflecting those famous cruises that had been undertaken by the "Millionaires' Yacht", the Cunarder *Caronia* - the fabled "Green Goddess" - in the 1950s and 60s. In those heady days passengers took the whole of the World Cruise, not just parts of it as many would in later years.

The 5th of August involved the *Queen Elizabeth 2* in a double celebration in Southampton. Her Majesty the Queen had travelled to the city port with her son, Prince Andrew, to join in the 175th anniversary of the British Sailor's Society that had been founded at the instigation of business and clergy interests in London to look after neglected sailors dismissed after the then long periods of naval warfare. An old naval wooden-wall, HMS *Speedy*, had been purchased and converted into a floating chapel, being moored at Wapping, and the Society commenced, as Her Majesty - the Patron of the Society - said during the commemoration, "...providing practical and down-to-earth help to seafarers everywhere".

After the service, attended by 3,000 specially invited guests, Her Majesty boarded the Royal Yacht *Britannia* to a twenty-one gun salute and progressed around the Port of Southampton accompanied by HMS *York* and the Trinity House Vessel *Patricia* to review various units of the Merchant Fleet, including the *Queen Elizabeth 2* alongside the QEII Terminal. Serenaded by the Yacht's band The Queen waved to the people lining the ship's rails and they waved back. The Royal Yacht then returned to Cowes for the remainder of the yachting Week.

An article in a popular magazine quoted "....oceanographers have lately noted that waves off the south coast at Lands End have grown a third taller over the past three decades, perhaps due to influences in the atmosphere". Not only had oceanographers noted this change but mariners, including Captain Woodall, had noted it too. And not just off Lands End. The Captain believed that the weather on the North Atlantic in general was getting worse : "No longer do we have just good old-fashioned 35-knot gales, they're all Force 10 now - storms, winds of 40, 50 knots". It was about to be proved.

Queen Elizabeth 2 had left New York for Southampton on 22nd September and before she had sailed the Captain informed the passengers, including entertainer Rolf Harris, that they were going to run into bad weather in the eastern Atlantic. Seamanlike precautions were taken to secure loose items, etc, as the ship got underway.

By four o'clock in the morning of 1st October the ship had run into a Force 8 to 9 ("...a nasty gale...") blowing in from the northwest by west. Although the seas were rough the *QE2* was riding them easily at 28.5 knots. By 8am the wind had increased slightly to Force 9 and was now from the northwest. The day was otherwise fine and sunny and passengers were on deck, some of them videoing the dramatic seas with waves from 25 to 30-feet high around the

Moored at Southampton in 1993. *Author* ship.

Then, around mid-morning, the *Queen Elizabeth 2* rolled 19º to starboard. Nothing, not even a passenger, fell over and the ship rolled easily. By noon the wind had gone back to northwest by west and the sea was still rough with a heavy swell.

Passengers Mrs Allflatt and her husband, returning home to the Isle of Wight, had just finished lunch in the Princess Grill when, without any warning, the ship heeled over to starboard. This time the inclinometer registered 21º - only 2º more than the morning's roll but the results were severe. Mrs Allflatt recalled "People and everything else slid across the floor. Two people were badly cut by breaking glass. Every piece of china and glass was broken and there was a tremendous noise from the kitchen....Glass-topped tables in the bars were broken and one grand piano was smashed....Gaming tables were overturned and the one-armed bandits were torn from their mountings". Structurally, however, the *QE2* was sound.

The *Queen* had apparently been hit by a wave that was probably steeper than its brethren or, as the Captain said, it could have been a rogue cross-swell that sometimes occur. He remembers: " The water just fell away from the starboard side of the ship... and she just fell into the hole!"

After the roll the liner recovered sharply and the resultant whip action caused most of the damage. A lot of furniture had rolled around and there were quite a few injuries with about fifty people receiving treatment for cuts and bruises. Two people suffered broken limbs.

Veteran but versatile entertainer Rolf Harris gave an impromptu concert to help allay the feelings of terror from which many of the passengers were suffering after the ship had taken everybody so much by surprise.

The liner carried on at 28.5 knots. During the evening the wind fell slightly to Force 8 and the ship was again riding comfortably. By the time the *QE2* reached the English Channel and The Solent the sun was shining and the sea was "...like a mill pond".

The liner arrived on time at Southampton and some of the injured were taken to hospital. Because of her speed the *QE2* had arrived on schedule so the press assumed that the accident had occured off Lands End and not to the southwest of Ireland where it had actually happened.

1993 finished for the *QE2* with her, almost by now traditional, Christmas and New Years Caribbean cruise.

Above left: The lady receives attention to her make-up prior to taking the Atlantic stage in August 1993.   *Author*
Below: Arriving at Liverpool in 1993 on a Round Britain cruise. *QE2* is one of the very few ships that can attract a crowd!

Chapter Twenty

D-Day and Disappointments

Ever since her introduction into service the *Queen Elizabeth 2* had undergone many refits, with both major as well as smaller changes being made. During this time her interiors had been subjected to a policy of piecemeal improvement and by 1994 her interiors lacked any unity of style.

Since the early '90s, the brochures issued by Cunard had used small vignettes, usually in a mock-art deco style, amongst the illustrations of public rooms, cabins and exotic ports-of-call to nostalgically recall the days of the golden era of when ocean liners - of which *Queen Elizabeth 2* was a late but superb example - were "The Only Way to Cross". Latterly amongst these evocative drawings were placed small reproductions showing old Cunard postcards, reflecting an awoken interest in the companys own history.

In the plans that were being formulated for the *QE2* (and which would be made public in the coming May) the interest shown in the history of Cunard (as exemplified in the 150th anniversary celebrations) would be exploited to the full and the theme of nostalgia would permeate much of the ship. The Mauretania Restaurant already did this with its

wonderful collection of photographs of the building of the restaurant's namesake and in the large, glass-encased model of the old liner displayed in the restaurant's midst.

But before this major announcement was made, the *QE2* was continuing her increasingly busy schedule. During her World Cruise it was reported that she had been in collision with one of the ferries that take commuters across Sydney Harbour. Apparently, the wash from the three tugs that were attending to the *Queen* apparently pushed the ferry against their huge counterpart.

At the beginning of the year *Queen Elizabeth 2* celebrated her three-millionth mile! A magnificent achievement that exceeded the total number of miles travelled by both of the old *Queen Mary* and *Queen Elizabeth*.

Then, a few months later, the ship was commemorating yet another anniversary and, deservedly again, it was another of her own! On 2nd May, 1969, and after many trials and tribulations, the *Queen Elizabeth 2* had left Southampton on her maiden voyage - the start of her active life. So it was "Happy Silver Anniversary, QE2!" and many of the hopes - if not all! - that had been wished for the

The *Queen Elizabeth 2* at the Queen Elizabeth II Terminal in her home port as seen from a tug in 1994.   *Doug Toogood*

ship at that time had been more than fulfilled. She had achieved one such hope in grand style as one sentiment expressed at the time of her inaugural voyage was that she would be good enough to last Cunard for at least twenty-five years! A thankful Silver Anniversary Gala dinner was held on board on 11th May and the famed Red Arrows flying formation team of the Royal Air Force gave her a spectacular display of their skills in Southampton. She then sailed on a special anniversary cruise to the Baltic in June.

June 1994 was a particularly important month for *Queen Elizabeth 2*. The fruits of many months of planning for a major refit would be announced and she would take a leading role in another very special review at Spithead.

The important Review was to be a spectacular but moving commemoration of the seaborn Allied Invasion of Normandy - "D-Day" - and would be held on 5th June to enable the memorial services to take place off the beaches off Normandy on the actual anniversary of the 6th.

Queen Elizabeth 2 had arrived in Southampton on 4th June from New York carrying guests and contingents of wartime veterans. Steaming up Southampton Water and slowing as she approached the port she had found herself being overtaken by the first contestants to finish the Whitbread Round the World Yacht Race that had started in Southampton the previous year.

Following some cold, wintry showers on what turned into the bright, windy evening that preceded the Review, the great ships started to assemble off Fort Gilkicker on the Hampshire coast near to Gosport. A few miles away in Portsmouth services of remembrance were being held on Southsea Common in a "Drumhead Service" attended by many heads of state and members of the British and other Royal Families.

Spectators on the shore had seen the United States Navys giant aircraft-carrier, the *USS George Washington* arrive a few days before the event and she was already anchored in the Number 2 position. Then, from the direction of Southampton came the *Vistafjord* and next to her anchored the restored Victory-ship *Jeremiah O'Brien* and the *USS Guam*. The ever-popular P&O liner *Canberra* also arrived from Southampton and she was soon followed by the same company's *Sea Princess* (later to be renamed *Victoria*) but she sailed by the assembling fleet on her way out on a cruise.

The United States Training Vessel *State of Maine* also arrived then, almost the last to arrive that evening, the *Queen Elizabeth 2* made a grand entry from Southampton and took her place in the Number 1 anchorage to the west of the fantastic line that was gathering in readiness for the next day's Review that would commemorate the gathering of the enormous Allied Invasion Fleet. These same waters had sheltered thousands of ships carrying tens of thousands of men and equipment of all kinds when they had assembled here in 1944.

5th June dawned slightly overcast but this cleared as the Royal Yacht *Britannia*, flying the Royal Standard to denote that Her Majesty Queen Elizabeth II was on board, and again led by the *THV Patricia*, left the South Railway Jetty in Portsmouth Dockyard. As she approached the entrance of the harbour several fly-pasts occured with many veteran aircraft from the Second World War flying in salute. One formation of twenty Hawk aircraft flew overhead forming the number "50" in honour of the anniversary being celebrated below them.

The aircraft went on to overfly the assembled ships and, as a special mark of distinction, the Royal Navy's venerable Swordfish bi-plane, streaming a White Ensign, flew past the *QE2* at Bridge height and its officer, standing in the aircraft's aft cockpit, stood and saluted the *Queen Elizabeth 2*.

The beaches overlooking Spithead and The Solent were thick with excited crowds and they were not to be disappointed with the spectacle unfolding before them. Other vessels had arrived and over eighty ships were there to be reviewed by the Royal squadron. The new cruise-ships *Seabourne Pride* and *Silver Cloud* sparkled brilliantly white in the sunlight and many representatives of navies and merchant ships of all sizes and nationalities from the mighty *QE2* to the small, restored steamship *Shieldhall*, all looked their best.

The Solent, too, looked its best in the late, bright Spring sunshine. A rather windy, slightly cloudy day, had created a lively chop and the green sea, banded in dark blue from cloud shadow, was literally churned into a mass of white foam as hundreds of small craft manouevred around the area hoping, perhaps, to catch a glimpse of HM the Queen and the Duke of Edinburgh and also perhaps Queen Elizabeth the Queen Mother; Diana, Princess of Wales; President Clinton; Prime Minister John Major and other world leaders on board the *Britannia*, as well as to see the wealth of shipping and to savour and understand the atmosphere of the day. There were many Heads of State present on this most noble of ocassions coming as they did from the United States, New Zealand, the Czech Republic, Australia, Poland, Norway and many other countries representing the fourteen nations who participated in the invasion.

After the Royal Yacht had sailed around

QE2 on the morning of the 50th Anniversary of D-Day. The liner was the last major vessel to arrive in The Solent for the event.

James Vinter

Profile showing the planned new livery that would be applied during the liner's 1994-95 major refit.   *Cunard*

the outer perimeter of the fleet, using the *QE2* as a marker to make her turn, the vessel with her royal passengers and very important guests made her way eastwards towards the Nab Tower, heading for Cherbourg. A mere eighteen days later an announcement was made that the magnificent Royal Yacht, a product of the same shipyard as the *QE2* and similarly a great ambassador overseas for Great Britain, would be decommissioned in 1997, subsequently to spend her retirement at Leith in Scotland.

The ships in the D-Day Commemoration Review dispersed and many, along with the *Canberra*, the *QE2* sailed for the waters off the Normandy Beaches.

The *Queen Elizabeth 2*'s ability for speed enabled her to overtake the *Britannia* and join the flotilla comprising "Operation Ramsay" (named after the Commander-in Chief of the operation in 1944) that would take its station for a mid-Channel review.

To the *Canberra* fell the honour of leading the mid-Channel service that would celebrate "Operation Neptune", the Allied Invasion of Europe, and to remember those who gave their lives during the Channel operations. During this ceremony the liner was showered with huge clouds of poppies dropped from a Lancaster aircraft.

Queen Elizabeth 2 made her way to Cherbourg (five other cruise ships would also dock there) where the US veterans that she was carrying disembarked for further events on French soil. Whilst she was in harbour a concert took place on board that was recorded for television. Wartime US journalist Walter Cronkite and the BBC's Richard Baker linked a programme which included comedian Bob Hope and singer Vera Lynn ("The Forces Sweetheart"), both of whom had entertained the troops during the War, popular singer Chris de Burgh and many others. The show was recorded mainly in the Grand Lounge and from a specially constructed stage on the Helicopter Deck, aft of the funnel.

Sailing from Cherbourg the next day the *Queen* headed for Le Havre. *En route* she passed by the Normandy beaches,

the scenes of so much bitter fighting and valour fifty years previously, and the Captain took his ship in towards the coast, as closely as he dare. The course that he took was the "Big Ship Gun Line" that the bombarding battleships used prior to the D-Day landings. Her subsequent departure from Le Havre was accompanied by a fireworks display.

One of the following Southampton arrivals of *Queen Elizabeth 2*, on 28th October, marked a very special occasion for her Captain. On his retirement Robin Woodall ("I've travelled 3,193,371 miles! That's not bad in 45 years!") left the ship to great applause and to three blasts from the siren of his companion and command of seven years (he had also been with her intermittently as an officer since he had stood by her during her fitting-out). He and his wife, Eileen, were driven to their home on The Wirral in a chauffeur driven Rolls Royce. One of his post-retirement ambitions? "... to go for a cruise on the *QE2*!"

John Burton-Hall became *Queen Elizabeth 2*'s Senior Captain with Keith Stanley and Ronald Warwick his Reliefs. The new Master, when still a Second Officer, had also stood by the "Q4" when she was building at Clydebank and then sailed with her on her maiden voyage. He would be the last captain in command to have done so.

The *Queen* made a "Round Britain" cruise in the August and her arrival on the Mersey on this ocassion was again received with a great deal of enthusiasm. As the ship departed accompanied by another flotilla of small craft in torrential rain the huge crowd of spectators on shore were delighted to hear the "Liverpool Sound" of the Beatles and Gerry & The Pacemakers (some 'Ferry 'Cross the Mersey' the great Cunarder made!) emanated from her broadcast system. Her second visit to the Clyde since her initial sailing on trials was accompanied by sunshine and, again, hundreds flocked to see her from the banks of the great river. Waterford and Brest completed the cruise before she returned to Southampton.

Many months of careful planning and of the

endeavours of many people in both artistic and technical fields came to a climax on 13th November when *Queen Elizabeth 2* arrived in New York and, after disembarking her passengers, was taken out of service and sailed directly to Blohm + Voss shipyard in on the River Elbe in Hamburg, Germany. Her scheduled sailing to Southampton did not materialise.

Here she was to have a radical refit involving her interiors (furnishings and layouts), structural alterations, and a new overall look. It would, as the publicists' had said earlier in the year when initial designs had been published, enable the ship to "....sail into the Twenty First Century....". It was also said that, as the *QE2* had been "....twenty-five years ahead of her time...", she had really caught up with herself and that it was time to enable her to compete in the market place not in direct competition with much younger, glitzier cruise ships but as a by-now classic liner in her own right.

For many weeks prior to the ship's withdrawal from paying passenger service contractors had systematically sealed off blocks of cabins and, after the cabins had been checked for "fibre", started to prepare the rooms for the forthcoming refurbishment and structural alterations. All 963 cabins were intended to have new bathrooms, a huge logistical undertaking in itself - and one that would lead to problems in the future weeks - and work was also planned to be undertaken on minor stairwells during these preceding voyages. From July, up to 120 skilled men completed preparations in sixty units in each ten-day period, and over three hundred items (many from other suppliers who in turn had to be sub-contracted) required for each cabin's update were stored in a dockside shed in Southampton in readiness for transference to the ship during her short turn-arounds.

At around this time the ship's doctor, Nigel Roberts, author in 1988 of "C-Six: Ten Years as the Doctor of the *QE2*" (C-Six being not only a pun for *mal-de-mer* but also the location of the ship's well-equipped hospital) was made "redundant". This was, he believed, a result of protesting against the lack of protection given to crew members during the removal of residue asbestos from the ship.

The refurbishment was planned to complete so that the *Queen Elizabeth 2* could undertake a two-day shake-down cruise before leaving Southampton on her scheduled 17th December sailing for New York prior to the start of her 1995 world cruise. £30-million was the expected cost of the whole work. The four weeks alloted was a very short time indeed for such a major job and left no room, it seemed, for delay. Accountancy appeared to have the upper hand once again over ship husbandry.

Two teams of specialist designers had been employed by Cunard to undertake the interior re-styling of their world-famous ship - MET Studio Ltd., and John McNeece Ltd., - both companies, a statement said, "...working together to create a unified design concept which will re-establish the rhythm and harmony of the ship's spaces in keeping with the spirit of this unique, ocean-going liner".

Both companies would also, continued the statement, "...work on aspects of the interior design, with MET Studio (MET was headed by Alex McCuaig who had begun his career with James Gardner, the original masterplanner for the ship) responsible for the masterplanning and interior design and (John) McNeece responsible for project management and (also) interior design". A unity of interior design and an easy flow of passengers were the keys to the new-look QE2.

Structurally the changes to the *Queen*'s internal layout

Always an impressive image, a mighty ocean liner high and dry in a floating dock.   *Cunard*

would reflect the foresight of her designers in arranging her public rooms (except for the theatre and the Grand Lounge, ex-Double Down Room) on one deck level which gave greater flexibility should the need arise to reconfigure these spaces. That time had arrived.

Included amongst the many changes planned were:

Sun Deck- a small bar and toilets aft of the superstructure block were built for the convenience of the sun worshippers using this delightful sheltered deck.

Boat Deck- additional shops were built around the well of the Grand Lounge, the "International Shopping Concourse" being renamed the "Royal Promenade" and the floors were given inlays of woods in compass form; the Conference Room was renamed the Boardroom; theatre balcony refurbished; and the Queen's Grill and Lounge were also refurbished.

Upper Deck- the Yacht Club Bar was destined to become even more popular with its refit. Expanding forward the Club extended to spaces previously occupied by the Tour Office, the Teen Club; whilst various toilets and stairways were dispensed with. A foyer to the Club was also built and would boast some of the Cunard Heritage Trail artefacts including a portrait of Samuel Cunard and the sumptuous silver loving cup (presented to him with other silver by the grateful citizens of Boston after the first arrival there of the paddler *Britannia*) that had been previously displayed in the Colombia Restaurant on Quarter Deck. The Players Casino, portside amidships was given a small bar and paintings of interiors of the *Queen Mary*; the Theatre Bar, starboard, was changed into a British pub, called the "Golden Lion" in honour of the rampant creature on the company's flag; and the after end of the Mauretania Restaurant disappeared to create a transverse meeting area, the Crystal Bar with *Art Deco* motifs, including a reproduction of a flying horse based on a relief previously used on the old *Queen Elizabeth*. A small, attractive stairwell was installed on the port side, to match that on the starboard side that served the Princess Grill Starboard (now renamed the Britannia Grill) to give access to the Princess Grill. The remainder of the Mauretania Restaurant underwent a remarkable transformation and was restyled to become the 580-seat Caronia Restaurant, decorated in a colour scheme to reflect the colours of the "Green Goddess". The partitions along each side were given large, glazed curves and a large aluminium sculpture by Althea Wynne was placed in the middle of the room. This depicted several horses in wave-like action and reflected the horse motifs used extensively on the *Caronia*, of 1949. A mural of the "Goddess" by Jane Human adorned the rooms forward bulkhead whilst the builders model of the *Caronia* along with her original builders plate and a superb painting of that ship at Cape Town by master marine artist Stephen Card greeted diners as they made their entrance.

Quarter Deck- the Magrodome that had been fitted over the Lido area in 1983 to make the swimming pool usable even on the Atlantic run was removed. This retractable cover had had a mixed reception; one of the main criticisms was that, after rain, the cover showered passengers with water when it was retracted! The Lido Cafe was decked over, the decking above providing additional sunning area; the pool was removed; and stairways were constructed to One Deck below to a new, airy, enclosed Pavilion self-service hamburger grill and bar overlooking the One Deck swimming pool. The Cafe would be used for informal dining and the famous Midnight Buffets! Self-service buffet bars port and starboard were replaced by a new Tour and Travel Office; a Social Director's Office; and new toilets.The twin stairways forward of the Grand Lounge were removed to

Above: The magnificent silver Loving Cup that was bestowed on Captain Woodruff of the Cunard paddle steamer *Britannia* by the grateful citizens of Boston, Massachusetts, in 1840. The cup's location outside the Yacht Club bar makes a splendid spot from which to start the on-board Heritage Trail that was installed during the 1994 refit. *Author*

Below: Decorating a panel in the Crystal Bar outside the 1994 Caronia Restaurant is this bas relief that reflects those installed on the *Queen Elizabeth* of 1939. *Author*

make way for a larger stage and a new, sprung dance floor was sited further aft towards the stage; a smaller stairway placed aft was in a similar position to the original spiral stairway of 1969 and the Lounge was refurbished to give better views of the stage. The tan-brown leather cubist armchairs were disposed of (one always had a propensity to slide out of them!) and replaced with smaller chairs in a light mustard yellow. Carpeting was also changed. Wood veneers lined the Lounge, reflecting a return to this traditional material in other areas of the ship. Forward again and, starboard, the Midships Bar (always dark and cosy with its green suede walls) was opened up and brightened with a new bar, more artefacts (including Captain Peter Jackson's sextant on a five-year loan); and a grand piano, hailing from the *Queen Mary*, transferred from the Midships Lobby. Port, the popular Library was extended forward using the Card Room to become the Book Shop, doubling the Library's overall capacity. A corridor leading to a stairway divided the two rooms. A vaulted, glazed ceiling gave one the feel of a social hall on a nineteenth century steamer. The *QE2's* Librarian remained the only full-time librarian at sea and a second would be employed. Columbia Restaurant became the 464-seat Mauretania, the latter having been transferred from the deck above. The large painting of the four-funnelled *Mauretania* was hung here having been transferred from a corner of the Quarter Deck outside the old Card Room entrance where it had been hopelessly out of scale with its surroundings. Princess and Britannia Grills completed the public rooms on this deck.

One Deck- the Beauty Salon was enlarged; and the Princess Grill (Port) Lounge was dispensed with as the attractive Crystal Bar on Upper Deck would suffice both Grills for pre-dinner cocktails.

Other than alterations to the *QE2* Spa and Gymnasium the other major alteration involved the spectacular, circular Midships Lobby which has always served both as the main entrance to the ship and as a room for small or recorded concerts whilst at sea. Built with a space-age ceiling and decorated in dark green and black it would be altered with wood burr veneered, quadrant balustrades enclosing the central recessed well. Long murals painted by Peter Sutton depicting events in the history of the Cunard Line in a montage style were displayed on the surrounding walls, giving embarking passengers an instant appreciation of the traditions that lay behind the company's history, including a picture of the "Q4" on the slip as shown earlier in this book. It had been intended to raise the ceiling of the Lobby through two decks with a balcony around the One Deck level but this (perhaps fortunately) did not happen.The *QE2* Computer Learning centre on this deck was also reduced in length.

Although it was regretted that, by now, the United Kingdom had lost the shipyards with the necessary skills to perform such work more than half of the workforce of skilled men came to Germany from Britain under contract. Blohm + Voss were ideally placed to undertake the work as they had worked on the *Queen* several times before. But Ron Connolly, Cunard's senior Technical Director, and others had misgivings about completing such a heavy workload in the short time available. Work continued around the clock and in crowded conditions on the ship as she lay in Floating Dock 11 in an attempt to meet the very tight deadline.

As with much construction and complex plumbing work (and ships notoriously present unexpected problems in such areas) the timetable for the refit fell enough behind schedule to delay the finishing trades (upholsterers, soft furnishings, etc) from starting their work and by the time that the *Queen Elizabeth 2* arrived in Southampton the work was far from complete. A lady writing to the London "Times" said "Sir, Renovations on our bathroom started in 1993, three weeks before Christmas.... I had my first shower in July 1994 and the floor has yet to be laid. I offer Cunard...... my heartfelt sympathies." Understanding came from other informed quarters (including journalist Alan Coren, the son of a plumber and himself a one-time plumbers mate, also writing in "The Times") but the Cunard management was criticised for demanding such heavy expectations from project managers in the various sub-contracting firms.

Plumbing work in some cabins was still being worked on; carpets in some areas lay still rolled; boxes - full and empty - were piled all over the ship; rubbish skips adorned the after decks ready for being craned off. Workmen and women were busy everywhere - sitting on floors sewing curtains, attempting to finish the Grand Lounge with scaffolding platforms filling the dancefloor; chairs and cardboard boxes crowding the Queen's Room.

Captain Ron Warwick toured his ship wearing a look of resigned disbelief. Meanwhile passengers were eagerly congregating in the Queen Elizabeth II Terminal ashore waiting to board the ship, not yet knowing that the seeming chaos that prevailed on board was worse than anticipated. Workmen could be seen through the ship's windows working on bunches of trailing cables that hung in bunches from open ceiling panels.

Originally a two-day celebration cruise to the English Channel had been scheduled on the ship's return to the UK on 14th December but this jaunt was yet another victim of the existing unhappy state of affairs.

Between 15th and 17th December stability tests were carried out, the ship being inclined with heavy weights moved from one side of the vessel to the other in order to establish her metacentric height.

Meanwhile, formalities still had to be observed and HRH Prince Andrew, The Duke of York, arrived at Southampton on sailing day, 17th December, to unveil two royal portraits temporarily sited in the Queen's Room for the occasion. The larger of these portraits was of HM Queen Elizabeth the Queen Mother (painted when she was still Queen), painted by Sir Oswald Birley, and had hung in the Main Lounge of the *Queen Elizabeth*. After that great ship's sale to American interests, the picture was given on permanent loan to Southampton City Council and hung in the Mayor's parlour.

The other painting, by Edward Halliday, portrayed Queen Elizabeth II when, as Princess Elizabeth, she had married Lieutenant Philip Mountbatten RN. The painting, mounted in a contemporary, specially carved frame, showed them arm-in-arm as the Duke and Duchess of Edinburgh and had been originally hung in the Main Lounge of the legendary *Caronia*. This latter oil-painting had also been handed into the care of Southampton's council on that ships decommissioning from Cunard and was eventually placed above the magnificent stairway inside the entrance hall of the town's post-war Civic Centre.

Twenty five years previously Cunard's deputy chairman, Lord Mancroft, had handed the paintings over to Southampton "...for all time". Now a Cunard spokesman said "They are Cunard's paintings and while we are happy for them to be in Southampton we feel that the *QE2* is the embodiment of Southampton". With that an intimation was dropped that the pictures would be returned to the city should the *QE2* be de-commissioned.

It nevertheless came as a blow to Southamptons civic pride when Cunard asked for the return of the paintings for the *Queen Elizabeth 2*. They were subsequently hung either side of the forward main stairwell landing between Upper and Quarter Decks.

As the Duke of York pulled the cord to unveil the paintings the curtains stuck. A royal tug only managed to dislodge the rail holding the curtains, one side of which collapsed like a dipped flag over the side of the exposed painting of The Queen Mother! Captain Burton-Hall undoubtedly did his best to make light of the situation. The shambles of the occasion only seemed to reflect the seeming chaos that the unfinished state of the liners interior presented to the press.

The Duke, who had previously toured the ship and had seen the unfinished state of a vessel in refit - a condition that he sympathised with from his own experiences in the Royal Navy - was quietly taken off the ship in order to avoid protests from the increasingly impatient passengers waiting to board the liner for their Christmas cruise to New York.

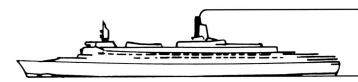

Chapter Twenty One

Transmutation to Magnificence

Three hundred people from just over one thousand booked for the crossing had had their transatlantic Christmas voyage tickets cancelled before they had left home but several hundred more had arrived at the Terminal expecting their cabins to be ready. But disappointments were again in store as one hundred and sixty more were informed that they could not sail with the ship. The workload still remaining and the state of many cabins had convinced the local Inspector from the Marine Safety Office that the ship should only sail with a thousand passengers - and this number would have to include the army of skilled workmen who would, of necessity, travel with the ship to complete their work. He issued a certificate to that effect. Refunds and promises of a free cruise were offered, but some of the erstwhile passengers baulked at the idea of the free cruise. Six hundred fare-paying passengers would board the liner. The liner's post-refit capacity should have been around 1,760.

Eighty passengers boarding the ship knew that when the ship sailed they still would not have been allocated cabins. Frequent floods had occurred and some cabins were deep in water. Two maritime authors who had been visiting the ship disembarked and, as they did so, were met by two reporters from the local BBC television station, one of whom was obviously upset - as were many other members of the press - at having her ticket cancelled. On being asked about the condition of the ship one of the authors responded "She's in a state typical of a ship under refit. But when she is finished she will be magnificent!"

And magnificent she would be. Through the current state of the liner's interior the prospect of a new, integrated decor could be seen that would live up to the company's expectations. Gone were the remnants of piecemeal refits and an unified interior gave the impression of a ship that would again achieve her old popularity as soon as the embarrassments, disappointments, inconveniences and "anti-Cunard" press had been forgotten.

The use of wood veneers (beech, American cherry, mahogany, etc,), and of carefully chosen colours in the carpeting was the first impression of the new layout. Then the awareness of the history of the Cunard unfolded as displays and models were discovered on the new Heritage Trail. A huge model of the old "*Maury*" stood outside the new Mauretania Restaurant, its case supports not yet enclosed with panelling; a statue, "The Spirit of the Sea", that used to grace the First Class Lounge of the second *Mauretania*, was displayed near the Midships Lobby, itself in stark contrast to its predecessor; the new Caronia Restaurant with its models, paintings,

After such a major overhaul the QE2 was famously not ready for her 1994 Christmas Cruise to New York much to the disappointment - and annoyance - of many. However, the promise of a magnificent new look shone through the apparent disarray.
Southern Newspapers

sweeping glass partitions, a huge, illuminated sculpture of horses with a fountain at its base, a mural on the aft bulkhead showing the "Green Goddess" in an exotic location; the Crystal Bar; the new Midships Bar perhaps not quite so intimate now as it had been although it now boasted the piano from the *Queen Mary* that had been transfereed from the Midships Lobby and a case of navigational memorabilia including ex-Captain Peter Jackson's sextant displayed on loan for five years.

Artworks were also added, but the gallery created on the bulkheads of a corridor proved to be unpopular as it made the location look like a small shop without adequate viewing space. Paintings by artists Stephen Card, Harley Crossley and Simon Fisher graced the after stairwell where their paintings positioning and space gave them a greater impact.

In the attractive, rebuilt and extended Library and Bookshop the staff bravely worked like Trojans within the unfinished rooms, polishing and tidying as well as stocking the shelves. Six hundred additional volumes were added to the six thousand already on the shelves. A second Librarian was employed as a result of the expansion.

Ease of passenger movement and access had been a prime remit in the designers' brief and passenger flow around the ship, including ramps and toilets for the disabled, was vastly improved as a result. Lighting, too, was an important element, which was used to great effect with the *Art Deco* inspired interiors.

Externally the *Queen Elizabeth 2* looked magnificent in her new colour scheme, although her brilliant white superstructure had been given what could only be described as a "Go Faster Stripe" in red, gold and royal blue. Self-adhesive and two hundred metres long it was placed along a level between One and Quarter Decks extending fore and aft

from below the Bridge to the Lido Cafe. At the forward end of the stripe was the Cunard lion, painted in gold outline with the existing legend "CUNARD" emblazoned in red above; over the line at the after end, was the beflagged Trafalgar House logo. The stripe itself was in Trafalgar House colours and was of the type that could be seen stuck onto hoardings surrounding the company's building sites. Appropriate, perhaps, because at this particular moment in time the QE2 herself resembled a building site!

Quite stunningly, the hull of *Queen Elizabeth 2* had been painted in royal blue. The boot-topping remained the standard red anti-fouling but, between boot-topping and dark blue hull a waterline was painted of a surprising yellow/gold. As this thin line was usually painted a smart white the new colour gave a feeling of oily, faded neglect. In spite of that, the *Queen* looked the superliner that she was.

With workmen still on board, the ship sailed several hours late leaving many disgruntled passengers ashore. As the embarked workmen had to be accommodated somewhere they were given cabins on Five Deck (which, of course, decreased further the number of fare-paying passengers that could be carried), sharing facilities as work was proceeding around the clock.

Passengers were inconvenienced during the crossing by floods (ship's staff being notified of such events over the broadcast system by the call "Niagara! Niagara!"), dripping water, uncarpeted floors, piles of bedding in the theatre (which were soon cleared), toilets and washing facilities that ran with rusty brown water, erupting toilets, etc, etc,. One of the few finished spaces was the Britannia Grill which was described as "...an oasis", offering a haven of peace from the uproar around the ship. A Force 8 during the trip also took its toll on some of the workmen who, suffering from sea-sickness, delayed their work even more.

Both crew (many of whom were upset at what had befallen their ship), supernumery staff such as superintendants and officers, and the Safety Inspector kept a vigilant watch to ensure that satisfactory levels of safety were maintained and advising appropriate action where doors and corridors were found to be temporarily obstructed by equipment, waste materials, etc. Barges had been ordered ahead of arrival in New York to ship away the accumulated garbage which was stored aft on One Deck, a convenient location in readiness for off-loading.

The ship arrived in New York twelve hours late because of the bad weather experienced and, to save time, United States Coast Guard personnel boarded the ship earlier than expected to inspect the ship prior to issuing their certificate of "Control Verification for a Foreign Vessel". Cunard's chairman John Olsen, appointed by Trafalgar Houses main shareholder - Hong Kong Land - also boarded to negotiate with angry and disappointed passengers.

One of the passengers to sail on the *QE2* in 1997 was 85 year old Millvina Dean. At just a few weeks old she had been the youngest survivor of the foundering of the *Titanic* in 1912. The *Queen Elizabeth 2* is seen here (with Millvina on board) passing the ancient castle at Calshot at the entrance to Southampton Water. It would be Millvina's first ocean voyage since returning from America all those years ago.   *Author*

Queen Elizabeth 2 moored at her usual berth in Southampton during 1995. She is sporting her new deep blue hull with the Trafalgar House
'go-faster' stripe on the superstructure.
Roger Hardingham

The conditions that the USCG found gave rise to concern. The expected barges were now unavailable so the rubbish had to be manhandled down through the ship to a shell door in the ship's side and this task started a few hours before the ship arrived in New York. The USCG's impression was that the rubbish had been piled inside the ship all through the voyage.

Without meeting any senior staff to discuss the reasons and solutions for the problems that the Coastguards found and to put the problems into context, the USCG wandered unaccompanied and freely about the vessel speaking to members of the crew, therefore not receiving an authoritative overall picture of the prevailing conditions. By the time that senior staff were eventually consulted the USCG had "...already become convinced that the ship was in a dangerous condition".

Even so, the required Certificate was issued after it was ascertained that certain work would be undertaken, such as disposal of the garbage (a major job which was already underway) and that fire-doors that had been wedged open for ease of working (but had been kept monitored during the voyage) were safe. The certificate restricted access to certain areas of the ship. The MSA had issued the ship with a full term Passenger Certificate in Britain on the understanding that the garbage would be cleared before sailing from New York on the World Cruise and that certain other works (mainly revolving around the new Lido) would be completed as soon as possible during that trip.

The USCG inspectors presented the company with six pages of requests to remedy safety violations some of which, without their knowledge, had been previously verbally highlighted by the MSA. The certificate for a reduced number of passengers that had been issued in Southampton was intended to keep passengers out of the rebuilt Lido area but the USCG was not aware of this restriction and declared that passengers should be restricted completely from using the vertical "Fire Zone 7" which included not only the Lido but the decks above and below it as well. The MSA inspector also thought that the USCG had the impression "....that most of the work carried out in New York would not have been done had they not specifically asked for it" although it had been already planned or was even underway.

The press had a field-day and it was not only Cunard and the *Queen Elizabeth 2* that received their attention. Personalities within Cunard unfortunately got drawn into the mud-slinging; the MSA inspector, too, was slated for having his wife accompany him (the reports omitted to mention that

she also worked for the MSA - one punny headline read "*QE2* Waives the Rules") and for several weeks the mere mention of the ship's name brought forth negative comments from a generally unempathetic press. At least, many of the newspaper cartoons expressed an amusement over the reports in the media.

Another difficulty arose before the ship was able to leave New York. Because of the USCG report - and also unbeknown to Cunard - the ship had been prohibited from sailing until all the defects in the report had been rectified. A Detention Notice was usually issued to the ship but, in this case, it was not. Instead an unlogged telephone call had been made to the British Consulate in New York and its recipient at the Consulate later remembered receiving the call but not the message that a Notice had been issued. It was only when a letter was received from Admiral Card of the USCG that the seriousness of the situation became apparent and a series of meetings were hurriedly held in Washington and New York in order to resolve the *impasse*.

The ship was eventually permitted to sail - twenty four hours late (the work remaining being completed over the following few days) on her World Cruise leaving behind recriminations, claims and counter-claims. A lawyer who had experienced the Christmas cruise and representing several other passengers went to Cunard's London office to picket the company and to lodge his complaints. The early television news showed him rattling an office door and claiming that Cunard had locked him out (good television!) Unfortunately, he was rattling the secure, corner door that was only used by staff: he was shown on a later news bulletin entering Cunard's offices through the large revolving doors at 30-35 Pall Mall! He later expressed his satisfaction with his compensation.

Hard lessons had been learned and improvements in communications, surveys and line management would result. The final "victim" of the whole unhappy episode was John Olsen, Cunard's chairman since 1993. He had approved the refit and had been the man with the courage to exploit Cunard's history in such a grand way on the ship. He admitted in January that the *QE2* should not have sailed before the refit had been completed and was dismissed from the company the following May with a compensation for "...loss of office..." of £232,000. Olsen was replaced by Peter Ward, lately chairman of Rolls Royce, who was apparently not so keen on the Heritage aspects of the ship and rumours of the planned removal of the increasingly popular artefact cases abounded on the waterfront.

In one way the *Queen Elizabeth 2* had grown in stature during the refit. Her Gross Tonnage (1 Gross Ton = 100 cubic feet) had changed over the years since her design (58,000gt projected); entry into service (65,862); increasing after various refits to 67,139 in 1985; reducing slightly (66,450) in 1988: 69,053 (1991) and, in 1994, she was entered in Lloyd's Register as being of 70,327 gross tons. Some things had remained as they were: her call sign "GBTT" and her Official Number 336703.

Perhaps because of the adverse publicity that *QE2* had received from the post-refit press, she would achieve a new popularity in the months and years to come.

There seemed to be nothing more appealing to the travelling public in 1995 than a *Queen* with a tarnished reputation!!

Part of the refit work that continued at Southampton and during the Christmas Cruise.   *David Ellery*

Above: The Midship's Bar in 2000. Gone is the more inimate darker look but a brighter bar for cruising is now evident.　*Peter Seden*
Below: Stylish vaulted ceilings in the Library give the room a feel of the old Cunarders. *Inset:* The same room as it appeared at the end of the 1994 refit immediately prior to the Chrismas cruise!　*Cunard/David Ellery*

Above: The Lobby to the Caronia Restaurant still boasts the large model of the *Mauretainia*.
Below: The new-look port Caronia Restaurant in 2000. Wood encased columns contribute to a more traditional look.   *Both, Peter Seden*

Above: The Midship's Lobby, the first interior that greets boarding passengers as they came aboard, was completely redesigned in the 1994 refit.

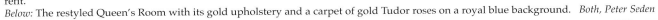

Below: The restyled Queen's Room with its gold upholstery and a carpet of gold Tudor roses on a royal blue background.   *Both, Peter Seden*

Above: QE2's boat deck with the sparkling evening lights of Liverpool's famous buildings during its visit in 1990.

Left: The Britannia Grill. The print on the wall depicts the paddle steamer *Britannia* leaving Boston after a channel had been cut out of the ice by its citizens thus helping her to maintain a mail contract with the city.   *Cunard*

Below: The massive interior of the Engine Room during the 1987 refit. This panoramic photographic illustrates the vastness of the area and the complexity of the work involved. The first of the new engines can be seen already in place. Removed inner bottom plates to the left expose the structure beneath.   *Meyer Werft*

Above: The liner at Capetown with the dramatic Table Mountain overshadowing the southern-most city of South Africa.

Below: Another of *QE2*'s ports of call on her World Cruise schedule is San Francisco.

Cunard

Marvin Jensen

Chapter Twenty Two

Storms Abating and Arising

After passing through the Caribbean where some on-board problems still persisted (resulting in around six hundred other passengers having their cruises cancelled), the outstanding work from the refit was completed and the furore was generally left behind her. It was now hoped that the *Queen Elizabeth 2* could complete her 1995 World Cruise free of adverse publicity. But the eyes of the world's press were still on her, waiting in the sidelines for her next transgression.

Even whilst the ship was away, newspapers were full of American legal proceedings against Cunard amounting to claims of $100,000 for each American passenger (120 of them) as compensation, £7.5-million was put aside by Cunard as a contingency to cover compensation claims. A year later settlements were reached, paying the UK to New York passengers $5,000 each and the New York to the Caribbean passengers $2,000.

Viscount Gochen, British Governmental Minister for Shipping, was also kept busy in the House of Lords responding to questions tabled by various Members of Parliament. The Viscount's reply began: "A report on the *QE2* incident has been completed by the Director of Operations and Seafarer Standards of the Marine Safety Agency. The Director's report discloses serious deficiencies in the shore and ship management of the vessel by Cunard; it also identifies failings on the part of the Marine Safety Agency". Criticism of the MSA fell short of the inquiry that MPs had demanded but did recommend several improvements in the Agency's procedures.

Passing into the Pacific Ocean the "new look" *QE2* was delighting recently-joined passengers but she was sailing into yet more controversy when she arrived at anchorage in Hawaiis Kailua Bay. Whilst there she was accused of spilling sewage into the sea. Hawaiis Maritime Law Enforcement Division rightly investigated and it was found that the muddy, swilling discharge was permitted waste pumped from the ship's garbage macerators possibly mixed with rusty residue from the water tanks.

The early Spring brought with it the news that James Gardner, who had designed much of the *QE2's* interiors and co-ordinated the ship's external original aesthetic appearance, had died at the age of 87.

The 117-day 1995 World Cruise (fares from £12,495 to £117,230 for the full cruise) ended in Southampton on 13th April, 1995. The year was divided into her by-now usual transatlantics; cruises down the US East Coast or to the Caribbean; North Cape to see the midnight sun in July and, in late August, the *QE2* made her first complete circumnavigation of the British Isles, calling at Guernsey, Waterford, Liverpool, Greenock and then Invergordon and the Tyne *en-route* down through the North Sea to Le Havre before returning to Southampton. However, the call into the Tyne (where a shipyard had made a bid for the 'Q3' contract) was cancelled due to the

Left top: The large, impressive and inwardly illuminated model of the old *Mauretania* of 1906 that stands in the foyer to the 1994 installed Mauretania (now Caronia) Restaurant.

Left below: This portrait of the then Princess Elizabeth shows her as the Duchess of Edinburgh with her new husband, the Duke of Edinburgh, and originally hung in the *Caronia*, the 'Green Goddess'. The painting, still in its original specially carved frame, now graces a stairwell on the *Queen Elizabeth 2. Both by Peter Seden*

prevailing rough conditions. The Mayor of Newcastle-on-Tyne and other local dignitaries were most disappointed as the liner steamed by in the gloom and the eagerly awaited reception on board disappeared with the liner.

It was also in April that Captain Warwick had the bow crest of the Cunard Lion removed from the *Cunard Countess*, which had been sold, and had it remounted on *QE2's* Bridge front when he joined her in September.

The fiftieth anniversary of the Allied victory over Hitler's Nazism - Victory in Europe (VE Day) - was celebrated in a special "VE Day Commemoration" cruise which took *QE2* to Gibraltar, Lisbon and then on to anchor off Plymouth (8th May), thereby making her maiden call at the famous Devonshire port and home of Sir Francis Drake, sailed on to Guernsey in the Channel Islands and returning home to Southampton.

June saw another sad departure when Captain William Law died on the 4th. Captain Law had been in command of the *QE2* during the bomb hoax of 1972 and had been in command of all three "Queen" liners. Later that month, during a transatlantic, Captain John Burton-Hall gave permission to hold and then led a small, early morning private commemoration service held to remember those lost in the Atlantic and Russian convoys during the Second World War. A wreath was cast into the sea.

The North Cape was visited again in July and as part of this cruise *QE2* called at Edinburgh on 17th July. HRH The Princess Anne came aboard for lunch. When the ship sailed around 3pm, the next day she led the sailing ships partaking in the "Cutty Sark" Tall Ships Race out through the Firth of Forth.

In mid-season the *Queen Elizabeth 2* celebrated another remarkable achievement - her One Thousandth voyage. This was achieved appropriately during an eastbound voyage between New York (an aircraft here towed a banner reading "NY salutes *QE2* on her 1000th voyage") and Southampton, 14th to 19th June, with fireboats sending up plumes of water in salute on both sides of the Atlantic. Special certificates and enamelled lapel badges in the form of the liners funnel were issued to both passengers and crew and a celebratory dinner was held during the crossing. 3.8-million miles were "on the clock" and some 1.7-million passengers had been carried during *QE2's* remarkable career.

The *Queen's* 1001st voyage took her to the Baltic calling at Copenhagen, Stockholm and Oslo. She was sent off from Southampton in gala style and similar gifts and dinners were enjoyed during this special cruise. Veteran singing star Edmund Hockridge was booked to perform in the Grand Lounge. He had sung there on *QE2's* maiden voyage when this room was the then brand-new Double Down Room.

On 7th September the *Queen* had left Southampton under the command of Captain Ron Warwick on another of her "Transatlantic Classic" voyages to New York. The usual Great Circle route was followed and soon the progress of Hurricane "Luis" (coming up from the Caribbean) was being carefully monitored and plotted on the Bridge. It was soon realised by the navigators that "Luis" would pass close to the course of the *QE2* and, on 10th September, the ships course was changed to the south-west in an attempt to distance the ship from the storm. The Captain reckoned that "Luis" would pass ahead of the *Queen* at eleven o'clock that evening and had accordingly informed the passengers, updating the information during the course of the day.

By late evening (Sunday, 10th September), with the "eye" of "Luis" still 140-miles, away the wind speed

had increased from 50 to 100 knots, giving the ship a heel of 7° to starboard. The wind then came from ahead creating very heavy head seas that continually broke over the ship's bow leaving it awash for minutes at a time. The seas had made it unadvisable for the hotel staff to set out the Midnight Buffet.

Speed was reduced and in the early hours of the morning the *QE2* hove-to, riding 30 to 40-foot waves. At 2.10am a rogue wave was sighted.

In her cabin Librarian June Applebee, prepared by the Captain's bulletins, prepared for the worst: "...I took the usual seaman-like precautions and put away any loose objects, even putting the telephone in the drawer, and settled down for a bumpy night.

"At about 2am I awoke with a start to find that both my wardrobe doors and the bathroom door had burst open! Never had that happened before".

"I turned on the television to Channel 3 - the TV camera above the Bridge (that gave a continuous view over the bow) - and turned off all the lights in the cabin. Being night time the screen was dark...gradually my eyes became accustomed to the darkness and I was able to make out a very dim definition of the bow of the ship".

"It was possible to see the waves breaking over the bow - which, in a storm, I have often seen in daylight - this was a very grey shadow around the darker bow...suddenly the screen appeared to be filling up with grey shadows - the ship was bumping around and I thought this was not normal - so I tried to put a pillow over my head and tried to get to sleep".

"The next morning we were told of the ...wave!"

On the Bridge Captain Warwick had kept a vigilant watch with his navigators and watchkeepers. He recalled the heart-stopping moment as hundreds of tons of water thundered down onto the foredeck of his ship: "The wave seemed to take ages to reach us, but it was probably less than a minute before it broke with tremendous force over the bow of the *QE2*. An incredible shudder went through the ship followed a few moments later by two smaller shudders. At the same time the sea was cascading all over the fore part of the ship, including the Bridge, and it was several seconds before the water had drained away from the wheelhouse windows and vision ahead was restored".

Cruise Director Brian Price was in his cabin on 2 Deck, way above the waterline. He was amazed to see water rushing past his port!

The Captain would later add: "It looked as if we were going straight into the White Cliffs of Dover!"

Visually, and from data gleaned from Canadian weather monitors in the area, the wave had been from 95 to 98-feet in height and around 1,200-feet wide. Railings around the foredeck had been buckled and the deck plating of the tip of the foredeck had been buckled downwards to show the lines of the beams and longitudinal stiffening underneath.

As June Applebee summed up her feelings: " ...An amazing experience to have been on board....*QE2* is an amazing ship and one feels confident in any situation that the elements care to throw at her" - a sentiment echoed by everybody on board from the Master downwards.

Storm Certificates were issued the next day as a memento.

By going through that ordeal the *Queen Elizabeth 2* proved herself to the press and, in the waters of the rogue wave, seemed to slough the bad feelings generated by her December refit. Once again she was Queen of the Seas.

Above: The liner positioned on the Blomm + Voss floating dock at Hamburg during her 1994 refit.
Below: A splendid painting of the *Queen Elizabeth 2* surrounded by fleets of racing yachts off Cowes.

Harley Crossley
Painting by Robert Lloyd

Chapter Twenty Three

Sailing On

"Mediterranean Medley" was the title of the cruise that left Southampton on 15th October, 1995. Barcelona was the first stop-over followed by Villefranche, Genoa, Palma, Gibraltar and Lisbon. What made this cruise so particular to many British people was that many of the cast from the top-rating television soap "Coronation Street" were on board to film a Christmas special. Curly, Rita, Alec, Raquel, *et al* performed their stuff but it appeared that it was filmed mostly late at night as the spacious but normally busy *QE2* seemed strangely deserted in the final film. Members of the cast have often travelled on the ship as part of the on-board entertainment talking to passengers and giving autographs.

At the beginning of 1996 Cunard announced that they had received a record number of bookings for the year in spite of, or probably because of, the adverse publicity stemming from the so-called "Christmas Cruise From Hell"!

It was all too late for Trafalgar House. Heavy losses over the previous year and a recent stranding and fire on the *Sagafjord* led them finally to accepting a bid from the Norwegian construction and engineering group of Kvaerner

and, in March, Trafalgar was sold for £904-million. At first it was thought that, although Kvaerner appeared to be happy with the cruising side of the business, Cunard might be sold on. The collision of their super-luxury *Royal Viking Sun* with a Red Sea coral reef probably did nothing to make them change their minds. Kvaerner's chief executive said bluntly: "Cunard falls outside our core business". But it was later announced officially that Cunard was not for sale although Carnival, P&O and Sea Containers expressed interest. Cunard was valued at above £200-million but would need a substantial investment if Kvaerner could not sell it. Cunard's London address was moved to Berkeley Street.

At the same time, as seems to be periodically usual, there were rumours that the *QE2's* base would be moved from Southampton either to America or Japan. This rumour was based on a fall in *QE2* profits over recent years and it was felt that a more lucrative base market could be found where the ships great reputation could be exploited.

It was whilst she was on her 1996 World Cruise - her twentieth - that another milestone was reached in the story of the remakable *Queen Elizabeth 2*: or rather her four-

The *Queen* in the spectacular setting of Invergordon during her inaugural call there at the developing cruise port.

Courtesy of Cromarty Firth Port Authority

QE2 in the Geiranger Fjord, Norway, in 1999. The other two liners are the *Maxim Gorky* and *Black Prince*. The Cunarder's anchor went down a long way!

Len and Margaret Thompson

A brace of handsome Cunarders together off Barbados. *Queen Elizabeth 2* and *Caronia* met again at the turn of the Millenium.

Cunard

The 1996 refit was carried out, after an absence of several years, in Southampton. The structural work that was carried out included the removal and relacement of the bow plates buckled after the liner's encounter with a 90 foot wave! The discarded piece of fore deck can be seen on the edge of the King George V dry dock where the work was carried out.

millionth-milestone! An extraordinary achievement.

During the time that the company she belonged to was being sold to a non-British owner the *Queen Elizabeth 2* was still on her 1996 World Cruise. Entitled "Voyage to Distant Empires" it lasted from 4th January (New York) to 8th April (New York) and, as usual, segments of the voyage were sold as shorter cruises (fares from $24,230 each for an inside cabin sharing to $537,800 for each of the Queen Mary/Queen Elizabeth suites for the whole cruise).

Beating off fierce competition it was announced in May that the Southampton ship-repair firm of A&P Southampton (part of the A&P Group) had won the bid to refit the *Queen* during the coming December with a £12-million contract. Southampton was jubilant, realising again how important this ship was to the city.

1996 turned out to be a remarkably uneventful year for the *Queen Elizabeth 2*. No doubt, her owners were glad of this and it gave the ship time to renew her old popularity.

Some family nostalgia was commemorated in a special transatlantic and Bermudan cruise to recall the sixtieth anniversary of the maiden voyage of perhaps the most famous ocean liner ever - the *Queen Mary*. 18th May saw *QE2's* departure from Southampton celebrating that famous, historical voyage that had captured the imagination of the world.

The American "leg" of this cruise took the *QE2* to Bermuda and she was booked to capacity - there was even a

waiting list! In what would be described as "...one of the most exciting and successful cruises in recent years...", the trip had all the right ingredients for a trip of nostalgia: good weather, a beautiful destination, good rates and a ship full of ocean liner enthusiasts from various shipping societies and museums.

The day to Bermuda and the day returning were filled with lectures by noted maritime authors John Maxton-Graham and Bill Miller, and displays - and sales - of memorabilia were provided by Richard Faber in the Boardroom. Captain Warwick's only chance of seeing the displays and to avoid a lengthy queue was to find his way through the Queen's Grill kitchen! The *QE2's* own new Heritage Trail was also eagerly explored.

On 5th August, during a "Northern Capitals" cruise, the *Queen* assumed a fifty-foot dent after breaking free of her tugs in Copenhagen and ramming the quay wall. A September cruise to the Iberian Peninsula that had been scheduled in the brochure for 1996 had been cancelled almost as soon as the brochure had been issued. One hundred early bookers had refunds or the chance to take a cruise of greater value plus generous compensation. The liner had been chartered for £1-million to act as a floating hotel during the Ryder Cup golf tournament which was held at Valderrame, near Cadiz.

Prince Edward was once again on board *QE2* (28th September) hosting another Royal Ball in aid of his father's

Special Projects Group, which was celebrating its tenth anniversary. Tickets cost up to £300 and the entertainment included supper, a fireworks display and plenty of music. The partying finished at 4am.

Bizarrely, in September, the ship rammed and killed a whale, an event not unknown at sea as the *Caronia* had similarly done so off the East African coast in 1958.

Kvaerner finally admitted in November that they were intending to sell their interests in Cunard (the company had lost £16.5-million in 1995) but it would be several months before negotiations were completed and a buyer could be announced.

The big refit of 1996 started on 21st November and the *Queen Elizabeth 2* was dry-docked in the King George V Graving Dock, the first time for nine years, that had been built to accommodate the *Queen Mary* during her annual overhauls. A&P (Southampton), who were chosen to undertake the work against stiff competition, had to temporarily increase their workforce from their normal 130 to 1,000.

Over the previous three months the company had already refitted the *Black Prince*, *Black Watch* and the mighty *Norway* (ex-*France*) that had made a special North Atlantic voyage of nostalgia to travel to Southampton for her refit. Amongst the work to be done on the *QE2* was to finish forty-three top grade bathrooms (marble and gold in best art deco style) that remained to be completed after her last refit and refurbish several public rooms as well as 160 cabins. Passenger capacity would again be reduced, this time to fifteen hundred giving more space per passenger and reducing sittings to one in the Mauretania Restaurant.

In anticipation of new SOLAS (Safety Of Life At Sea) regulations that would be coming into force the following year, four thousand fire and smoke detection devices were also fitted. This equipment (including detectors, interface modules and call-points) linked to controllers placed in the Wheelhouse and safety centre. Mimic displays were installed to give a clear indication of which call points on the ship were in alarm. Fire doors on crew stairways were also refitted and the remaining asbestos was removed. Other technical work included propellers, stabilisers, the overhaul and replacement where necessary of five miles of pipework, classification society survey of anchors and chains, hull blasting and repainting, etc. The work was completed on time and to budget.

Other work included the fitting of a new six-inch thick, English Oak, sprung dance floor in the Queen's Room, replacing the original that had been there for nearly thirty years. A new foredeck section replaced the area of buckled deck that remained as a souvenir of Hurricane "Luis". The Mauretania Restaurant, an increasingly attractive room with new lighting and a new suspended glass-fibre ceiling, had its seating capacity increased to cater for a single sitting and the telegraph from the first *Mauretania* was moved to the entrance of the officers' Wardroom. The One Deck branch of Harrod's was changed to a Gift shop, later becoming the "Cunard Collection Shop".

Both the Queen Mary and Queen Elizabeth suites were enlarged being extended to incorporate the adjacent cabins which became new bedrooms and dining rooms with six chairs.

Veteran of 38 *QE2* cruises, Sir Jimmy Savile, had been given a special tour of the ship on 4th December whilst she was still in dry-dock. Impressed with what he saw he told the local Southampton "Daily Echo": "She is like a relative to me so I have come to see how she is getting on. I can't wait to get back on board afterwards. In fact, I might just stow away on the next cruise!"

After the experiences suffered after the 1994 refit A&P and the hard-working ship's staff ensured that the ship, was "spic-and-span" by the time that passengers boarded on 12th December in readiness for a three-day party cruise. These three days would either prove the ship or they could be cancelled to allow any outstanding work that was required to be completed. As it was, A&P had finished ahead of time which allowed the high standard of preparedness in readiness to embark passengers to be achieved and sea trials were carried out on the 11th. Relief Captain Keith Stanley was justifiably proud of his ship as he showed the shipping press around his vessel.

After the three-day party cruise a transatlantic (these were now scheduled to take six instead of five days) was followed by a Caribbean Christmas Cruise returning to New York for the start of the 1997 World Cruise leaving the city on 4th January under the command of John Burton-Hall who was making his last round-the-world cruise before retiring.

When the *Queen* called at Hong Kong she embarked sixteen government officers and seventeen dependants. This would be the liner's last call there before mainland China took over the British colony. The *QE2* had always been looked after in Hong Kong, receiving a mid-world cruise paint "make-over" there and even appearing on one of the colony's postage stamps.

The cruise during its final stages from 21st March, was also sold as smaller cruise segments, the longest being as the *Queen Elizabeth 2* made her maiden call into Dubai (in the United Arab Emirates) who was hoping to develop into a cruise ship centre. Fly/cruise passengers could join her here on her westward "Odyssey Through the Ancient World". The liner was met in the Strait of Hormuz by HMS *Southampton*, then on the Armilla Patrol in the Persian Gulf, which escorted the *Queen* into port.

1997 bought in a change to the transatlantic voyages. In future they would include six nights at sea instead of the more hectic five as before. This was partly due to passenger demand but it would also save Cunard the cost of the oil-fuel used in high-speed crossings and would also provide a "cushion" for any delays (caused, for example, by inclement weather) thereby giving an allowance in which, if necessary, to make up lost time.

In mid-March Kvaerner's chairman, Antti Pankakoski, spoke about the possibility of building a running mate for the *QE2* but the company would no longer own Cunard by the time that such a decision would be made. Peter Ward had resigned in September, taking with him any threat to remove the Heritage Trail; his position as President would be taken the following June by Captain Paris Katsoufis.

Arriving home in Southampton on the morning of 11th April the *Queen Elizabeth 2* sailed the next day at noon on a 22-day Spring circular tour of the Atlantic. On board she carried the ashes of the late Commodore of the Cunard Line, Geoffrey Marr, one-time captain of the fabled *Queens* as well as of the *Caronia*, *Mauretania*, etc, for committing to the deep waters of the North Atlantic on 14th April. Relief Captain Roland Hassel officiated with Chief Officer Ian McNaught in attendance. After a remarkable career - which had included witnessing the sinking of the German battleship *Bismark* from an advantageous point on *HMS King George V* - the Commodore had lived in retirement at Redlynch in the New Forest (where he had written his eminently readable "The Queens And I"). A move to Devizes preceeded a lengthy transfer to his daughter's farm in Scotland. He had been taken ill whilst visiting his son near London and had spent his last days in the Royal Alfred Home For Sailors in Surrey. Away from his old friends that he missed in and around the New Forest there were very few at his funeral.

On 11th April too, rather strangely and inexplicably, the Mauretania and Caronia Restaurants were swapped around (the Mauretania was reinstated back to where it used to be pre-1994). The name boards around the entrances were the only items to be exchanged in the exercise whilst the *QE2* was alongside her Southampton terminal. The *Caronia* model, painting and mural remained where they were in the Upper Deck restaurant as did the horse sculpture and fountain. The large model of the *Mauretania* remained outside what now became the Caronia Restaurant. This anomaly could never be explained to the curious enquirer.

"Where on Earth will you be at midnight on December 31st, 1999?" was the question already being posed by Cunard's publicists in advance material issued for the Millenium. Discounts, as usual, were being

offered on bookings taken in advance. The *Queen's* new millenium would be spent, it was said, in Barbados.

The *QE2* settled down to her varied and very busy schedule and thankfully remained free of any major negative occurences that would have caused instant press reaction.

July 1997 marked a major event when the British dependent territory of Hong Kong was reverted back into Chinese Sovereignty. But this favourite amongst the ports of call during her world cruises (usually staying there for a lengthy three days at the beginning of March during each world cruise) would still remain on her future itineraries. Hong Kong now came under the care of the son of C Y Tung (Tung Chao Yung), the man who had bought the venerable old 'Lizzie', converting her into a floating university, Seawise University. The old ship on the brink of a new lease of life burnt out and capsized just prior to her entering service in 1970. She was broken up on the spot. Tung Chee Hwa, CY's son, would become Chief Executive, Hong Kong Special Administrative Region Peoples' Republic of China, when the old British colony was returned to the Chinese Government. Some had taken the *QE2*'s final trip to Hong Kong prior to the handover before 'they' took over but the liner would continue to use the port in the years that followed.

Top: A captain's view of the Bridge of the Americas, Panama Canal.
Cunard

Left: The names of the Caronia and Mauretania Restaurants were inexplicably transposed even though artifacts relating to the liners after whom the restaurants were named remained where they stood! Here the Mauretania Restaurant is being renamed Caronia - and not as an honour to Captain Ron Warwick! *Author*

In August westbound the ship missed a call at Cobh on the 8th because of fog leaving some passengers stranded (which caused a mild disturbance in the lurking press). Some of the disappointed passengers prefered the enforced wait for the ship's next call on the 25th rather than fly. On arrival the *QE2* sailed from New York to spend two nights anchored off Newport, Rhode Island, during that towns famous Jazz Festival.

Later the *Queen* hosted a special group of people that provided one of the many theme cruises that Cunard regularly organise. The transatlantic westbound from Southampton that began on 24th August carried a group of thirty of the worlds top chefs, many of them in the service of world leaders. Called "Le Club des Chefs des Chefs" they were hosted by Cunard's Executive Chef, Rudi Sodamin. The passengers dined with an even greater luxury and variety on the trip.

At the end of August Cunard relocated its worldwide corporate headquarters from 555 Fifth Avenue, New York (which it had occupied for many years) to Dade County in

An upward drift of 1,159 balloons (one for each voyage) hastened by a brisk breeze colorfully speckle the sky at the start of the liner's 30th Birthday celebratory voyage to New York. *Mick Lindsey*

Miami, Florida (it was rumoured that this was done because the Chief executive lived in that area!) As a result the Cunard fleet switched from using Port Everglades to the Port of Miami. The new port of call was inaugurated by the *QE2* on her visit on 15th November which meant a change in her published schedule.

The *Queen Elizabeth 2* has carried the rich and the famous and the prominent during her sea-going career but on 7th August she sailed from Southampton carrying a lady whose claim to fame lay elsewhere and who had not been on the Atlantic - or even on a large ship - for eighty-five years. At nine weeks old she had disembarked in New York, carried by her mother and accompanied by her elder brother Bertram, from the Cunard liner *Carpathia*. Little Millvina Dean had left Southampton on 10th April 1912, with her family headed by her father. The ship on which they sailed towards a new life in America that never materialised was the *Titanic* and Millvina, the youngest survivor of that tragedy, was now going to the States as the principal guest of the Titanic Historical Society.

A rare photograph of the Cunard liner *Carpathia* of 1903 in dry-dock. It was this 13,500-ton liner that made a gallant dash on the morning of 15th April 1912, to rescue the survivors from the White Star liner *Titanic*.
Collection of the Author

At the end of the month, on 31st August, the United Kingdom and the world had been stunned at the news from Paris that Diana, Princess of Wales had died as a result of a car accident. Two minutes silence was held on the QE2 which was westbound for New York. The following month a special luncheon was held on the ship in aid of the British Red Cross campaign against landmines, a cause in which the late Princess had an abiding interest, still went ahead on 1st October both in memory of the Princess and as part of the liner's celebrations of the thirtieth anniversary of her own launching.

The Princess had been due to attend the fund raising lunch (for which 300 people had paid £350 per ticket) which was also attended by Lord Richard Attenborough; former hostage Terry Waite; Elizabeth Dole (President of the American branch of the Red Cross); and Cherie Blair (wife of the British Prime Minister). The guests were greeted by Captain Ron Warwick and £70,000 was raised from the occasion. Cunard's Chief Executive, Antti Pankakoski, also announced that the Red Cross would become the company's official charity until the year 2000.

Helping to celebrate the liner's anniversary the QE2's Grill Class accommodation was awarded, in September, a Five-star accolade by the "Berlitz Complete Guide to Cruising and Cruise Ships", becoming Number One in the large ship category.

20th September saw celebrations on board Queen Elizabeth 2 during Voyage 1,104 en-route for Southampton in honour of the actual anniversary of her launching.

Meanwhile, negotiations were quietly continuing between Kvaerner and agents, the ship-owning and managing Vlasov Group of Monaco, for the sale of the Cunard once again, this time to an as yet undisclosed buyer.

An American Thanksgiving cruise left New York on 13th November for a 9th December return, turning around at Los Angeles on 26th November. Thanksgiving, 27th November, was spent at sea. Before joining the ship at LA passengers had lunch on board the old Queen Mary, permanently berthed in retirement at Long Beach. There were two attractions on this particular cruise: a double transition of the Panama Canal and the presence on board of American comedian and actor Bill Cosby.

The ship returned to Southampton on 15th December prior to her depature for New York at the outset of her World Cruise, "Exploration of Distant Lands", that took her to Pacific islands, New Zealand, Australia, Japan, China (Hong Kong), Vietnam, Singapore, Indonesia, India, Africa and around the Horn to Portugal, arriving back in Southampton on 15th April, 1998. It was on this cruise that retired Captain and Mrs Robin Woodall fulfilled one of his ambitions for retirement - to sail on his beloved old command as passengers!

During QE2's call in to Durban, South Africas President, Nelson Mandela, boarded the liner and journeyed with her to Cape Town. A luncheon was held on board during this voyage around the Horn of Africa in aid of The Nelson Mandela Childrens Fund. Also during the trip the President was interviewed during a live televised broadcast by David Frost for his programme "Breakfast With Frost". Mr Mandela unveiled a plaque to commemorate his visit before leaving the ship.

Whilst the Queen Elizabeth 2 was completing her World Cruise it was announced that Kvaerner had sold its interests in Cunard to a joint venture between Norwegian investors holding 32% and the mighty Carnival Corporation (68%) of Miami. Exciting plans were unveiled for the new company

(Cunard Line Limited) after its merger with Carnival. Seabourn Cruise Line would join with Cunard with QE2 and Vistafjord (to be renamed Caronia) being British flagged and officered whilst the Seabourne ships (Seabourn Goddess(es) I and II - ex-Sea Goddess(es) I and II - and Seabourn Sun, ex-Royal Viking Sun) would similarly be Norwegian registered. The British government had recently at long last decided that the country's merchant fleet had dwindled to unacceptable levels and were providing tax concessions to companies to re-flag their fleets. QE2, however, already flew the Red (or Blue) Ensign and in herself made up a large proportion of the British fleet.

Not only was a corporate indentity to be given to the Cunard ships by using a recognisable livery (and the traditional naming suffix of "...ia" in Cunard's case) in each component company but ambitious plans for a new ship were announced in June. This would be for the biggest, most expensive transatlantic liner ever to be built and was given the project name of "Project Queen Mary". An unique feature of the new 150,000gt ship would be the proposed inclusion of privately-owned apartments on board for the mega-rich!

Larry Pimentel, Cunard's new president, said: "The project will lead to the development of the grandest and largest liner ever built - the epitome of elegance, style and grace.

"It is our objective to build a new generation of ocean liner that will be the very pinnacle of the shipbuilders' art; the realisation of a dream of another time. Our goal is nothing less than to create a new Golden Age of Sea Travel for those who missed the first!"

Early artists' impressions of the proposed new Queen Mary showed a vessel larger but not dissimilar to the QE2. This would be the first new-building for Cunard for many years and the exciting news was welcomed by observers who had noted that Cunard, unlike its competitors who had commissioned new ships, had relied on "taken-over" tonnage for far too long. Cunard's short-lived headquarters in Blue Lagoon Drive, Miami, would also be moved again, this time to Fort Lauderdale.

Meantime, the QE2 carried on with a transatlantic return voyage that preceded a 16-night cruise to Istanbul and back. Caribbean and Baltic cruises followed and on 19th July, at the end of a return from New York, the Queen Elizabeth 2 anchored in beautiful Falmouth Bay to allow her passengers to see the start of the 1998 "Cutty Sark" Tall Ships Race. After three hours of the parade of sail passing the huge liner the QE2 followed the race for a further three hours.

Another popular "Round Britain Discovery" cruise was operated in August with the Queen again sailing clockwise around the UK.

October brought two revelations in the press. Firstly, that a wealthy businessman had been booking the top two suites for himself and his wife on world cruises for the past eight years (along with other staterooms for their luggage!) and that a special book had been planned about the ship. The top edition of a mere thirty copies was soon sold out. This would have a bejewelled cover by Asprey's of London and would cost £25,000! Other editions would have a silver porthole as its cover motif (nearly £600); another edition at almost £250 and an 'edition ordinaire' at less than £20! The author of the planned book would be Carol Thatcher, journalist daughter of the late Prime Minister, who had given lectures aboard the ship on previous voyages.

1998 ended with the traditional Caribbean christmas cruise terminating in New York on 5th January, 1999.

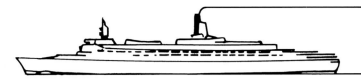

Chapter Twenty Four

For Sale - or Good for Thirty Years?

The New Year would prove to be an important one for the *Queen Elizabeth 2*. Her World Cruise (£18,770 to £193,410 for the complete 99-days) started from New York on 5th January and finished in Southampton on 14th April. Since the introduction of her six-day transatlantic schedule the *Queen* was always timed for a 7am arrival in Southampton (although this was more usually 6am) and the same stood for her return from World Cruises. A 5pm sailing invariably (bar delays) followed.

Terminal in Southampton docks were not in the least bit dampened. Several ex-*Queen Elizabeth 2* captains were present for this most unusual but joyful event including Peter Jackson, Robin Woodall, Bob Arnott, Douglas Ridley, Mortimer Heier, Lawrence Portet and Keith Stanley. Captain Roland Hassel was also in attendance as was Ron Warwick as the Senior Captain. Unhappily Ron Warwick's father, retired Captain 'Bil' Warwick, had been due to attend but his death, at 86, had occured only a few weeks before the

Surrounded by a festive throng the 30-year old *QE2* sails from Southampton *en-route* to New York.   *Author*

14th April commemorated two notable shipping events. The 'big one' was the anniversary of the White Star liner *Titanic* striking an iceberg in 1912 that led to her foundering with great loss of life in the early hours of the following morning. The second event, in 1999, was the celebration in Southampton of the *Queen Elizabeth 2's* thirtieth anniversary of her maiden voyage. Although the actual anniversary would not be until 2nd May it had been decided to hold her birthday party in her home port on the day that she arrived home from her World Cruise.

The party day stated in a typically changeable manner for April - cloudy, rain, sleet and lightning - but the spirits of those joining *QE2* alongside the Queen Elizabeth II

event. A few moments silence during the on-board presentation would be held in his memory.

Many famous personalities from British show business and the media were also present, representing the hundreds of top name people who had lectured on board the ship at some time in the past. Those fortunate few, numbering less than five hundred, who were on board to mark the *QE2*'s special anniversary were given a presentation by Larry Pimentel, Cunard's new president under the Carnival Corporation, and he spoke of Carnival's plans for the line's future. The fabulous 'Project *Queen Mary*' was not only officially launched but plans for a second such vessel were also announced as were plans for a major £19-million refit for the *QE2* which would take place later in the year, giving her and the 'new' *Caronia* (ex-*Vistafjord*) a corporate identity in company livery. Mr Pimentel said: 'We are very proud to own this ship, and very well aware of its place as a national institution and the affection it holds throughout the world'.

After the presentation a large cake depicting the *QE2* was wheeled onto the stage and Captains Ron Warwick and Roland Hassel (standing in for 'Bil' Warwick) made the first cut.

After lunch in the Caronia Restaurant (during which each guest was presented with a copy of Gary Buchanan's superbly illustrated '*QE2* - A Magnificent Millennium' which photographically traced the various internal alterations that the ship had undergone). *QE2*'s famous fan, Sir Jimmy Saville, spoke on behalf of the guests and proposed the well-deserved toast to the *Queen Elizabeth 2*.

During the afternoon the inclement weather abated leaving a sunny but blustery, Spring afternoon in its wake. At 5pm the *QE2* pulled away from her berth as 1,159 red, white and blue balloons were released, peppering the sky with pin-pricks of colour, each balloon representing a voyage made during her 4.5-million miles of ocean travel. The liner then sounded thirty blasts on her siren as the tugs around her sent tapering plumes of water upwards into the air with apparently much of Southampton Water apparently landing on the liner as a result! Meanwhile, spectators both on shore and on the myriad of small craft surrounding the liner cheered and waved the *QE2* yet another *Bon Voyage* as she sailed for the United States. She arrived in New York to be greeted by the press and a glorious gold and red sunrise six days later.

Associated British Ports had placed a full-page advert in a special *QE2* anniversary supplement of the Southampton 'Daily Echo' proclaiming 'Many Happy Returns *QE2*' and showing a photograph of the ship with thirty superimposed pink candles alight on her superstructure. A few months later, in October, ABP and Cunard were involved in their almost traditional three-yearly joust about the 'high costs' of berthing fees. The Cunard as per usual, threatened to take *QE2* away from the port and a vigorous campaign ensued in the Southampton paper to keep the ship in the city. The campaign appeared to be successful with Cunard even committing to using the Port of Southampton for their prestigious new *Queen Mary 2*.

Another of *QE2*'s milestones another was reached on Sunday 13th June whilst *en-route* between Southampton and Madeira. The ship's siren was sounded to mark twenty years - or 175,296 hours - of actual steaming time, making the *Queen Elizabeth 2* the hardest working vessel in the history of the Cunard Line.

In stark contrast to the celebrations of 1999 it was revealed from recently released papers that Cunard had barely survived the upheavals that it had faced in the mid-sixties. It was also revealed that it was even contemplated

Left: A huge cake representing the *QE2* was wheeled onto stage during the on-board celebrations in Southampton and ceremoniously cut by Captains Ron Warwick and Roland Hassle.

Below: During the Millennium World Cruise the *Queen Elizabeth 2* met the recently renamed *Caronia* (ex-*Vistafjord*) off Barbados.

Cunard

that the company might be liquidated and the then new *Queen Elizabeth 2* sold after her launch in 1967, perhaps to a Greek shipping company. However, in August 1969, the magazine 'Shipbuilding and Shipping Record' quoted Lord Mancroft, then Cunard's deputy chairman as publicly giving an assurance that '....the ship would be remaining under Cunard's flag throughout her career, estimated to be 27 to 30 years'. He also commented on the fact that a number of people had been worried about the prospect of the ship being sold to P&O or to an American company, especially in view of the sale of her predecessors, but these worries were unfounded.

QE2 followed her usual cruise pattern for the rest of the year and her pilgrimage to the North Cape in July almost following those similar cruises undertaken by her illustrious predecessor, the *Caronia*, during the fifties by including several UK and Irish ports in her itinerary.

The British mercantile marine that had been in decline for many years was given a fillip in August 1999 when the British Deputy Prime Minister, John Prescott, (himself an ex-steward on board liners such as *Caronia* and *Queen Mary* and staunch union member and official), introduced tax concessions for shipowners. This action attempted in some way to undo some of the severe damage that his old union had caused the merchant navy in 1966 when he had personally assisted in the great Seamens' Strike by, amongst other actions, exhorting fellow seamen on board the *Queen Mary* to walk off the ship on strike. The Strike, which crippled British sea trade, would eventually bring about the virtual collapse of Britain as a seafaring nation.

Now, with the new concessions, shipowners were encouraged to recommence training future seamen and thus help to alleviate an impending world shortage. The *QE2*, until now by far the largest vessel to fly the Red Ensign under British registry, was joined by fifty units of the mighty P&O fleet. The presence of the Red Ensign upon the oceans of the world was practically doubled in a very short time. Britannia had started to regain her lost crown.

On Trafalgar Day, 21st October, the Carnival Corporation wholly acquired the Cunard. They thereby achieved what their fellow Americans had failed to do at the turn of the century when financier J. Pierpoint Morgan's giant International Mercantile Marine Company was taking over many North Atlantic shipping companies, including Cunard's arch-rival - the White Star Line. The world-wide fame of Cunard's long and often distinguished history, now the jewel in Carnival's crown, would later be lauded in 'corporate-speak' by the new owners as 'global brand equity'

On her arrival in Southampton on 10th November from a Panama and Caribbean cruise the *QE2* disembarked her passengers and sailed for her promised £19.5-million refit. This again would be undertaken at the German Bremerhaven yard of Lloyd Werft which was also refitting the *Royal Viking Sun* (to be renamed *Seabourn Sun*) and the *Vistafjord*, shortly to be renamed *Caronia*.

Whilst in Bremerhaven the liner became the target of protest by the environmental group Greenpeace. In common with many hundreds of other ships the *QE2*'s underwater hull was painted with an anti-fouling paint that had, as a chemical biocide, a high tin content known as tributyltin (TBT). This effectively prevented algae and molluscs from growing on ships' hulls, thus slowing them down and increasing fuel bills. It also prevented undesirable foreign marine life from being spread from one world location to another. Equally, it was a toxic pollutant, released when water blasted during hull cleaning as well as by erosion due

to its self-polishing capabilities. The pollution persisted in water and had become a prime concern as it killed sealife, harmed the environment and possibly entered the food chain.

To make their protest against TBT Greenpeace had chosen their world-famous target well. A flotilla of small inflatable craft sped around the ship as she sailed through Bremerhaven harbour and fifty protesters dived into the water to prevent the vessel from moving forward or astern. Two hundred other protesters waved banners that proclaimed 'Stop TBT!' and the crew of one inflatable drew up alongside the towering hull and spray-painted 'God Save the *Queen* from TBT' along her hull just above the waterline.

The protest worked as Cunard officials gave an assurance that TBT-based paints would no longer be used on the *QE2* nor on any of their other ships.

Since then the International Maritime Organisation (IMO), the maritime regulatory body of the United Nations, has put into its agenda a suggestion that TBT based paints should not be used after 1st January 2003 and that hulls painted with the deadly organotins should be repainted or sealed by 1st January 2008. More acceptable coatings would be recommended such as a silicon rubber compound that provides a 'non-stick' surface that allows marine growth to attach itself to a ship's bottom but is then washed off once the vessel is underway.

Over the next month the *QE2* would undergo the third most important refit of her life and one that would establish her place amongst the vanguard of the world fleet of liners and cruise ships. £12-million would be spent on her redecoration brilliantly masterminded by Tillberg Design whilst £7.5-million would be expended on the technical aspects of the work.

New carpets, furnishings, decor, lighting and re-upholstery would enhance the three grillrooms. The Mauretania Restaurant would receive new furnishings and carpets as well as chandeliers and new glass doors and the *Caronia* mural was replaced with one depicting a lily pond at evening which seemed to reflect the warm tones of the room's furnishings. The Caronia Restaurant was redesigned to create an '.... English country house feel'. Mahogany panelling and mahogany encased pillars and beams that highlighted a white ceiling would recall the elegance of the earlier Edwardian steamers. New lighting, including chandeliers, carpets, curtains and chairs along with an enhanced music system made the room into a superb dining area. Anomalies still existed between the themes of the two restaurants that perhaps provided the only discordant note of the whole refit.

The Queen's Room received new furniture and a luxurious carpet in royal blue with a woven motif of Tudor roses in gold. Mahogany panelling was applied to the bulkheads. Oscar Nemon's bust of HM The Queen was prominently relocated. Unfortunately it still retained its heavy gold leafing and had not been returned to its original *vert-de-gris* finish. The Grand Lounge received a new stage, chairs, curtains and carpet and the Theatre and balcony were rejuvenated with new upholstery and carpeting. Stairs were no longer evident in the Lounge, thus creating more useful space.

The Yacht Club, Chart Room, Crystal Bar and Golden Lion pub were all modified during the refit and 106 bathrooms were renewed to complete the work commenced in 1994. New luxury suites were created or enlarged and given - or renamed with - the names of historical Cunarders, thus maintaining the ship's theme of company heritage. One

The longest and the last of the ocean liners designed and built for the North Atlantic run meet in their cruising capacities in Miami. The *Norway* (ex-*France*) had long been converted from her liner role to one of cruising.

Richard Weiss

of the new suites, the Caledonia (575 square feet) on the Boat Deck, had been built using space formerly occupied by the Radio Room. The arrival of GMDSS had helped to obviate the requirement for such a large room and a new, compact, communications centre was located in the Purser's Office on 2 Deck. Corridors and stairways around the ship were also refurbished with new wall coverings and carpets.

As a welcome return to traditional comforts - and perhaps influenced by the recent blockbuster movie 'Titanic' - the *QE2*'s deck furniture was replaced with new teak-wood steamer chairs of classic design.

Externally the *Queen* had been given the new, almost traditional, Cunard livery. Her hull had been blasted to remove the accumulation and weight of fifty-two layers of paint. The Trafalgar House 'Go-faster' stripe disappeared from the superstructure as did the quite attractive golden lion at the line's forward end above the legend 'CUNARD'. The Trafalgar House emblem of signal flags astern of the stripe had disappeared previously when Kvaerner had taken control of the Line.

It is planned at some future overhaul to completely clear the aluminium superstructure of its old layers of paint and perhaps repair the athwartships cracks forward of the funnel and over the Queen's Grill. The latter crack has been problematical, as it has at various times seeped water on to the diners below. A temporary solution has been to fit some grey household guttering below the split to drain away such unwelcome water!

At the outset of the refit Larry Pimentel had said: 'This refit is the first stage of an overall master-plan we are developing for QE2. The ship has a long life ahead of her and we are committed to maintaining, and improving even further, the already high standards for which she is known'.

Arriving back in Southampton on 9th December the *Queen Elizabeth 2* sailed on a three-day shakedown cruise entitled 'Pre-Millennium Celebration'. On her return to Southampton early on the morning of Sunday 12th December the *Queen* was made ready to welcome her companion in the Cunard Line, the 'new' *Caronia*.

The *Caronia* had been re-named as such at a

spectacular ceremony in Liverpool the previous Friday and had sailed south with a group of very special guests - Lord Lichfield (the Queen's cousin) amongst them, personalities (including many characters from television programmes such as 'Coronation Street' and 'Keeping Up Appearances') and journalists (Jenny Bond, Sir Michael Ingram, Michael Buerk, etc,) on board. A Force 9 in the Irish Sea had been encountered (laying many of the passengers low) but this had reduced in its effect as the liner turned into the English Channel. On arrival at Southampton her passengers were taken to the *Queen Elizabeth 2* that lay ahead of her to inspect the larger liner's new interiors.

A special celebratory luncheon was held for them, appropriately in the Caronia Restaurant, during which a *QE2* cookbook was presented to the ladies and a copy of Captain Ron Warwick's own magnificent volume, '*QE2*', was given to the gentlemen.

The thirty-year old liner, rejuvenated and redesigned over several major refits was now looking her magnificent best.

And so the *Queen Elizabeth 2* had achieved what had been wished for her (and only a few could have realistically hoped for realisation) in her early and subsequent years - both her thirtieth year of service in the Cunard and to sail into a New Millennium.

The liner sailed the same day for New York on the outset of her Millennium World Cruise entitled 'Circling the Water Planet' (fares from £14,550 to £153,030 per person for the full sixty-nine days). Arriving and departing from New York on 18th December the *QE2* circumnavigated the globe from west to east, again rounding the Cape of Good Hope at the southern tip of Africa before heading north for Southampton via St. Helena, Agadir and Lisbon. Maiden calls were often made during the World Cruises and during this cruise the *QE2* made maiden calls at Zihuatanejo in Mexico; Port Douglas, Australia; Madang in Papua, New

Guinea and at Pointe des Galets on the Indian Ocean island of Reunion. New Year's Eve for the year 2000 had been spent at Bridgetown on the Caribbean island of Barbados where she met up with the *Caronia* on her maiden Caribbean cruise.

4th July, Independence Day, 2000 saw the Cunarder being eased into her berth in New York after providing a grandstand view of a three-day spectacular maritime event during which time the *QE2* had been anchored. In a high wind and with adjacent berths crowded with ships that had taken part in the festival the liner was being assisted out of her dock when the three tugs accompanying her momentarily lost control causing the ship's stern to veer ultimately colliding with a Japanese National Defence vessel, the *Kashima*. Just prior to the collision a startled Japanese sailor rushed to the impending collision point, hastily lowering a small, plastic fender over his ship's side! The collision caused the loss of paint on both ships and a buckled rail on the *QE2*. As a reaction to the collision the *Kashima*'s mooring ropes snapped and sent her forward to collide with the British destroyer, HMS *Manchester*!

Officers from *Queen Elizabeth 2* later went aboard the Japanese vessel to make their peace with their counterparts but were told that 'It had been an honour to be kissed by such gracious a lady!'

The *Queen*'s own damaged paintwork was soon repaired by a painting party lowered over her side.

There have been many that, taken by flights of fancy, have tried to stow away on the *Queen* with varying degrees of success. Not least are the many birds, some rare, which have settled on the liner's decks to rest in mid-flight only to find themselves transported many miles away from their intended destinations. In July, 2001, a pair of racing pigeons settled down to rest on the ship during a foggy race from France to England and subsequently found themselves *en-route* for New York. Taken into care on board the liner the birds sailed to the Caribbean via New York and back before being reunited with their owners in Southampton in a flurry of publicity.

The oft-times consort of the *Queen Elizabeth 2*, the sleek, supersonic Concorde (originally specially chartered but later used on scheduled flights), also celebrated its 30th Anniversary in 1999. But, on 25th July, 2000, one of the aircraft belonging to Air France suffered a catastrophic tragedy on take-off from Paris' Charles de Gaulle airport. A piece of debris on the runway ruptured the aircraft's starboard wing fuel tank, causing the plane to catch fire and crash with the tragic loss of 109 lives. The Concordes of both the British and French fleets were

One of the super-luxury suites. The *QE2* boasts her own butler to serve the de-luxe accommodations.
Cunard

withdrawn from service for sixteen months whilst improved safety features were built into their fuel tanks. Much improved, the aircraft were reintroduced into service during November, 2001. Concorde and *QE2* were soon to offer a joint service to create once again 'the ultimate transatlantic travel experience.'

An eastwards September 2000 sailing headed the *QE2* into some very rough weather. The P&O cruise vessel *Oriana* had left the States a day previously and had diverted her course to go to the assistance of 76-year old lone sailor, Jack Nye, whose yacht had been dismasted in the prevailing gale. During her rescue mission the *Oriana* suffered structural damage with cabins well above the waterline being severely flooded. Several passengers and members of the crew were injured by glass broken by the 40-foot wave. *QE2* sailed unscathed through the bad weather and arrived in Southampton a day ahead of the P&O ship.

The 2001 World Cruise, billed as the 'Voyage of Great Discoveries', was preceded after her departure from Southampton on November 14th by a cruise to the Caribbean and started in earnest from New York on 5th January, 2001. During the course of the world cruise the liner called into Dubai, a Gulf port that was endeavouring to become a major cruise destination and was planning to build a huge leisure island in the form of a palm tree.

Staying overnight between 25th and 26th March the *QE2* was the principal guest vessel amongst other cruise ships at the opening of the Dubai Cruise Terminal at Port Rashid.

Trouble hit the liner on 26th May shortly after leaving Southampton *en-route* for the Mediterranean. At 2am that night, whilst still in the English Channel, difficulties were experienced with the steering gear and the liner came to a halt, drifting in misty conditions, whilst her engineers worked through the night to rectify the fault. Warnings were sent out to other ships in the area to take extra care but the ship was underway once again before many passengers had awoken. Captain Paul Wright, however, made a broadcast that morning to keep the passengers informed of what had happened.

On an April Atlantic cruise to Madeira and Lisbon from New York shortly after the end of her 2001 world cruise the liner received a distress call when an emergency had arisen on board a Spanish fishing vessel. One of the fishing boat's crewmembers had received a wound to his head so, in response, the Cunarder turned in her tracks and retraced her course for 150 miles, arriving at the scene at around eight in the evening.

The ship's surgeon, Dr Martin Carroll, was taken in one of the *QE2*'s boats and, deciding that the head wound was serious enough, had the fisherman transferred to the waiting liner. As a result the ship missed her scheduled call at Madeira on the 28th April and proceeded straight to Lisbon. The rescued sailor received many cards from both passengers and crew and apparently made a full recovery.

Between the loss of the French airline's Concorde and its sisters' reintroduction into service a greater tragedy occurred, the ramifications of which had - and, at the time of writing, still has - enormous effect on the West and on the industry in which the *QE2* is involved.

On 10th September, 2001, the *QE2* left Southampton at 5pm on one of her scheduled voyages to New York where she was due to arrive early on the morning of the 16th. A fine early summer's evening saw the liner sailing eastwards through The Solent, the still bright evening sun of late summer picking out her size and livery to its best effect.

But, as with her predecessor - the *Queen Mary* - sailing westwards in September of 1939 on the eve of the outbreak of the Second World War, international affairs would take a drastic, unexpectedly tragic and violent turn of events before her journey's end.

On the second day of her voyage the security of the world was changed for ever as three aircraft, loaded with innocent passengers and piloted by Islamic fundamentalist terrorists' hands, slammed with spectacular eruptions of consuming flame, acrid smoke and destruction into American and international confidence. On one of the brightest and clearest days of the year, two of the highjacked aircraft found prime targets in the imposing twin towers of the World Trade Center in the financial heart of New York. The third passenger aircraft was crashed into the nerve centre of US defence in Washington, the Pentagon. A fourth 'plane crashed prevented from reaching its target by heroic passengers who overpowered the terrorists on-board.

'September the Eleventh' subsequently became by-words for infamy and horror.

Those on board the liner shared with the rest of the civilised world feelings that combined horror, shock and a disbelieving fascination as the dreadful spectacle was replayed over on television screens. There was no possible

A sight often seen in the past but one that will never again reoccur - the *QE2*, outward bound, slips by the twin towers of New York's World Trade Centre.   *Cunard*

way that the *Queen Elizabeth 2* could proceed to New York so, as on other occasions in her past, the ship was diverted to Boston. Even her arrival - and that of the similarly diverted *Caronia* - was delayed because telephoned bomb threats caused the closure of the harbour. The two ships were held outside the port whilst their terminal was inspected.

As the smoke still rose from hundreds of thousands of tonnes of rubble that marked the ruins of the twin towers and the graves of the thousands that had died Pier 92, near to the *QE2*'s usual berth at Pier 90 in New York, was occupied in the month that followed the attack by the United States Naval Ship *Comfort* (T-AH 20). This big, white ship with three red crosses painted on each side was used to provide assistance to the search and rescue teams and to provide food and short-term lodging space for firemen and disaster recovery personnel. The cruise terminal used by *Queen Elizabeth 2* was used by the Federal Emergency Management Agency as a command centre and as a departure point for boats transporting bereaved families so that they could view 'Ground Zero' from the river.

The WTC towers had collapsed appallingly quickly and the after-shock of the terrorism that caused their disintegration created a loss of confidence in air and sea travel. Major airlines saw demand for seats plummet and a few companies actually went out of business. Although the severe losses in cruise line share values (Carnival Corporation - Cunard's parent company - had millions wiped off their stock market value) had recovered by 20% by mid-November it was too late for some cruise lines as they suffered a sudden loss of trade. With massive numbers of cancellations due to both 11th September and a general slowdown in the world economy Renaissance Cruises filed for bankruptcy with their ships ceasing operations immediately; the entire fleet being eventually offered for sale. American Classic Voyages' two new 1,900-berth cruise-ships that were being built in the United States (the first to be constructed there for many years) were cancelled whilst only 40% and 55% complete. It was later suggested that the vessels could be completed as troopships.

It would not take long for Carnival's own fortunes to be revived as by mid-January, 2002, the cruise company was reporting record levels of bookings and were planning to operate a 24-hour day booking system.

Other cruise companies were requesting shipyards to slow down on the completion of newbuildings until a hoped-for recovery in demand for berths commenced, but the Cunard (under the guardianship of the Carnival Corporation) did exactly the opposite. Not only were Carnival/Cunard going ahead with their exciting new project but the company actually brought forward the start date of their prestigious new 150,000gt, 345-metre, £538million *Queen Mary 2* at the French yard of Chantiers de l'Atlantique at St. Nazaire.

The first steel for this, the first true liner to be built for decades, was cut at a ceremony attended by the Line's new President and Chief of Operations, Pamela Conover. (The previous President and CEO of Cunard Line Limited, Larry Pimentel, had resigned his position as of February 2001 to become co-owner and CEO of a new cruise line, SunDream Yacht Club). The cut shapes of plate and section will be welded into panels and these panels will, in turn, be formed into blocks (sections of ship). These blocks, previously fitted out with piping, cables, etc, will eventually be erected on the building berth to gradually form the hull of the liner. Amazingly, the entire hull and funnels of the 'old' *Queen Mary* could fit inside the massive hull of her intended

The US Naval ship *Comfort* (T-AH 20) at berth in Pier 92. The *QE2*'s berth 90 is on the far right.
US Navy photo by Cheif Photographer's Mate Eric J. Tilford

namesake, as could almost the whole of the *QE2*!

For the three months following the 11th September attack the *Queen Elizabeth 2* would make Boston her American destination for the three calls that she had been scheduled to make. New York Harbour was effectively closed to external passenger traffic as work on clearing 'Ground Zero' continued and the threat of further terrorist attack was evaluated. The piers along the Hudson were blocked-off by a fleet of barges.

On 12th November, however, the first cruise-ship to call into the port for a month, the new Royal Caribbean Cruise Lines' *Adventure of the Seas* (at 137,300 gross tons she and her sisters were the current largest cruise-ships in the world) arrived on her delivery voyage (without passengers) from her builders. The ship lay alongside Berth 1 at Pier 88 to be named by representatives of the New York Police and Fire Departments (both of which had lost many of their members in the early stages of rescue at 'Ground Zero') and by the City mayor, Rudolph Giuliani, who spoke at the naming ceremony. Mayor Giuliani would later, in February 2002, receive an honourary Knighthood from the hand of HM Queen Elizabeth II for the way in which he had handled the emergency in Manhattan. He received the accolade on behalf of the Police, Firefighters and other heroes of New York.

The newly christened *Adventure of the Seas* then took 2,800 relatives and friends of emergency service employees who had been killed on 11th September on a complimentary two-day cruise. At the cruise's end the officers amongst them were called to duty almost immediately to attend American Airlines flight 587 that had crashed onto the Rockaway Beach area in the Borough of Queens shortly after take-off from JFK Airport. Fearing another terrorist attack the vessel, in the high state of emergency that was declared for the city, was immediately ordered out of the port. She returned the following day (after the crash had proved to be an accident) to pick up those members of her crew stranded by her sudden departure.

After the horrific events of 11th September it may be a respite to recall a few of many amusing incidents that have occurred on board the *Queen Elizabeth 2*. One of the ship's officers recalled an occasion when an elderly lady passenger became trapped in a jammed lift. Using the lift's emergency

An artists impression of the new Cunarder, *Queen Mary 2*. Alonside you can see the first ship of the fleet, the Britannia. *Cunard*

telephone her call was quickly answered by an officer on the Bridge. Eager to effect a quick rescue the officer asked the passenger where she was. The reply came back, 'On a big liner in the middle of the ocean.' Unperturbed, the officer informed the stranded passenger that a rescue team would be with her in five minutes. 'That's very quick as you have so far to come' the lady replied, assuming that the rescue team had to come from the shore!

The imposing figurehead of Britannia that used to grace the original Britannia Restaurant had for some time been placed in the foyer just forward of the Mauretania Restaurant on Upper Deck. A broad band of steel bolted the figurehead to the adjacent bulkhead, but this was not to prevent the old lady from falling over in rough seas but to prevent roguish colleagues from once again removing her to the more comfortable confines of some unsuspecting officer's bed!

The *QE2*'s steering wheel had evoked many comments when the liner had first appeared because of its small diameter. After a visit to the Bridge by a group of school children the wheel was found to be missing. Too late to locate another before sailing the mighty *Queen Elizabeth 2* was navigated safely across the North Atlantic and back using a pair of mole grips in lieu of the missing wheel!

October brought forth at least one happy occasion on board when Captain Warwick had the pleasure of officiating at his daughter's wedding, although it happened in Boston rather than the hoped for location of New York. A special permit was obtained from the office of the Governor of Massachusetts for, as a layman, to perform the ceremony and the happy couple also obtained a rushed-through marriage licence. Since that marriage it has been proposed in Great Britain that laws that have prevented weddings being conducted on board ships had to be reformed, an action that will hopefully encourage more owners of cruiseships to re-register their vessels under the Red Ensign.

From 21st November, 2001, prior to her World Cruise that began on 11th December, the *Queen Elizabeth 2* underwent her annual refit, again undertaken at the Bremerhaven yard of Lloyd Werft.

At a reported £19.5m the work carried out included refurbishment of the two Grand Suites. A total revamp of the uninspiring work that had been previously carried out in the Queen's Grill and adjoining Lounge included the addition of a decorative glass-reinforced gypsum frieze contained within an alcove complete with oil gilded lattice work, all being illuminated by concealed lighting. The restaurant's columns were encased in sycamore, ebony and maple burr veneered panelling. Similar panels were fitted to the window surrounds in the Grill Lounge showing off the new curtains. Furniture in both rooms was also reupholstered. New, specially designed chandeliers were also fitted.

The Yacht Club was redecorated, furniture reupholstered and carpets renewed with new joinery work enhancing windows, etc, as in the restaurant area.

After starting her 2001/2002 World Cruise, 'Voyage of Exploration' (from Southampton to Southampton in 127 Nights' from 11th December) the *Queen Elizabeth 2* arrived at New York on 7th January after her usual preliminary cruise to the Atlantic and Caribbean Isles. On her arrival in the Hudson, the first major passenger liner to enter the port on a scheduled cruise since the destruction of the twin towers, the *Queen Elizabeth 2* made a ceremonial stop opposite 'Ground Zero'. Beautifully and impressively illuminated by her on-board lights in the semi-darkness of early morning a moment of remembrance of the events of 11th September was held. The liner, surrounded by the lyricism of the whispering ocean, lowered the Stars and Stripes to half-mast and a wreath gently dropped over the side into the river.

After transitting the Panama Canal a traditional call into Honolulu preceded the vessel's progression across the Pacific which introduced a change from other world cruises when a call into Fiji was omitted.

This stemmed from 19th May 2000 when a group of dissatisfied indigenous islanders, led by George Speight, removed the then Prime Minister (of Indian extraction of the Fijiian island of Suva) from power and held forty two island

Members of Parliament hostage. The prevailing political problems continued for some time with a resultant negative effect on tourism. The *Queen*'s itinerary was subsequently altered on this current cruise calling instead into Papeete, the Tahitian capital, and the nearby island of Moorea.

At the time of writing it has been announced that Cunard has expressed an interest in building yet another new ship. This newbuilding, to be constructed in Italy, will be around the 85,000 gross tonnes mark - similar to the long-held record of the tonnage of the old *Queen Elizabeth*! It also seems likely that the *QE2* will now make only one transatlantic round voyage in conjunction with the new *QM2* in 2003, thus providing an unique opportunity to re-enact the times when the *Queen Mary* and *Queen Elizabeth* used to spectacularly pass each other in mid-Atlantic within a mile of each other. Stephen Payne, Carnival Corporation's chief Naval Architect, can not as yet decide whether to be onboard the *QE2* to see his latest ship in mid-Atlantic or to be on board the *QM2* to see his old favourite from her successor! The *QE2*, then relinquishing her epithet of 'The Last Great Ocean Liner', will then be transferred to full-time cruising whilst 'exploring new liner markets', perhaps being retained in this role for another ten years!

The sistership mooted for the 150,000gt *Queen Mary 2* (the first true liner to be built for almost three decades and under construction at the French shipyard of Chantiers de l'Atlantique, the yard that had built the beautiful *Normandie* - the arch-rival to the old *Queen Mary*) may bear the name *Queen Victoria*, a name originally envisaged by Cunard for the first *Queen Mary*. A suggestion has also been put forward that, on her 'retirement', the *Queen Elizabeth 2* could possibly join the venerable old *Queen Mary* in her retirement at Long Beach near to the proposed Carnival Cruise Terminal that is planned for the area. An idea put forward by a business consortium in Southampton to use the *Queen Mary* as a hotel for passengers embarking on the *Queen Elizabeth 2* had the bid for the Long Beach based liner not been thwarted by her withdrawal from sale in 1991 will now become a reality in California.

In November 2001 it was announced that P&O Princess Cruises and Royal Caribbean Cruises Limited were planning an amalgamation of interests thus forming the world's largest cruise line, thereby taking that distinction away from the Carnival Corporation.

Towards the end of December Carnival entered the fray and expressed their intention to make a hostile bid for P&O Princess Cruises and over the ensuing weeks would four times increase their offer to over £5 billion.

The ensuing 'battle' has produced some startling proposals, not least was the indication that Carnival would be willing to appease European legislation by relinquishing their European holdings. This would mean disposing of Holland-America and their prestigious new acquisition - the Cunard!

So, at the time of writing, the future of the Cunard Line and its ships seems uncertain. A question mark would also seem to hover over the future of the biggest passenger liner ever to be built - what will become of the *Queen Mary* Project?

The last chapter for the *Queen Elizabeth 2* has obviously yet to be written. By the time that this comes to fruition the 'New Cunarder' will undoubtedly have travelled many more thousands of miles, bringing pleasure to untold numbers of people, both on board or wistfully watching her from a distance.

May the *QE2* continue to enjoy (hopefully, in spite of the current uncertainties) that which Her Majesty Queen Elizabeth II wished the ship during her launching speech on 20th September, 1967:

'A long life and good fortune'.

Whether sailing through the vagaries of Nature or Accountancy, the *Queen Elizabeth 2* more often than not reaches a safe haven on a tide of good management, great care and goodwill.
Cunard

Acknowledgements

In this necessarily brief but updated account of the career of the *Queen Elizabeth 2* I have tried to paint a broad picture, highlighting some events whilst briefly touching on others. I apologise if I have missed out any particularly favourite story about the ship but space, of course, precluded the inclusion of everything! The *Queen* still continues with an amazingly action-packed career and, for some of the headline stories of her thirty years of sailing the oceans of the world, I have endeavoured to obtain first-hand accounts of some of those particular incidents. For these I am particularly grateful to: Cunard's Public Relations Department (notably Eric Flounders and Michael Gallagher); Boyd Haining (ex-Shipyard Manager at John Browns, Shipbuilders and Engineers); Captain Peter Jackson; Captain (then First Officer) Philip Rentell; and last, but in no means least, Captain Robin Woodall not only for his wonderful recollections but for his patient reading of the manuscript, for contributing an excellent Foreword and for suggesting corrections to the original book.

Cunard's shore staff of two continents should also be mentioned. Theirs is a job which goes largely unsung but without them, between the enormous organisation that culminates in the endless stream of brochures that initiate many voyages and the final offloading of baggage at the end of a voyage, the *QE2* would not be run so efficiently. Amongst the many others whom I would wish to thank are the authors of many invaluable most informative books including; Messrs. Potter and Frost; Captain Ron Warwick; my good and knowledgeable friend, William H Miller and his co-author Luis Miguel Correia; and Gary C Buchanan whose own book wonderfully captures in photographs the many changes that have occurred to the *QE2* over the years.

In addition to the above I would like to express my appreciation (posthumously , I regret to say, in the cases of a few since the appearance of the first edition) to the following people and their respective organisations for either their time and patience during my interrogations or for loaning precious photographs or artefacts: Fabian Acker ("Motor Ship"); Wally Adams; Nigel Allan; June Appleby; Brian Atkinson; Mr. Ballard (GEC Electrical Projects Ltd.,); Bob Bantock; Len Betts; John T. Brown; Wyn Coombe; Robert Cove; Department of the Navy (US), Frank B. Randall jnr; Captain Ian Dunderdale (Cromarty Forth Port Authority); Audrey and Steve Dymock: Richard Faber (Ocean Liner Memorabilia of 230 East 15thSt., NY, NY10003); Michael A. Findlay; Barney Gallagher; George Gardner; Lilian Gibson: Bob Bruce Grice; Les and Thomas Gough; Charles Haas; Jenny Haining; John Havers; Imperial War Museum, London; Norman Jackman; Marvin Jensen; Tim Jone; Diana Johnston (of MaGregor-Navire Publications Ltd.,); P. A. Kroehenst; Katherine Leiper (daughter of John Rannie); Terry Little; Liverpool University; Staff Captain Ian MacNaught; Commodore Geoffrey Marr; Gordon Matthews (GEC Turbines Ltd.,); William H. Miller; Peter Newall; Nigel Overton; Royal Torbay Yacht Club; Scottish Records Office; Peter Seden (for his wonderful additional photographs of the liner's 1999 interiors); Southampton Central Library; Southampton Maritime Museum; Southampton Daily Echo (especially Peter Ashton and Keith Hamilton); Liz Stephens; "Titanic" International (PO Box 7007, Freehold, NJ 7728-7007, USA); University of Glasgow Business Archives; Cedric Wasser; John Watson (MAN-B&W Diesels Ltd.,) and Peter Weiss.

My publisher, Roger Hardingham, I thank for his perseverance after requesting three additional chapters to update my original book but received 30,000 words in return!

Bibliography

Arnott, Captain Robert, Captain of the Queen (New English Library, 1982).

Bonsor, N.R.P., North Atlantic Seaway, Vol. 1 (David & Charles, 1975).

Buchanan, Gary C., Queen Elizabeth 2 - A Magnificent Millennium (Past and present Publishing Ltd., 1996).

Cunard Line, The Cunarders 1840-1969 (Peter Barker Publishing Ltd.,); - Pleasure Island (1969?); - Sailing Into a Great Tradition (1982 souvenir World Cruise book).

Hutchings, David F., RMS Queen Mary - 50 Years of Splendour (Kingfisher Railway Productions, Southampton, 1986).

Hutchings, David F., Caronia - Legacy of a Pretty Sister (Shipping Books Press, 2000).

Hyde, Frances E., Cunard and the North Atlantic (The MacMillan Press Ltd., 1975).

Johnson, Howard, The Cunard Story (Whittet Books, 1987).

Kludas, Arnold, Passenger Ships of the World, Vol. 5, 1951-1976 (Patrick Stephens, Cambridge, 1977).

Lloyd Werft, Bremerhaven, Queen Elizabeth 2 - The History of a Conversion.

Marine Accident Investigation Branch, Report of the Investigation Into the Grounding of Passenger Vessel Queen Elizabeth 2 on 7 August 1992 (HMSO, The Department of Transport, 1993).

Marine Safety Agency, Queen Elizabeth 2 - Voyage From Southampton to New York, December 1994 (MSA, The Department of Transport, Southampton, 1995).

Marr, Commodore Geoffrey T., The Queens and I (Adlard Coles, 19730.

Maxtone Graham, John, Tribute to a Queen (Berltz Publications, 1987).

Miller, William H., Great Cruise Ships and Ocean Liners from 1954 to 1986(Dover, 1988).

Miller, William H., Transatlantic Liners 1945-1980 (David & Charles, 1984).

Miller, William H. and Correia, Luis Miguel, RMS Queen Elizabeth 2 of 1969 (Liner Books, Lisbon, 1999).

Miller, William H. and Hutchings, David F., Transatlantic Liners at War - The Story of the Queens ((David & Charles, 1985).

National Transportation Safety Board, Grounding of the United Kingdom Passenger Vessel RMS Queen Elizabeth 2 Near Cuttyhunk Island, Vineyard sound, Massachusetts, August 7, 1992 (NTSB, Washington DC 20594, USA).

Potter, Neil and Frost, Jack, Queen Elizabeth 2 - The Authorised Story (Harrap, 1969).

Ransome-Wallis, P., North Atlantic Panorama 1900-1976 (Ian Allan, 1977).

Rentell, Philip, Historic Cunard Liners (Atlantic, 1986).

Roberts, Dr. Nigel, C-Six - Ten Years as the Doctor of the QE2 (Sidgwick & Jackson, 1988).

Southampton Corporation, The Queens (Harvey Barton-St. Stephens Publication, 1969).

Taylor, Arthur, Great Liners (Southern Newspapers, Southampton).

Villar, Captain Roger, Merchant Ships at War Conway/Lloyds of London Press, 1984).

Wall, Robert, Ocean Liners (Collins, 1978).

Warwick, Captain Ronald, QE2 (W.W. Norton & Company, revised edition 1998).   **Newspapers** Daily Telegraph; Lloyds List; Portsmouth News; The Times; Southampton Daily Echo. **Journals and Periodicals** Bremerhaven Magazine No. 79, Mai/April 1987; CME (Journal of Chartrered Mechanical Engineers) May 1987; Cruise Digest reports, Vol 6 Special Issue No. 1, 1987; Cunard publicity brochures, Press Releases, etc.; Diesel and Gas Turbine Worldwide Engineering, 13 December, 1968; 100A1 (Journal of Lloyds Register of Shipping) July 1986; Lloyds Ship Manager, May 1987; ME/LOG, August 1986; MacGregor-Navire News, April 1986; Marine Propulsion, Special Issue Rebirth of a Queen, May 1987; MPS Review, September 1986;; The Motor Ship, June 1987; The Naval Architect (Journal of the Institution of Naval Architects), various dates; Sea Breezes; Sea Lines (journal of the Ocean Liner Society, 27 Old Gloucester St., London); Ships Monthly; Shipbuilding and Shipping Record, various but especially Supplement of 31 January, 1969; Shipping World and Shipbuilder; Shipping - Today and Yesterday.

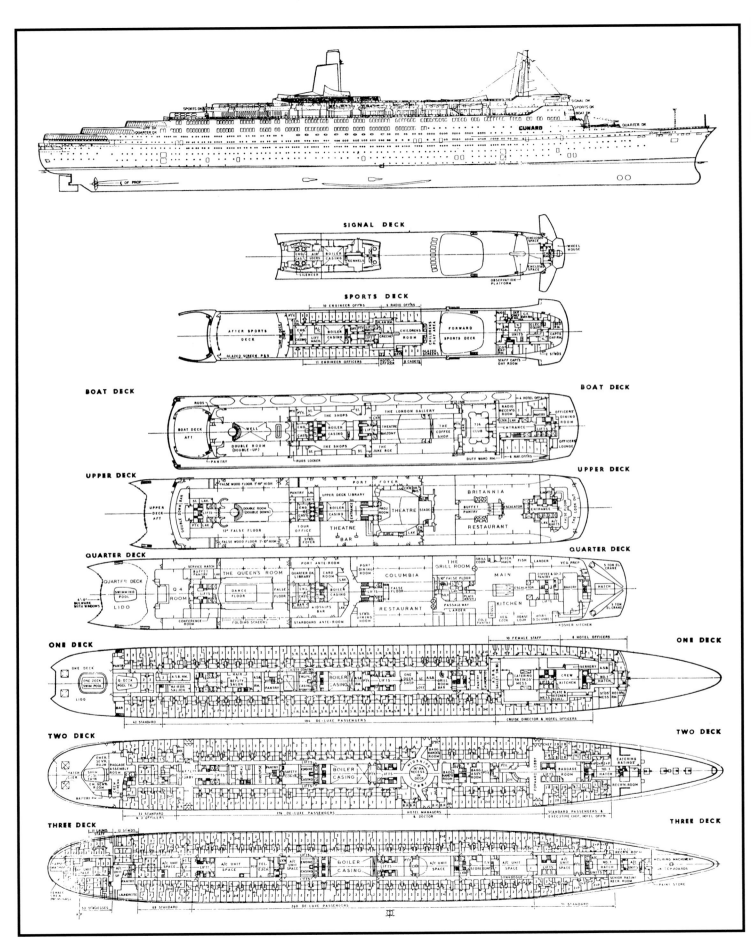